FIELDNOTES

FIELDNOTES

The Makings of Anthropology

Edited by ROGER SANJEK

CORNELL UNIVERSITY PRESS

Ithaca and London

First published 1990 by Cornell University Press.

International Standard Book Number 0-8014-2436-4 (cloth)
International Standard Book Number 0-8014-9726-4 (paper)
Library of Congress Catalog Card Number 89-46169

Printed in the United States of America

Librarians: Library of Congress cataloging information appears on the last page of the book.

⊗ The paper used in this publication meets the minimum requirements of the American National Standard for Permanence of Paper for Printed Library Materials Z39.48—1984.

*We dedicate this book to
the next generation of ethnographers.*

Contents

Contents

Preface

After a long American Ethnological Society board of directors session on the first day of the 1984 American Anthropological Association meetings in Denver, I met Shirley Lindenbaum, editor of *American Ethnologist* and a fellow member of the board, in the hotel lobby. We were later joined by James Clifford, a historian of anthropology. The three of us talked about current concerns in anthropology, including the growing interest in ethnographies as texts.

By eleven o'clock in the evening we were all hungry and decided to eat in the hotel. We descended several flights to the one restaurant that was still open. The service was slow and uncoordinated. As Lindenbaum and Clifford sat eating their dinner and I sat waiting for mine, Clifford brought up the subject of fieldnotes. He said that in all the recent discussion about writing ethnography and about ethnographies as writing, no one had addressed what anthropologists write *before* they write ethnographies—fieldnotes. This led our conversation to a chain of associations, comments, and ideas about fieldnotes and about why ethnographers have written so little on the subject.

When I learned at the next day's AES board meeting that I was to chair the program committee for the AES Invited Sessions at the Washington AAA meetings, in 1985, I immediately thought of doing a panel on fieldnotes. In the next two days, I discussed this with Lindenbaum and AES president-elect Judith Shapiro, both of whose ideas on themes and potential panelists were extremely helpful. Clifford also was amenable, and willing to do a paper.

The next step, early in 1985, was to write to a score or so of anthropologists, to gauge their interest in joining the Washington symposium. I approached people of substantial ethnographic accomplishments, people I believed would be able to reflect upon such work. Some I knew well; others only slightly; some not at all. My bait was a sketch of topics and issues to consider:

> Unlike historians, anthropologists create their own documents. We call them fieldnotes, but we speak little about them to each other. This symposium seeks to open up discussion about fieldnotes within the profession. The aim is less to concretize what various theoretical schools think ought to go into fieldnotes than to examine what anthropologists do with fieldnotes, how they live with them, and how attitudes toward the construction and use of fieldnotes may change through individual professional careers.
>
> We hope contributors will present a variety of perspectives. Among the topics that might be considered are these:
>
> 1. What are the relationships between fieldnotes and ethnographies? Are ethnographic writings written "from" fieldnotes, from fieldnotes plus other sources, or does one or more intermediate stage of writing follow between fieldnotes and ethnographic product? How do fieldnotes provoke and animate memory?
>
> 2. What are the different "kinds" of fieldnotes an ethnographer produces—running accounts of events, texts, reports, impressions, and other forms? How do these fit together in providing the first-stage ethnographic record?
>
> 3. When they are available, what is the impact of earlier ethnographers' fieldnotes on later researchers? Should access to such fieldnotes be a regular process of professional courtesy? If so, why, and how; if not, why not? How successfully may one ethnographer's fieldnotes be used by another in writing ethnography?
>
> 4. How does an ethnographer "live with" fieldnotes over time? What sense of responsibility to one's notes do anthropologists feel? Do fieldnotes become a burden from which one must win freedom before going on to new work? How long can fieldnotes remain useful to an anthropologist? How does the ethnographer's reading of her or his own fieldnotes change with professional development and maturity? Can ethnographic writings become "obsolete" but fieldnotes remain a source for new ethnography?
>
> 5. How do ethnographers in return visits change their conceptions of what fieldnotes should be? How do such conceptions change as anthropologists take on second or third fieldwork projects?

6. How is access to fieldnotes handled when two or more ethnographers work cooperatively—in team research, or in parallel investigations?

7. What uses may be made of fieldnotes—directly—as part of ethnographic writing? How do canons of scientific method, responsibility to informants, and desires to write persuasively and authoritatively all intersect in the use of fieldnote material?

8. Should fieldnotes become available to anyone (including non-anthropologists) other than the ethnographer? When; to whom; in what forms?

I appended a list of useful sources, including Srinivas's *Remembered Village* and Pehrson and Barth's book on the Marri Baluch; papers by Clifford, Larcom, and Marcus and Cushman; and the collection of essays on field research edited by Foster and others.

The bait worked. Fourteen contributors prepared papers, and eleven of those papers, in revised form, are included in this volume (the press of other commitments prevented Emiko Ohnuki-Tierney, Triloki Nath Pandey, and Michael Silverstein from revising their papers for inclusion here).

The topic of fieldnotes proved to be timely. A report on the symposium followed in the *Chronicle of Higher Education* immediately after the Washington meetings (see Ellen K. Coughlin, "Anthropologists' Archives: Scholars Examine the Problems and Possibilities of Field Notes," December 18, 1985, pp. 5, 7). In the next three years, several works on ethnographic writing appeared, some dealing directly and some indirectly with the uses of fieldnotes (including books by Agar, Clifford, Clifford and Marcus, Friedrich, Geertz, Marcus and Fischer, Van Maanen). Pointed and controversial pieces on ethnographic writing by Richard Schweder in the *New York Times Book Review*—"Storytelling among the Anthropologists," September 20, 1986, pp. 1, 38–39; "The How of the Word," February 28, 1988, p. 13—provoked reactions in anthropological circles and beyond.

When my work on this collection of essays began in 1985, a two-decade mix of theoretical, political, methodological, and fieldwork experiences had primed my thinking about the role of fieldnotes in doing anthropology. I teach at Queens College in Powdermaker Hall, named for Hortense Powdermaker, who taught there for many years. Soon after I arrived in 1972, I read her book *Stranger and Friend: The Way of an Anthropologist* (1966). What stayed with me most from this fascinating personal history was the sense of drudgery involved in diligently typing up fieldnotes from handwritten notes on observations and informants' statements.

This resonated with the feelings I had during my own fieldwork in Adabraka, Ghana, in 1970–71. I had kept a small notebook in my back pocket, a suggestion made by Lambros Comitas in a field training seminar in 1965. I wrote in this notebook all kinds of things seen and heard and struggled to keep my typing from it up to date. It resulted in 397 single-spaced pages of fieldnotes covering eighteen months, although the last one hundred pages were not typed until the Watergate summer of 1973, a year after my Ph.D. thesis was completed. That thesis and my publications on Adabraka since have been based on nearly as many pages of network interviews and other systematic records, kept separate from my wide-ranging fieldnotes. The notes remain to be used, someday perhaps, in as yet unbegun ethnographic writing.

The attention to records in my Adabraka fieldwork and writing is a product of my times. I first did fieldwork in 1965 in Bahia, Brazil, as part of a Columbia University undergraduate summer program. This was preceded by a field training seminar, led by Comitas and Marvin Harris, in which the focus was on the practicalities of getting to and around in Brazil, and on establishing rapport with informants. Several students from the previous year's program spoke about their experiences. The assigned reading from Adams and Preiss's *Human Organization Research* washed over me. (*Stranger and Friend* was not yet published, nor were Epstein's *Craft of Social Anthropology* and Jongmans and Gutkind's *Anthropologists in the Field*; they would appear in 1966 and 1967, and begin the flood of fieldwork and methods literature in the 1970s.) I was more concerned about Brazilian ethnography and the ethnoscience literature to which my planned fieldwork on racial vocabulary related. Others in the Brazil group I met that year—Dan Gross, Maxine Margolis, David Epstein, Conrad Kottak, Betty Kottak—mentioned Lévi-Strauss's *Tristes Tropiques,* but I did not read it then.

In Brazil I took no fieldnotes; I tried, but had no idea of what to write. Instead, I collected records of interviews, and responses to a set of drawings of varying combinations of skin color, hair, and nose form. This led to my second published paper.[1] My first, written in the

---

[1] Brazilian Racial Terms: Some Aspects of Meaning and Learning, *American Anthropologist* 73 (1971): 1126–43.

aftermath of the Columbia revolt of 1968, captured the intertwined concerns with ecology, underdevelopment, political engagement, science, and method which influenced me in my 1967–69 graduate student days.[2] It reflected Harris's teaching and writing. I was especially impressed by how his field encounter with racial inequality in Moçambique had led to his thinking about the emic-etic contrast, and how this in turn shed light on understanding the sacred role of the cow in preventing even greater immiseration in India.

Politics, science, and rigorous data-gathering were all one piece for me. My concerns about race, ethnicity, and class were crystallized in my Adabraka research on whether "tribe" or class was more important in daily life, and in my interest in testing the plural society separatist thesis that M. G. Smith and others had applied to Africa. The careful study of the daily life and interactions of Adabraka women and men which Lani Sanjek and I conducted was rooted in Harris's *Nature of Cultural Things* (1964), a theoretical book that I read as having political implications.

I was also strongly influenced by what I saw as a parallel interest in charting interaction among the Manchester anthropologists. Comitas had turned me on to British social anthropology, in which I read widely. I was fortunate also to work with Jaap van Velsen at Columbia in 1968. His *Politics of Kinship* (1964) was a demonstration of how careful fieldnotes on actual behavior could be analyzed to throw light on larger questions of process and social structure; his paper in the Epstein volume, and Epstein's own 1961 paper on network analysis, I saw as a next step from Harris's theoretical approach. Thus, detailed attention to daily activity marked both my Adabraka network records and my fieldnotes. George Bond and Allen Johnson, who came to Columbia in 1968 and served on my dissertation committee, reinforced this combination of intellectual elements for me. The importance of dedicated perseverance in fieldwork was also impressed upon me by Simon Ottenberg, who was in Ghana while we were.

The mix of political concern, respect for systematic data, and methodical attention to detail, which I have tried to make evident in my Adabraka publications,[3] has continued to be important to me. This

2Radical Anthropology: Values, Theory, and Content, *Anthropology UCLA* 1 (1969): 21–32.

3What Is Network Analysis, and What Is It Good For? *Reviews in Anthropology* 1 (1974): 588–97; Roger Sanjek and Lani Sanjek, Notes on Women and Work in Adabraka, *African Urban Notes* 2, no. 2 (1976): 1–25; New Perspectives on West African

mix also marked my writing in the 1970s about the employment of
women in anthropology.[4] The victory achieved on this issue, however, had as much to do with the political experience I gained in 1976–
78 at the Gray Panthers' Over 60 Health Clinic in Berkeley[5] as with
methodological and quantitative skills. My two years as an applied
and advocacy anthropologist in Berkeley, however, produced few
written fieldnotes, though they did result in a large file of other
documents.

I continued as a Gray Panther activist on health, housing, ageism,
and economic justice through the 1980s after I returned to New York.[6]
In 1981 I decided to write a book about the Berkeley Gray Panthers
and their health clinic. I discovered, however, a treasure of documents
on the origins and history of the Gray Panther movement at the
Presbyterian Historical Archives in Philadelphia, and my plan shifted
to a study of the national organization, with the local Berkeley story as
one chapter. In working on this project in 1981–82 and the summer of
1985, I reflected often that the documents were my fieldnotes. Though
I had not been present at the formative 1970–76 events detailed in
them, I knew all the major actors, had seen the places where events

Women, *Reviews in Anthropology* 3 (1976): 115–34; Cognitive Maps of the Ethnic
Domain in Urban Ghana: Reflections on Variability and Change, *American Ethnologist* 4
(1977): 603–22; A Network Method and Its Uses in Urban Ethnography, *Human
Organization* 37 (1978): 257–68; Who Are "the Folk" in Folk Taxonomies? Cognitive
Diversity and the State, *Kroeber Anthropological Society Papers* 53 / 54 (1978): 32–43; The
Organization of Households in Adabraka: Toward a Wider Comparative Perspective,
Comparative Studies in Society and History 23 (1982): 57–103; Female and Male Domestic
Cycles in Urban Africa: The Adabraka Case, in *Female and Male in West Africa,* ed.
Christine Oppong, 330–43 (London: Allen & Unwin, 1983); Maid Servants and
Market Women's Apprentices in Adabraka, in *At Work in Homes: Household Workers in
World Perspective,* ed. Roger Sanjek and Shellee Colen (Washington, D.C.: American
Ethnological Society, 1990).

[4]The Position of Women in the Major Departments of Anthropology, 1967–1976,
American Anthropologist 80 (1978): 894–904; Roger Sanjek, Sylvia H. Forman, and
Chad McDaniel, Employment and Hiring of Women in American Departments of
Anthropology: The Five-Year Record, 1972–1977, *Anthropology Newsletter* 20, no. 1
(1979): 6–19; The American Anthropological Association Resolution on the Employment of Women: Genesis, Implementation, Disavowal, and Resurrection, *Signs: Journal of Women in Culture and Society* 7 (1982): 845–68.

[5]Anthropological Work at a Gray Panther Health Clinic: Academic, Applied, and
Advocacy Goals, in *Cities of the United States: Studies in Urban Anthropology,* ed. Leith
Mullings, 148–75 (New York: Columbia University Press, 1987).

[6]*Crowded Out: Homelessness and the Elderly Poor in New York City* (New York:
Coalition for the Homeless and Gray Panthers of New York City, 1984).

occurred, and had participated in similar events in Berkeley, in New York, and at national Gray Panther meetings. To me, the process of building ethnographic description and analysis from these documents was similar to van Velsen's extended case method and to the account of Adabraka life which I had built more quantitatively in my network analysis dissertation and in papers.

My thinking about fieldnotes was stimulated, as well, by the part-time, long-term fieldwork I began in Elmhurst-Corona, Queens, in late 1983, which continues at present. In this incredibly diverse neighborhood of established white Americans of several ethnic backgrounds, newcomers since the late 1960s have included Latin American and Asian immigrants of many nationalities, Black Americans, and white not-quite yuppies. With a team of researchers as diverse as the local population, I have been studying changing relations among these varied groups. My fieldnotes cover mainly meetings of political bodies and associations, public festivals and ceremonies, and services and social occasions at three Protestant churches, with scores of descriptive accounts of events in each of these three categories. My chronological fieldnotes to date amount to 930 single-spaced pages, with more notes from ethnographic interviews. My analyses of these three domains begin with the fieldnotes. They have more in common with van Velsen's extended case approach than with the quantitative analysis of behavioral records of my Adabraka network study. Political concerns about the future of racial, ethnic, and class differences continue to give meaning and purpose to this work.

Most of the revised essays for this volume reached me during 1986. In June of that year my father died, and in the following two years several responsibilities overtook me. It was not until 1988–89 that I was able to return to the introduction for *Fieldnotes: The Makings of Anthropology*. Once started, the introduction seemed to take on a life of its own; it is now divided into essays that address the issues raised in each of the book's five sections.[7] The eleven other authors are not entirely blameless for this extended "introduction." They raised so many compelling issues that adequate treatment of the wider literature

[7]For reading and commenting on sections of my contribution to this book I thank Lani Sanjek, David Plath, Robert J. Smith, Simon Ottenberg, Peter Agree, Linda Wentworth, James Clifford, Nancy Lutkehaus, Rena Lederman, Carol Greenhouse, David Holmberg, Judith Goldstein, Moshe Shokeid, and Jean Jackson, who always sent just the right signal at just the right time.

and context—the proper job of an introduction to an edited collection—proved a formidable task. With their joint examination of anthropology from fieldnotes "up" rather than from theory "down," the whole history of the discipline looked different. Theoretical concerns were very much present, but they were extended to include questions of "when theory," "where theory," "why theory," in addition to "which theory."

Several writings have been extremely helpful to my work on this book. They include Clifford Geertz's "Blurred Genres: The Refiguration of Social Thought," in *Local Knowledge: Further Essays in Interpretive Anthropology,* pp. 19–35 (New York: Basic Books, 1983); Peter C. W. Gutkind and Gillian Sankoff's "Annotated Bibliography on Anthropological Field Work Methods," in *Anthropologists in the Field,* ed. D. G. Jongmans and P. C. W. Gutkind, pp. 214–72 (New York: Humanities Press, 1967); Nancy McDowell's aptly titled "The Oceanic Ethnography of Margaret Mead," *American Anthropologist* 82 (1980): 278–303; and several essays by the historian George W. Stocking, Jr.—anthropology is blessed that he has devoted his professional attention to our discipline.

But most valuable of all are the essays in this book by George C. Bond, James Clifford, Jean Jackson, Allen and Orna Johnson, Rena Lederman, Nancy Lutkehaus, Christine Obbo, Simon Ottenberg, David Plath, Robert J. Smith, and Margery Wolf. Every one of the authors surprised me, doing much more than I expected, revealing sides of themselves to the world, or dealing with themes and issues far beyond what I imagined back in 1984. As editor, I am honored. As reader, you are in for a treat.

ROGER SANJEK

New York City

PART I

Living with Fieldnotes

A significant attribute of writing is the ability to communicate not only with others but with oneself. A permanent record enables one to reread as well as record one's own thoughts and jottings. In this way one can review and reorganize one's own work, reclassify what one has already classified, rearrange words, sentences, and paragraphs in a variety of ways. . . . The way that information is organized as it is recopied gives us an invaluable insight into the workings of the mind of *homo legens*.

—JACK GOODY

JEAN E. JACKSON

"I Am a Fieldnote": Fieldnotes as a Symbol of Professional Identity

This essay began as an exploration of my own relationship to my fieldnotes in preparation for a symposium on the topic.[1] When I began to chat with anthropologist friends about their experiences with fieldnotes, however, I found what they had to say so interesting that I decided to talk to people in a more systematic fashion. My rather nonrandom sample of seventy is composed of all the anthropologists I contacted; no one declined to be interviewed. Interviewees are thus mostly from the east coast, the Boston area being especially overrepresented. With the exceptions of one archaeologist, one psychologist, two sociologists, two political scientists, and one linguist (each of whom does research "in the field"), all are card-carrying anthropologists by training and employment. The only representativeness I have attempted to maintain is a reasonably balanced sex ratio and a range of ages. To protect confidentiality, I have changed any potentially identifying details in the quotations that follow.

Given the sample's lack of systematic representativeness, this essay should be seen in qualitative terms. The reasonably large sample size

[1] An earlier version of this essay was read at the 84th annual meeting of the American Anthropological Association, Washington, D.C., December 4–8, 1985, in the symposium on fieldnotes.

3

guards against bias in only the crudest fashion, since so many complex variables are present. While I cannot claim to represent the entire field, I do think the sample represents practicing anthropologists living in the United States. Some are famous, others obscure; some have reflected on fieldwork and fieldnotes a great deal (a few have written about these topics), while others describe themselves as having been fairly unconscious or even suspicious of such matters. My sample is thus more representative of the profession than if I had written a paper based on what anthropologists have published about fieldnotes—the last thing many of my interviewees contemplate undertaking is writing on this topic. I believe that the fact that some common themes have emerged from such a variety of individuals is significant.[2]

Although readers might justifiably want to see connections made between an interviewee's opinions about fieldnotes and his or her work, I provide none because I very much doubt that many anthropologists would have spoken with me if I had indicated that I was endeavoring to write up the interviews in journalistic format, or write biographical sketches, or compare different anthropological schools represented by named or easily recognizable individual scholars. Thus my "data" prove nothing, divorced as the quotations are from the context of the interviewee's personal background, personality, fieldwork project, and published ethnographies or essays on theory and method. The quotations given are illustrative anecdotes and nothing more. Rather than write a polemic about what is wrong with our methods, I hope to gently provoke readers, to stimulate them to ask questions about their own fieldnote-taking. Hence, this essay is to be

---

[2]Although this essay is inspired by the current interest in "ethnographies as text" (see Marcus and Cushman 1982; Clifford and Marcus 1986; Geertz 1988; Clifford 1988), my methodology necessarily produces findings that differ from these and similar work in two crucial respects. First, most of the anthropologists I interviewed are not enamored of the "anthropology as cultural critique" (Marcus and Fischer 1986) trend, even though all of them had very interesting comments to make about fieldnotes. Second, given the frankness and the strong feelings—especially the ambivalence and negativity—that emerged in the interviews, I doubt that some of what my interviewees said to me would ever be said in print, even by those who might be inclined to write about fieldnotes one day. For all I know, some might later have regretted being so frank with me, although this does not necessarily make what they said any less true. Thus, while I certainly do not think I got the *entire* truth from anyone, given that the confidential interaction of an interview setting can pull out of people ideas and feelings they might not come up with by themselves, I believe that the material I did get is different from what I would get from a literature search about fieldnotes, even given that authors make extremely negative comments about fieldnote-taking from time to time.

seen as neither a philosophical nor a historical treatise on anthropological epistemology but rather as a somewhat lighthearted exploration of the emotional dimension of one stage of the anthropological enterprise, one that heretofore has not received much attention.

With a few exceptions, my procedure has been, first, to ask interviewees to tell me whatever they might want to say about the subject of fieldnotes. Almost all have been willing to comment. Then I ask about (1) their definition of fieldnotes; (2) training—preparation and mentoring, formal and informal; (3) sharing fieldnotes; (4) confidentiality; (5) disposition of fieldnotes at death; (6) their feelings about fieldnotes, particularly the actual, physical notes; (7) whether "unlike historians, anthropologists create their own documents."[3] I also try to query those who have had more than one field experience about any changes in their approach to fieldnotes over the years and to ask older anthropologists about changes over the span of their careers.

Interviews last at least an hour. Lacking funds for transcription, I do not tape them, but I do try to record verbatim as much as possible. Along the way, of course, I have discovered other issues that I wish I had been covering systematically: for instance, the interdependence of what Simon Ottenberg terms "headnotes" (remembered observations) and written notes. In more recent interviews I have added questions about a possible mystique surrounding fieldnotes, and whether fieldnotes are connected to anthropologists', or anthropology's, identity.

Whatever their initial attitude, by the end of the interview all interviewees seem to have become interested in one or two of the deeper issues that the topic introduces. Most comment that my questions and their answers have made them realize that fieldnotes are not by any means limited to nuts-and-bolts matters. The subject is clearly complex, touchy, and disturbing for most of us. My interviewees have indicated their unease by using familiar words from the anthropological lexicon such as *sacred, taboo, fetish, exorcise,* and *ritual,* and by commenting on our tendency to *avoid* talking about fieldnotes or only to *joke* about them (comments reminiscent of the literature on avoidance and joking relationships).

Anthropologists have many insights to offer, even in discussing the nuts-and-bolts issues connected to the actual recording of notes. Field-

[3]This phrase was part of Roger Sanjek's abstract for the 1985 symposium; see Preface.

notes seem to make a remarkably good entry point for obtaining opinions and feelings about bigger issues (such as this paper's topic, the relationship between fieldnotes and professional identity), probably better than point-blank questions about these larger issues. The monologues I encourage at the beginning of the interviews seem to put informants at ease, reassuring them that I am genuinely interested in whatever they have to say and piquing their interest in the topic. All the interviews have gone smoothly—although one interviewee said he was "leaving with a dark cloud" over his head: "How am I going to get ready for class in the next ten minutes?"

Why has this project turned out to be so interesting, both to me and seemingly to all those I interview? For one thing, because at least one of my questions (although *which* one varies) arouses each interviewee, the dialogue becomes an engaged one. Also, while some responses are well-formulated answers, at other times the reply is anything but prepackaged, neat, and tidy, allowing me to see thinking in action.

Overview of Answers to the Specific Questions

Let me try to summarize the perplexing and challenging variety of responses to the specific questions. This section does not address professional identity per se, but it provides necessary background.

Definition

What respondents consider to be fieldnotes varies greatly. Some will include notes taken on readings or photocopied archival material; one person even showed me a fieldnote in the form of a ceramic dish for roasting sausages. Some give local assistants blank notebooks and ask them to keep fieldnotes. Others' far more narrow definitions exclude even the transcripts of taped interviews or field diaries. It is evident that how people feel about fieldnotes is crucially linked to how they define them, and one must always determine just what this definition is in order to understand what a person is saying. Clearly, what a "fieldnote" is precisely is not part of our profession's culture, although many respondents seem to believe it is.

Most interviewees include in their definition the notion of a running log written at the end of each day. Some speak of fieldnotes as representing the process of the transformation of observed interaction to written, public communication: "raw" data, ideas that are marinating, and fairly done-to-a-turn diagrams and genealogical charts to be used in appendixes to a thesis or book. Some see their notes as scientific and rigorous because they are a record, one that helps prevent bias and provides data other researchers can use for other ends. Others *contrast* fieldnotes with data, speaking of fieldnotes as a record of one's reactions, a cryptic list of items to concentrate on, a preliminary stab at analysis, and so forth.

Some definitions include the function of fieldnotes. Many people stress the mnemonic function of notes, saying that their purpose is to help the anthropologist reconstruct an event. Context is often mentioned.

> You try to contextualize. I never did it and I regret it bitterly. I don't have people's words on it.

> I don't have a daily diary. There are a lot of things that became a part of my daily life I was sure I'd remember and I didn't. Things you take for granted but you don't know why any more. Pidgin words, stuff about mothers-in-law. You can recall the emotional mood, but not the exact words.

One interviewee commented that at the beginning of her fieldwork she generated fieldnotes in part because doing so reassured her that she was doing her job. An insight that she could use materials her informants were generating (memos, graffiti, schedules) as fieldnotes greatly aided her fieldwork. Here a shift in definition seems to have been crucial.

Most anthropologists describe different kinds of fieldnotes, and some will rank these according to the amount of some positive quality they possess. But what this quality is, varies. For some, those notes containing the hardest data rank highest; others have found their diaries to be the best resource:

> That journal, of course, is also a kind of data, because it indicates how to learn about, yes, myself, but also how to be a person in this environment. Subsequently I see it as part of the fieldnotes.

> The category "hunch" is something anthropologists don't bring to the field. This is why you should take a journal.

A moral evaluation often colors the definition itself and how respondents feel about fieldnotes in general. Clearly, those who see fieldnotes as interfering with "doing" anthropology, as a crutch or escape, or as the reason we are not keeping up with the competition (e.g., sociology) in rigor, differ from those who characterize fieldnotes as the distinguishing feature separating superior anthropologists from journalists, amateurs, and superficial, number-crunching sociologists.

Training and Mentors

The question of training often elicits strong reactions.[4] Virtually all respondents complain in some manner, most saying they received no formal instruction in fieldnote-taking, several pointing out that their graduate departments are proud to "do theory" only. Some approve of this state of affairs, and some do not. Many speculate about how to improve the situation; a few interviewees spoke approvingly of the training received by students in other social science and clinical fields. But the complaints from those who *did* receive fieldwork training reveal this to be an extremely thorny issue. Designing a course on fieldwork and fieldnotes that will be useful for all anthropologists, with their different styles, research focuses, and fieldwork situations, appears to be a challenge few instructors meet successfully. One interviewee said that much of what is published on fieldwork today is not "how-to" material so much as reflections on why it is so difficult to tell people how to do it. The best tack would appear to be to provide a smorgasbord of techniques for students to learn about, without insisting on a particular approach. Many of those most adamant about the worthlessness of whatever formal advice they received nonetheless report that little bits and pieces picked up along the way have been extremely useful.

Sharing Fieldnotes

Interviewees are very touchy on the topic of sharing notes. Questions of privacy, both one's own and one's informants', enter in.

[4] Several readers of earlier drafts of this paper have commented on how a number of the responses quoted seem quite "studenty." As noted above, I have obtained a roughly representative range of ages for interviewees, and I have avoided overrepresenting recently returned graduate students in the quotations I have chosen to present. Yet regardless of interviewees' age, stature within the field, and number of separate field-work projects, most of them chose to answer my questions by referring to their early fieldwork experiences. My conclusions suggest some reasons why these initial research periods were most salient in interviewees' minds.

Also, because we don't demand access to fieldnotes, people don't demand, "Look, you say such-and-such, I want to see the notes." . . . It's
like saying to a student, "We don't trust you."

I haven't, and I'd be of two minds . . . who they are and what they'd
want it for. Fieldnotes are . . . it's strange how intimate they become and
how possessive we are.

Yet many recognize the myriad potential values of sharing:

It would be such an advantage . . . to enter a place with some of that
background.

I think for someone else who's gone there, your notes can be an aid to
his memory, too. They are still helpful, sort of like another layer of
lacquer to your own notes.

An eminent anthropologist's fieldnotes can be a valuable source of
information about both the person as a scholar and a culture greatly
changed in the interim. One interviewee commented on Franz Boas's
diary:

The notes reveal a lot and for that reason they are valuable documents.
Does the anthropologist see the culture, or see himself in the culture . . .
see the social context from which he comes as somehow replicated in
the culture?

Interestingly, this respondent thinks she will eventually destroy her
own fieldnotes.

Many speak of the privacy of fieldnotes with a touch of wistfulness,
saying they have never seen anyone else's:

There are strong rules in anthropology about the intensely private
nature of fieldnotes. I'd like to have this protection. . . . "It's in my
notes," or "It's not in my notes," and hide behind this.

I'd show mine to people and they'd say, "Oh, wow, I've never seen
notes like that. Fieldnotes are really holy."

Confidentiality

Comments about the confidentiality of notes depend in large part
on the field situation and type of research conducted. Worries about
promises made to informants emerge, as do ethical considerations

about revealing illegal activities or giving ammunition to groups who do not have one's field site community's best interests at heart. Waiting until one's informants die may not be a solution:

> I'm working with people who have a lot of interest in history as a determinant force, and therefore for someone to read about a scandal his family was in a hundred years ago is still going to be very embarrassing.

On the other hand, some anthropologists' informants wanted to be mentioned by name. And members of some communities disagreed among themselves about how much should be made public.

Death

Several anthropologists, particularly the ones who took few fieldnotes and relied a lot on their memories, commented on what would be lost when they died:

> It's not a random sample, it's much better designed. But because the design and values are in my head, it's dead data without me.

Very few interviewees, even the older ones, have made any provisions for the disposition of their fieldnotes. Many worry about compromising their informants, and a large number say their notes are worthless or undecipherable. Some speculate about possible ways to preserve the valuable information in them, but apart from systematically organizing and editing for the express purpose of archiving the notes themselves, no other practical solutions have been described.

Feelings about Fieldnotes

The subject of fieldnotes turns out to be one fraught with emotion for virtually all anthropologists, both in the field and later on. I found a remarkable amount of negative feeling: my interview transcripts contain an extraordinary number of images of exhaustion, anxiety, inadequacy, disappointment, guilt, confusion, and resentment.[5] Many in-

---

[5]It has occurred to me that since anthropology provides no forums for discussing some of these issues, except anecdotally during "corridor talk" or at parties, one reason so much emotion comes out during an interview is that it provides a rather rare opportunity to express such feelings confidentially and reflectively. (Even in field methods courses that systematically explore fieldnotes, one's defenses are likely to be in

terviewees feel that writing and processing fieldnotes are lonely and isolating activities, chores if not ordeals.

Many mention feeling discomfort taking notes in front of the natives:

> I think part of that process is forgetting your relationship, letting them become objects to some extent. . . . The way I rationalize all that is to hope that what I publish is somehow in their interest.

Others mention discomfort when at times they did *not* take notes and an informant responded: "Write this down! Isn't what I'm telling you important enough?"

Working with fieldnotes upon return can also evoke strong memories and feelings, and a number of interviewees discuss this in fetishistic terms:

> The notebooks are covered with paper that looks like batik. I like them. They're pretty. On the outside. I *never* look on the inside.

Several people have remarked that since fieldnotes are a jog to memory about such an important time in their lives, strong feelings are to be expected.

Some interviewees comment on how writing fieldnotes can make you feel good, or proud to be accumulating lots of valuable data. Others remark on the reassurance function of taking notes, particularly at the beginning of fieldwork:

> You go there, a stranger. It gives you something to do, helps you organize your thoughts.

Still others mention the value of fieldnotes in getting an idea off one's mind or using the notebooks to let off steam—what we might call the Malinowskian garbage-can function.

> Fieldnotes allow you to keep a grip on your sanity.

> Of course I couldn't show that I was unhappy. My diary helped me talk about myself—my angst, my inadequacy. I wasn't experiencing the exhilaration I was supposed to.

---

place.) A number of respondents commented at the end of the interview that they felt relieved and appreciated having been able to talk at length about the topic.

Fieldnotes can reveal what kind of person you are—messy, pro-crastinating, exploitative, tidy, responsible, generous. Some inter-viewees find this valuable; others find it upsetting:

> Rereading them, some of them look pretty lame. How could you be so stupid? Or puerile?

> You could do an archaeology of my understanding . . . but that's so hard to face.

And a number of respondents discuss how fieldnotes, in tandem with their emotions, produce good anthropology:

> I try to relate the analysis to the fieldnotes and my gut sense of what's going on . . . do you *feel* male dominance?

Quite a number of respondents mention feeling oppressed by their fieldnotes:

> I experience this still when I listen to them. A horror, shock, and disorientation. Paranoia, uncertainty. I think I resisted looking back at the journal for that reason.

> If I look in them, all this emotion comes out, so it's like hiding some-thing away so it won't remind you.

> Sometimes I've wished they just weren't there.

> So they aren't just physically unwieldy, but mentally as well.

And others' fieldnotes invite invidious comparisons:

> I had a sense of insufficiency. I hadn't done it as well. I wouldn't be able to access mine as easily as she had hers. She, on the other hand, felt the same way.

For one respondent who "wondered how it felt to be responsible for so much [written] material," the contrast between having something written down rather than stored in memory is troubling. The written notes become more separated from one's control, and their presence increases one's obligations to the profession, to posterity, to the na-tives.

> It sort of makes me nervous seeing those file drawers full of notes. It reifies certain things, to get it into boxes. For me . . . a lot gets lost when they're translated onto these cards.

Several interviewees mention the problem of having too much material, of feeling dominated or overwhelmed.

> They can be a kind of albatross around your neck.

> They seem like they take up a lot of room . . . they take up too much room.

Several find this to be particularly true of audio tapes.

Issues of worth, control, and protection often figure prominently. An entire study could be devoted to whether fieldnotes are thought of as valuable, potentially valuable, or worthless. Anxiety about loss emerges in many interviews. The notion of burning fieldnotes (as opposed to merely throwing them away) has arisen quite often. I have also been struck by how many interviewees mention, sometimes with great relish, legends (apocryphal or not) about lost fieldnotes. Though fieldnotes in general have received little attention until recently, this is not true for the theme of lost fieldnotes in the profession's folklore.

> So maybe the people who lost their notes are better off.

> [Without notes there's] more chance to schematize, to order conceptually . . . free of niggling exceptions, grayish half-truths you find in your own data.

Several interviewees spoke of the physical location of their notes and meanings attached; one admitted

> a strong awareness of the physical notes, in a symbolically important place next to my desk at home . . . a mana quality.

And quite a number of respondents report feeling great pleasure, in some cases visceral pleasure, at thinking about their notes, looking at them, reading them (sometimes aloud):

> I do get pleasure in working with them again, particularly my notes from my first work. A feeling of sort of, that is where I came in, and I can sometimes recapture some of the intellectual and physical excitement of being there.

> So a feeling of confidence that if one could manage this, one could manage almost anything.

> For example, you write about a sacrifice, how it's done. When reading my notes I remember how it smelled . . . everyone's really pleased when it comes time to eat it.

Black ink, very nice; blue carbon, not so nice.

Some respondents seem to see their fieldnotes as splendid in themselves and invaluable for helping with recall; others say their fieldnotes are rubbish compared to their much more real memories of the events. These memories may be described in terms of visual or aural qualities that fieldnotes cannot provide. One interviewee said his fieldnotes were not real for him until he combined them with his memories, the theory he was working on, and his wife's critiques to make a published work.

For some reflective types, fieldnotes possess a liminal quality, and strong feelings may result from this alone. Fieldnotes are liminal—betwixt and between—because they are between reality and thesis, between memory and publication, between training and professional life (see Jackson 1990).

It seems that fieldnotes may be a mediator as well. They are a "translation" but are still en route from an internal and other-cultural state to a final destination. And because some anthropologists feel that fieldnotes change with each rereading, for them that final destination is never reached.

Fieldnotes as Documents "Created" by the Anthropologist

Despite being the premise of the 1985 AAA symposium on fieldnotes, the statement that anthropologists create their own documents elicits quite varied and usually strongly opinionated responses. Some say this is absolutely true:

Yes, you do create data in a self-conscious way that is quite special.

Each anthropologist knows it's a dialectic. The informant creates it; you create it together. There must be a tremendous sense of responsibility in it, that is, a sense of political history, one version.

It seems plausible . . . one is creating some special kind of fabricated evidence. Especially after time has passed, and you go back and it's as if they're written by someone else.

So we do more than historians . . . we create a world, not just documents.

Fieldnotes are my creation in the sense that my energies saw to it in some sense that they be recorded.

It's creating something, not creating it in the imagination sense, creating it in terms of bringing it out as a fact.

In some senses we do. We see ourselves. Malinowski . . . says as he's coming into Kiriwina, "It's me who's going to create them for the world."

But some consider "create" as a pejorative term:

This [statement] says that anthropologists fudge and historians don't. I don't agree.

I tend to believe my notes reflect reality as closely as possible.

A large number of interviewees object to the implication that anthropologists use only those documents they have created. To others, the statement seems to disparage the natives:

The reason why I'm having a hard time responding is I never think of my fieldnotes as a document. I feel the people are sort of a document. I did not create these people, and they are the documents.

Maybe I just view my task not so much as creating but transmitting, being a broker, an intermediary, a partner. . . . It's their words.

Still others disagree with the contrast made between anthropologists and historians:

Of course anthropologists create their own documents. The argument would be to what extent historians do that.

Fieldnotes, the Anthropologist, and Anthropology

Having sketched in some necessary background, we can now explore the extent to which the interviewees see fieldnotes as symbolizing the anthropological endeavor. Some make very direct statements:

It's a symbol of your occupation. A material symbol.

Anthropologists are those who write things down at the end of the day.

It's our data, it comes in chronological order. Not neatly classified the moment you receive or generate it.

Clearly, one reason for the strong feelings my questions frequently elicit is that "fieldnotes" is a synecdoche for "fieldwork." One woman described the differences between anthropology and other social sciences in terms of how we do fieldwork, saying that ours was feminine and osmotic, "like a Scott towel soaking up culture."[6] Another female respondent said that she found fieldwork and traditional fieldnote-taking *too* feminine, and this was why ethnoscience was so appealing: it promised to introduce rigor into fieldnotes, eliminating the touchy-feely aspects (see Kirschner 1987).

Yet several others saw no special link between being an anthropologist and taking fieldnotes:

> No. I've read the fieldnotes of sociologists and psychologists. They're very similar.

> I don't feel they're unique. In order to collect data, you have to take notes of some kind.

> No. Our fieldnote tradition comes out of naturalist explorer-geographer background. Lewis and Clark . . . [were] not that different.

> This is a way anthropologists have of alienating themselves from other disciplines because we are alienated from number-crunching sociologists.

> We just feel superior to social psychologists because we say this isn't social. They don't do fieldwork, we say.

Still, the majority of interviewees do say that fieldnotes are unique to anthropology, even if they disagree as to why. It is in their own varied definitions of fieldnotes that we find clues about how fieldnotes are seen as unique to anthropology and therefore emblematic of it. For almost all, fieldnotes are limited to the field (it is perhaps significant that the few nonanthropologists I interviewed did not make this distinction):

> Notes taken in the field. Hard-core fieldnotes are written records of observations and interviews.

> Anything I wrote down in the field. And didn't throw out.

> Before going I read about the place and take notes. I keep the notes but I don't consider them as fieldnotes.

[6]Lévi-Strauss comments: "Without any pejorative intent—quite the contrary—I would say that fieldwork is a little bit 'women's work,' which is probably why women succeed so well at it. For my part, I was lacking in care and patience" (Eribon 1988: 3); see also Caplan (1988).

Another ingredient found in many definitions is the notion that field-notes come from primary sources:

> Notes taken on a book in the field are not fieldnotes. But if a Kwakiutl brought down Boas's book, then yes.

> I suppose, strictly speaking, fieldnotes are the records of verbal conversational and observational kinds of work you did, rather than archives.

However, as always seems to happen with this topic, ambiguity soon enters the picture:

> The question is: is it only notes on the interviews, or everything else? Or what I'm note-taking in Bahia versus New York City? I'm not sure there's a neat distinction . . . in Brazil I'm in the field. But what if I'm doing research in New York City? It's sort of an infinite regress.

> For example, in Nicaragua, it's such an ongoing event, and I can't say, "Something's happening but it's not of relevance."

Several interviewees commented on the problem of defining the field, particularly those working in nontraditional settings:

> Sometimes I don't take notes on purpose. Around here I use it as a protective device. My way of turning off.

For many respondents this "field" component of the definition, while historically and sociologically important, is not the only reason field-notes are unique to anthropology. But "the field" for the majority is seen as exclusive to anthropology, for it is characterized by various criteria that are not seen as applying to the research sites of other disciplines. While fieldwork is carried out in other behavioral sciences, anthropology is seen by many as having imparted a special quality to "the field" tied up with the intensive, all-encompassing character of participant-observation, which is not found in notions about field-work in related disciplines.

> Your try hard to be socialized. Your measure of success is how comfortable you feel. We try like mad.

> I feel now that I am prepared to not finally become "one of the locals." I did have that expectation.

This attitude toward the field has consequences for fieldnote-taking:

I think [fieldnotes are] unique . . . because of the kind of data being collected and because of the kind of relationships. The fieldnotes are the record of these. . . .

I don't think the fact of notes is unique, but the type of notes is. Maybe not unique, but special. We try so hard to get close to the people we're working on. Most anthropologists are not really satisfied until they've seen them, seen the country, smelt them. So there's a somewhat immediate quality to our notes.

The sense of intimacy we pretend to develop with people we work with. I think if it's done correctly, then you get good information, not the trivial stuff that frequently comes from surveys. For example, the theory of the culture of poverty is worthless, but *Children of Sanchez* [Lewis 1961] will survive.

Dialogic considerations enter the picture for some:

In many ways I see anthropology as the art of listening to the other.

Doing fieldwork happens when you expose yourself to the judgment of others.

Several interviews indicate that the anthropological fieldworker frequently worries about intellectual exploitation. Having material in one's head is somehow less guilt-inducing than having it on paper. Some of this may be the "two-hat" problem: one is in some ways a friend of the natives, yet one is also a student of them, and one cannot wear both hats simultaneously. Writing fieldnotes can make repressing the contradictions in this balancing act more difficult:

I found [troubling] the very peculiar experience [of] getting to know people, becoming their friend, their confidant, and to be at the same time standing on the side and observing. . . . So when I came back from the field, it was, yes, years before I was able to write up that experience.

In traditional types of "deep bush" fieldwork, the category "fieldnotes" can be conceptually opposed to "the natives" (usually seen as illiterate).[7] Many interviewees revealed complicated opinions and feelings about colonialism and cultural imperialism, literacy and power, and their own image of themselves both as hardworking observers and sensitive, moral persons.

[7]Not all field situations fit this stereotype. Some interviewees plan to leave their fieldnotes on file in a local museum run by the people they study.

A general pattern for most interviewees is to couch their answers in terms of how their fieldwork—and hence fieldnote-taking—differs from the stereotype. I think in part this signals a defensiveness about one's fieldwork not living up to an imagined standard. It may also reflect what we might call the Indiana Jones syndrome: a romantic individualism, an "I did it my way" attitude. A substantial number of interviewees expressed pride in the uniqueness of their field sites, in their own iconoclasm, and in being autodidacts at fieldnote-taking.

The stereotypical research project involves isolation, a lengthy stay, and layers of difficulty in obtaining information. One needs to arrive, to get settled, to learn a language, to get to know individuals, and so forth. Overcoming such difficulties is seen as demanding a near-total marshaling of one's talents and resources. These and other characteristics of fieldwork turn any written notes into something valuable, because to replace them is difficult if not impossible.

> [Given] the whole aspect of remoteness, remote areas, not much written, your fieldnotes become especially precious.

One factor is the conditions of traditional fieldwork, the role of isolation and loneliness in producing copious fieldnotes that the researcher will be attached to. In modern urban settings this factor may not apply, yet it appears that at least for some "marginal" anthropologists - people carrying out research in nontraditional settings—fieldnotes are an important symbol of belonging to the tribe.

Another often mentioned characteristic of traditional fieldwork is the attempt to supply context, to get the whole picture. This is spoken of in many ways, often with ambivalence.

> I suppose I had a desire to record the complete picture. The ideal is like a video in my mind.

> I have trouble with my students. I say, "Write down what they're wearing, what the room looks like."

> I guess what strikes me is that for all the chaos I associate with fieldnotes, there's also a richness, and that somehow that is distinctive to anthropology.

Another important idea is that the investigator is a crucial part of the fieldwork/fieldnotes project:

> Fieldnotes enbody the individual fieldworker's reactions. It's O.K. for

me to be part of [anthropological] fieldnotes, but not O.K. if I'm part of [notes from] a child observation [in a psychology research project].

Often, notions of personal process, of the investigator's own evolution and investment, enter in:

> In that case, the interview transcripts wouldn't count [as fieldnotes; they are] data but not fieldnotes. They're more inseparable from you, I guess.

> An aura, an intensely personal experience, an exposure to the other, a reluctance to reduce to or translate, so unwilling to do this [to write down fieldnotes].

The individual is further tied to the fieldnotes because he or she "sweats blood" for them in the field. This is often remarked on in connection with reluctance to share notes. Frequently mentioned too is fieldnotes' mnemonic function; they become "a document of what happened and device for triggering new analysis."

All these personal aspects of fieldnotes bring us far from formal, spatial, and temporal definitional criteria. A frequently mentioned theme does seem to be that of the anthropologist-as-participant-observer in the very process of reading and writing from fieldnotes, revealing the close ties between fieldworker and fieldnotes:

> That might be closer to a definition of a fieldnote: something that can't be readily comprehended by another person. A newspaper clipping can be interpreted. The clipping has more validity of its own, but it can be a fieldnote if it needs to be read by me. . . . It's what I remember: the notes mediate the memory and the interaction.

This tie is illustrated by one anthropologist's reactions when her notes were subpoenaed:

> "They're dog's breakfast!" they [opposition lawyers] would say. "How can you expect anything from this?" . . . [They] had been written on the back of a Toyota [i.e., scribbled on paper held against the trunk of a car in the field] and were totally incomprehensible to anyone but me. But it was an attack on my credibility . . . I said, "This is a genealogy." "*This* is a genealogy?" Our lawyer would jump in, "Yes, of course."

Securing the document's acceptability as a genealogy demonstrated her credibility as a professional anthropologist.

Some people see the centrality of the personal component in field-work and fieldnotes as a strength:

> Something about the identity of anthropology, first of all, concerns the subjectivity of the observer. Being a social science doesn't exclude this . . . the definition of fieldnotes is a personally bounded [in the field] and personally referential thing.

> [Fieldnotes are] personally referential in terms of this dialectical relationship with memory. Otherwise you're dealing with "data"—sociological, demographic, computer card, disks.

A political scientist notes:

> Anthropologists are self-conscious about this process called the creation and use of personal fieldnotes. I think it's dangerous that political scientists aren't.

Yet many interviewees are reluctant to see fieldnotes in overly subjective terms:

> They're unique to anthropology because anthropology has consciously made it a methodology and tried to introduce some scientific methods. . . . in anthropology we don't see it only as an extension of someone's self but also a methodology of the discipline.

> If I felt that ethnography just reflected internal states, I wouldn't be in this game.

The personal issue emerged strongly when interviewees considered the interdependence of fieldnotes and memory:

> An event years later causes you to rethink. . . . What is the status of that material? Is this secondary elaboration? . . . the memories one has, we have to give some credence to, and the notes themselves are subject to distortion, too.

> Are memories fieldnotes? I use them that way, even though they aren't the same kind of evidence. It took a while for me to be able to rely on my memory. But I *had* to, since the idea of what I was doing had changed, and I had memories but no notes. I had to say, "Well, I saw that happen." I am a fieldnote.

This interviewee's willingness to state "I am a fieldnote" reflects the shifting, ambiguous status of fieldnotes. At times they are seen as "data"—a record—and at times they are seen as "me." I create them but they also create me, insofar as writing them creates and maintains my identity as a journeyman anthropologist.

A number of anthropologists link the uniqueness of their fieldnotes directly to issues of privacy:

> I've never systematically studied anyone else's, which says something about anthropologists.

> It comes from the British teaching of keeping one's personal experiences private. You can read all through *Argonauts* without finding out how many natives Malinowski talked to about painting canoes.

> I do think about what to do with them. I would hate for it to come to light if something happens to me. The people being observed forget you're there. There is something unethical about that: they go on about their business, and you're still observing. So to have fieldnotes that reflect your direct observations become public property is to me a betrayal of trust.

> It's secret. Part of it is a feeling that the data is unreliable. We want to be trusted when we say "the X do Y"; we don't want them to be challenged.

Many respondents point out that the highly personal nature of fieldnotes influences the extent of one's willingness to share them:

> Fieldnotes can reveal how worthless your work was, the lacunae, your linguistic incompetence, your not being made a blood brother, your childish temper.

But several note that such secrecy is unacceptable in other fields:

> Think of how it would be for a graduate chemistry student saying "You'll have to take my word for this."

> We've built up a sort of gentlemanly code dealing with one another's ethnography. You criticize it, but there are limits, social conventions . . . you never overstep them or you become the heavy.

A number of anthropologists mentioned that field notebooks serve as reminders that one is an anthropologist and not a native:

> I'm not just sitting on a mountain in Pakistan drinking tea.

> [I had] to write something down every day. To not accept everything as normal.

They can also be a reminder to informants that the information will be used:

> I feel better taking notes and tape recording, because it's clear that we're interviewing.

But others saw the notebooks as hindering the researcher from obtaining information and creating distance between the observer and the observed:

> The record is in my head, not on paper. The record on paper, it, because it's static, it interferes with fieldwork . . . keeping fieldnotes interferes with what's really important.

> First, it took up far too much time, like the addiction to reading the *New York Times*.

> Fieldnotes get in the way. They interfere with what fieldwork is all about—the doing.

> *This* is what I would call fieldwork. It is not taking notes in the field but is the interaction between the researcher and the so-called research subjects.

One interviewee criticized at length the profession's mythology about fieldwork, saying that most anthropologists throw away their original research proposals. They begin without a clue as to how to do it, or if they have a clue, it turns out not to work. Most of the time in the field is wasted, and many unsavory emotions emerge. Not only are you not "living like one of the natives" much of the time, he said, but the anthropological enterprise requires that you do not; your wife and kids will probably go more "native" than you. This man concluded that many people know their fieldnotes are worthless, but, as with the emperor's new clothes, mutual deceit is necessary to underpin the fate of the empire. Another man noted:

> One always doubts. Anthropologists mask their doubting with a certain amount of masculine bravado.

The ways a number of interviewees discuss the mystique of fieldnotes reveals the problematic association between fieldworkers and their notes. Many speak, usually ironically, about the fieldnotes as sacred, "like a saint's bone." Some even volunteer that their fieldnotes are fetishes to them. The legends about lost notes and the frequent theme of burning suggest the presence of a mystique.

The high degree of affect expressed by many interviewees is probably also evidence of a fieldnotes mystique. That some do not feel this
way, or at least say they do not, does not necessarily argue against the
existence of a mystique, for these anthropologists note that their
feelings are not shared by others; they "don't have the same kind of
mystical attachment" that some people do.

Linked to the issue of mystique is the frequent observation that
graduate school is an apprenticeship period and fieldwork an initiation
rite. Student-advisor interaction can provoke long-standing problems
of authority, sometimes for both student and advisor. Mentors were
identified as the generous givers or mean withholders of fieldnotes
advice. Strong feelings about advisors also emerged when several informants discussed how they "liberated" themselves from their fieldnotes—or at least from the variety they had initially attempted to
produce—using such phrases as "the illusion of control," "positivism," "empirical trap." One called fieldnote-taking "a self-absorption,
a way of retreating from data."

Many interviewees comment that their training reflected the mystique of fieldwork and fieldnotes. The following explication of this
connection summarizes and "translates" their remarks.

   1. The only way you learn is through the sink-or-swim approach.
"You go to the field with Hegel and you do it or you don't." (I went
through hazing week; you should too.)
   2. The only way that you become attached, cathected, truly initiated
is through the sink-or-swim approach. (An important feature of becoming a professional anthropologist is to discover that the standard
operating procedure is wrong, and then modify it.)
   3. Each research site is different, each research project is different,
each anthropologist is different. (So *any* fieldnotes training will resem-
ble the "take a big stick for the dogs and lots of marmalade" jokes. Any
advice will eventually have to be thrown away.)
   4. Anthropology is not at a stage where it knows the Best Way.
   5. Tailor-made solutions are the way to go, to be worked out between graduate student and advisor.
   6. There is always competition between the Old Guard and the
Young Turks regarding theory and method, and so any beginnings of a
continuous tradition of training about fieldnotes will be sabotaged.

We can argue that first-fieldwork fieldnotes are a diploma from
anthropology's bush school, even if it is almost never displayed. Further, insofar as being a member in good standing of the anthropologi-

cal club requires continued research, continued production of field-notes is evidence that one is not letting one's membership lapse. But we have seen that a few interviewees speak of fieldnotes (and here again, definition is crucial) less as tools of the trade than as tools of the apprentice. For these anthropologists—a small minority—fieldnotes are a beginner's crutch, to be cast aside when one has learned to walk properly. While most anthropologists, by far, do not hold this view, it is a remarkably clear, albeit extreme, illustration of the ambivalent emotions revealed in many interviews.

Some interviewees suggested that one reason fieldnote-taking is rarely taught may be that part of the hidden curriculum of graduate training in anthropology is to promote a mystique about writing and ethnographic documentation. Perhaps in some ways it is necessary to *unlearn* assumptions about the connections between observing and recording to become a good fieldworker. One respondent spoke of receiving an insight into Australian Aboriginal symbolism about the ground while *on* the ground:

> You notice in any kind of prolonged conversation, people are squatting, or lie on the ground. I came to be quite intrigued by that, partly because *I'd* have to, too . . . endless dust.

This is participant-observation, ethnography-by-the-seat-of-your-pants par excellence. The lesson this anecdote imparts about how to do fieldwork would be difficult to teach explicitly. The important insight that followed his paying attention to the ground is quite divorced from formal academic models of observing and analysis.

In part, what interviewees are talking about is that the writing versus the doing of ethnography creates a tension sometimes difficult to bear. Thoreau wrote that he could not both live his life and write about it. Some anthropologists grapple with the problem by becoming heavily involved with recording and even analyzing their field data in the field. For them, "fieldwork" includes data-sort cards, audio tapes, even computers:

> I sometimes felt like a character in a Mack Sennett comedy trying to manipulate the camera, tape recorder, pens. A mental image of myself trying to write with the microphone and point the pen at someone.

> I always managed to justify it to myself that it was more important to analyze while you're still in the field so you can check on things. . . . But it's also a preference.

But others become convinced, at least at times, that the road to success is to minimize these trappings of academe and the West.

Clearly, many anthropologists suffer during fieldwork because of this tension, which is exacerbated by not knowing what the methodological canons are:

> We ought to have the kinds of exchanges of methods and technologies that scientists do rather than the highly individuated kinds people do in the humanities. It would make life interpersonally more comfortable if you knew others were having to make this kind of decision.

The lack of standard methodology is also revealed in the huge variety of definitions of fieldnotes offered by interviewees. While in our "corridor talk" we anthropologists celebrate and harvest anecdotes about the adventure and art of fieldwork, playing down and poking fun at our attempts to be objective and scientific in the deep bush, the tension remains—because at other times we use our fieldnotes as evidence of objectivity and rigor. Fieldnotes, as symbol of fieldwork, can capture this tension but not resolve it.

> They are a mystery to me . . . I never know what is material.
>
> How do you know when you know enough? How do you know when you're on the right track?
>
> If there was something happening, I'd write it down. Not very helpful information, and I was looking to the lists of words to get a clue as to what to do.
>
> You have no criteria for determining what's relevant and what isn't.
>
> And collecting notes: what do you write down?

Some anthropologists connected this lack of explicitness and agreement regarding methods to the anthropological enterprise as a whole, and to its position vis-à-vis other social sciences.

> What is lost in that, I feel, is that there is a sense that disciplines are cumulative in their knowledge. We're not just collecting mosaic tile and laying them next to each other. [Yet] anthropology has performed a real service in being [politically and intellectually] slippery. So I feel a certain ambivalence.

Such feelings—of loss of control, inadequacy, or confusion about what one is supposed to do—influence the stance one takes regarding fieldnotes.

Fieldnotes and the Individual Anthropologist's Identity

The topic of fieldnotes sooner or later brings up strong feelings of guilt and inadequacy in most of my interviewees. I wish I had recorded how many of them made negative statements (using words like "anxious," "embarrassing," "defensive," "depressing") when I first asked to interview them. Some even accused me of hidden agendas, "of trying to make me feel guilty my fieldnotes aren't in the public domain." Most often, people worried about the inadequacy of their fieldnotes, the disorder they were in, their indecipherability:

> Oh, Christ, another thing I don't do very well, and twenty years later I still feel this quite strongly.

Fieldnotes can bring up all sorts of feelings about one's professional and personal worth. Several interviewees have commented on how disappointed they are when rereading their notes: they are skimpy; they lack magic:

> I went back last year and they were crappy. I didn't have in them what I remembered, in my head, of his behavior, what he looked like.

And yet

> What the field is is interesting. In Africa I [initially] wrote down everything I saw or thought, whether I understood it, thought it significant, or not—300 photographs of trees full of bats. How people drove on the left side of the road. . . . Having sent [my advisor] back all that crap, he didn't say anything.

In one case the fieldnotes are inadequate because they are skimpy; in another they are inadequate because of an "everything including the kitchen sink" quality.

With interviewees opinions on training and preparation, and sometimes with the fieldnotes-as-fetish issue, come expressions of attachment to one's first fieldnotes:

> They're like your first child; you love them all but your first is your first, and special.

> I do like my fieldnotes from the very beginning. There's more freshness, excitement. The sense of discovery of things which by now seem very old hat.

> My fieldnotes of the '50s, that's where I have my emotional investment, even though my work in the '70s was superior.

> I still have my 1935 Zuni notes. I couldn't bear to throw them away.

A number of interviewees commented to the effect that "an important part of myself is there"; they find it natural to be anxious about the notes because they represent a period of anxiety, difficulty, and great significance to which their career, self-esteem, and prestige may appear to be hostage. Several made direct links between fieldnotes and their own professional identity:

> When I think of activities I do, that's a lot closer to the core of my identity than most things. I'm sure the attitude toward the notes themselves has a sort of fetishistic quality—I don't go stroke them, but I spent so much time getting, guarding, and protecting them . . . if the house were burning down, I'd go to the notes first.

> I have a lot of affection for my notes in a funny way . . . their role here—in the U.S.A., my study, in terms of my professional self. Something about my academic identity. I'm not proud of everything about them, but I am proud of some things about them . . . that they represent. Probably in a less conscious way some motive for my not wanting to make them too public.

> My primary identity is someone who writes things down and writes about them. Not just hanging out.

> That particular box is my own first real claim to being a scholar and gives me the identity of a person doing that kind of work.

> Looking at them, when I see this dirt, blood, and spit, it's an external, tangible sign of my legitimacy as an anthropologist.

A number of anthropologists saw their field notebooks as establishing their identity in the field: "a small notebook that would fit into my pocket" became "a kind of badge."

Frustrations in the field regarding which intellectual economies to make add to the complexity: fieldnotes can be a validation of one's worth or a revelation of how much one is a fraud. But how to decide whether one is or is not a fraud is far from clear. As we have seen, fieldnotes are not done by filling in the blanks. Advisors can tell you only what they did and what you should do, but one person's method does not work for most others, and many advisors and graduate schools refuse to cover these topics. Doing fieldwork properly apparently involves strategies other than following well-specified rules. It appears that one must create some of the rules, predissertation research proposals with impressive methodology sections notwithstanding. To some extent, perhaps, one is expected to define or design the problem in the field and is subsequently judged according to how well one has lived up to those expectations.

These interviews make it almost seem that fieldwork involves the discovery of one's own True Way. The advisor-shaman can only provide some obscure warnings, like the aids in a game of Dungeons and Dragons. If the initial period of fieldwork is part of a coming-of-age process, then the fieldnotes aspect of it seems a well-designed and effective ordeal that tests the anthropologist's mettle. Clearly, insofar as first fieldnotes symbolize first fieldwork, they represent a liminal period in our preparation as professionals. As in other initiation rites, items associated with such activities take on a heavy emotional valence and sacredness.

We need some answers as to why many interviews do offer evidence of a fieldnotes mystique, for although a minority of interviewees assert that their fieldnotes are just a tool, most respondents relate to field-notes—their own and as a concept—in an ambivalent and emotionally charged manner. Despite some anthropologists' apparent nonconfusion about what fieldnotes are and how to teach about them, one could make an overall argument that ambiguity and ambivalence about fieldnotes are promoted in the occupational subculture.

Perhaps the idea that fieldwork requires one to invent one's own methods explains why such advice as is given is so often joked about, even when it was originally offered in utter seriousness.

> You know, "Take plenty of marmalade and cheap tennis shoes."

> [Alfred] Kroeber said to take a big stick for the dogs. [That was the extent of his advice to me.]

The numerous complaints about useless advice concerning stenographer's pads, data-sort cards, or multicolored pen sets—all of which were spoken of favorably by other interviewees—need a deeper analysis than merely that only some advice works for only some people only some of the time.

During fieldwork one must work out one's relationship to the field, to the natives, and to one's mind and emotions (as data-gathering instruments and as bias-producing impediments). Working out a relationship to one's field notebooks is a part of this process, and since fieldnotes are material items that continue to be used upon one's return, they apparently often come to symbolize these other important processes. Furthermore, since the writing of fieldnotes validates one's membership in the anthropological subculture, fieldnotes symbolize relations with one's fellow professionals: "You have to do something to justify your existence as an anthropologist." Those interviewees who exasperatedly disagree with this view do for the most part acknowledge its hold on their fellow anthropologists. Even the most adamantly anti-fieldnote respondent indicated that he did not consider himself a true anthropologist in a number of respects. Another said:

> I remember reading a novel by Barbara Pym where one character burned his fieldnotes in a ritualistic bonfire in the back yard. It was inconceivable . . . someone doing that and remaining an anthropologist. I found this passage to be fascinating and very provocative.

My material on competitive feelings, in the form of smugness or anxiety, shows that people are curious and judgmental about each other's fieldnotes:

> I've been astonished at the amount, both more or less, of fieldnotes people have come back with.

This accounts for some of the expressed reluctance to share, even though interviewees see value in sharing:

> The irony in anthropology is that [because fieldnotes are private,] we're really exercising acts of faith a lot of the time.

Perhaps some anthropologists see their fieldnotes as a sort of holy text which, like the tablets Moroni gave to Joseph Smith, need to be deciphered with golden spectacles or a similar aid; otherwise, the possibility arises of one's fieldnotes leading to misunderstanding—by colleagues and by natives. In part, fears about notes being used without their author's supervision are fears about potential abuse, but they may also go deeper: how could something so much a part of you be (potentially) so alienated from you? In this, Bronislaw Malinowski's diary (which many interviewees referred to one way or another) stands not only as evidence that all gods have feet of clay but as a dire warning. His diary was deciphered without his permission or participation, and most of us want to feel comfortable and secure about a text so linked to our identities.

We are also pulled in the opposite direction, urged to archive our notes, to be responsible scientists about them:

> It's taken me four years to turn this over to an archive . . . I'm about to do it.

The interviews provided many examples of how the boundaries between the anthropologist and his or her fieldnotes are fuzzy. One interviewee, who commented on how useful Boas's diary is because of its revelations about his motives, concluded:

> On the other hand . . . by taking fieldnotes we're reporting on the public and private lives of the natives. To what extent are the documents our own? And for either side, the observer and the observed. I don't think there's an easy answer.

As we have seen, some respondents consider themselves to be a kind of fieldnote, speaking of both written notes and memory in similar fashion.

As noted above, for some interviewees fieldnotes from the beginning of a fieldwork period are "all garbage," yet for others these are "the most valuable" because one has not yet become too socialized; one has not yet come to take things too much for granted:

> Right at the beginning [taking copious notes] is important because later on you'll see your mistakes.

> Watching people's fieldnotes over the years, the first impressions are very important, very revealing. Because you become socialized to the culture . . . although some scorn this and think it's dangerous, most pride themselves on this.

One respondent regarded fieldwork as a social process whereby we learn to formulate questions that the members of the cultures being studied find interesting and appropriate, yet even "boring" questions can have interesting answers that fieldnotes provide a record of. Many interviewees commented on how changing research topics, methodology, or theoretical orientation can make rereading fieldnotes an eye-opening experience: "You get this eureka experience: there it was and I didn't notice at the time." In a number of respects, then, fieldnotes are a synecdoche for the anthropologist. Probably those who are both pro- and anti-fieldnotes are so in part because of how they want to think of themselves as anthropologists.

Some of those I interviewed also contrasted fieldnotes with the questionnaires and standardized instruments of sociologists and political scientists, portraying fieldnotes as individualistic, authentic, impossible to replicate—the art and poetry of anthropology. When these anthropologists link fieldnote-taking with their professional identity, romantic and adventurous themes appear. Perhaps some of those who feel negative about fieldnotes reject what they see as the Western tendency to valorize the record over "reality." They are unhappy with the fact that in a modern bureaucratic state a document can have a major role in creating the reality: whether you're married or not finally depends on the validity of the marriage license, rather than on your intentions and assumptions at the time. Expressions such as "I needed to carry things to keep alive; the last thing I needed was a bunch of notebooks" perhaps contains a wish to be free of the power of the written word; free from the way writing, bureaucracy, and academe can control one's life; free, like the noble natives, to experience life directly with no interfering intermediaries, external (notebooks) or internal (the symbols that the enemy—inauthentic literacy—uses to maintain outposts in one's mind). Of course, those anthropologists who believe that fieldnotes fairly unproblematically reflect reality do not feel this way at all.

Conclusions

My interviews have illustrated that the topic of fieldnotes is often one of deep significance for the anthropologist who writes and subsequently works with them, as well as the anthropologist who speculates about someone else's notes. The answers to the questions I asked reveal strongly held and varied opinions and feelings about many of the issues linked to fieldnotes. Many interviewees believe that more consensus on fieldnotes (e.g., definition) exists in the profession than is actually the case. Our profession perhaps has an unusually large proportion of people who view themselves as rugged individuals; I have argued that fieldnotes and fieldwork do represent an individualistic, pioneering approach to acquiring knowledge, at times even a maverick and rebellious one. I have argued that the hints of a deliberate know-nothing spirit in graduate training, which emerge in discussions of lack of preparation for ethnographic fieldwork and fieldnote-taking, may even be part of a hidden curriculum designed to force the student to become an active creator, or re-creator, of anthropological technique. As one interviewee put it: "There was the image that each anthropologist was going into terra incognita and had to reconstruct, or reinvent, anthropology."

I have argued that anthropologists' opinions and feelings about fieldnotes can tell us much about the anthropological enterprise: how it straddles the fence between science and the humanities; how it distinguishes itself from its sister social science disciplines; and how it creates its own pecking orders, prods, rewards, and justifications for doing "good" fieldwork. Planning field research, carrying it out, and reporting on the results necessitates planning, writing, and using fieldnotes. If "the field" is anthropology's version of both the promised land and an ordeal by fire, then fieldnotes symbolize what journeying to and returning from the field mean to us: the attachment, the identification, the uncertainty, the mystique, and, perhaps above all, the ambivalence.

REFERENCES

Caplan, Pat. 1988. Engendering knowledge: The Politics of Ethnography (Part 2). *Anthropology Today* 4 (6): 14–17.
Clifford, James. 1988. *The Predicament of Culture: Twentieth-Century Ethnography, Literature, and Art.* Cambridge, Mass.: Harvard University Press.
Clifford, James, and George E. Marcus. 1986. *Writing Culture: The Poetics and Politics of Ethnography.* Berkeley: University of California Press.
Eribon, Didier. 1988. Lévi-Strauss Interviewed (Part 2). *Anthropology Today* 4 (6): 3–5.
Geertz, Clifford. 1988. *Works and Lives: The Anthropologist as Author.* Stanford, Calif.: Stanford University Press.
Jackson, Jean. 1990. Déjà Entendu: The Liminal Qualities of Anthropological Fieldnotes. *Journal of Contemporary Ethnography* 19 (1): in press (special issue on ethnographic research writing).
Kirschner, Suzanne R. 1987. "Then What Have I to Do with Thee?": On Identity, Fieldwork, and Ethnographic Knowledge. *Culture Anthropology* 2:211–34.
Lewis, Oscar. 1961. *The Children of Sanchez: Autobiography of a Mexican Family.* New York: Random House.
Marcus, George E., and Dick Cushman. 1982. Ethnographies as Texts. *Annual Review of Anthropology* 11:25–69.
Marcus, George E., and Michael M. J. Fischer. 1986. *Anthropology as Cultural Critique: An Experimental Moment in the Human Sciences.* Chicago: University of Chicago Press.

ROGER SANJEK

Fire, Loss, and the Sorcerer's Apprentice

As Jean Jackson's anthropologist natives revealed to her, the very thought of fieldnotes is "fraught with emotion . . . both in the field and later." Fieldnotes may "reveal the kind of person you are." Their existence summons up feelings of professional and personal competence and obligation. Destruction or loss of fieldnotes is the worst thing that can happen to an anthropologist.

How appropriate, then, that the image of fieldnotes afire came up in so many of Jackson's interviews. This has its feared but practical side: "If the house were burning down I'd go to the notes first," one anthropologist told her. Yet I suspect that with such deep, emotional feelings about identity involved, the purging by fire also conveys a lure of finality where one must live with ambivalence.[1]

The shackles that fieldnotes may be to an anthropologist and the release the anthropologist might feel when they are gone are ingredients in the wild scene of fieldnote burning near the end of Barbara Pym's novel *Less than Angels* (1955), mentioned by one of Jackson's informants and epigraphed by David Plath for his essay in this book.

[1] Fire does bring finality. When Margaret Mead received a letter in Samoa from Edward Sapir telling her he had fallen in love with someone else, she burned all his letters to her. This was uncharacteristic; Mead's habit was to save all her letters, from nearly everyone (Howard 1984: 73).

Pym knew her anthropologists well; she was from 1958 to 1974 editorial assistant to International African Institute director Daryll Forde, and assistant editor of the journal *Africa*.

Fire has indeed threatened the work of flesh-and-blood anthropologists. On Nigel Barley's second Cameroons field trip, the hum and glow of fire over the village he was working in filled him with panic. "It was probably a hut on fire. I felt with strange certainty that it was mine. All my notes on local healing techniques, my camera and equipment, my documents and records were now doubtless disappearing in a pall of smoke" (1986: 91).

A false alarm—but not so for David Maybury-Lewis. As flames approached the Sherente village in Brazil where he and his wife Pia were conducting fieldwork in 1955–56, "I met Pia hurrying back towards our hut. 'We had better decide what we want to take out,' she said, 'I don't think we've got much time.' I grabbed my notebooks and pencils. She took the camera. On the second trip we took the hammocks" (1965: 77).

After the interrogation of Paul Rabinow by a French-speaking policeman while he was doing fieldwork in a Moroccan village in 1968–69, his key informant Malik was shaken: "He asked me to burn the notes we had made." Rabinow instead gave the fieldnotes to Malik to hold until the tempest subsided (1977: 85–89, 105). They were safely returned—nothing ventured, nothing burned.

Fire did more than threaten the fieldnotes of Winifred Hoernle, the first professional anthropologist to conduct fieldwork in South Africa and Namibia. In 1931 a fire at the University of the Witwatersrand library destroyed her 1912, 1913, and 1922–23 fieldnotes on the Khoikhoi (Carstens 1987: 1). Fortunately, several papers based on this work had already been published, and her journals survived (Carstens et al. 1987; Hoernle 1985). Four months into M. N. Srinivas's residence at the Center for Advanced Study in the Behavioral Sciences at Stanford University, on April 24, 1970, "all three copies of my fieldwork notes, processed over a period of eighteen years, were in my study at the Center when a fire was started by arsonists. My own study, and a neighbour's, were reduced to ashes in less than an hour, and only the steel pipes forming the framework stood out with odd bits of burnt and twisted redwood planks of the original wall sticking to them" (1976: xiii). Srinivas's mother had died in India only five days earlier, and his despair was overwhelming. Sol Tax suggested that he write his planned ethnography of Rampura village from memory, and this he began immediately to do, producing *The Remembered Village,* published in 1976 (Srinivas 1976: xiii–xv; 1978: 134–36; for appraisals of the book, see Madan 1978).

The notes lost were those that Srinivas had developed from his original fieldnotes, which had been written in Rampura and were safe in Delhi. These original notes were quickly microfilmed and airmailed to Stanford. With his long-time research assistant joining him, Srinivas was able to compare the paper fragments remaining after the fire with the original notes and reconstitute "a good part of the processed data." Yet *The Remembered Village* was written, in the main, from neither the original nor the salvaged notes. Srinivas began writing by hand from memory. He soon switched to dictaphone, and the draft of the book was completed by November 1970. The fieldnotes were consulted only to check certain details and to locate a passage on consulting a Rampura deity (Srinivas 1976: 326–28).

Fire may be the most dramatic and symbolic threat to fieldnotes, but it is not the only one. Gunnar Landtman, a member of the pre–World War I "Cambridge School," spent two years doing fieldwork on the Papua New Guinea coast, and his fieldnotes "were actually lost in a shipwreck; it was only by hiring a diver that he was able to salvage the trunk that contained them" (Stocking 1983: 84). Robert Dentan lost part of his 1962–63 fieldnotes on the Semai of Malaysia "when our canoe tipped over during a tricky portage over a fallen log on our last trip downstream" (Dentan 1970: 95). Following Stanley Diamond's 1958–59 fieldwork among the Nigerian Anaguta, "the larger part of my notes were stolen in October, 1960" (Diamond 1967: 363). No wonder many anthropologists store their fieldnotes in trunks and metal boxes (Lévi-Strauss 1955: 33; Perlman 1970: 312).[2]

Legends about lost fieldnotes were recited by several of Jean Jackson's anthropologist informants. A few even suggested that those who lost their notes might be better off. (I doubt that Srinivas, Dentan, or Diamond would agree.) Richard Schweder, in a front-page *New York Times Book Review* essay, "Storytelling among the Anthropologists," went even further:

[2]Two anthropologists have made light of losses, or near losses, of fieldnotes. "It was dawn. . . . I had clearly been woken by a large goat that was pensively devouring my field notes" (Barley 1983: 139–40). "Little boys grabbed my data to make kites" (Werner 1984: 61). This rings of "the travails of fieldwork" cocktail-party chatter. Those who write of fire and loss convey a different emotional tone.

The idea is that the best way to write a compelling ethnography is to lose your field notes. Sir Edmund Leach, the British anthropologist, did this. While in Southeast Asia during the Second World War, he lost his field data as a result of enemy action. Made free, quite by mishap, to speak on behalf of the facts, Sir Edmund went on to write a classic ethnography, "The [*sic*] Political Systems of Highland Burma." [1986: 1, 38]

Schweder was doing some storytelling of his own. Several acts of writing by Leach occurred between fieldnote-recording in the Kachin community of Hpalang, in 1939–40, and *Political Systems of Highland Burma*, published in 1954.

My Hpalang field notes and photographs were all lost as the result of enemy action. During 1941, however, I had found time to write up much of my Hpalang material in the form of a functionalist economic study of the Hpalang community. This manuscript is also lost but the effort was not entirely wasted. The fact that I had worked out this draft fixed many details in my mind which would otherwise have been confused. In 1942 when I reached India I sketched out notes of Hpalang as I then recollected it and I think the details were probably fairly accurate though some names and figures may have got confused. I took such notes as I could during my military tours of 1942–43 and these are preserved. . . . In 1946 I . . . was permitted by the University of London to prepare a thesis based largely on historical materials relating to the Kachin Hills Area. . . . I think I have at one time or another probably read nearly everything that has been published in English, French or German about the Kachin Hills Area during the past 130 years. [Leach 1954: 312]

Advocating "casuistry" in ethnographic writing, Schweder (1986: 38–39) follows his own advice. I read the first two sentences quoted from Leach to mean that he used his fieldnotes to write the 1941 "functionalist economic study" of Hlapang (see also Leach 1977: 196). That is ordinarily what British anthropologists mean by "writing up." Both fieldnotes and the draft study were then lost, in 1941 or 1942. Memory was prevailed upon only in 1942, in India, where Leach reconstructed a set of notes. These, plus his later 1942–43 notes and extensive historical materials, were used in writing *Political Systems*. To say that Leach was "made free . . . to speak on behalf of the facts" is to negate the efforts he indeed made to use, recall, and add to the fieldnotes that undergird his remarkable book.

Some anthropologists have also experienced fear that their fieldnotes might be lost not to them but to others, should the ethnographer
die before transcribing the notes into readable form. On leaving the
Mnong Gar village of Sar Luk in highland Vietnam in 1950, a hospi-
talized Georges Condominas learned, incorrectly, that "my days were
numbered. Since the worst could happen at any time, I had to take
advantage of my every living moment to salvage all the notes I could,
that is to say, to translate into French as much as possible of what I had
taken down directly in Mnong since I was, at that time, the only
person able to write the language" (Condominas 1972: 233).

Margaret Mead vowed early in her career that she would "write up
each trip in full before undertaking the next one" (1972: 184).

> I had been deeply impressed with the dreadful waste of field work as
> anthropologists piled up handwritten notes that went untranscribed
> during their lifetime and that no one could read or work over after they
> died. In New Zealand, Reo [Fortune] and I had called on Elsdon Best,
> that indefatigable chronicler of the Maori, and we had seen his cabinets
> full of notes. And every summer Pliny Earle Goddard took another
> lovely field trip to the Southwest and accumulated more notes that he
> never wrote up. [1972: 183]
>
> All of it is unique. All of it will vanish. All was—and will be—grist for
> some future anthropologist's mill. Nothing is wasted. He [sic] has only
> to record accurately and organize his notes legibly; then, whether he
> lives or dies, what he has done makes a contribution. [1977: 282]

Today's new fear, in addition to fire, loss, and death, is computer
wipeout. As anthropologists once moved from pencil to typewriter,
they are now, as Allen and Orna Johnson explain (in this book),
moving from typewriter to computer. Few computer users have not
lost text through error, careless attempts to overfill documents or
disks, or power failures. DOS-using anthropologists must master
BACKUP and COPY, and safeguard their second computer-readable
set of fieldnotes the way those of the typewriter era sent carbon copies
home for safekeeping.[3]

Fieldnotes cannot be produced without informants. Unless there are
"actions" and "utterances" (Ellen 1984: 214) to observe and hear, there

---

[3]In commenting on this essay, Moshe Shokeid told me of his unsettling experience of
learning that his fieldnotes would fade, then disappear. Max Gluckman provided
monies to photocopy and thereby preserve them.

is no ethnography. Evans-Pritchard (1940: 12–13) reproduced his famous conversation with Cuol to illustrate how noncooperative the Nuer could be. The act of recording fieldnotes stands for doing anthropology, for defining the ethnographer. But on a few occasions recorded in the fieldwork literature, anthropologists have revealed situations where their role has been challenged not by Nuer-like noncooperation but rather by the tables being turned.

"Mirth and horror" seized Ethel Albert when in 1956 her Rwandan field assistant Muntu failed to appear one morning,

> and I went to the kitchen to get my coffee for myself. He was there, leaning against his work-table, notebook and pencil in hand. He was talking to one of my informants and appeared to be taking notes. I asked what he was doing. "Anthropological research, like you. But I know the language, so my research will be better than yours." I asked if he meant to turn the notes over to me. He did not. This was his research. Happily, the professional rivalry between us did not last long. [1960: 369]

Muntu was literate; his challenge to Albert embodies the present reality of a world in which those whom anthropologists study, everywhere, can read (and write) fieldnotes, let alone ethnography. But such was not the case in the world anthropologists have lost, in the dreamtime when it was still acceptable to believe that there was "no more thrilling prospect for the anthropologist than that of being the first white man to visit a particular native community" (Lévi-Strauss 1955: 325–26).

Such romantic Western self-inflations, and their racist and sexist conventions, were dying—if slowly—by the 1930s, as Claude Lévi-Strauss's 1955 comment indicates. So does Rabinow's account (1977: 68–69) of his 1968–69 sexual conquest—symbolic domination—of a "Berber girl" in the field. Christine Obbo, siding perhaps with Muntu (a "research assistant on the cheap"), makes it clear in her essay here, however, that the last gasp of Western/middle-class/white/male (and female) ethnographic hegemony is still to be heard.

Lévi-Strauss's encounter with the Brazilian Nambikwara Indians in 1939 included this hint of the beginning of the end:

> As I had done among the Caduveo, I handed out sheets of paper and pencils. At first they did nothing with them, then one day I saw that they were all busy drawing wavy, horizontal lines. I wondered what they were trying to do, then it was suddenly borne upon me that they

were writing or, to be more accurate, were trying to use their pencils in
the same way as I did mine. . . . the chief had further ambitions. . . . he
asked me for a writing-pad, and when we both had one, and were
working together, if I asked for information on a given point, he did not
supply it verbally but drew wavy lines on his paper and presented them
to me, as if I could read his reply. . . . his verbal commentary followed
almost at once, relieving me of the need to ask for explanations. [1955:
296][4]

Decades earlier, in the 1890s, Franz Boas had already begun his
collaboration with the Kwakiutl-speaking *Metis* George Hunt; joint
effort and authorship were acknowledged. By the 1930s several "natives" were professional anthropologists. Sir Peter Buck (Te Rangi
Hiroa), a Maori, was staff ethnologist at the Bernice P. Bishop Museum in Honolulu, and from 1936 to 1951 its director (Keesing 1953: 3,
72, 101–2; Spoehr 1959). Jomo Kenyatta, a Kenyan; Fei Hsiao-tung, a
Chinese; and A. Aiyappan and D. N. Majumdar, both Indians, were
members of Bronislaw Malinowski's London School of Economics
seminar (Madan 1975: 133, 152; Malinowski 1938, 1939; Vidyarthi
1979a: 46, 171–73, 438–39; 1979b: 330–43, 352–55). The Mexicans
Manuel Gamio, Julio de la Fuente, and Alfonso Villa Rojas worked,
respectively, with Boas, Malinowski, and Robert Redfield and on
their own (Drucker-Brown 1982; Gamio 1930, 1931; Redfield 1934,
1941).

In the United States, American Indians William Jones, a Fox, and
Ella Deloria, a Dakota, were published students of Boas (Eggan 1955:
503–4; Jones 1939; Lesser 1976: 132; Liberty and Sturtevant 1978;
Mead 1959: 406). Under W. Lloyd Warner, African American anthro-
pologists Allison Davis did fieldwork in Massachusetts and Missis-
sippi, and St. Clair Drake in Mississippi and Chicago; Arthur Huff
Fauset, a student of Frank Speck and A. I. Hallowell, also studied
African American life ethnographically (Bond 1988; Davis et al. 1941;
Drake 1980; Fauset 1971; Szwed 1979). In sociology departments, Paul
Siu conducted a fieldwork-based study of the Chinese of Chicago (see
Tchen 1987), and S. Frank Miyamoto (1939) one of the Seattle Japa-
nese.

Today the promise and premise of a world anthropology in its

---

[4]In the late 1970s, Barley (1983: 84) found Dowayo mockery of fieldnote-taking
even more pointed. In a ritual performance, "the clowns were extravagant. . . . They
were delighted with me. They 'took photographs' through a broken bowl, 'wrote
notes' on banana leaves."

liberal or more radical universality is visible reality. Other-fucking in its more vulgar forms is drawing to a close. Yet the issue of to whom fieldnotes ultimately belong is not resolved. Their production requires local collaboration; their use, conversely, is mainly private, restricted to the ethnographer. Thorny issues of protection of informants remain, and the larger questions linger of authorship and of eventual access to cultures now lost by their immediate descendants.

Boas solved this problem as he scrambled to salvage the old Kwakiutl culture, studiously ignoring the commercial salmon industry and Christianity. His ethnography *is* his fieldnotes, and much if not most of it was published. But Boas is probably exceptional. As Sol Tax told Srinivas soon after the Stanford fire, "no social anthropologist, not even the most industrious . . . ever published more than a small portion of his data" (Tax 1976: xiv). Simon Ottenberg has arranged to deposit copies of his fieldnotes, to be made available after his death; Margery Wolf is aware of the complications in the short term but nonetheless believes that fieldnotes must in the long term become part of a public record. It was Margaret Mead's wish that her fieldnotes, with those of her colleagues, be accessible to future scholars (Bateson 1980: 276).

"All of it is unique. All of it will vanish," Mead wrote of the cultures that anthropologists study. In the short term an anthropologist's fieldnotes are her or his bread and butter. In the long term perhaps fieldnotes are like children, as envisioned by the Lebanese poet Kahlil Gibran (1923: 17–18):

> Your children are not your children. . . .
> They come through you but they are not from you,
> And though they are with you yet they belong not to you. . . .
> You may house their bodies but not their souls,
> For their souls dwell in the house of tomorrow, which you cannot visit,
>   not even in your dreams.

REFERENCES

Albert, Ethel M. 1960. My "Boy," Muntu. In *In the Company of Man: Twenty Portraits of Anthropological Informants,* ed. Joseph B. Casagrande, 357–75. New York: Harper Torchbooks.
Barley, Nigel. 1983. *Adventures in a Mud Hut: An Innocent Anthropologist Abroad.* New York: Vanguard Press.
———. 1986. *Ceremony: An Anthropologist's Misadventures in the African Bush.* New York: Holt.

Bateson, Mary Catherine. 1980. Continuities in Insight and Innovation: Toward a Biography of Margaret Mead. *American Anthropologist* 82:270–77.

Bond, George C. 1988. A Social Portrait of John Gibbs St. Clair Drake: An American Anthropologist. *American Ethnologist* 15:762–81.

Carstens, Peter. 1987. Introduction. In Carstens, Klinghardt, and West 1987, 1–15.

Carstens, Peter, Gerald Klinghardt, and Martin West, eds. 1987. *Trails in the Thirstland: The Anthropological Field Diaries of Winifred Hoernle.* Communication 14. Cape Town: Centre for African Studies, University of Cape Town.

Condominas, Georges. 1972. Musical Stones for the God of Thunder. In *Crossing Cultural Boundaries: The Anthropological Experience,* ed. Solon Kimball and James B. Watson, 232–56. San Francisco: Chandler.

Davis, Allison, Burleigh Gardner, and Mary Gardner. 1941. *Deep South: A Social Anthropological Study of Caste and Class.* Chicago: University of Chicago Press.

Dentan, Robert K. 1970. Living and Working with the Semai. In *Being an Anthropologist: Fieldwork in Eleven Cultures,* ed. George D. Spindler, 85–112. New York: Holt, Rinehart & Winston.

Diamond, Stanley. 1967. The Anaguta of Nigeria: Suburban Primitives. In *Contemporary Change in Traditional Societies.* Vol. 1, *Introduction and African Tribes,* ed. Julian Steward, 361–505. Urbana: University of Illinois Press.

Drake, St. Clair. 1980. Anthropology and the Black Experience. *Black Scholar* 11 (7): 2–31.

Drucker-Brown, Susan. 1982. Malinowski in Mexico: Editor's Introduction. In Bronislaw Malinowski and Julio de la Fuente, *Malinowski in Mexico: The Economics of a Mexican Market System,* 1–52. London: Routledge & Kegan Paul.

Eggan, Fred. 1955. Social Anthropology: Methods and Results. In *Social Anthropology of North American Tribes,* enl. ed., ed. Fred Eggan, 485–551. Chicago: University of Chicago Press.

Ellen, R. F. 1984. Producing Data: Introduction. In *Ethnographic Research: A Guide to General Conduct,* ed. R. F. Ellen, 213–17. San Diego: Academic Press.

Evans-Pritchard, E. E. 1940. *The Nuer.* Oxford: Oxford University Press.

Fauset, Arthur Huff. 1971 [1944]. *Black Gods of the Metropolis: Negro Religious Cults in the Urban North.* Philadelphia: University of Pennsylvania Press.

Gamio, Manuel. 1930 [1971]. *Mexican Immigration to the United States: A Study of Human Migration and Adjustment.* Chicago: University of Chicago Press. [New York: Dover]

———. 1931 [1971]. *The Mexican Immigrant: His Life Story.* Chicago: University of Chicago Press. [*The Life Story of the Mexican Immigrant.* New York: Dover]

Gibran, Kahlil. 1923 [1964]. *The Prophet.* New York: Knopf.

Hoernle, Winifred. 1985. *The Social Organization of the Nama and Other Essays,* ed. Peter Carstens. Johannesburg: Witwatersrand University Press.

Howard, Jane. 1984. *Margaret Mead: A Life.* New York: Fawcett Crest.

Jones, William. 1939. *Ethnography of the Fox Indians,* ed. Margaret Welpley Fisher. Bureau of American Ethnology Bulletin 125. Washington, D.C.: Smithsonian Institution.

Keesing, Felix M. 1953. *Social Anthropology in Polynesia: A Review of Research.* London: Oxford University Press.

Leach, E. R. 1954 [1965]. *Political Systems of Highland Burma: A Study of Kachin Social Structure.* Boston: Beacon.

———. 1977. In Formative Travail with Leviathan. *Anthropological Forum* 4:190–97.

Lesser, Alexander. 1976. The American Ethnological Society: The Columbia Phase, 1906–1946. In *American Anthropology: The Early Years,* ed. John Murra, 126–35. St. Paul, Minn.: West Publishing Company.

Lévi-Strauss, Claude. 1955 [1974]. *Tristes Tropiques.* Trans. John and Doreen Weightman. New York: Atheneum.

Liberty, Margot, and William Sturtevant. 1978. Appendix: Prospectus for a Collection of Studies on Anthropology. In *American Indian Intellectuals,* ed. Margot Liberty, 241–48. St. Paul, Minn.: West.

Madan, T. N. 1975. On Living Intimately with Strangers. In *Encounter and Experience: Personal Accounts of Fieldwork,* ed. Andre Beteille and T. N. Madan, 131–56. Honolulu: University of Hawaii Press.

———. 1978. A Review Symposium on M. N. Srinivas's *The Remembered Village.* *Contributions to Indian Sociology* 12:1–152.

Malinowski, Bronislaw. 1938. Introduction. In Jomo Kenyatta, *Facing Mount Kenya: The Tribal Life of the Gikuyu,* vii–xiii. New York: Vintage, n.d. (c. 1960s).

———. 1939. Preface. In Hsiao-Tung Fei, *Peasant Life in China: A Field Study of Country Life in the Yangtze Valley,* xix–xxvi. London: Routledge & Kegan Paul.

Maybury-Lewis, David. 1965 [1988]. *The Savage and the Innocent.* Boston: Beacon Press.

Mead, Margaret. 1959. *An Anthropologist at Work: Writings of Ruth Benedict.* Boston: Houghton Mifflin.

———. 1972. *Blackberry Winter: My Earlier Years.* New York: William Morrow.

———. 1977. *Letters from the Field, 1925–1975.* New York: Harper & Row.

Miyamoto, S. Frank. 1939 [1984]. *Social Solidarity among the Japanese in Seattle.* Seattle: University of Washington Press.

Perlman, Melvin. 1970. Intensive Field Work and Scope Sampling: Methods for Studying the Same Problem at Different Levels. In *Marginal Natives: Anthropologists at Work,* ed. Morris Freilich, 293–338. New York: Harper & Row.

Pym, Barbara. 1955 [1982]. *Less Than Angels.* New York: Harper & Row.

Rabinow, Paul. 1977. *Reflections on Fieldwork in Morocco.* Berkeley: University of California Press.

Redfield, Robert. 1934 [1962]. Preface. In Robert Redfield and Alfonso Villa Rojas, *Chan Kom: A Maya Village,* ix–x. Chicago: University of Chicago Press.

———. 1941. Preface. In *The Folk Culture of Yucatan,* ix–xiv. Chicago: University of Chicago Press.

Schweder, Richard. 1986. Storytelling among the Anthropologists. *New York Times Book Review,* September 20, pp. 1, 38–39.

Spoehr, Alexander. 1959. Foreword. In Peter H. Buck, *Vikings of the Pacific,* v–vii. Chicago: University of Chicago Press. Originally published as *Vikings of the Sunrise* (New York: Lippincott, 1938).

Srinivas, M. N. 1976. *The Remembered Village.* Berkeley: University of California Press.

——. 1978. *The Remembered Village:* Reply to Criticisms. *Contributions to Indian Sociology* 12:127–52.

Stocking, George W., Jr. 1983. The Ethnographer's Magic: Fieldwork in British Anthropology from Tylor to Malinowski. In *Observers Observed: Essays on Ethnographic Fieldwork,* ed. George W. Stocking, Jr., 70–120. Madison: University of Wisconsin Press.

Szwed, John. 1979. The Ethnography of Ethnic Groups in the United States, 1920–1950. In *The Uses of Anthropology,* ed. Walter Goldschmidt, 100–109. Washington, D.C.: American Anthropological Association.

Tax, Sol. 1976. Foreword. In Srinivas 1976, ix—xi.

Tchen, John Kuo Wei. 1987. Introduction. In Paul C. P. Siu, *The Chinese Laundryman: A Study of Social Isolation,* xxiii–xxxix. New York: New York University Press.

Vidyarthi, L. P. 1979a. *Rise of Anthropology in India: A Social Science Orientation.* Vol. 1, *The Tribal Dimension.* Atlantic Highlands, N.J.: Humanities Press.

——. 1979b. *Rise of Anthropology in India: A Social Science Orientation.* Vol. 2, *The Rural, Urban, and Other Dimensions.* Atlantic Highlands, N.J.: Humanities Press.

Werner, Dennis. 1984. *Amazon Journey: An Anthropologist's Year among Brazil's Mekranoti Indians.* New York: Simon & Schuster.

PART II

Unpacking "Fieldnotes"

Physically, the corpus of data I have acquired over the years fills 10 file boxes with 5 × 8 inch sheets of paper. Three boxes contain basic data of many types, classified according to the HRAF [Human Relations Area Files] indexing system, which I have used from the beginning of my Tzintzuntzan work, and which I feel is the most logical system for community studies. A fourth file contains nearly 400 dreams from more than 40 informants, while a fifth holds TAT [Thematic Apperception Test] protocols, all taken from tapes, of 20 informants. A sixth box contains data, much of it taped, on health and medical practices and beliefs. Two more boxes are filled with nearly 200 years of vital statistics, a near 100% sample of births, marriages, and deaths drawn from the parish archive and, since 1930, from the municipal civil registry as well. I have hand-transcribed from the original sources half or more of these data, a process requiring hundreds, and possibly thousands, of hours. . . . Finally, two boxes are filled with over 3000 slips, each of which contains basic data on a single person, all people whose names appear on any of the three 100% complete censuses taken in 1945, 1960, and 1970.

—George M. Foster

JAMES CLIFFORD

Notes on (Field)notes

This essay aims to complicate and decenter the activity of description in ethnography. It begins with three scenes of writing, photographs printed in George Stocking's *Observers Observed*.[1] The first, a recent photo by Anne Skinner-Jones, catches the ethnographer Joan Larcom glancing down at her notes while seated on a straw mat among women and children on the island of Malekula, Vanuatu. It is a moment of distraction. Larcom seems preoccupied with her notes. Two women look to the left, beyond the frame, at something that has caught their attention. Two boys stare straight into the camera. Another child's gaze seems riveted on the ethnographer's pen. The second image is a photograph from 1898 showing C. G. Seligman, Malinowski's teacher, in New Guinea. He is seated at a table surrounded by half a dozen Melanesian men. One of them sits rather tentatively on a chair drawn up to the table. Various ethnographic objects are scattered there. Seligman is intently writing in a notebook. The third scene, featured by Stocking on his volume's cover, finds Malinowski working at a table inside his famous tent in the Trobriands. He has posed himself in profile, turned away from a group of men who are looking on from just beyond the tent flaps.

[1] See Stocking 1983: 179, 82, 101. The volume contains other revealing scenes of fieldwork, more or less posed, which might be compared to the genre in realist painting which portrays the artist with model(s) in the studio.

1. *Inscription*. Joan Larcom with informants in Southwest Bay, Malekula, Vanuatu. Courtesy Ann Skinner-Jones.

2. *Transcription*. C. G. Seligman at work, Hula. Courtesy University Museum of Archaeology and Anthropology, Cambridge, England.

3. *Description*. Malinowski at work, Omarakana. Courtesy Mrs. Helena Wayne-Malinowska.

These three remarkable photographs tell a lot about the orders and disorders of fieldwork. Each would repay close attention. But I am using them here merely to illustrate and to distinguish graphically three distinct moments in the constitution of fieldnotes. (I can only guess what was actually going on in any of the three scenes of writing.)

I use the first to represent a moment of *inscription*. I imagine that the photo of Joan Larcom glancing at her notes records a break (perhaps only for an instant) in the flow of social discourse, a moment of abstraction (or distraction) when a participant-observer jots down a mnemonic word or phrase to fix an observation or to recall what someone has just said. The photo may also represent a moment when the ethnographer refers to some prior list of questions, traits, or hypotheses—a personal "Notes and Queries." But even if inscription is simply a matter of, as we say, "making a mental note," the flow of action and discourse has been interrupted, *turned* to writing.

The second scene—Seligman seated at a table with his Melanesian informant—represents a moment of *transcription*. Perhaps the ethnographer has asked a question and is writing down the response: "What do you call such and such?" "We call it so and so." "Say that again, slowly." Or the writer may be taking dictation, recording the myth or magical spell associated with one of the objects on the table-top. This kind of work was the sort Malinowski tried to dislodge from center stage in favor of participant-observation: getting away from the table on the verandah and hanging around the village instead, chatting, questioning, listening in, looking on—writing it all up later. But despite the success of the participant-observation method, transcription has remained crucial in fieldwork, especially when the research is linguistically or philologically oriented, or when it collects (I prefer "produces") extended indigenous texts. Boas spent quite a few hours seated at a writing table with George Hunt. Indeed a large part of Malinowski's published ethnographies (their many myths, spells, legends) are the products of transcription. In *Return to Laughter* Laura Bohannan (Bowen 1954) advised prospective fieldworkers: "You'll need more tables than you think."

The writing evoked by the scene of Malinowski inside his tent may be called *description*, the making of a more or less coherent representation of an observed cultural reality. While still piecemeal and rough, such field descriptions are designed to serve as a data base for later

writing and interpretation aimed at the production of a finished account. This moment of writing in the field generates what Geertz
(1973) has called "thick descriptions." And it involves, as the Malinowski photo registers, a turning *away* from dialogue and observation
toward a separate place of writing, a place for reflection, analysis, and
interpretation. Stories of fieldwork often tell of a struggle to preserve
such a place: a tent with the flaps closed, a private room in a house, a
typewriter set up in the corner of a room, or, minimally, a dry,
relatively quiet spot in which to spread out a few notebooks.

   The three scenes of writing are, of course, artificially separated: they
blend, or alternate rapidly, in the shifting series of encounters, perceptions, and interpretations called fieldwork. The term "fieldwork" has
a misleading unity, and breaking it up in this way may at least have a
defamiliarizing effect. Moreover, it should be apparent that, as I am
using them here, these "scenes" are less representations of typical
activities than images, or figures, standing for analytical abstractions.
The abstractions refer to basic processes of recording and constructing
cultural accounts in the field. I have found it useful to take these
processes, rather than fieldnotes as such, as my topic. For it is clear
from Jean Jackson's survey, as well as from the diversity of observations contained in this volume, that there can be no rigorous definition
of exactly what constitutes a fieldnote. The community of ethnographers agrees on no common boundaries: diaries and journals are included by some, excluded by others; letters to family, to colleagues, to
thesis supervisors are diversely classified; some even rule out transcripts of interviews. The *institution* of fieldnotes does exist, of course,
widely understood to be a discrete textual corpus in some way produced by fieldwork and constituting a raw, or partly cooked, descriptive database for later generalization, synthesis, and theoretical elaboration. But within this institution, or disciplinary convention, one
finds an enormous diversity of experience and opinion regarding what
kind of or how much note-taking is appropriate, as well as just how
these notes are related to published ethnographies. A historical account of this diversity (linked to influential teachers, disciplinary exemplars, and national research traditions) would be revealing. There
is, however, a problem of evidence: most of the actual practice and
advice is unrecorded or inaccessible. Fieldnotes are surrounded by
legend and often a certain secrecy. They are intimate records, fully
meaningful—we are often told—only to their inscriber.

Thus, it is difficult to say something systematic about fieldnotes, since one cannot even define them with much precision. The three processes marked off in this essay account for a good deal of ethnographic production without exhausting the subject. And it should be stressed at the outset that a focus on the interrelations of inscription, transcription, and description need not imply that writing is the essence of fieldwork. Its importance is suggested by *-graphy* in the word ethnography, but there is no point in replacing the misleading formula "participant-observation" with an equally simplistic "participant-inscription."[2] Fieldwork is a complex historical, political, intersubjective set of experiences which escapes the metaphors of participation, observation, initiation, rapport, induction, learning, and so forth, often deployed to account for it. The frankly graphocentric analysis that follows merely brings to center stage processes that have until recently been simplified or marginalized in accounts of ethnographic research.

Fifteen years ago Clifford Geertz asked—and answered—the crucial question underlying this collection of essays: "What does the ethnographer do—he writes" (1973: 19). His influential discussion went a long way toward opening up a broad domain for debate (see also Crapanzano 1977; Dumont 1978). But I will suggest in what follows that Geertz and the mainstream of "symbolic anthropology" unduly narrowed the domain of ethnographic writing to processes of inscription and interpretive description. My three scenes of writing are an attempt to complicate matters.[3]

---

[2]Jean Jackson and Simon Ottenberg (this volume) discuss the crucial function of memory as a (re)contextualizing process making fieldnotes (re)intelligible. The role of fieldnotes as mnemonic artifacts largely escapes my graphocentric analysis. Nor do I deal with the full range of documentary materials produced and gathered in the field— maps, photos, documents, objects of diverse sorts.

[3]In his book *Works and Lives: The Anthropologist as Author,* which appeared after this essay was completed, Geertz writes of cultural description with a good deal more hesitation than he did fifteen years before—"now that anthropologists are caught up in the vast reorganization of political relationships going on in the world and the hardly less vast rethinking of just what it might be that 'description' is, . . ." (p. 141) "The moral asymmetries across which ethnography works and the discursive complexity within which it works make any attempt to portray it as anything more than the representation of one sort of life in the categories of another impossible to defend" (1988: 141, 144). Description as a perhaps impossible goal is not rejected in *Works and Lives.* But there is a new emphasis: thick description becomes contingent description, caught up in history, politics, and the imperfect arts of writing and translation.

Scene One

What is most extraordinary in the image chosen by Joan Larcom to represent her fieldwork in *Observers Observed* is the sense of confusion it registers. Data inscription appears not as an orderly process of collecting or recording but as an improvisation in the midst of competing, distracting messages and influences. The photo's play of gazes suggests (1) that the focused ethnographic moment always leaks beyond its frame into other "irrelevant" events; (2) that the ethnographic observer is always her- or himself observed; and (3) that any representation of this messy event, as here the photograph, is itself part of the event. The gazes, directed to the act of writing, to something outside the scene, and to the photographer, signal the confusion of fieldwork, its inescapable reflexivity, and the *struggle* to register data.

The photo is also appropriately ambiguous concerning the ethnographer's activity. Is she writing something down or looking something up? Are we witnessing the birth of a new, jotted text or a recourse to some notes that have been brought into the field, a prefiguration of what will count as important in the swirl of potentially meaningful discourse and activity? In the Anne Skinner-Jones photograph we cannot tell. Recent literary and textual theory argues that the ambiguity can, in fact, never be resolved. Inscription is both the making and remaking of texts. Writing is always to some degree rewriting. This is also the burden of Larcom's essay (1983), which analyzes her engagement with, simultaneously, the Mewun of Malekula and the unfinished texts of her predecessor in the field, A. B. Deacon. Larcom's essay portrays ethnographic fieldwork as fully historical: drawing on prior inscriptions to portray local customs over time *and* temporally situating its own interpretations of events and documents in an ongoing series. The critical and inventive use of prior written sources enmeshes ethnography in the history of ethnography. As Emiko Ohnuki-Tierney reminded us in her paper at the 1985 symposium, the rapprochement of ethnography and history in recent years diversifies the range of appropriate textual sources. The archive encroaches on the field; historical readings can no longer be seen as mere background for the essential work of firsthand discovery.[4]

_____

[4] The latest convergence of history and anthropology has been widely discussed; see, among others, Cohn 1981; Davis 1981; Sahlins 1985; Thomas 1963; Wolf 1982. For the

The belief in ethnography as an original production, a process of pure inscription most perfectly embodied in the fieldnote, is shaken. For of all the data used by fieldworkers, the texts created in the field have seemed most authentic, least tainted by prejudice. Fieldnotes embody cultural facts apparently under the control of their inscriber. Malinowski expressed the notion of originality a little too clearly, as usual, in his field diary (1967:140): "Feeling of ownership: it is I who will describe them or create them." But ethnographers can no longer claim this sort of originary or creative role, for they must always reckon with predecessors (and no longer only those most easily dismissed: missionaries, travelers, administrators). The field is more and more littered with "serious" ethnographic texts. One writes among, against, through, and in spite of them. This predicament undermines fieldnotes as the privileged empirical basis for a descriptive practice.

Indeed, one has, less and less, the illusion of control over the construction of any written corpus. Many literary analyses of intertextuality (e.g., Barthes 1970; Bloom 1975; Kristeva 1969) have made us confront the *un*originality of writing.[5] And recent studies of ethnography as a genre (Pratt 1986; Thornton 1983, 1985) bring out the many tropes it shares with unscientific, lay forms such as travel writing. Moreover, the originality of "primary" inscriptive practices has been challenged by theories of prefiguration and pre-encoding, most notably those of Hayden White.[6] Even to notice an event or fact, to find it important, White argues, is to presuppose some prior inscription or grid. The class of phenomena taken to be "the field" can be grasped— in sequence or separately—according to at least four modes of figuration: (1) as an image or pattern (metaphoric), (2) as a collection of empirical facts (metonymic), (3) as a hierarchical, functional, or organ-

use of historical texts by anthropologists, see Evans-Pritchard's severe strictures (1971) on the Seligmans. "Ethnographic" topics and rhetoric have been adopted by social and cultural historians (see Rosaldo 1986), but as yet no systematic analysis exists concerning the differences and similarities of research *practice*, juxtaposing "the archive" with "the field"—seen both as textual, interpretive activities, as disciplinary conventions, and as strategic spatializations of overdetermined empirical data.

[5] In Kristeva's words, "Every text takes shape as a mosaic of citations, every text is the absorption and transformation of other texts" (1969: 146).

[6] See esp. White's *Metahistory* (1973) and *Tropics of Discourse* (1978). Daniel Defert's analysis (1982, 1984) of *grilles de description* in early travel accounts identifies "obvious" units, or "natural" entities, which are projected prior to even the most detailed and accurate accounts. Thornton (1988) takes a similar approach to early ethnographies.

ic whole (synecdochic), or (4) as a temporal, usually passing, reality (ironic). Kenneth Burke's four master tropes are here deployed to account for the dominant forms of historical narrative. White makes a strong claim that any historical or cultural "fact" can be registered as meaningful only by virtue of some prior code or figuration of the whole in which it belongs.

Robert Thornton (1988) makes an equally strong argument for the textual/rhetorical prefiguration of the facts in ethnographies that purport to describe social or cultural wholes. A classificatory rhetoric orders the most elementary items of behavior and experience included in the textual "corpus." (Thornton makes visible the commonsense metaphors of body, architecture, and landscape that underpin ethnographic co-constructions of text and society.) The most simple description, or even statistical counting, in the field presupposes that the items recorded are parts of larger social or cultural units whose imaginary configuration in terms of explicit or implicit wholes relies on rhetorical means.

Another account of the pre-encoding of facts has been offered by Johannes Fabian (1983). He argues that the differences constituting "us" and "them" in ethnography, a complex play of distances in each moment of inscription (visible in the photo of Joan Larcom), have been mastered and simplified in the form of an overriding *temporal* distance. "They" are placed in either a historical past or a mythic, oral (non-historical) condition. Fabian's critique makes us aware that every perception and inscription of an "event" implies a temporal positioning with political implications. Very concrete decisions of what to record in the field can follow from these prior assumptions. If one perceives an event—a performance or ritual—as a traditional survival, one may "naturally" exclude from one's data the modern, commercial, or evangelical forces that are everywhere in the culture but "peripheral" to the event. If, however, one sees the performance or ritual as emergent, predominantly located not in a past but in a possible future, modern things become interesting and will be much more prominent in one's corpus of inscriptions.

Of course, few ethnographers believe that the facts "speak" for themselves, or that the scientific observer merely collects or records them. But it is still widely assumed that inscription, the passage of experiential phenomena into writing, is at the origin of ethnography's more or less realistic descriptions. What I have said so far suggests that this is too simple a view of the writing, prefiguring, and remembering that occur in the field. Inscription is intertextual, figurative, and historical all the way down to the most "immediate" perceptions.

Scene Two

Theorists who see ethnography as beginning with a process of inscription generally rely on Ricoeur's influential formulation (1971). Clifford Geertz gives a quick version in his introduction to *The Interpretation of Cultures,* an essay which I am rewriting here and to which I thus owe a great deal: "The ethnographer 'inscribes' social discourse; *he writes it down.* In so doing, he turns it from a passing event, which exists only in its own moment of occurrence, into an account, which exists in its inscriptions and can be reconsulted" (1973: 19; original emphasis). I have suggested, drawing on White, Thornton, and Fabian, that the very noting of an "event" presupposes a prior inscription. Moreover, my second scene of writing suggests further the limits of inscription as a model for what ethnographers do. The photograph of an ethnographer doing extended textual work with an indigenous collaborator reveals a kind of writing in the field that is often not a matter of catching "passing events" of social discourse as much as it is a process of transcribing already formulated, fixed discourse or lore. A ritual, for example, when its normal course is recounted by a knowledgeable authority, is not a "passing event." Nor is a genealogy. They are already inscribed. The same is true of everything paradoxically called "oral literature." A myth recited and taken down, a spell or song recorded in writing or on tape—these involve processes of transcription and explicit translation. I have suggested elsewhere the difference it makes when transcription and indigenous forms of writing are moved toward the center of ethnography (Clifford 1983: 135–42). For example, if writing in the field is not seen as beginning with inscription, then the ethnographic writer less automatically appears as a privileged recorder, salvager, and interpreter of cultural data. Greater prominence given to transcribed materials can produce a more polyphonic final ethnography. This effect already existed in the early works of Boas, Lowie, and others who, seeing their task as importantly philological, translated and commented on indigenous texts, many of them written by native "informants." (Even the term *informant* implies a story of inscription: "They tell me, I write it down.") The image of transcription (of writing over) interrupts the smooth passage from

writing down to writing up, from inscription to interpretive description. The authority of the researcher who brings passing, usually oral,
experience into permanent writing is decentered.[7]

I do not mean to suggest, however, that transcription is an innocent,
ethically superior, or nonauthoritative form of writing. It distributes
authority differently. Authority is neither bad nor good in itself, but it
is always tactical. It enacts power relations. The range of possible
readings differs according to whether a cultural account presents itself
as a description, for example, or as an exercise in philology. Fieldnotes, less focused or "cooked" than published ethnographies, reflect
more diverse, often contested, contexts of authority. (This is perhaps
one of the reasons why they have become interesting at a time like the
present, when styles of scientific description and analysis are being
intensely debated.) Fieldnotes contain examples of my three kinds of
writing: inscription (notes, not raw but slightly cooked or chopped
prior to cooking), description (notes sautéed, ready for the later addition of theoretical sauces), and transcription (reheated leftovers?). But
the cooking metaphor, so tempting when it comes to fieldnotes, is
inexact, because there are no "raw" texts. Transcription, which as a
kind of copying appears to involve the least transformation, is in no
way a direct or innocent record. The process may have the political
effect of making canonical what is simply one telling of a myth or item
of cultural lore. And transcription always raises questions about *translation*.

In a very acute essay, Talal Asad (1986) argues that the rather commonly invoked model of ethnography as translation hides the fact that
cultures are not like coherent languages or texts but are composed of
conflicting discourses. Moreover, the apparently neutral act of translating is enmeshed in global power inequalities. There are persistently
"strong" and "weak" languages, he observes, and the vast majority of
ethnographies are written in strong languages. Asad's analysis of how
a strong language of ethnography overrides other languages adds a
political dimension to our attention to fieldnotes.

The texts produced in the field are often polyglot. They include
large quantities of the local vernacular plus diverse pidgins, short-
hands, and languages of translation, along with the language or lan-

---

[7] I have analyzed critically this mode of authority, which identifies ethnography with
a fraught passage from oral to literate, from event to text; see Clifford 1986b: 109–19.
For a recent look behind the scenes of Boas's textual production which shows his
Tsimshian collaborator, Henry Tate, "on a tightrope between oral and literary storytelling," see Maud 1989: 161.

guages of the ethnographer. The final "written-up" ethnography smooths over the discursive mess—or richness—reflected in the fieldnotes. Is this inevitable? To a degree, yes. Who would want to read unimproved fieldnotes? But there are alternative uses and formats for these texts produced in the field. I have called attention elsewhere (Clifford 1986a: 15–17) to a recent series of publications from the University of Nebraska Press: the papers of James Walker (1980, 1982, 1983), who worked with the Lakota Sioux around the turn of the century. Thirty-eight Lakota "authorities" are listed at the back of the first volume, *Lakota Belief and Ritual*. Each section of the book is presented as the work of one or another of these authorities, interspersed with Walker's own notes and reflections. In the normal transition from fieldnotes to final ethnography, utterances tend to lose their individuated quality. Quotations from indigenous sources are often not given proper-name attribution, and even when they are, they merely serve to confirm or exemplify the ethnographer's general line. Two Crows is seldom heard denying things, as he more often does in contradictory, heterophonic fieldnotes.[8] Of course, vernacular expressions do appear in many ethnographies, according to protocols with which we are all familiar; for example, they often stand for problematic native "concepts." But we seldom encounter in published work any cacophony or discursive contradiction of the sort found in actual cultural life and often reflected in fieldnotes. A dominant language has overridden, translated, and orchestrated these complexities.

A culinary relapse: I am reminded of Roland Barthes's image of the sauce or glaze, the *nappe,* which in French cuisine smooths over and hides the productive, transformative processes of the cooking. Barthes makes this into an image for ideological, naturalizing discourse. I have the impression, as I try to find out about fieldnotes, that I can sometimes see through the *nappe* of the finished ethnography—beneath the unifying glaze, chopped meat.

Scene Three

Any systematic analysis of fieldnotes is hampered by the problem of access to a broad sample of texts. Moreover, individuals' reflections on

---

[8]The issue of what to do with disagreeing, or heterophonic, Lakota voices was specifically confronted by Walker in writing up his fieldnotes for what would become his classic monograph, *The Sun Dance* (1917). In a revealing exchange of letters, Clark Wissler (of the American Museum of National History), urged Walker not to write too

their own practice are limited in obvious ways.[9] The fullest published compendium of fieldnotes that I know is Geertz's *Religion of Java,* a work unusual to the extent that it is openly constructed from texts written during primary research. The book contains hundreds of indented passages identified as "transcriptions from the author's field notes" (1960: 15). These fieldnotes are largely of my third sort: composed, thick *descriptions.* Almost any example will give the flavor:

> We spoke about the difference between village and town patterns of *duwé gawé,* and she said the *buwuh* pattern was different. She said that the people on the Pohredjo row (this is the elite section of town, inhabited almost entirely by *prijajis*) wouldn't accept *buwuh.* They only accept gifts (called *cadeau,* following Dutch usage), and then they note down the price of the gift, and when the giver has a *duwé gawé* they return something of exactly the same value. [1960: 67]

The passage is indirect, summarized speech about custom, with parenthetical additions by the ethnographer, and this is a dominant mode throughout the book. The passage continues with a directly quoted interjection by the informant's brother, her own comments about how the exchange system doesn't work perfectly, and more parenthetical information about her class standpoint. The fieldnotes quoted in the book—often taking up as much as half the page—include a mixture of discursive positions and distinct viewpoints while maintaining, overall, a homogeneous tone.

Geertz provides an unusually specific appendix, which clarifies just how these notes were constructed and, to a degree, cleaned up for publication. Writing in the late 1950s, Geertz was far ahead of the field in textual self-consciousness. He would say things rather differently now, and it is unlikely that he would assert without hesitation, as he did then, that his book was "nothing more than a report," that his extensive use of fieldnotes was a way for the ethnographer "to get out of the way of his data, to make himself translucent so that the reader can see for himself something of what the facts look like and so judge

---

ideal or unified an account of the sun dance. He made a subversive suggestion, not followed by Walker: "I often feel that the ideal thing would be to publish all the statements of informants together with an estimate and summary by the investigator" (Walker 1980: 29).

[9]Jean Jackson's interviews provide ample evidence of the highly personal, and often ambivalent, feelings of individual researchers to their own precious and flawed productions in the field.

the ethnographer's summaries and generalizations in terms of the ethnographer's actual perceptions" (1960: 7). But despite its sometimes too simple notions of transparency, this is one of the few ethnographies that give us a real glimpse of the making of cultural descriptions in fieldnotes. It embodies a kind of textual empiricism, rather different from Geertz's later position of textual interpretationism. If *The Religion of Java* does not provide us with a direct view of its author's "actual perceptions" in the field, it does offer an unusual, if partial, access to his construction of ethnographic facts.

Consider the book's first quoted fieldnote, which ends the short opening chapter. It is an ethnographic set piece sketching a typical *slametan,* the "simple, formal, undramatic, almost furtive little ritual" that lies "at the center of the whole Javanese religious system" (1960: 11). After setting out the "pattern" of events (when the ceremony is given, who cooks, who gets invited, what is chanted, how the food is distributed and received), Geertz then quickly elucidates the ritual's "meaning." He does this in a familiar ethnographic way, quoting and explicating the statements of unnamed Javanese. Sometimes he creates a collective persona, as in this definition of the ritual's psychic goal: "The wished-for state is *slamet,* which the Javanese defines with the phrase '*gak ana apa apa*'—'there isn't anything,' or, more aptly, 'nothing is going to happen (to anyone)'" (1960: 14). Then, at the end of a paragraph on Javanese beliefs about the omnipresence of spirits— against which *slametans* provide protection—the book's first indented fieldnote makes its appearance, introduced simply "As a Javanese put it."

> At a *slametan* all kinds of invisible beings come and sit with us and they also eat the food. That is why the food and not the prayer is the heart of the *slametan*. The spirit eats the aroma of the food. It's like this banana. I smell it but it doesn't disappear. That is why the food is left for us after the spirit has already eaten it. [1960: 15]

With this lucid and engaging statement, the chapter on *slametan* closes.

Like all direct extracts from fieldnotes the text "shows" the ethnography's representational data. In his paper at the 1985 AAA symposium, Michael Silverstein nicely analyzed this rhetorical function and added that rather like photographs in the text, quoted fieldnotes are "reality-close"; they have a "you are there" quality (for example, in the quotation above: "It's like *this* banana"). A reading of *The Religion of Java* which focused on its ways of establishing authority might see the opening chapter as an elaborate staging of its final quotation. The last word on a "basic core ritual" (1960: 14) is given to a Javanese making an explicit cultural interpretation. This interpretation, presented *as a transcribed fieldnote,* associates the book's database with a direct access to the Javanese viewpoint. At the same time, the citation accomplishes a subtle fusion of native and ethnographic subjectivities in a common interpretive project. The passage, for all its "spoken" immediacy, is not surrounded by quotation marks. Geertz explains in his appendix (1960: 385–86) that such marks are reserved for more or less literal, or close, translations of things actually said. The passage in question is thus not an exact rendering but in some degree a reconstruction. It is an enunciation neither *by* a specific Javanese nor *by* Clifford Geertz; it falls somewhere between direct and indirect discourse, accomplishing a rhetorical fusion of viewpoints. It is the enunciation of an ethnographic persona speaking *cultural* truths.

The passage, endowed with both the personal presence of speech and the empirical function of a fieldnote, is an enunciation of *Javanese* knowledge. It does what any "good" ethnographic interpretation does, making a difficult custom or belief concretely comprehensible. Geertz chose it in part, certainly, for this reason: to show that his empirical data was a record not only of his observations but also of indigenous interpretations. Later he would explicitly argue that cultural facts are always already interpretations (Geertz 1973: 3–30). Moreover, since culture is prefigured as a complex but coherent whole, Javanese interpretations will not systematically contradict those of the ethnographer of Java. Geertz will account for all the interpretations he chooses to quote in *The Religion of Java.* And as we have seen, Javanese direct statements will, in their constitution as fieldnotes, have already been selected, focused, contextualized as "cultural" enunciations.

The book regularly presents its informants as interpreters giving lucid explanations of their beliefs and acts, sometimes with a laudable cultural relativism: "I don't know how it is in America, but here . . ." (1960: 14). Moreover, as in the first fieldnote quoted above, the research process is continually made manifest: "I asked her," "she said," then "he said," then a parenthesis on her personal background, and so forth. One might object that Geertz's notes smooth over a great deal, that they do not contain much on the ethnographer's subjective states, that reported interpretations seldom conflict radically, that a certain "ethnographic" tone suffuses all the purportedly individual voices. But how many ethnographies (let alone those written in the late 1950s, at the height of American social-scientific positivism) can satisfy such objections? What makes the fieldnotes selected for inclusion in *The Religion of Java* especially useful for my present purpose is the variety of ways in which they show cultural interpretations being constructed as fieldnotes. Javanese discourses and those of the ethnographer (descriptions, translations, contextual comments) are fused or, better, *orchestrated* to produce rich descriptions. Geertz's fieldnotes may be "thicker" than most. But the kind of selecting, narrating, contextualizing, and translating visible in them is in some degree practiced by any ethnographer who sits down to record and begin to make cultural sense of a busy day's impressions.

Travels with a Typewriter

Geertz's fieldnotes are, of course, anything but "raw." He tells us in his appendix (1960: 385) that they were carefully typed up every day or so. A short essay could be written about typewriters in the field (and soon, perhaps, one on word processors). There are intriguing glimpses in print. When Jean Briggs (1970) is ostracized by her Utku Eskimo hosts, she finds solace in her typewriter. Geertz represents the ethical ambiguities of fieldwork through a struggle over a typewriter with a Javanese informant (1968: 152–55). Colin Turnbull reveals somewhere in *The Forest People* (1961) that he has the machine with him (forcing us to reimagine his Mbuti villages, adding to the calm suffusion of forest sounds the tap-tap of fieldnotes in the making). To illustrate my third scene of writing I almost chose the famous photo that appears on the cover of this volume: Mead and Bateson in the Iatmul "mosquito room," facing each other from behind separate typewriters.

This moment of initial ordering, the making of a neat record (whether in type or script), must be a crucial one in the fieldwork process. "Good data" must be materially produced: they become a distanced, quasi-methodical corpus, something to be accumulated, jealously preserved, duplicated, sent to an academic advisor, cross-referenced, selectively forgotten or manipulated later on. A precious, precarious feeling of control over the social activities of inscription and transcription can result from creating an orderly text. This writing is far from simply a matter of mechanical recording: the "facts" are selected, focused, initially interpreted, cleaned up.

Most writing is sedentary activity. Unlike storytelling, it cannot be done while walking along a path. The turn to the typewriter involves a physical change of state, a break from the multisensory, multifocal perceptions and encounters of participant-observation. Writing of this sort is not "situated" like discourse or an oral story, which includes— or marks in the performance—the time/space of the present moment and audience. Rather, the present moment is held at bay so as to create a recontextualized, portable account. In crucial respects this sort of writing is more than inscription, more than the recording of a perception or datum of "evidence." A systematic reordering goes on. Fieldnotes are written in a form that will make sense elsewhere, later on. Some may even, like the notes included in *The Religion of Java,* pass directly into a published book. Turning to typewriter or notebook, one writes for occasions distant from the field, for oneself years later, for an imagined professional readership, for a teacher, for some complex figure identified with the ultimate destination of the research. Facing the typewriter each night means engaging these "others" or alter egos. No wonder the typewriter or the pen or the notebook can sometimes take on a fetishistic aura.

As we have repeatedly seen, fieldnotes are enmeshed in writing and reading that extends before, after, and outside the experience of empirical research. A fundamental question emerges. "The field," seen as a place of writing, leaks. Once one complicates and historicizes the "notes" in "field/notes," the boundaries of the first term, "field," begin to blur. How is the field spatially and temporally defined? Can one, properly speaking, record a field note while not physically "there"? Would a remembered impression first inscribed at one's home university count as a fieldnote? Or, what about a "thick description" written not at the site of research but while sojourning in the capital city of the host nation? Fieldnotes are by definition written "in" the field. But with increased coming and going, better global transport and mobility, where does the field begin and end? Indeed, the very identity of "fieldnotes" as a discrete corpus depends on a spatialization more and more difficult to maintain, a historically specific set of distances, boundaries, and modes of travel. As the historical and political relations of different parts of the planet shift, as cultures interpenetrate, and as ethnography turns back on its own culture, "the field" becomes more and more evidently an ideal construct.

It would be useful to trace a genealogy of the term "field," as used to designate a site of professional activity. While this is beyond my present scope, it is worth mentioning a few points of departure (Bertrand Pullman [1988] develops some of them in his analysis of the French term *terrain*). In various Western discourses "field" is associated with agriculture, property, combat, and a "feminine" place for ploughing, penetration, exploration, and improvement. The notion that one's empirical, practical activity unfolds in such a space has been shared by naturalists, geologists, archaeologists, ethnographers, missionaries, and military officers. What commonalities and differences link the professional knowledges produced through these "spatial practices" (De Certeau 1984)? What is excluded by the term "field?" The modern traveler, unlike the ethnographer, has no field, only a route; no body of classified data, only a narration. The primary "descriptions" of travelers are recorded in journals, not fieldnotes. How have these generic and professional differences been constituted and maintained? How has one set of practices come to be coded "objective," the other "subjective?" Such questions open up a larger domain of research concerned with the history of Western modes of travel, occupation, and dwelling. Within that general history professional ethnography appears as a particular, contested, spatial practice.

Arjun Appadurai (1986: 337) has raised similar spatial/historical questions with regard to the articulation of theory.

> At least since the latter part of the nineteenth century, anthropological theory has always been based on the practice of going *somewhere,* preferably somewhere geographically, morally, and socially distant from the theoretical and cultural metropolis of the anthropologist. The science of the other has inescapably been tied to the journey elsewhere. But the question of what kind of elsewhere is tied in complicated ways to the history of European expansion, the vagaries of colonial and postcolonial pragmatics, the shifting tastes of Western men of letters. In turn, changes in anthropological theorizing, influenced in ill-understood ways by these shifting loci of investigation, have themselves influenced fashions in anthropological travel. Places (i.e., particular areas, locations, cultures, societies, regions, even civilizations) are the objects of anthropological study as well as the critical links between description and analysis in anthropological theory.

The issues raised here are far-reaching and will require, as Appadurai has said, considerable development.[10] I can only suggest, in a passing

---

[10] Appadurai organized a session on place in anthropological theory and practice at the December 1986 meetings of the American Anthropological Association. Many of the papers presented there appeared in *Cultural Anthropology* 3 (February 1988).

way, how they impinge on the *topos* of fieldnotes. Appadurai's crucial point is that description and analysis are systematically linked (and distinguished) by specific historical *spatializations*.

From this perspective, a corpus called *field*notes serves the function of reifying and naturalizing a "place" to be kept separate from the various operations of theorizing, fictionalizing, and writing up that conventionally occur elsewhere. The largely unexamined distinction between "fieldnotes" and other forms of ethnographic writing (the intimate journal; or letters home; or more openly analytic, interpretive, or explanatory styles of writing) serves to constitute and protect a bounded "object" of study, a collection of textualized cultural facts that will serve as a fairly stable base for interpretation and theorizing even long after the field research has been accomplished. This spatially defined corpus resists the historicity of the long-term writing and rewriting processes involved in making an ethnography. Once recognized, however, the inescapable temporality of writing and rewriting unravels synchronic spatializations. And it blurs conventional frontiers separating, for example, "fieldnotes" from "writing up."

The problematic corpus, the disciplinary convention "fieldnotes," tends to dissolve into more general processes of writing—inscription, transcription, and description. And as one questions the specificity of writing done in "the field," one is led to confront the ways a cultural science defines and maintains its objects of study. I have suggested that ethnography—a practice fused, after the 1920s, with academic fieldwork—has tended to construct its object as something to be *described*. There are alternatives. A dominant paradigm of *transcription* (closer to the practice of Boas or Lowie, for example) constructs the other philologically, as a collection of discourse requiring translation and exegesis.[11] Or an ethnography less concerned to separate itself from "subjective" travel writing might adopt an openly *inscriptive* stance, registering the circumstantial situations of a perceiving, interpreting subject, noting events and statements as part of a passing sojourn of research. (Indeed, many recent autobiographical, reflexive, ethnographies can be seen as signs of a rapprochement between ethnographic and travel genres.) I have argued that all three modes of writing are active in fieldwork. But they have been hierarchically organized, under a dominant rhetoric of description, in ways that are now in question.

[11] The Walker collections mentioned above are recent examples (see also Evers and Molina 1987). For an ethnography (written by an anthropologist and a linguist) which combines description with extensive textual exegesis, see Bensa and Rivierre 1982.

Toward a Decentering of Description

The fieldnotes cited throughout *The Religion of Java* are typed-up, constructed, and written-over "descriptions." Actually, they contain little description in the strict sense. (Description is a specific, rather uncommon, form of writing.)[12] But their overall effect is descriptive: they select and foreshorten perceptions and statements in ways that constitute an objective, uncontested world of interpretations, indigenous and scientific. In the process, interpretations cease to be primarily debates, dialogues, transcriptions, or circumstantial inscriptions. I have argued that the construction of "thick" cultural descriptions involves a *turning away* from inscription and transcription to a different form of writing. The photo of Malinowski stages rather precisely this moment of turning away from encounter, speech, participation, and observation toward the writing table, the notebooks, the typewriter. A crucial line—in the photo, the shadowy threshold between the tent's inside and outside—must be maintained, crossed and recrossed. Various rituals and conflicts surround this transition. And as Jean Jackson's survey confirms, the turning toward solitary writing can be the focus of strongly ambivalent feelings: "It takes you away from the action" or "It keeps you from going native."

The process of field research is potentially endless. One can never have enough conversations, learn the language well enough, grasp all the "hidden" and emergent domains of indigenous life. Yet one must arrive at some baseline or adequate corpus of facts. The writing of descriptive fieldnotes, "good" data oriented toward a coherent cultural object, provides a body of knowledge prefigured for theoretical development. This textual (portable and permanent) corpus offers a conventional "empirical" ground, or starting point, in a situation where, as Geertz intimates, "it's interpretations all the way down" (1973: 29).

But descriptions are not merely interpretations. They are *written* rhetorical constructions. A fieldnote featured by Geertz (1973: 7–9) in his influential essay on "thick description" provides a particularly clear example: the story of Cohen the Jewish merchant in French colonial Morocco leading a raid against maurauding Berbers and claiming five hundred of their sheep as an indemnity. An ironic colonial tale, replete with Conradian touches (the French captain says to Cohen: "If you get killed, it's your problem!"), the tale is presented as a "not-untypical"

[12]See particularly the work of Hamon (1981) and Beaujour (1981).

excerpt from Geertz's field journal. Its composed, narrated quality is
patent. And it is, one assumes, derived from interlocution, narration,
and rewriting. The events take place in 1912, their source an unnamed
"informant." The field journal excerpt—"quoted raw, a note in a
bottle"—brings us to *see* the events. For example, after the conflict is
settled, a sharply etched scene:

> The two armed Berber groups then lined up on their horses at opposite
> ends of the plain, with the sheep herded between them, and Cohen, in
> his black gown, pillbox hat, and flapping slippers, went out alone
> among the sheep, picking out, one by one and at his own good speed,
> the best ones for his payment.

Here is description. But who saw this scene? Not Cohen. The "informant"? *His* informant? Or, as I suspect, the ethnographer as he sat at
his writing table, pulling together jottings, memories, transcriptions
of the account (or accounts) he heard?

Geertz cites this "fieldnote"—obviously complex and literary—to
show that ethnographic data are always constructions of other people's
constructions ("winks upon winks upon winks"). His point is important and trenchant. But Geertz's well-known formula for ethnography, "thick description," is more ambiguous. It can either be read as an
oxymoronic critique of the very notion of description ("interpretations all the way down") or be taken as a charter for an interpretive
science (which describes, with hermeneutic complexity, a cultural
object). By associating ethnographic construction with description,
however thick or problematic, Geertz limits a possibly far-reaching
critique. For description inevitably suggests a specular, representational relation to culture. I have argued that such a relation is always
rhetorically (also historically and politically) mediated. Ethnography
cannot, in practice, maintain a constant descriptive relationship to
cultural phenomena. It can maintain such a relationship only to what is
produced in fieldnotes, and especially in the most "focused" products
of writing in the field, those of my third scene. Other forms of
writing, inscriptive and transcriptive, may register quite different
relationships to the people, discourses, and events studied in fieldwork. One form of ethnographic writing, description, has too often
been made to stand for the entire ethnographic process. But whether it
is writing down, writing over, or writing up, the work of ethnography is intertextual, collaborative, and rhetorical. It is possible to be
serious, truthful, factual, thorough, scrupulous, referential—without
claiming to be describing anything.

REFERENCES

Appadurai, Arjun. 1986. Theory in Anthropology: Center and Periphery. *Comparative Studies in Society and History* 28:356–61.

Asad, Talal. 1986. The Concept of Cultural Translation in British Social Anthropology. In Clifford and Marcus 1986, 141–64.

Barthes, Roland. 1970. *S/Z*. Paris: Le Seuil.

Beaujour, Michel. 1981. Some Paradoxes of Description. *Yale French Studies* 61:27–59.

Bensa, Alban, and Jean Claude Rivierre. 1982. *Les chemins de l'alliance: L'organisation sociale et ses représentations en Nouvelle-Calédonie*. Paris: Société d'Etudes Linguistiques et Anthropologiques de France.

Bloom, Harold. 1975. *A Map of Misreading*. New York: Oxford University Press.

Bowen, Elenore Smith [Laura Bohannan]. 1954. *Return to Laughter*. New York: Anchor Books.

Briggs, Jean. 1970. *Never in Anger: Portrait of an Eskimo Family*. Cambridge, Mass.: Harvard University Press.

Clifford, James. 1983. On Ethnographic Authority. *Representations* 1:118–46.

———. 1986a. Introduction: Partial Truths. In Clifford and Marcus 1986, 1–26.

———. 1986b. On Ethnographic Allegory. In Clifford and Marcus 1986, 98–121.

Clifford, James, and George E. Marcus, eds. 1986. *Writing Culture: The Poetics and Politics of Ethnography*. Berkeley: University of California Press.

Cohn, Bernard. 1981. Anthropology and History in the 1980s: Toward a Rapprochement. *Journal of Interdisciplinary History* 12:227–52.

Crapanzano, Vincent. 1977. The Writing of Ethnography. *Dialectical Anthropology* 2:69–73.

Davis, Natalie. 1981. Anthropology and History in the 1980s: The Possibilities of the Past. *Journal of Interdisciplinary History* 12:267–75.

De Certeau, Michel. 1984. *The Practice of Everyday Life*. Berkeley: University of California Press.

Defert, Daniel. 1982. La collecte du monde. In *Collections passion*, ed. Jacques Hainard and Roland Kaehr, 17–31. Neuchâtel: Musée d'Ethnographie Neuchâtel. [Trans. in *Dialectical Anthropology* 7 (1982).]

———. 1984. Un genre ethnographique profane au XVe siècle: Les livres d'habits (Essai d'ethno-iconographie). In *Histoires de l'anthropologie XVI–XIX siècles*, ed. Britta Rupp-Eisenreich, 25–42. Paris: Klincksieck.

Dumont, Jean-Paul. 1978. *The Headman and I*. Austin: University of Texas Press.

Evans-Pritchard, E. E. 1971. Sources, with Particular Reference to the Southern Sudan. *Cahiers d'Etudes Africaines* 11:129–71.

Evers, Larry, and Felipe S. Molina. 1987. *Yaqui Deer Songs: Maso Bwikam*. Tucson: Sun Tracks and University of Arizona Press.

Fabian, Johannes. 1983. *Time and the Other: How Anthropology Makes Its Object*. New York: Columbia University Press.

Geertz, Clifford. 1960. *The Religion of Java*. New York: Free Press.

———. 1968. Thinking as a Moral Act: Ethical Dimensions of Anthropological Fieldwork in the New States. *Antioch Review* 27:139–58.

——. 1973. *The Interpretation of Cultures.* New York: Basic Books.

——. 1988. *Works and Lives: The Anthropologist as Author.* Stanford, Calif.: Stanford University Press.

Hamon, Philippe. 1981. *Introduction à l'analyse du descriptif.* Paris: Hachette.

Kristeva, Julia. 1969. *Semiolikè: Recherches pour une sémanalyse.* Paris: Le Seuil.

Larcom, Joan. 1983. Following Deacon: The Problem of Ethnographic Reanalysis, 1926–1981. In Stocking 1983, 175–95.

Malinowski, Bronislaw. 1967. *A Diary in the Strict Sense of the Term.* New York: Harcourt, Brace & World.

Maud, Ralph. 1989. The Henry Tate–Franz Boas Collaboration on Tsimshian Mythology. *American Ethnologist* 16:163–68.

Pratt, Mary Louise. 1986. Field Work in Common Places. In Clifford and Marcus 1986, 27–50.

Pullman, Bertrand. 1988. Pour une histoire de la notion de terrain. *Gradhiua* 5:21–30.

Ricoeur, Paul. 1971. The Model of the Text: Meaningful Action Considered as a Text. *Social Research* 38:529–62.

Rosaldo, Renato. 1986. From the Door of His Tent: The Fieldworker and the Inquisitor. In Clifford and Marcus 1986, 77–97.

Sahlins, Marshall. 1985. *Islands of History.* Chicago: University of Chicago Press.

Stocking, George, ed. 1983. *Observers Observed: Essays on Ethnographic Fieldwork.* History of Anthropology 1. Madison: University of Wisconsin Press.

Thomas, Keith. 1963. History and Anthropology. *Past and Present* 24:3–24.

Thornton, Robert. 1983. Narrative Ethnography in Africa, 1850–1920. *Man* 18:502–20.

——. 1985. "Imagine Yourself Set Down . . . .": Mach, Conrad, Frazer, Malinowski, and the Role of Imagination in Ethnography. *Anthropology Today* 1 (5): 7–14.

——. 1988. The Rhetoric of Ethnographic Holism. *Cultural Anthropology* 3:285–303.

Turnbull, Colin. 1961. *The Forest People.* New York: Simon & Schuster.

Walker, James R. 1917. *The Sun Dance and Other Ceremonies of the Oglala Division of the Teton Dakota.* Anthropological Papers 16; pt. 1. New York: American Museum of Natural History.

——. 1980. *Lakota Belief and Ritual,* ed. Raymond J. DeMallie and Elaine A. Jahner. Lincoln: University of Nebraska Press.

——. 1982. *Lakota Society,* ed. Raymond J. DeMallie. Lincoln: University of Nebraska Press.

——. 1983. *Lakota Myth,* ed. Elaine A. Jahner. Lincoln: University of Nebraska Press.

White, Hayden. 1973. *Metahistory.* Baltimore, Md.: Johns Hopkins University Press.

——. 1978. *Tropics of Discourse.* Baltimore, Md.: Johns Hopkins University Press.

Wolf, Eric. 1982. *Europe and the People without History.* Berkeley: University of California Press.

RENA LEDERMAN

Pretexts for Ethnography: On Reading Fieldnotes

Anthropologists do many things in the field and out, and while writing is one of those things, it is surely not the distinguishing characteristic of our work. Writing sets us apart neither from people in other disciplines and lines of work nor, always, from the people we seek to understand. Nevertheless, a focus on anthropological forms of writing can reveal something about the strengths and limits of anthropological knowledge.

Recent analyses of the conventions of ethnographic writing (e.g., Clifford 1983; Clifford and Marcus 1986; Marcus and Cushman 1982; Sperber 1982) are just part of a sustained exploration of the largely tacit dimensions of our work. During the past twenty years anthropologists have published detailed descriptions of the personal experience of fieldwork. While such accounts have not always been self-critical or analytical, they have been reflexive in a particularly direct manner and have occasionally pursued epistemological and ethical or political issues merely named in manuals on research technique.

I thank Michael Merrill, Hilly Geertz, Roger Sanjek, and Julie Taylor for comments on an early version of this chapter, and also Jim Clifford, whose paper I read in 1986 as I was drafting this one and whose arguments helped to provoke mine. I do not take account of a number of important, recent works (e.g., Clifford 1988; Geertz 1988; Strathern 1987).

The "I" is generally not present in more recent considerations of ethnographic writing, as Rabinow (1986) notes. However, analyses of unspoken conventions—such as how an authoritative or persuasive voice is created in ethnography (Clifford 1983; Geertz 1988; Rosaldo 1986)—may pose a more systematically critical challenge to anthropological self-understanding than do descriptions of field experiences, a challenge akin to that raised by earlier exposés of the relationship between anthropology and colonialism or by the feminist critique of anthropological knowledge.[1]

This volume's consideration of fieldnotes must be seen in the context of such reflexivity and critique. While fieldwork (the typification of anthropological practice in the popular mind) has been a focus of disciplinary attention, and while ethnography (anthropology's official public medium) is now also an object of unsettling critical analysis, fieldnotes remain largely obscured from view, even among practitioners. They are a "muted" medium, seeming to be merely a means to an end, or an end to the day. One wonders whether fieldnotes constitute a topic worth writing about at all and casts about for a proper analogy: are they like historians' archives, or like the notes historians take when they are in the archives? In view of the obvious centrality of fieldnotes to our work, professional silence on the matter ought at least to raise suspicions.

It is no wonder that fieldnotes are hard to think and write about: they are a bizarre genre. Simultaneously part of the "doing" of fieldwork and of the "writing" of ethnography, fieldnotes are shaped by two movements: a turning away from academic discourse to join conversations in unfamiliar settings, and a turning back again. As a kind of communication addressed primarily to oneself, they are unlike both the face-to-face but ephemeral sociability of fieldwork and the indirect but oddly enduring published exchanges at home. What is more, many (perhaps most) anthropologists have never actually read any before creating their own; they have well-established models neither for how fieldnotes are written nor for how they are used. Despite being created for oneself, fieldnotes are not meant simply as a diarylike record; however, neither are they a public archive. While they are supposed to be a reconsultable record of field experiences—an

---

[1] But see Rabinow 1986 and also Clifford's (1986) self-critical remarks. Textual concerns may also lead one in a direction antithetical to feminism and anticolonialism.

anchor for the crafty frames of memory and possibly a resource for other researchers—their value as such is sometimes questioned: "The idea is that the best way to write a compelling ethnography is to lose your fieldnotes" (Schweder 1986).

They are in fact ambiguous in form, content, and intention, neither here nor there (or, perhaps, both Here and There). Smudged by gritty fingers and squashed bugs, any day's sheaf of notes might include a series of chain and compass readings, jotted fragments of interrupted conversation, a typed-up interview transcript with marginal comments, a dense description of some event or person (suitable for publication), an outline for a dissertation or journal article, a comment on a book or letter recently read, an expression of personal feelings. Produced and still smelling of There—musty, smoky, spicy evocations of people and places—fieldnotes, like ethnography, are simply a form of writing.

Discomfort with their personal side makes reading and writing about one's own notes difficult (as this volume's papers reveal). But reading fieldnotes is discomfiting not just because of their revelations about one's personal anxieties and inadequacies or because of their ambiguity: fieldnotes are *dangerous*. Observations are noted or written down in order to aid memory, but reading fieldnotes can challenge memory. It threatens to return one to uncertainty about what was what; it acts against the sense of the whole that one carries around in one's head. Fieldnotes can contradict the single, anthropological voice we are all encouraged to adopt in our formal ethnographic writing at home by recording—however indirectly—the voices of the people we lived with when doing fieldwork. In this way, while fieldnotes mediate fieldwork and ethnographic writing and are shaped by both, they also subvert ethnography as surely as they are at odds with other aspects of the fieldwork experience.

In this essay I first describe my own fieldnotes to illustrate more concretely their particular form of fragmentation and their relations to the worlds of field and academy; the description is offered with the expectation (or hope) that my notes are typical—if not in details, then in function or sense. I go on to discuss some of the ways in which I have read and used fieldnotes. I conclude by considering the impact of different audiences and communities on the evaluation of fieldnotes. By the end, it ought to be clear that the dangers of fieldnotes are positive, even essential to critical cultural analysis.

Fieldnotes: Orientations and Disorientations

I agree with James Clifford (in this volume) that distinctions must be made among kinds of "field work"; the term is unwieldy and needs to be unpacked. While Clifford's scriptive categories are thought-provoking, I will need to unpack it differently because my focus is less on the contexts in which notes are written down than on how they are read and used.

I did field research in the Mendi Valley (Southern Highlands Province, Papua New Guinea) during 1977–79 and again for a few months in 1983; my research concerned sociopolitical aspects of the relationship between production and exchange and focused on understanding Highland pig festivals from the perspective of community history (see Lederman 1986c). I also became interested in gender relations and in local economic and political innovation.

Over the course of my fieldwork in Mendi, I produced three main kinds of written fieldnotes: daily logs, typed files, and personal journals.[2] Each kind is both orienting and disorienting for the reader in its own way. For example, an extended "description"[3] in a logbook can be quite readable and provide apparently easy access to "what things were like"; it orients the reader by presenting an account that seems comprehensible in itself, or else by having traceable connections to other notes. At the same time it is disorienting insofar as it derives from heterogeneous, sometimes contradictory sources and documents a shifting perspective (more on this below). More fragmentary notes such as my census data are relatively meaningless in themselves and need to be cross-referenced to be usable. They are disorienting insofar as they are so obviously incomplete. One needs to know more in order to interpret them, but they do not themselves point out a direction in which a reader must travel to complete them, and in fact, many directions are possible. At the same time, a census *format* does orient the reader to a single topical context.

---

[2]I do not discuss tapes and photos here; their different mediums need separate consideration. I do not mean to imply that they are not "fieldnotes" too; both are quite relevant to any consideration of how fieldnotes preserve the "voices" of an anthropologist's research subjects, a central theme of this essay. But it would be wrong to literalize and reify the notion of "voices" by asserting that they are necessarily preserved better on tape than in written notes. A process of selection is at play in taping just as much as in written note-taking, and that process can be engineered (consciously or not) to create a kind of univocality in any record.

[3]See Clifford, this volume, for a discussion of the inadequacies of this term.

While the feeling of being oriented is useful to a reader of notes, it is also misleading. The special value of fieldnotes is their capacity to unsettle, to cause a repositioning of existing boundaries and centers. In order to realize this value, one must recognize the qualified character of the orientations provided even by one's more holistic notes.

Among my own notes, my personal journals are the most orienting and accessible because they contain long, synthetic passages on particular topics. But perversely, they are also the most private of my notes. They are, in fact, what I imagine I would never want to make public, since they are as much a diary "in the strict sense" as they are a record of reflections on my reading and my field observations and interviews.

The journals are most orienting precisely because they were my meta-notes: in them I wrote about my fieldnotes and recorded my sense of how things fit together.[4] But despite the orientedness of particular passages, the journals also make quite clear—clearer than the other kinds of notes—that my sense of the whole was hardly coherent: not only did it keep changing, but it had many sources. In the case of the journals, these sources include both the reading I did in the field and the conversations I had there with my husband and other Westerners: my familiar Here brought temporarily into relation with another world. They also include telling incidents or subtle accumulations of detail: the unfamiliar There translated and brought provisionally under conceptual control through many, many pages of writing.

Thus, reactions to the books and articles I was reading—some anthropology, some history, and some other things—were usually entered in the journal in the form of ideas for a dissertation/book or

[4]There I also wrote about what I considered, at the time, to be my not officially noteworthy field experiences. One's topical and theoretical interests constitute an explicit basis for choosing what to include in and exclude from one's notes. But what of the tacit choices? I have found personal journals an important source of information concerning my own unstated assumptions about what constitutes an "anthropological" observation; this is an important reason for considering them as fieldnotes here. Although they were meant as a place for reflecting on material already noted elsewhere, they contain accounts of conversations and observations I reported nowhere else because, at the time at least, I was not treating them "anthropologically." Of course, the inclusion of even those items had its own determinations, but they were of a different (and perhaps more variable) sort than those shaping inclusions and exclusions in the potentially public notes. Insofar as any kind of writing implies a background of culturally structured understanding—tacit and explicit—that shapes what we perceive to be notable, it is probably a good idea to have various kinds of writing routines in the field.

for articles. More general notes on readings (before and after field-work) were kept separate from the fieldnotes. Part of the underlying motive for recording reactions to the books in the journals as well as separately was a fear I had, familiar to many graduate students, that I would not have "enough data" from the fieldwork itself to produce an adequate ethnography.

Whatever the motive for including them, the journal passages concerning readings demonstrate how non-field (and, in particular, textual) sources suggested lines of in-field questioning and defined in-field topics. For example, when I was living in Mendi town and had not yet decided on a rural community in which to base my research, I became aware that the leaders in one of the villages I was considering were in conflict concerning their group's Pig Festival date. I wrote in my journal that such a conflict was just the thing I needed to be able to observe in order to understand the politics of pig kills, a "topic" in the anthropological literature on the Highlands and a focal point of my research proposal. In other words, whether or not it was as notable locally (and at that stage of the research, I was in no position to tell), the conflict was of some ethnographic interest. Similarly, as I was preparing to leave my rural field community, I planned to organize my report to the Southern Highlands Province's Research Committee around a criticism of assumptions contained in the earlier report of a former provincial development planner about the relationship between leadership and land ownership. That report was the text to which several journal passages comparing the landholdings of "big-men" and ordinary men obliquely referred.[5]

Another significant type of journal entry summarized conversations with my husband about our shared interests and reflected his sense of historical methods and wide reading in social and economic theory, his research experience in colonial American history, and his practical experience in labor education. My reports of our discussions often concerned ways to translate familiar abstractions like "exploitation" or "reciprocity" into an alien idiom and social-historical context.

[5] Intertextual references in the journals are mostly explicit, more so than in any other kind of notes I took. But my emphasis on external and literary references in this description of my journals is not meant to deny the existence of other sorts of references. As fieldwork progressed, my own previous fieldnotes on local affairs, as well as previously unnoted (un-"inscribed") conversations, observations, and interactions, became an increasingly important context within which each new happening became a notable "event." The gradual emergence of this new context and the deformations it produced in my interpretive language are evident in the journal, just as they are in my other notes.

Paralleling these references to homeward-oriented readings and conversations were journal passages about what I was learning through conversations with my Mendi village hosts, observations of local events, and more structured research routines. Many of these passages speculated about connections between observations made in different field contexts—especially when there were discrepancies or confusions—and planned strategies for following through. Not a few of these passages were also composed as a counterpoint of Here and There. For instance, when it began to be clear to me that my husband and I were going to have no trouble talking with Mendi women about gift exchange and other things, my journal contains ungenerous mutterings concerning the research and writings of other Highlands ethnographers. These thoughts were notable because they had a bearing on anthropological "conversations" concerning gender in the Highlands.

As my experience in Mendi deepened, an important theme connecting many disparate journal entries was my discomfort with the categories and analytical structures discussed in the passages about my readings and non-Mendi conversations. It became less easy to find adequate translations for key ideas from each context. In effect, it was here that I played with alternative ways of extending the categories of the various disciplines and literatures I worked with to conjure up the Mendi concepts I imagined I'd want to write about once I returned home. The journal documents just how powerful my resistance was to giving up familiar, orienting categories, how very clever I was at coming up with fresh alternatives, and how difficult it was simply to hear what my Mendi acquaintances were telling me (see Asad 1986).

Despite their overtly synthetic intent, the journals are disorienting. While particular passages record my attempts to harmonize what I heard around me in Mendi, to read the journals through is to hear a dissonance of shifting keys, for my sense of the whole kept changing over the course of fieldwork. What is more, any day's entry contains diverse, distracting items; the strictly diary-style entries are particularly discordant. During the first few years after they were written, the journals were sufficiently disturbing to induce me to avoid them almost totally.

I also kept a daily log, of which (unlike the journals but like all the other notes I took) I sent carbons home for safekeeping—perhaps a sign that these were part of my "public" record. The log-books contain reports of conversations I had had or had listened to each day, descriptions of whatever events in the area came to my attention, and responses to my questions (concerning local events or linguistic points, for example). Whenever conversations became interviews—as they often did when talk turned to local history or to exchange practices— or whenever an event was so involved as to require an extended account, the log refers readers to my typed files. Like the census and interview material described below, these extended, log-style accounts were typed up and stored in ring binders, whereas entries in both the personal journals and the daily logs were handwritten in bound books.

As did the personal journals, daily log entries derived from various sources, although this is perhaps less obvious than in the journals, since these sources were more likely to be local (Mendi) ones—neither literary nor familiar to most potential readers—and, in any event, log entries contain little explicit information about them. For example, because I worked on the transition zone between two language areas, some of my frequent informants spoke a language with which I was not familiar; as a result, some log notes were based on direct discussions between me and my interlocutors, others on interpreter-mediated discussions. The logs do not always identify my interpreter (though that information may be recorded in my journal), and when they do, they rarely offer information about that person's particular biases and active interventions.[6]

Another reflection of their diverse sources is that some of the log notes were written while people were talking, and others were written up afterward with the help of abbreviated jottings taken down in the steno pads I always carried with me. I did not distinguish between these two note-taking methods in the log.[7] Rewritten notes usually contained more information than the original jottings, but the press of events or the limits of lighting—not to say my inadequate recognition of their importance—often led to uneven levels of detail concerning settings, my own and my assistants' moods, and our respective relations with our interlocutors. My personal journals contain much of this missing background information, an indication that I did not then consider it to be of strictly "anthropological" interest.

In any case, even when I rewrote my abbreviated, nearly illegible

---

[6]I agree with Obeyesekere (1981), who noted that much of interest could be written about the "interpreter effect."

[7]An extended discussion could probably be written about what goes on when personal shorthand notes, written in the midst of a conversation or event, are transcribed for one's permanent records. There are no doubt many ways of doing this when it is done at all.

steno-pad notes in the logbooks, expanding them in a legible script while I could still decipher them, I made no effort to compose and consolidate entries on a particular topic but rather transcribed them in the same order as I had recorded them. As a result, they contain interruptions and interjections: notes on so-and-so's explanation for the fuss he made at a public meeting; a list of other meetings planned; some Mendi terms; more notes about the fuss. All the while, place names and personal names are explained only if I did not know them at the time of the note-taking.

Many a day's log entries contain a series of unrelated items—a sentence reporting that a friend had gone off to his wife's father's place to repay a gift, a paragraph describing an interaction overheard on a village path that morning, a longer report summarizing several conversations bearing on a land dispute, a list of names of people who had contributed to a mortuary prestation a week or so before—all with only sporadic mention of where related items might be found. Very often there is no clear indication of why any particular item was deemed noteworthy at the time. Neither could a naive reader tell whether what is contained in an entry is complete in itself, as an item either of local concern or of anthropological interest. The gift repaid that day might have been controversial or might become so; the repayment might help to clarify an exchange rule previously (or soon to be) described.

To some extent, the log's chronological organization is orienting, at least when what one is looking for is the story of a dispute or anything else that is played out over time, yet this mode of reading is inefficient. As the author of the log, with a reasonable memory of where things are and an index for each logbook, I nevertheless find myself reading over many items of no direct relevance to my immediate goals whenever I consult it. The eye wanders; unsought facts make their appearance, and unanticipated connections suggest themselves, leading the eye further astray. With all these juxtapositions, the daily log is the most disorienting of my notes.

But chronology is key in another way. These disorientations—collages of apparently unrelated items, ambiguities as to why certain items were included (or excluded) and whether (or on what basis) any item is complete—engender reading problems because log notes increasingly presuppose, and subordinate themselves to, the context of understandings created through long-term sociable exchanges with people in one's field community. Over the course of fieldwork one becomes party to conversations and situations defined not only by an interpreting observer's autonomous eye, or by external criteria of interest, but also by deepening relationships with some of the people with whom one is living. Happenings become notable (events) against a background of one's friends' and neighbors' not always convergent concerns.

These in-field matters have their own logics which, played out over time, may gradually shift the emphasis of one's notes away from preexisting, comparative frames of reference and toward diverse "colloquial" ones (Fernandez 1985). Any item newly noted in a logbook may have many unnoted but significant antecedents that made its coming-to-(note)-consciousness possible. Just as one has limited control over the intertextual shaping of one's attention, one has only partial control over these changing colloquial influences. Yet while colloquial contexts for the interpretation of events are the special vantage points that fieldwork opens up, they probably cannot be fully recorded. Consequently, reading notes requires remembering (or discovering) the various local biases and partialities that formed an important but largely tacit rationale for inclusions and exclusions. This inevitable incompleteness is what makes reading one's own old notes, not to mention *other* people's, so difficult.

In addition to the handwritten journals and logs, I typed up notes taken during long interviews and complex events (my own observations and reports of what other observers and participants told me on the spot or afterward). Some interviews arose spontaneously out of informal conversations concerning events or topics of particular concern to me or to my hosts; these were the same, except for level of detail, as the sorts of items found in the log. Apart from these extended log-style accounts, my typed notes include the results of a community-wide household census, responses to systematic interviews concerning marriage and bridewealth, mortuary prestations, land tenure histories, exchange partnership histories, daily "gift-debts" and "gift-credits" and other matters, and descriptions and measurements of the community's gardens, garden production, and pigs. The results of each of these investigations were typed up every day or so; back in the States, each was filed in its own ring binder.

My typed surveys are simultaneously the least readable and the most orienting and formal of my notes. While my personal journals are orienting on the level of the part but not of the whole, the reverse is true of the surveys. They are hard to "read" because they contain decontextualized responses to questions: the rationale for the questions is contained in the log and the journal, but the question-and-answer "situation"—the participants and their mutual relationships at the time of interviewing—is not described in the typed notes themselves. Nevertheless, any set of interview notes is composed of the responses of individuals to questions on a relatively coherent topic; it orients the reader to a single topic and involves few of the distractions that are rife in the journals and the logs.

Despite their apparent coherence, the survey notes are a precipitate of the dialectical relationship between intra-anthropological discourse and the interactions of fieldwork. For many of my interview projects I first defined topics and outlined questions with the anthropological literature on other Highlanders in mind: that is, with the desire to address topics with which other Highlands researchers were also concerned. But I worked out the boundaries of the topic, and the details and phrasing of the questions included in even the most general survey, with the help of my field assistants, my closest friends in the community, and the people I interviewed in each case.

For example, after talking and corresponding with a number of Highlands researchers before I arrived in Mendi in 1977, and having talked with my husband during the preceding few years about his own historical research on the account books of eighteenth- and nineteenth-century American farmers, I decided to create monthly gift exchange "accounts" for a sample of the female and male residents of my field community. The idea was to get a sense of the everyday gift exchanges of ordinary people in Mendi to complement my investigation of public "ceremonial" exchange. As a follow-up to that work, about a year into the research we interviewed all members of the "accounts" sample concerning the history of each of their partnerships. Considering that an average member of the sample might have a network of about forty exchange partners, we needed a way to organize the interviews meaningfully, so as to facilitate memory and to maintain interest.

The first people I interviewed were two of my closest friends in my field community: my village sponsor, Nare (a local leader), and Mel, my main field assistant. Both of them were comfortable enough with me and proprietary enough about the work I was doing to tell me how they thought I ought to conduct the interview. In separate conversations they each explained how they remember their own exchange obligations, and how those mnemonic devices might be employed in this unfamiliar context. My questions and what they each chose to explain during their partner-by-partner histories helped me to develop explicit "prompts" in subsequent interviews. The interview format remained flexible as I spoke with the people I knew best (people most likely to speak without "prompting" questions and most likely to offer unsolicited advice and commentary) and gradually became more formal as I went along. Consequently, the results reflect both anthropological and local frames of reference. All the surveys my husband and I carried out in Mendi originated in this sort of interactive process and bear its traces—though it might be hard for anyone else to reconstruct, since the diachronic dimensions of the surveys are obscured by the way I have filed them.

Using Fieldnotes

A written ethnography is not just a summary or selection of "what's in the notes." The point of ethnography is not, after all, to describe one's fieldnotes (as I am doing here) or to reconstitute the anthropologist's day through a chronological collation of notes but rather to enable one's audience to understand something of interest about a corner of the world they have not experienced directly themselves; to share that to which one's field experience has given one access. Something of interest to one's audience: what that is depends on the audience and how far one believes they are willing to travel.

I used my notes for self-clarification when I was still in the field. While my personal journal entries record reactions to field experiences, they are also the products of a critical reading of the log and other notes. In the field I used journal writing as a time for exploring connections between the various things I was learning about and for reciprocal translations of the terms of my anthropological and Mendi knowledge. This work invariably generated questions; the effort to orchestrate my knowledge clarified some of what was missing or discordant. Such frequent summarizing and rethinking was a check on the complacent sense of everyday competence and familiarity that long-term fieldwork can engender (Lederman 1986b). After all, frustrating or confusing interactions with informants, assistants, or friends and shifts in the sense of how things fit together are often repressed in the interest of carrying on.

In my case the journals became the place where these things were preserved for conscious reflection. My journals inform me, for example, that I was not fully aware of the significance of exchange partnerships—a central component of my present understanding of Mendi social relations—until the last month of my first period of research, even though I had been focusing on them all along. This realization enables me to read my log and survey notes more critically and warns me of the need to compare my early reports of conversations and incidents with those written toward the end of the research.[8]

When I first returned from the field in 1979, I planned to index my notes but soon changed my mind. I was dissatisfied with the categories I was imposing on them and wanted to give myself more time to understand what I had learned in Mendi. For the same reason, I held off tabulating and summarizing the information contained in the surveys. In short, I was not at all sure how to read and use my own notes. Viewed as a whole—as shelves of ring binders and journals, and as stacks of paper on the floor near my desk—the notes were inaccessible. Journal writing, my in-field vehicle for exploring the other notes, no longer seemed appropriate; its thematic pacing had been too closely linked to the daily rhythm of fieldwork.

Another method of using the notes had begun to assert itself, however, even before I left the field. It was occasioned by the need to address audiences and contexts quite different from those that had shaped my journal writing and other fieldnote-taking. Several months before leaving Mendi I prepared an abstract and outline for a paper I hoped to read at the American Anthropological Association meeting later that year, and during my last week in Mendi in 1979 I presented a research report to the Southern Highlands Province Research Committee. These writing projects focused on issues defined for me by preexisting "conversations" among people who were not members of my field community. The research report addressed questions raised by provincial and national development planners about the rural political economy in Mendi; the meeting paper concerned the participation of Highlands women in gift exchange, a topic of general as well as

---

[8]Two points ought to be spelled out, though they may be obvious. First, as I have indicated, the notes themselves develop during fieldwork: one's use of terms shifts in subtle ways as one's understanding of local concepts and relations changes. Second, during any rereading of the notes—in the midst of fieldwork or subsequently—one's current sense of the whole imposes certain consistencies on this heterogeneous source. As Ottenberg, Wolf, and others in this volume point out, one's changing sense of the whole is registered in the changing interests and perspectives expressed in the writings produced during an anthropological career. Clearly, this process may not be evident at any single moment in any particular writing.

regional interest in ethnography. While the terms of those conversations shaped my participation in them, I joined in with the hope that introducing the Mendi case might shift the terms a bit.

Other events intervened to influence the ways I used my notes after I had returned from Mendi to New York. Like the two writing projects already mentioned, those events involved addressing specific audiences and entering conversations that already had histories. Reading the newsletter of the Association for Social Anthropology in Oceania in the fall of 1979, I found descriptions of two symposia to be held at the association meeting the next spring. Since both symposia were still open to the inclusion of new papers, and I felt that I had observations relevant to the topics, I set to work writing them up.[9]

Not only did participation in these symposia help me to use my notes by orienting me to a specific audience and topic (just like the cases cited above), but it also suggested a particular *place* of entry into the notes. For both papers—one involving the political uses of language (Lederman 1980) and the other concerning the relationship between "sorcery" and social change (Lederman 1981)—I planned to address the symposium topics by analyzing events I had studied in Mendi: a political meeting, a curing ceremony. As the work progressed, of course, I had to go far beyond simple description of the events themselves, tracing out connections to other events and collating what many informants had told me about related matters.

In retrospect, it seems that "events" were good modes of entry into fieldnotes.[10] Events happen at particular times, and can therefore be found easily in chronologically organized notes, whether one has a good index or not. They also have an apparent "wholeness"—a superficial sense of boundedness—that facilitates initial description. Event-based topics helped to orient me in my notes because they "made sense" in three ways: each occurrence had been a focus of local interest and discussion in my field community, but it also related to some domain of anthropological discourse, and from a practical standpoint it directed me first to my most readable notes.

Starting with events that had been of concern in my field community helped to preserve a local logic, but the integrating rationale for

[9]Each ASAO symposium is meant to be the last stage in a collective process that also (ideally) involves informal face-to-face discussion of ideas, followed by an exchange and discussion of working papers.

[10]The question of what constitutes an "event" in this or that culture (or cultural context) is complex; for a suggestion with regard to Mendi, see Lederman 1986a.

these inquiries was at least as much comparative as it was local. As I confronted ethnographic questions I had not explicitly thought about in the field, notes about events guided my search through the less immediately readable surveys, bits of conversation and observations recorded in the logbooks, and so on. Unlike a project of indexing, of tabulating survey results, or of explicating concepts I knew to be important when I was in the midst of research, rereading my record of events maximized the possibility of discovering relations and connections within the notes of which I had not previously been aware. This experience, which effectively turned the notes into an archive for me by suggesting questions different from those around which the notes were collected, finally enabled me to do the indexing and tabulating without which a longer writing project would not have been possible.

I will discuss one last use of fieldnotes here: their incorporation into ethnographic writing. Ethnography issues from an "argument" ("dialogue" may sometimes be too genteel a term) between comparative and local voices. While the comparative voice is usually the more influential (given the demands and capacities of ethnography's readership), the textual echo of local voices may be privileged in certain styles of ethnographic writing (as in life histories and transcripts of native texts). If my experience is at all typical, this argument has its clearest written expression in fieldnotes. It is there that the comparative attitude is humbled in the effort to understand an immediate but unfamiliar and confusing reality. That is not by any means to say that it disappears. But at least some balance is achieved, in the very course of fieldwork, between transcriptions, paraphrasings and reports of what some others are saying and doing, and the ethnographer's composed description and commentary.[11]

One can bar this argument from one's formal ethnographic writing. Or one can choose to introduce it into the text by allowing fieldnotes to break through at critical points to advance the argument or even to

[11] Transcriptions and paraphrases obviously involve interpretation, even when informants and ethnographer speak the same language; and changing contexts of interpretation and of reflexivity may foreground as "interpretation" that which was previously unrecognized as such. It may be that fieldnotes provide more ready access than ethnographies do to the interpretive *process,* regardless of the ethnographer's commitment to "experimental" ethnographic writing. Description in the notes is more clearly the product of a concrete social process involving particular people. Even if one works to compose some of one's notes in the form of finished (publishable) descriptions, the balance is likely to evince a specific voice and perspective, the rough edges of uncertainty, and questions and answers with named others.

constitute it (as, for example, Clifford Geertz has done; see Clifford, this volume). Allowing fieldnotes to break through does not necessarily require direct quotation from the notes, but it does demand that some of the fragmentation of knowledge—some of the contradictions and polyvocality characteristic of fieldnotes—be represented for readers to consider, alongside the writer's interpretive efforts of orchestration.

In other words, ethnographic writing is all about directing readers toward novel modes of seeing the world (an effect achieved by maintaining authorial control, one way or another). Our claim to a right to write this way is based on bouts of successfully disorienting field research (and, presumably, on discovering a way of taking down and using equally disorienting notes). Bringing the field home is only fair; to disorient readers is sometimes an effective way to encourage a rethinking of received categories and a reorientation of perspective.

I have tried several times to incorporate disorientations into my ethnographic writing. After composing a brief, univocal community history of a Mendi pig kill in a book mostly devoted to exploring the social structural background of such events (Lederman 1986c), I wrote a paper (Lederman 1986a) that discusses some of the local sources of historical knowledge in Mendi, by way of arguing that while the Mendi have a dynamic past and present, they do not necessarily use "historical" arguments (as Europeans and Americans often do) to assert their agency in the world. That paper catalogued disparate observations I had made in the field concerning Mendi representations of the past, less to orchestrate an interpretation than to create a sense of possibilities. The point of presenting the material in a relatively disjointed fashion was to encourage readers to rethink the meaning of "history" as applied to contexts like that of Mendi.[12]

Similarly, in several places in my ethnography, *What Gifts Engender* (1986c: 40–41, 47–52), I present descriptions of what are essentially fieldnotes. They paraphrase or quote statements by my Mendi informants that either contradict one another or else do not fit existing ethnographic paradigms—or "gatekeeping concepts," in Arjun Appadurai's (1986) useful phrase. In this case the issue was the form and significance of male collectivities ("clans") in Mendi. Using as my

[12] As Clifford (1986) has pointed out, Richard Price's study of the Saramaka, *First Time* (1983), uses a similar device: the *form* of his book makes a substantive point about local Saramaka historical representations. Writing a coherent history of the Saramaka would have misrepresented the insistent and self-conscious polyvocality of local history, so Price chose to *demonstrate* this complexity instead. His "texts" became his text.

model a paper by Roy Wagner (1974), which questions whether there are "groups" in the New Guinea Highlands, I tried to clear a space for such a question about the Mendi by discussing my "sources" rather directly. In a later paper dealing with a related issue (Lederman 1989), preserving the contradictory perspectives of Mendi men and women as I found them in my notes rather than giving them a unifying "glaze" enabled me to raise questions about the relevance and implications of a general model of the social structure.

It would be interesting to discover how frequently fieldnotes are employed in this way in published ethnographies. Their use to bring the disorientations of fieldwork home to readers—the better to shift the terms of existing anthropological conversations—may be more common than it seems, although it may be missed if we look only for deliberate and direct quotation. Because of the dangers and ambiguities of fieldnotes, and because of their privatization (which encourages each of us to interpret our confusions primarily in personal terms, as signs of inadequacy, rather than in terms of cultural disjunctures), the notes themselves may be disguised and detectable only indirectly as a force acting against received comparative categories.

Communities and Audiences

To historians who read anthropology, "being there" is anthropology's distinct advantage insofar as it gives us a sense of the whole and the conviction that we have understood a place and a people. But that easy sense of the whole is treacherous; from this point of view, historians are lucky that their convictions clearly are conscious and hard-won acts of imagination. The ease with which we can claim to know the worlds we invent—the fact that we can claim to "remember" them rather than having to admit always that we have fashioned them—is dangerous. We might do better to be suspicious of that ready familiarity, that implied factuality, even as we strive to convince readers, in authoritative and not so authoritative ways, of the plausibility of the worlds we write about.

Anthropological research practices do not automatically check the human tendency to familiarize strange circumstances, but they offer the possibility of doing so, and we can choose to emphasize it. To that end, it is interesting that fieldnotes can have the reverse effect "at home" from the one Clifford (this volume) describes for them in the field.

In the field, living with an alien reality, every new day offers us

opportunities for a confrontation between our existing ways of understanding the world and those of our neighbors. In the midst of our
research, many of us work to create contexts for long-term (post-
research) dialogue with the people we live with and study—whether
simply by building close personal friendships or by making practical
or political commitments of one sort or another—even when we do
not write about these efforts. Whether personal or political, such
involvement can help rein in the tendency to interpret what we see and
hear solely from our own perspective. But both the anthropologist
and his or her informants continue to have their own interests as well;
not all the projects of either are necessarily of moment to the other. For
many, though certainly not all, anthropologists this separation (or,
more strongly, this active disengagement) is palpable in the everyday
movement of writing in the field: looking away to write something
down while others continue to argue; turning one's back to type
something up while around the hearth the rest are still laughing.[13]

To understand the role of fieldnotes *in the field,* one has first to
acknowledge that being in the field involves placing oneself deliberately in a context of commitment doubly different from the normal
one. As we all know, this act need not involve any traveling at all: it
sometimes involves simply a shifting of attention and of sociable
connection within one's own habitual milieus. From this perspective
"the field" is not so much a place as it is a particular relation between
oneself and others, involving a difficult combination of commitment
and disengagement, relationship and separation. That one is writing
about what one is simultaneously living is part of the separation and
difficulty. But there is more to be said: the question is, for *whom* do we
write?[14] The point is that writing in the field is more often than not a
very tangible sign of our double lives, of sociable connections in two

[13]Performing dual, apparently contradictory roles in the field as friend or engaged
participant on the one hand and as note-taker, photographer, recorder, or transcriber
on the other—as close and as distanced—is a central experience for many anthropologists. The disquiet engendered by that experience helps to motivate professional
reflexivity. Engagement ought not to be thought of as a means to the end of better note-
taking, nor ought note-taking to be thought of either as a justification for being there or
as something that gets in its way. As *anthropological* activities, these are two moments of
the same process. Note-taking is not anthropological (field)note-taking without long-
term participation in everyday life, and that participation is a less anthropological
experience without the discipline of systematic comparison between alternative, im-
pinging realities which keeping notes encourages.

[14]The separation is quite clear when we write ethnographies for anthropologists and
for the anthropologically trained. It is less so when those we write about will form a
large part of our readership.

directions. To the extent that our two worlds are distinct, our loyalties are divided, and we may feel compromised. But that is the price we pay for a unique voice.

Once we are home, however, the scales tilt overwhelmingly in one direction. The commitments we have made to people in our field community are subjected to intense if contradictory competition with commitments to our professional community, which for most of us exerts a more persistent influence. Our conversations, formal and informal—in seminars, conferences, and hallways, and indirectly on the pages of journals and books—are constrained by common anthropological idioms. As Appadurai (1986: 357) has emphasized, "gatekeeping concepts" (such as "honor and shame" in the Mediterranean) can virtually create ethnographic "places" and suffuse our ways of talking about them; insofar as they frame our theorizing about the places where we do our research and "define the . . . dominant questions of interest in the region," these concepts necessarily affect how we use our fieldnotes. How we read our notes is also affected by habits of thought that transcend approaches to particular ethnographic "places": Western presuppositions concerning gender, for example (see Wolf in this volume).

These sorts of influences may even be felt in the midst of field-work—while presenting a seminar report during a research break, perhaps. Certainly, many of us can tell stories about our traumatic resocialization to academic discourse en route home from the field. Along the way, local realities—Alcome's dream, the death of Miribip—frequently become exemplifications chosen to illustrate a point whose rationale lies outside Alcome's world, in a context in which Alcome does not laugh with others around the hearth just a few paces from one's typewriter.

Once we are home, our written styles encourage narrative closure and a final analysis: in conventional ethnography, decisions need to be made about what's what. Now, fieldnotes can be party to that. As a corpus, the notes may give us the sense that, for the moment anyhow, they contain the basis for all that can be written about a place: the fundamental intangibility and infinite complexity of social experience reduced to a "thing" which, even when very bulky, has finite dimensions. Given this finiteness, we can talk about how efficiently or inefficiently fieldnotes are used in this or that case in the production of ethnography (see Plath, this volume). And their concreteness restores our confidence in the possibility of "grasping" social reality.

But simultaneously, fieldnotes can defamiliarize our knowledge of the field, and perhaps that is one reason why they disturb us so much (see Jackson, this volume), why some of us avoid using our notes when we write, and why stories about lost or destroyed notes (such as that of Leach's *Political Systems of Highland Burma*) take on mythic dimensions. *Having* notes—all neatly typed or bound, all stored safe and sound—is one thing: it validates our anthropological communications. But *using* notes is quite another: that activity shows fieldnotes to be not a fixed repository of data from the field but a reinterpretable and contradictory patchwork of perspectives. We rightly fear that immersion in them might cause us to doubt our conviction about what's what and (even worse!) lose our putative advantage over the historians.

In this way, fieldnotes can have an effect at home quite opposite from their effect in the field. While one may indeed have to turn away from direct engagement with people in one's field community in order to "inscribe" notes and type them up, at home one has to disengage from ethnographic discourse in order to consult them. While this movement is not exactly like returning to the field, still it does put one back in touch—mediated and imperfect though it may be—with another set of categories, commitments, and values.

Moreover, it preserves the tension between what we talk about with our interlocutors in the field and our dialogue with our fellows at home. But after all, that tension is what animates an anthropological sensibility. Anthropology can no longer claim to produce descriptions of cultural traditions through an imaginative separation of Self and Other. A recognition that connections between the two cannot be factored out—that they are constitutive both of our scholarly practice and of the phenomena we study—has helped motivate the recent scrutiny of ethnographic writing. These connections are no less evident in fieldnotes than anywhere else. Thus it makes sense to extend that scrutiny to fieldnotes, as the corpus of still largely unexamined texts in which much of the significant work of decontextualizing and recontextualizing cultural categories and idioms takes place. This essay urges that equal attention be paid to the scenes of reading notes as to those of their writing, the better to appreciate those texts' critical potentialities.

REFERENCES

Appadurai, Arjun. 1986. Theory of Anthropology: Center and Periphery. *Comparative Studies in Society and History* 28:356–61.

Asad, Talal. 1986. The Concept of Cultural Translation in British Social Anthropology. In Clifford and Marcus 1986, 141–64.

Clifford, James. 1983. On Ethnographic Authority. *Representations* 1:118–46.

———. 1986. Introduction: Partial Truths. In Clifford and Marcus 1986, 1–26.

Clifford, James, and George E. Marcus, eds. 1986. *Writing Culture: The Poetics and Politics of Ethnography.* Berkeley: University of California Press.

———. 1988. *The Predicament of Culture: Twentieth-Century Ethnography, Literature, and Art.* Cambridge, Mass.: Harvard University Press.

Fernandez, James. 1985. Exploded Worlds: Text as a Metaphor for Ethnography (and Vice Versa). *Dialectical Anthropology* 10:15–26.

Geertz, Clifford. 1988. *Works and Lives: The Anthropologist as Author.* Stanford, Calif.: Stanford University Press.

Lederman, Rena. 1980. Who Speaks Here? Formality and the Politics of Gender in Mendi, Highland Papua New Guinea. *Journal of the Polynesian Society* 89: 479–98.

———. 1981. Sorcery and Social Change in Mendi. *Social Analysis* 8:15–27.

———. 1986a. Changing Times in Mendi: Notes Towards Writing Highlands History. *Ethnohistory* 33 (1): 1–30.

———. 1986b. The Return of Redwoman: Fieldwork in Highland New Guinea. In *Women in the Field,* 2d ed., ed. Peggy Golde. Berkeley: University of California Press.

———. 1986c. *What Gifts Engender: Social Relations and Politics in Mendi, Highland Papua New Guinea.* New York: Cambridge University Press.

———. 1989. Contested Order: Gender and Society in the Southern New Guinea Highlands. *American Ethnologist* 16:230–47.

Marcus, George E., and Dick Cushman. 1983. Ethnographies as Text. *Annual Review of Anthropology* 11:25–69.

Obeyesekere, Gananath. 1981. *Medusa's Hair: An Essay on Personal Symbols and Religious Experience.* Chicago: University of Chicago Press.

Price, Richard. 1983. *First-Time: The Historical Vision of an Afro-American People.* Baltimore, Md.: Johns Hopkins University Press.

Rabinow, Paul. 1986. Representations Are Social Facts: Modernity and Post-Modernity in Anthropology. In Clifford and Marcus 1986, 234–61.

Rosaldo, Renato. 1986. From the Door of His Tent: The Fieldworker and the Inquisitor. In Clifford and Marcus 1986, 77–97.

Schweder, Richard. 1986. Storytelling among the Anthropologists. *New York Times Book Review,* September 21, pp. 1, 38–39.

Sperber, Dan. 1982. *Le savoir des anthropologues.* Paris: Hakluyt.

Strathern, Marilyn. 1987. Out of Context: the Persuasive Fictions of Ethnography. *Current Anthropology* 28:251–81.

Wagner, Roy. 1974. Are There Social Groups in the New Guinea Highlands? In *Frontiers of Anthropology,* ed. Murray Leaf, 95–122. New York: Van Nostrand.

ROGER SANJEK

A Vocabulary for Fieldnotes

Anthropologists often characterize themselves as mavericks and individualists, holding an "I did it my way" attitude about fieldwork, as Jean Jackson confirmed in several of her interviews. Despite this iconoclastic "Indiana Jones syndrome," as she calls it, there is considerable order and pattern in the ways anthropologists operate, more than many may wish to believe. Patterns in fieldnote practice have changed from the 1880s to the 1980s, as I show in "The Secret Life of Fieldnotes" (in Part III). But first we need to establish a vocabulary for the discussion of fieldnotes.

"What are fieldnotes?" George Bond asks (this volume). He answers that they are first, certainly, texts; they are documents with "the security and concreteness that writing lends to observation . . . immutable records of some past occurence." Yet fieldnotes are written, usually, for an audience of one. So they are also "*aides-mémoire* that stimulate the re-creation, the renewal of things past," Bond explains. Fieldnotes can make difficult reading for anyone other than their author, as Robert J. Smith discovered in his first reading of Ella Lury Embree's fieldnotes about the Japanese village of Suye Mura. Fieldnotes are meant to be read by the ethnographer and to produce meaning through interaction with the ethnographer's headnotes.

Headnotes and Fieldnotes

"Headnotes," the felicitous term coined by Simon Ottenberg, identifies something immediately understandable to ethnographers. We
come back from the field with fieldnotes and headnotes. The fieldnotes stay the same, written down on paper, but the headnotes continue to evolve and change as they did during the time in the field.
Ethnography, Ottenberg explains, is a product of the two sets of
notes. The headnotes are more important. Only after the anthropologist is dead are the fieldnotes primary.

Other anthropologists have written about headnotes without using
the term (Davis 1984: 304–5; Ellen 1984b: 279; Holy 1984: 33; Van
Maanen 1988: 118). On her third visit to Manus in 1965, Margaret
Mead was struck by the importance of her headnotes: "Because of my
long acquaintance with this village I can perceive and record aspects of
this people's life that no one else can. . . . It is my individual consciousness which provides the ground on which the lives of these people are
figures" (1977: 283).

Niara Sudarkasa (Gloria Marshall), while working in another field
site, wrote a rich account of her 1961–62 fieldwork in the Yoruba
community of Awe. Her fieldnotes, diaries, and letters remained at
home; only her dissertation and a few photographs were with her.
"What follows, therefore, might best be described as remembrances
of, and reflections upon, my efforts as an anthropologist in the making. These are the encounters, the evaluations, the episodes that are
chiseled in memory" (Marshall 1970: 167). She relied on her headnotes.

Martin M. C. Yang's 1945 classic, *A Chinese Village,* was written
from headnotes alone. In China during 1931 he drafted a paper about
his home community which was later published. Still later,

> early in 1943 Ralph Linton invited me to work on a project entitled
> "The Study of Modern Chinese Rural Civilization" in the department
> of anthropology at Columbia University. . . . The project, which lasted
> about sixteen months, resulted in my writing *A Chinese Village.* . . . In
> my imagination I almost completely relived my boyhood and adoles-
> cent years. I did not merely recall facts or occurrences, but mentally and
> emotionally retraced my role in the life of the community. All came
> back to me—my parents, brothers, sisters; the people of adjacent neigh-
> borhoods, of the village, the market town, the market-town school;

their personalities, lives, and work; their relations with each other. [Yang 1972: 71–72]

Srinivas wrote *The Remembered Village* also primarily from head-notes. And like Yang, but more extensively, he had done earlier writing about Rampura (see Srinivas 1987 for several of these papers). A. C. Mayer raised the question about Srinivas's book:

> Has not that memory been "mediated" by diary-writing and note-taking . . . by the later "processing" of the field notes, and for some of the data, by the writing up in articles? . . . The question is, then: how far was Srinivas able to forget his field notes and other writings? . . . He may have had his memory "shaped" by these other data, in much the same way, though to a much lesser extent, as might the person working openly with notes in an orthodox way? . . . Perhaps, then, Srinivas has not so much used a new method of providing ethnography . . . as varied the mix—of memory and written aids—in the usual one? [Mayer 1978: 43–44]

Mayer is correct, of course. Srinivas's headnotes of 1970, his memories at the time he wrote the book, were different from the headnotes formulated in Rampura at the time of his fieldwork in 1948 and 1952. All the episodes of writing and thinking about Rampura between these points in time affected the headnotes and led to *The Remembered Village*.

Several of the authors in this volume comment on the headnotes-fieldnotes relationship. Jean Jackson mentions that for many anthropologists, changing topical interests and theoretical orientations "make re-reading fieldnotes an eye-opening experience." Margery Wolf writes that feminism brought new questions to the fieldnotes she and Arthur Wolf had produced in Taiwan. Nancy Lutkehaus's post-fieldwork headnotes provoked a reading of Camilla Wedgwood's Manam Island fieldnotes different from that preceding Lutkehaus's residence there. Rena Lederman considers extensively the tensions between fieldnotes and the evolving "sense of the whole," both during and after fieldwork. George Bond concludes, "When we review our notes we fill in gaps, we give order to the immutable text."

The Field and Writing

Fieldnotes are produced in the field, but where is the field? Clifford asks: "Can one, properly speaking, record a field note while not physically 'there'? Would a remembered impression first inscribed at one's home university count as a fieldnote?" And what of the increasing number of anthropologists who do fieldwork "at home," often in their home communities?

Lederman offers an answer. Being "in the field," she says, "need not involve any traveling at all: it sometimes simply involves a shifting of attention and of sociable connection within one's own habitual milieus." Fieldnotes are "of" the field, if not always written "in" the field.

But *what,* physically, are they? Anthropologists bring back a variety of objects from fieldwork, including much paper. Jackson found no defining consensus on what to include; notes on readings, photocopied archival material, a ceramic dish, even the ethnographer her- or himself ("I am a fieldnote," stated one storer of headnotes)—all were considered fieldnotes by some. Anthropologists also bring back photographs, films, videotapes, audio recordings, and recovered documents of many sorts, including informant letters or diaries.

Here our focus is on what the anthropologist *writes* in the field: " 'What does the ethnographer do?'—he writes" (Geertz 1973: 19). We shall identify scratch notes, fieldnotes proper, fieldnote records, texts, journals, diaries, letters, reports, and papers written in the field (cf. Davis 1984: 297–304; Ellen 1984b).[1] We will briefly discuss also taped interviews and informant statements, which are often transcribed outside the field but then become written documents used in writing ethnography, like field-produced fieldnotes.

Scratch Notes

For many anthropologists, a first step from field perception to paper is handwritten "scratch notes," to use another of Ottenberg's well-chosen phrases (cf. Ellen 1984b: 279–80, 282). Scratch notes are sometimes produced in the view of informants, while observing or talking with them, and sometimes out of sight.

William Partridge, in Colombia, felt uncomfortable carrying a notebook early in his 1972–73 research, but with time he was able to record

[1]Ottenberg's and Clifford's essays guided my analysis of the fieldwork literature. I read Ellen's edited volume (1984a) after writing the first draft of "A Vocabulary for Fieldnotes." All of our views of fieldwork writing are gratifyingly coincidental, even if we, or other authors in this volume, do not always use the same terms for conceptualizing different types of field writings. I wish to acknowledge the published priority of Ellen's typology (1984b) and of Davis (1984).

notes in front of his informants (Kimball and Partridge 1979: 52, 171). Lederman always carried a steno pad; sometimes she wrote fuller notes as people were talking, and at other times she reconstructed her observations later, from "abbreviated jottings" on the pads. In outdoor observation among the Skolt Lapps in 1958–59, Pertti Pelto was often prevented by cold weather from producing more than bare scratch notes (1970: 265–66). Edward Norbeck, in Japan in 1950–51, choosing to "devote as little time as possible to writing while in the presence of informants," produced his scratch notes afterward; during long interviews he often excused himself "to go to the toilet, where I hastily jotted down in Gregg shorthand key words to jog my memory later" (1970: 255).

Morris Freilich, in 1956 research among Mohawks in Brooklyn and Canada, soon learned that open note-taking would not be tolerated: "[I] had to keep a small notebook in my hip pocket and periodically go to the men's room in the bar or the outhouse at Caughnawaga and write notes to myself. As frequently as possible, I would go to a coffee shop to write down longer statements" (1970b: 193. See also Gupta 1979: 113; Keiser 1970: 230). William Sturtevant (1959) even published a short statement about his technique of writing scratch notes un-observed during long ceremonial events: he used a two-inch pencil on two- by three-inch slips of paper held together by a paperclip in his pants or jacket pocket. Some of Hortense Powdermaker's fieldnotes in Mississippi were written with similar surreptitiousness (1966: 175, 178).

Scratch-note production is what James Clifford calls *inscription*: "A participant-observer jots down a mnemonic word or phrase to fix an observation or to recall what someone has just said." It might also record fuller observations or responses to questions the ethnographer brings. Either way, as Clifford observes, "the flow of action and discourse has been interrupted, *turned* to writing." For some of Jackson's anthropological informants, inscription disrupts participant-observation: "Fieldnotes get in the way. They interfere with what fieldwork is all about—the doing."

Inscribing scratch notes, usually on a small pad contemporaneous with or soon after the events observed or words heard, *is* anthropological fieldwork (Boissevain 1970: 74–75, 79; Freilich 1970b: 200–201; Gonzalez 1970: 171; Gulick 1970: 133–34; Kobben 1967: 42; Marshall 1970: 190; Powdermaker 1966: 94–95; Whitten 1970: 351; Yengoyan 1970: 416). But so is the "typing up" Ottenberg speaks of, the production of an enhanced and expanded set of fieldnotes (see Beals 1970: 50;

Beattie 1965: 41; LeClair 1960: 34–35; Marshall 1970: 190; Powder-maker 1966: 95; Wolff 1960: 241).

Scratch Notes to Fieldnotes

This second stage of fieldnote production is epitomized in the photograph on the cover of the paperback edition of this book, Margaret Mead and Gregory Bateson at work in "the mosquito room" in the Iatmul village of Tambunam in 1938. They sit opposite each other at a small desk, each behind a typewriter. Bateson is looking to his left at a small notebook, his handwritten scratch notes. Mead, her notebook to her right, next to Bateson's, is either reading her typewritten page or thinking. They are busy in *description,* as Clifford characterizes it: "the making of a more or less coherent representation of an observed cultural reality . . . for later writing and interpretation aimed at the production of a finished account."

The scratch-notes-to-descriptive-fieldnotes writing act must be timely, before the scratch notes get "cold" (Mead 1977: 202). But more than preserving their warmth is involved. As Ottenberg notes, other ingredients are added in the process. Aneeta Minocha, whose circumstances of field research in a women's hospital in Delhi made taking scratch notes relatively easy, is precise about her additions in writing second-stage descriptive fieldnotes.

> During my talks I scribbled key words on a small notebook. Later I wrote extensive reports of my conversations, and also recorded my explanations and interpretations as they occurred to me at that time. I also recorded the contexts in which particular conversations took place, as well as the general physical and emotional condition of the informants, their appearance and behavior, and the gestures they used. Usually it took me three to four hours to put on paper five to six hours of field work. It was because of such immediate recording of my field experiences that I was able to recreate the atmosphere in which each conversation or event took place. Even now, as I write, I can vividly feel the presence of the participants. [1979: 213]

John Gulick, in a Lebanese village in 1951–52, used brief scratch notes in conjunction with his memory of conversations to produce his fieldnotes.

> Often . . . I would have to wait until the evening to do this, and tired though I usually was at the end of the day, I found that it was essential to write the day's notes before going to sleep. If I failed to do this and

postponed note writing till the next day, I found that the notes were useless, except insofar as they might contain simple factual information. The subtleties of cues and responses—some of which one can catch in notes if one writes them soon enough—became lost in sleep, and what I wrote the next day was essentially a second-hand account, an over-simplified version, in which the events and my reactions to them were truly blurred. [1970: 134]

Other anthropologists may handwrite fuller, longer-lasting, scratch notes (Powdermaker 1966: 95), though these also vary in completeness from one time to another (Beals 1970: 55; Honigmann 1970: 44; Wagley 1977: 18). Few are as candid about the compromises they make as Pelto:

My plan was to type up the day's field notes each evening, or, at the latest, the next morning. However, I was frequently at a roundup or other activity for as long as two weeks at a time, which meant that on returning to home base I would have to schedule lengthy typing sessions to catch up on back notes. While typing up my notes, I often recalled significant events that I had not jotted down in my notebook. I wrote up these additional notes in the same manner as the information from the notebook, although the nature of the materials often made it clear which data had been written on the spot and which were later recollections. [1970: 266]

A backlog of scratch notes to be typed plagues more anthropologists than Pelto—probably most anthropologists (see Briggs 1970: 33; LeClair 1960; Powdermaker 1966: 170). When possible, some ethnographers take short periods away from their fieldwork location to catch up on processing their scratch notes (Norbeck 1970: 25; Shah 1979: 32). Mead comments on the pleasure that being caught up brings, if only momentarily: "For the first time in two months I am almost up to date in writing up notes, which is the nearest I can ever come to affluence. It's impossible to get on the credit side of the matter, but just to be free of the knowledge that there are pages and pages of faintly scratched, rapidly cooling notes waiting for me is almost affluence" (1977: 228–30).

The disposition of scratch notes is probably the wastebasket in most cases. Ottenberg kept his for some years, then threw them out. Norbeck apparently kept his longer. He wrote in 1970 about his fieldwork in Japan: "My handwritten field notes consisted of two very slim notebooks more or less filled with cryptic symbols. My typewritten notes consisted of a file of 5 by 8 inches equal to perhaps 2000 manuscript pages. The slim notebooks contained . . . the basis for typing lengthy accounts" (1970: 256).

Fieldnotes Proper

When Solon Kimball arrived in West Ireland in 1933, it had been "drilled" into him that success "would be evident in fat piles of field notes" (1972: 183). The "lengthy accounts" brought back from the field—Norbeck's 2,000 cards, for example—are the heart of our concern with fieldnotes. It is this body of description, acquired and recorded in chronological sequence, that I shall term "fieldnotes proper," though others have different names for it: "journal," "notebooks," "daily logs." Scratch notes precede fieldnotes, and other forms of writing in the field are arranged around them.

At the core of the more specialized fieldnote records and journal from Margery and Arthur Wolf's 1958–60 research in Taiwan are, on five- by eight-inch cards, "some 600 closely typed pages of what we came to call G data, or general data. These notes include detailed descriptions of funeral ceremonies, intensive interviews with unhappy young women, lengthy explanations by village philosophers, and rambling gossip sessions among groups or pairs of women and men." Simon Ottenberg's 1952–53 Afikpo fieldnotes are similar—"a thicket of ethnography." Rena Lederman's New Guinea "daily logs" were handwritten, from her steno-pad notes, in chronologically kept bound books: "Very often there is no clear indication of why any particular item was deemed noteworthy at the time. Neither could a naive reader tell whether what is contained in an entry is complete in itself."

Nancy Lutkehaus and Robert Smith, coming across other ethnographers' fieldnotes, have found in them the properties and problems that Wolf, Ottenberg, and Lederman ascribe to their own. Following Malinowski's advice to produce "a chaotic account in which everything is written down as it is observed or told," Wedgwood kept her 1933–34 fieldnotes in "thirty-four neatly bound notebooks" that record "observations of daily activities, genealogical data, fragments of texts with interlineal translations, narrative descriptions of events and processes, and drawings diagramming such things as house construction and the various parts of an outrigger canoe" (Lutkehaus, this volume). Among the Suye Mura field materials were "two typescript journals. John Embree's contained 1,276 pages; Ella's 1,005." Ella Embree, reports

Smith, "wrote down what she had seen and heard, and often what she thought about it, at the end of every day. The journal . . . begins on December 20, 1935, and ends on November 3, 1936. The difficulty was that increasing familiarity led the journal's author to use short-hand references to individuals and places."

Allen and Orna Johnson (this volume) suggest solutions to the problems of unevenness and haphazard organization that may characterize comprehensive fieldnotes. They also point out, provocatively, that the "interpretive" and "scientific" camps of contemporary anthropology have had little to say about the implications of their positions for the fieldnotes that anthropologists produce: "We suspect that both humanistic and scientific anthropologists keep their journals in roughly comparable ways. . . . Open discussion of our fieldnotes . . . might reveal more similarities between varieties of anthropologists, illuminating the bases that link us as a unified profession."

Whether in handwritten bound books or typed on five-by-eight cards or full-sized typing paper ("I . . . use the best rag-content paper" [Mead 1977: 11]), a substantial corpus of sequentially produced, wide-ranging fieldnotes is at the heart of the ethnographic enterprise (Barnett 1970: 4–5, 28; Boissevain 1970: 79, 81; Ellen 1984b: 283; Fenton 1972: 109; Gulick 1970: 133, 134; Honigmann 1970: 40; Wolcott 1981: 256; Wolff 1960: 241). Extracts from such fieldnotes have been published in several books discussing fieldwork (see Boissevain 1970: 75; Conklin 1960: 119–25; Freilich 1970b: 197–98; Kimball and Partridge 1979; Kobben 1967: 37–38, 43–47, 50, 53–54; Mitchell 1978: 101–3, 107–8, 160, 172–76, 185, 232–33; Wagley 1977: 90–93; Whiting and Whiting 1970: 293, 299–311).

Fieldnote Records

Some of Jean Jackson's anthropological informants contrasted "fieldnotes," in the sense of "a running log written at the end of each day," with "data." For these ethnographers, fieldnotes are "a record of one's reactions, a source of background information, a preliminary stab at analysis." Data, for them, are sociological and demographic materials, organizable on computer cards or disks.

The Johnsons point to the differences in design and use between fieldnotes and more specialized field materials—both the "question-naires and surveys" of quantitatively oriented anthropologists and the "folktales, life histories, or taxonomies" of the humanistically inclined. Robert Maxwell (1970: 480), reviewing his 1964 research in Samoa, distinguished "thesis-relevant information" ("tests and systematic observations that provided me with enough data for a dissertation") from "soft data" (his fieldnotes, recorded on 1,500 five-by-eight cards, concerning "the sociological characteristics of the village, the dreams of the inhabitants, . . . general information on the way people in Laovele pattern their lives," and a mass of details on the lives of two individuals).

In an organizational sense, these contrasts are between fieldnotes proper and fieldnote records—information organized in sets separate from the sequential fieldwork notes that anthropologists produce (Ellen 1984b: 286). While Jackson and the Johnsons identify a strain of contemporary anthropological thinking in which fieldnote records, or "data," are a more important goal than wide-ranging fieldnotes, and Maxwell provides an example, the point here is larger than "scientific" models of fieldwork.[2] Records, as the Johnsons note, are produced by all brands of anthropologists; this was the case for many decades before anthropology became a "behavioral science" in the 1950s.

In addition to the two sets of fieldnotes totaling more than two thousand pages from the Embrees' fieldwork in Japan, Smith was presented with their household census records, along with documents, letters, reports, photographs, and an informant's diary. The records from Margery and Arthur Wolf's 1958–60 Taiwan research were even more extensive: thousands of pages of timed observations of children, hundreds of pages of formal interviews of children and parents, and hundreds of questionnaires administered in schools, all in addition to their "G data" fieldnotes.

Other extra-fieldnote records that anthropologists have mentioned in accounts of fieldwork include household data cards, genealogies, and folders for information on "certain persons . . . and subjects such as kinship, godparenthood, church organization" (Boissevain 1970: 75, 77–78, 80); a list of personal names and their meanings, informant comments on a set of photographs, questionnaires, life histories, and a day-by-day record on political developments "in which every conversation, rumor and event was kept" (Codere 1970: 157–61); forms for data on knowledge of plants and animals and on material culture, and a

---

[2]Ottenberg writes in a personal communication, "There is a danger for some persons of overemphasizing records at the expense of fieldnotes. We had an ethnomusicology student who in his research did great work with the video camera but it so preoccupied him that he had few written notes."

World Health Organization form on household composition and possessions, economics, and health and nutrition (Dentan 1970: 95–96); a questionnaire on values and the Thematic Apperception Test (TAT), both adapted for local use (Diamond 1970: 138–39); topical notes on "change, children, communication, co-operatives, dances, employment, interpersonal relations, law, leadership, marriage, personality and recreation" and a "data bank" on individual community residents (Honigmann 1970: 40, 66); and Rorschach tests, a comprehensive "sociocultural index schedule," and an "expressive autobiographic interview" (Spindler and Spindler 1970: 280–82, 285, 293–95).

As these accounts explain, some fieldnote records are envisioned in "research designs" before fieldwork, and others are developed as the research progresses. Lederman carefully explains the evolution of her "daily log" fieldnotes and "typed files" records, and the relationship between them. Her records, kept according to topic in ring binders, included accounts of complex events, long interviews, a household census, land tenure histories, data on garden plots and pig production, gift exchange account books, and systematic interviews on exchange network memberships, marriage, bridewealth, and mortuary prestations.

In a valuable account of William Partridge's fieldwork in Colombia, the precise points at which systematic records emerged from fieldnotes are identified. Some six months after arrival in his research community, Partridge wrote Solon Kimball: "I am going to begin a series of directed interviews," choosing respondents from "the *costeño* [coastal] hamlet of laborers, the *cachaco vereda* [mountain settlement] La Piedra, and selected older people of the town's upper crust. I will record the interviews on five-by-eight-inch sort cards." Up to that point, information from these three groups had been included in Partridge's chronological fieldnotes. Six months later a new set of records—interviews on marijuana production and use—was begun. Again, this crystallized data collection already under way in Partridge's fieldnotes (Kimball and Partridge 1979: 131, 172).

The balance between fieldnotes and records is unique in each research project, and most if not all anthropologists produce both kinds of documents. Many ethnographers would probably feel uncomfortable speaking of research as fieldwork if it produced records but no fieldnotes. Yet the demands of particular subdisciplines and theoretical approaches increasingly drive fieldworkers toward more directed record collection. Attention to wide-ranging fieldnotes correspondingly recedes.

John Hitchcock, in his 1960–62 fieldwork in Nepal, used a carefully formulated interview guide, yet "much that we learned was picked up fortuitously" and recorded as fieldnotes.

> On balance . . . it was a boon to have well-defined research objectives and easily drawn lines between relevance and irrelevance. Yet the situation was not without paradox. The same design that was guide and support . . . could become a demon rider . . . and I railed at it. . . . It did not truly lay to rest a conscience enhanced if not derived from written exposure to eminences like Boas. . . . The communal live sacrifice at the fortress described in *The Magars of Banyan Hill* [Hitchcock 1966] could not have been written without notes that from the point of view of the research design did not seem strictly relevant. [1970: 176]

Margery Wolf, in writing *The House of Lim* (1968) and *Women and the Family in Rural Taiwan* (1972), drew upon both fieldnotes and records. She was "gratified by all the seemingly purposeless anecdotes, conversations verging on lectures, and series of complaints that *had* been recorded. Clearly, the presence of unfocused, wide-ranging, all-inclusive fieldnotes was essential to the success of this unplanned project." During her 1980–81 interviews in China, it was impossible to produce much in the way of similar fieldnotes; in her view, a more restricted and limited book necessarily resulted.

"If we are to develop authentic descriptions of individual behavior and beliefs," the Johnsons write, "we must accompany the subject into the several significant settings that evoke the many facets of the whole person." They identify the dangers of records without fieldnotes: "The tight, deductive research designs of the behavioral scientist are necessarily reductionistic. . . . Anthropologists generally agree that most human behavior is overdetermined, serving multiple purposes or reflecting multiple meanings simultaneously." Among ways to balance record-oriented research with wide-ranging ethnographic fieldnotes, the Johnsons propose a "cultural context checklist" as a medium for constantly reintroducing holistic concerns into fieldwork routines— much as Honigmann (1970: 43) reports that reviewing Murdock's *Outline of Cultural Materials* was useful to him.

Texts

Among fieldnote records, "texts" are a particular kind, with their own long history in anthropology. They are produced by *transcription,* Clifford's third type of ethnographic fieldnote writing. Transcription, unlike inscribing scratch notes, usually involves an encounter between informant and ethnographer away from ongoing social action and conversation. Ideally, the ethnographer and informant sit alone together; the ethnographer carefully records answers to posed questions, or writes down in the informant's own words and language a dictated myth, spell, recipe, or life history remembrance. While handwritten transcriptions may be retyped and translated later, the point is to secure the informant's precise words *during* the fieldwork encounter, as they are spoken. The results of such fieldwork procedure are texts.

Texts figure prominently in the fieldnotes of Franz Boas. He published more than 3,000 pages of Kwakiutl texts and translations, many written by George Hunt, and some 6,751 pages of texts from all his fieldwork (Codere 1966: xiv; White 1963: 23–24). These texts give us "the lineage myth as its owner tells it, the potlatch speech as it was given, the point-by-point procedures in making a canoe," according to Helen Codere (1966: xxx), who knows as well as any anthropologist the full Boas corpus. Her three examples stand for three different social contexts of transcription: (1) a myth recited for the anthropologist—a text reproduced away from its normal context of recital; (2) a speech given during an event—a text recorded in the context of its social production, heard by natives and ethnographer alike; (3) an account of a technical procedure—a text created at the prompting of the ethnographer and not recoverable in such form elsewhere.

Although the second context—recording ongoing speech events—certainly results in texts, it partakes of both inscription and transcription. In a contemporary sociolinguistic appraisal of interview methods, Charles Briggs (1986) argues against imposition of the Western/middle-class interview speech event and in favor of culturally grounded forms of listening and talk, learned over time through participant-observation. His cautions are relevant to both the first, displaced mode of transcription and the third, fabricative one. His argument would favor the second inscription-transcription mode. Texts resulting from such ongoing speech events would also be more appropriate to the goals of text transcription professed by Boas.

These goals, according to Stocking, are well presented in a 1905 Boas letter on the importance of published texts:

> I do not think that anyone would advocate the study of antique civilizations . . . without a thorough knowledge of their languages and of the literary documents in these languages. . . . In regard to our American Indians . . . practically no such literary material is available for study. . . .

My own published work shows, that I let this kind of work take precedence over practically everything else, knowing it is the foundation of all future researches. Without it . . . deeper studies . . . will be all but impossible. Besides this we must furnish . . . the indispensable material for future linguistic studies. [Stocking 1974: 122–23]

The linguistic value of Boas's displaced and created texts is most useful in work on morphology, syntax, and semantics; it is less so for stylistics and pragmatics than the texts of actual speech events would be (Jacobs 1959). In "antique civilizations," texts and physical remains are all we have. In living societies, however, other anthropologists have not elevated text-recording in fieldwork to the height that Boas did; rather, they have valued participant-observation, with its other forms of note-taking. Nonetheless, it *is* the potential of texts to assist in "deeper studies" that has accounted for their continuing transcription.

For Boas, one aim of ethnography was to "disclose . . . the 'innermost thoughts,' the 'mental life' of the people," and texts were a means "to present Kwakiutl culture as it appears to the Indian himself" (Codere 1966: xi, xv). With fieldnotes and other kinds of records, texts have been used by other anthropologists to meet similar goals. On Manus Island in 1928–29, Reo Fortune "concentrated on texts, once he had trained Pokanau to dictate the contents of last night's seance. He took everything down in longhand" (Mead 1972:174). The limits of displaced transcription, however, were revealed to Mead in 1953 when Pokanau told her that her more rapid typing of his texts permitted him to "'put it all in.' The 'all' simply meant an incredible number of repetitions." But it is precisely "repetition" and other performative and paralinguistic features that today so interest analysts of transcribed texts of ongoing rituals and other speech events.

Like Mead (see also 1977: 297), Mandelbaum in India in 1937 transcribed texts directly by typewriter from his English-speaking Kota informant Sulli. Although "my notes and the quotations of his words usually preserve the structure of his utterance, ... as I typed I would repair, for the sake of future clarity, some of his direct speech" (1960: 279n). Sulli's texts covered a wide range of Kota culture. He also dictated texts for Murray Emeneau, who mentioned in *Kota Texts* (1944)—based entirely on Sulli's displaced oral productions—that he was a "fine storyteller who adjusted to the slow pace of dictation without losing the narrative and entertainment qualities which are characteristic of Kota tales" (Mandelbaum 1960: 306). In candor, Mandelbaum also adds that Sulli's narratives tended "to be neater and more integrated than was the historical actuality," and that he tended "to figure much larger in his account than he may have in the event" (1960: 307). Displaced and created texts are here certainly Kota "culture as it appears to the Indian himself." Like all texts, nonetheless, they and their creator are positioned in their local society.

Life histories turn around the disadvantages that such texts, created at the ethnographer's prompting, have for any general appreciation of "the mental life of the people." Instead, they purposely position the informant within her or his local society. In addition to large chunks of texts, life histories as genre present analysis based upon fieldnotes and other forms of records. John Adair (1960: 495–97) describes the life history fieldwork process, with an extract from his transcriptions once they reached a text-productive stage. Informative accounts of collecting life history fieldnote texts are provided by James Freeman (1979), Sidney Mintz (1960) and Edward Winter (1959). Langness and Frank (1981) offer a history and overview of this ethnographic option.

With literacy, the displaced oral productions and created accounts of informants may take on a self-edited form (Goody 1977, 1986, 1987) more like ethnography and, before recent interests in narrativity and rhetoric, well suited to the ethnographer's textual goals. Recalling fieldwork with the Copper Eskimo, Jenness conveys the frustration of many past text transcribers with nonliterate informants and their non–Western/middle-class speech conventions.

> We then closeted ourselves with two old men, whose hearts we warmed with some hard biscuits and cups of steaming chocolate. The comfortable tent and the unusual beverage loosened their tongues. . . . In the end it was not their secretiveness that hampered our researches, but our ignorance of their ways of thought and their own inability to narrate a story from the ground upward; for they invariably began with the crisis, so to speak, and worked backward and forward, with many omissions and repetitions, on the tacit assumption that our minds moved in the same groove as theirs and that explanations were needless. [1928: 202–3]

Sulli's texts no doubt reflect his schooling. So did the detailed, sequential account of the three-day Agarabi male initiation ritual dictated to James B. Watson on his second New Guinea field trip in 1963–64 by "a handsome, clean-cut youth" whose "clothing, his bearing, and his excellent pidgin, deliberately interspersed with English, betrayed that he had been to school and had also worked for a time in a town or on the coast."

> "The First Day," the young man announced like a title, flashing me a self-conscious smile. He began to detail the preliminaries of the ritual. . . . I finished the last unused leaf of the notebook and . . . continued the notes on the inside back cover, then on the outside. . . . He stopped to ask if I did not have another book. . . . I called out to the house . . . for someone to bring me the book. . . . We picked up where we had stopped. . . . My eyes were straining now from seldom looking up. Page by page we noted all the events of "The Second Day," finally reaching the third. . . . At last the session ended. . . . We had been at it for well over two hours. . . . My collaborator told me cheerfully that he would be available tomorrow for any further questions. . . . Sure that I knew the village well ten years ago, I had found no one like this. . . . No elder I had ever talked to could do what had just been done. [Watson 1972: 177–79]

The next step with literate informants, as Boas long ago learned with George Hunt, is to add texts written by the informants themselves to the ethnographer's own body of fieldnotes. This happened spontaneously for Mintz in 1953 after he asked Don Taso, a Puerto Rican sugar cane worker, if he could tape-record his life story. "He asked for time to think about it. . . . The following evening when we sat down together again, he produced from his pocket several sheets of lined paper, torn from a child's notebook, on which he had written down his story. . . . So the formal gathering of the data on Taso's life began with a written statement." Mintz published an English translation of this text, and reproduced a page from the handwritten Spanish original, in *Worker in the Cane: a Puerto Rican Life History* (1960: 27–31; illus. 4).

Letters from informants on ethnographic topics (Kluckhohn 1960: 450; Lowie 1960: 431–32) are another form of text, as is "The Diary of an Innkeeper's Daughter," found among the Suye Mura materials that accompanied the Embrees' fieldnotes when Smith received them. In Rwanda in 1959–60, in addition to transcribing forty-eight life histories, Codere (1970: 157) had a dozen Rwandan "reporters" fill many notebooks for her. Meeting the Boasian mandate, "the good notebook material does give a picture of the activities and preoccupations of the young Rwanda that year, of their mobility, and of their version of what they saw around them." Several of Jean Jackson's anthropological informants also gave their field informants notebooks to produce their own fieldnotes (see also Beattie 1965: 26–27, 30–34; Epstein 1961; Evans-Pritchard 1974; Lewis 1951: xix; Parsons 1917; Schapera 1935: 318). Perhaps the uncertainty of ownership between sponsor and author of these informant-produced texts is involved in the lack of clarity many of Jackson's informants expressed over what to include under the "fieldnotes" label.

Journals and Diaries

Journals and diaries are written products of fieldwork that serve indexical or cathartic purposes for ethnographers (Ellen 1984b: 289). Chronologically constructed journals provide a key to the information in fieldnotes and records (cf. Carstens et al. 1987); diaries record the ethnographer's personal reactions, frustrations, and assessments of life and work in the field. In some cases the same account will contain elements of both forms, as is evident of two extracts from S. F. Nadel's "diary" of his Nuba fieldwork (Husmann 1983; see also Turner 1987: 94). Latterly, the increasingly intertextual nature of post-field ethnographic writing has intruded on both journals and diaries. Journals may now record reactions to ethnographies read or reconsidered in the field; and diaries, one suspects, may be written with the aim of publishing a "personal account" of fieldwork (as with Barley 1983; Cesara 1982; Rabinow 1977; Romanucci-Ross 1985. See Geertz 1988: 89–91).

In her Pacific fieldwork Margaret Mead kept "a diary"—or *journal,* using the distinction I make here—"stripped of comment, as an index to events and records. This was an act of responsibility in case my field work was interrupted and someone else had to make sense of it" (1977: 11). Honigmann's 1944 and 1945 journals from his fieldwork among the Canadian Kaska Indians were similarly a daily record of activity; his fieldnotes were "on 4″ × 5″ slips of paper and categorized according to the advice in George P. Murdock's manual called *Outline of Cultural Materials*" (1970: 40). In Honigmann's case, there were no "fieldnotes proper"; the journal and topical fieldnote records together contain the information that more ordinarily appears in chronologically kept fieldnotes. Boissevain's 1960–61 Malta fieldwork journal—"a daily diary into which I entered appointments and a rather terse summary of persons and places visited during the day" (1970: 79–80)—is another example of the journal form.

Rosemary Firth's 1939–40 Malayan fieldwork diary was something different from these three examples of journals, or from that of her husband:

> [It] became for me a sort of lifeline, or checking point to measure changes in myself. I believe Raymond Firth kept a mainly chronological-record type of diary when he was in Tikopia [Firth 1936: 2] and Malinowski the more personal sort when he was in the Trobriands. Mine was used as an emotional outlet for an individual subjected to disorientating changes in his [sic] personal and social world. Perhaps ideally, both kinds should be kept; first the bare facts, the news summary as it were, then the personal reactions. [1972: 15]

Bronislaw Malinowski's *Diary in the Strict Sense of the Term* (1967) is certainly well titled. It has been the subject of many assessments, of which that of Anthony Forge—like Malinowski, an ethnographer of Melanesia—is both sympathetic and useful.

> It was never intended for publication. . . . These diaries are not about the Trobriand Islanders. . . . They are a partial record of the struggle that affects every anthropologist in the field: a struggle to retain a sense of his own identity as an individual and as a member of a culture. . . . Under these circumstances a diary is . . . your only chance of expressing yourself, of relieving your tensions, of obtaining any sort of cathar- sis. . . . The negative side of fieldwork . . . predominates in the diaries . . . a place to spew up one's spleen, so that tomorrow one can start afresh. [1972: 292–96. Also see Geertz 1988: 73–83; Mead 1970: 324n]

Other anthropological diarists, whose work we do not see in full as we do Malinowski's, stress the personal functions identified by Forge. When experiencing "despair and hopelessness" in her fieldwork in Mexico, Peggy Golde (1970a: 75) vented her feelings in her diary. Margery Wolf, ranging more widely, recorded her "irritation with village life, some wild hypotheses of causation, an ongoing analysis of the Chinese personality structure, various lascivious thoughts, dia- tribes against injustice, and so forth."

Diamond Jenness's 1913–16 Arctic fieldwork led to both diary (1957: 9, 88) and fieldnotes (1928: 14, 28, 41, 83–84). *Dawn in Arctic Alaska,* covering the first months of his research, portrays Alaskan Eskimos much more acculturated to Western society (1957: 100, 103, 122) than

the Canadian Copper Eskimo described in *The People of the Twilight*
(1928), one of the earliest and best of many personal ethnographic
accounts. *Dawn in Arctic Alaska* was written from Jenness's diary, he
tells us (1957: 8)—plus his headnotes, of course. An extract from the
diary is included (1957: 88–89), and the book incorporates both the
factual (journallike) and the personal (diarylike) qualities that his field
diaries clearly contain. No prefacing statement identifies Jenness's
textual sources for *The People of the Twilight,* but its chronological
structure must also be based on his diary; again, the factual and the
personal are comingled.

The intertextual environment of contemporary anthropology figures centrally in the extensive personal journals—"the most private of
my notes" which "I imagine I would never want to make public"—
that Rena Lederman kept along with her fieldnotes and records during
her New Guinea research: "There are reactions to the books and
articles I was reading—some anthropology, some history, and some
other things—usually entered . . . in the form of ideas for a disserta-
tion/book or for articles."

A textual influence on anthropological journals and diaries that has
registered powerfully in recent decades is Lévi-Strauss's *Tristes Tropiques* (1955), in English translation since 1961. Clifford Geertz says of it:
"Though it is very far from being a great anthropology book, or even
an especially good one, is surely one of the finest books ever written
by an anthropologist" (1973: 347; see also 1988: 25–48). While other
personal accounts of fieldwork predate it (Cushing 1882–83; Jenness
1928; Kluckhohn 1927, 1933; Osgood 1953; Wissler 1938), none except Laura Bohannan's *Return to Laughter* (Bowen 1954) has had nearly
the impact of Lévi-Strauss's work, as is evident from references to it in
several fieldwork accounts (Alland 1975; Rabinow 1977; Romanucci-
Ross 1985). One also suspects its inspiration or stylistic influence in
several others where it is not mentioned (Barley 1983, 1986; Cesara
1982; Gearing 1970; Maybury-Lewis 1965; Mitchell 1978; Read 1965;
Robertson 1978; Turnbull 1961; Wagley 1977; Werner 1984).

Stirred by this burgeoning genre since the mid-1950s, intentions to
write personal fieldwork accounts later have no doubt revivified a
fieldwork diary tradition that had been giving way to indexical journals under the growing influence of social anthropology and behavioral science models. Simon Ottenberg, writes of his 1952–53 Afikpo
fieldwork: "I did not keep a diary . . . which I very much regret today.

But we were brought up in a positivistic age where personal impressions were seen as less important than the 'facts out there.' "

Letters, Reports, Papers

Fieldnotes, records, texts, and journals and diaries remain in the field with their author and one-person audience. Many ethnographers mail carbon copies of fieldnotes home for safekeeping, but not, normally, for reading by anyone else. The exceptions are usually graduate students who send sets of fieldnotes to university advisors and mentors, as did William Partridge to Solon Kimball (Kimball and Partridge 1979).[3] Kimball's investment in Partridge's fieldwork via return letters was considerable—and unusual; in few other places in the fieldwork literature are similar involvements recorded. When advisors write to students in the field, it is more likely in response to those in-field compositions written to leave the field—letters, reports, and papers.

Probably most anthropologists in the field write letters to family members and friends, to mentors and professional colleagues. Letters, first of all, inform others that one is alive and well, or alive and recovering. They also allow the fieldworker to report on his or her psychological state and reactions—see Rosemary Firth's letter to her father (1972: 16)—although not as fully or cathartically as do personal diaries. "The long letters that Ruth and I wrote to our families are poor substitutes for a diary" (Dentan 1970: 89).

Perhaps more significantly, letters allow the ethnographer to try out descriptions and syntheses in an informal fashion. Hazel Weidman's 1957–58 field letters from Burma include evocative descriptions of Rangoon and of the hospital in which she conducted fieldwork (1970: 243–46). Buell Quain's 1938 letter from Brazil to his advisor Ruth Benedict (Murphy and Quain 1955: 103–6) is a rounded, rich description of Trumai Indian culture, more human in tone than the abstractions of fieldnotes.

Letters are a first step in committing headnotes to paper (e.g., Mitchell 1978: 96–101, 104–7). As Lutkehaus reveals, Camilla Wedgwood's letters from Malinowski, received while she was doing fieldwork in Manam, indicate that her letters to him were the beginnings of

---

[3]Triloki Nath Pandey's letters to his advisor Fred Eggan were indeed his fieldnotes: he did not take notes in front of his Zuni informants, but he could safely write to his "boss" (1979: 257).

her analyses. "Cut out certain portions of your information and publish them in *Man* as it might be easier to do it out of informal letters
than for you to stew over the writing up of an article," he advised her.
Letters certainly can be a useful tool in constructing a personal account
of fieldwork such as A. F. Robertson's for his 1965–66 research in
Uganda (1978: 1–2).

Like her ethnography, and her marriages, Margaret Mead's letters
from the field are monumental. A substantial selection of them (Mead
1977), published shortly before her death in 1978, form an essential
complement to her memoirs (Mead 1972) and Jane Howard's biography (1984) for an understanding of Mead's career in anthropology.
"Letters written and received in the field have a very special significance. Immersing oneself in life in the field is good, but one must be
careful not to drown. . . . Letters can be a way of occasionally righting
the balance as, for an hour or two, one relates oneself to people who
are part of one's other world and tries to make a little more real for
them this world which absorbs one, waking and sleeping" (Mead
1977: 7).

In her early fieldwork Mead wrote individual letters to relatives,
friends, and mentors Franz Boas, Ruth Benedict, William F. Ogburn,
and Clark Wissler. But from her first fieldwork in Samoa in 1925–26,
she also typed multiple carbons of letters addressed to a group; her
mother too retyped letters and sent them to others. This practice
netted Mead return mail of seventy or eighty letters every six weeks in
Samoa, as well as setting a pattern that continued through her field
experiences into the 1970s. By the 1950s her field letters were circulating to fifty or more persons (1977: 8–10).

The final two forms of fieldwork writing we will consider are
reports and papers. In preparation for such writing, as well as for later
dissertations and publications and to identify gaps in their fieldnotes,
many anthropologists report "rereading," "reviewing," "working
up," "going over," "organizing," and "thumbing through" their fieldnotes while in the field (Barley 1983: 91, 112, 169–70; Becker and Geer
1960; Ellen 1984b: 282; Firth 1972: 21; Gonzalez 1970: 171; Jenness
1928: 14; Lévi-Strauss 1955: 376; Pelto 1970: 263–64; Read 1965: 39;
Whitten 1970: 351; Yengoyan 1970: 417–18). On his own, Pelto "occasionally wrote short essays on such materials (sometimes in the form
of letters from the field)" (1970: 266).

Most reports, however, are directed outside the field, toward sponsors and overseers of the research. From Samoa, Mead sent the National Research Council a report (1977: 42). John and Ella Embree wrote "progress reports to the Social Science Research Committee of the University of Chicago which had funded the study," as Smith found in the cache of their Suye Mura materials. In the month before leaving Somaliland in 1957, I. M. Lewis wrote a report that "runs to 140 roneoed foolscap pages and is pompously titled *The Somali Lineage System and the Total Genealogy: A General Introduction to Basic Principles of Somali Political Institutions*" (1977: 236). Similarly, Lederman's first extensive writing was a report on Mendi rural political economy, written for the Southern Highlands Province Research Committee, and submitted before she left the field in 1979.

Reports, if read, may produce responses useful in later ethnographic writing. Boissevain sent the Colonial Social Science Research Council a 14,000-word, six-month report from Malta: "Writing the report forced me to rethink basic problems and to look at my material. . . . In doing so I discovered numerous shortcomings. . . . Moreover . . . I was able to elicit valuable criticism and comments from my supervisor [Lucy Mair] and her colleagues at the London School of Economics. This feedback was invaluable. . . . I should have been consolidating my data frequently in short reports" (1970: 80, 84). In addition to letters and fieldnotes, Partridge sent Kimball six-week and six-month reports (both reproduced in Kimball and Partridge 1979: 28–48, 136–48). Unlike too many supervisors, Kimball replied to Partridge with his reactions and suggestions.

Professional papers are occasionally written from the field, although the lack of library resources makes this difficult. Frank Hamilton Cushing wrote many papers while at Zuni pueblo between 1879 and 1884, several of which were published (Green 1979: 12–13), among them his personal fieldwork account, "My Adventures in Zuni" (Cushing 1882–83; Green 1979: 46–134). Ninety years later Partridge wrote "Cannabis and Cultural Groups in a Colombia Municipio" after a year in the field; flew to deliver the paper at the 1973 Ninth International Congress of Anthropological and Ethnological Sciences in Chicago; and returned to complete the final months of his research (Kimball and Partridge 1979: 190, 192, 220). The paper was subsequently published (Partridge 1975). While in Bunyoro, Beattie wrote a paper for an East African Institute of Social Research conference (1965: 44, 51). Also in the field, Lederman prepared an abstract and outline for a paper she presented at

the American Anthropological Association meeting later that year after
returning home, no doubt a more common experience than that of
Partridge.

Tape Transcripts

Transcripts of taped, dictated fieldnotes and texts may be typed out
of the field—by paid assistants in some cases—but the resulting documents work much like fieldnotes in relation to later forms of ethnographic writing. Dictating fieldnotes is by no means a common practice among ethnographers, though the technology to do so has been
available for decades (but see Barley 1983: 62; Warner and Lunt 1941:
69). Speaking into a microphone while one is alone would no doubt
appear a suspicious practice in many parts of the world. But I suspect
the missing scratch-notes-to-fieldnotes step is the primary reason that
dictation is rarely used. Sitting and thinking at a typewriter or computer keyboard brings forth the "enlarging" and "interpreting" that
turns "abbreviated jottings" and personal "shorthand" into fieldnotes.
Margaret Mead wrote in 1953, "I don't dare use tape because there is no
chance to work over and revise—or, if one does, it takes as long" (1977:
252). Untypically, Gertrude Enders Huntington and her family members, in a study of a Canadian Hutterite colony in the early 1960s,
dictated some fifty typed pages' worth of fieldnotes a week into a tape
recorder; they also kept written fieldnotes and records, but writing
time was at a premium in this communal society (Hostetler and Huntington 1970: 213). If tape-recording one's own fieldnotes has not
become a popular ethnographic practice—for good reason—taping
texts is another story. Laura Nader, in a short study in Lebanon in 1961,
tape-recorded informant accounts of cases of conflict; these proved
"much richer in contextual information" than similar cases recorded
by hand (1970: 108). R. Lincoln Keiser taped interviews and life histories with Chicago Vice Lord gang members in 1964–65: "I was able to
record highly detailed accounts of interviews that I could not have
written by hand. Transcribing the tapes was the main difficulty. It took
me months of steady work to finish" (1970: 230).
    Untranscribed tapes sit in many offices and studies. The disadvan-
tages mentioned by Keiser are real, but so are the advantages that he
and Nader found in having instant texts of the sort that Boas and
others labored for hours to record by hand, and with the oral features

that are often lost in written transcription encounters. Agar used participant-observation, documents, and taped "career history interviews" in his study of independent truckers. The lengthy interviews, "a format designed to let the interviewee have control," were the core of his research: "to work with this material, transcripts are necessary; their preparation is tedious work, since a clean hour of talk might take six to eight hours to transcribe. . . . Transcription was done on a word-processor to facilitate 'proof-listening'—going over the transcript, listening to the tape, and checking for errors" (1986: 178). Agar had an assistant transcribe most of the interviews, and his ethnography includes extensive quotations from these texts.

Current anthropological interests in political language and what Audrey Richards (1939; see also Briggs 1986) called "speech in action" require a good ear and a quick hand, or a tape recorder. The tape recorder is probably winning out. As David Plath reminds us, portable tape recorders are now a commonplace in rural villages as well as cities worldwide; their use by ethnographers in taping others no longer invites curiosity. New-fashioned styles of fieldwork are emerging in which transcriptions of taped texts are the primary if not the only form of fieldnotes produced (Agar 1980, 1986). Quinn's cultural analyses of American marriage (1981, 1982, 1987) are based on taped interviews— "patterned as closely as possible after ordinary conversations"—that average fifteen to sixteen hours for each partner in eleven married couples (1982: 776). As in Agar's work, extensive quotations from these texts appear in her publications, and the relationship between fieldnotes and analysis is as close as in any more traditional ethnography. Technology marches on, and taped texts are here to stay.

REFERENCES

Adair, John. 1960. A Pueblo G.I. In Casagrande 1960, 489–503.
Adams, Richard N., and J. Preiss, eds. 1960. *Human Organization Research*. Homewood, Ill.: Dorsey.
Agar, Michael H. 1980. *The Professional Stranger: An Informal Introduction to Ethnography*. New York: Academic Press.
——. 1986. *Independents Declared: The Dilemmas of Independent Trucking*. Washington, D.C.: Smithsonian Institution Press.
Alland, Alexander, Jr. 1975. *Where the Spider Danced*. New York: Anchor Press.
Barley, Nigel. 1983. *Adventures in a Mud Hut: An Innocent Anthropologist Abroad*. New York: Vanguard Press.
——. 1986. *Ceremony: An Anthropologist's Misadventures in the African Bush*. New York: Holt.

Barnett, Homer G. 1970. Palauan Journal. In Spindler 1970, 1–31.

Beals, Alan R. 1970. Gopalpur, 1958–1960. In Spindler 1970, 32–57.

Beattie, John. 1965. *Understanding an African Kingdom: Bunyoro.* New York: Holt, Rinehart & Winston.

Becker, Howard, and Blanche Geer. 1960. Participant Observation: The Analysis of Qualitative Field Data. In Adams and Preiss, 1960, 267–89.

Boissevain, Jeremy. 1970. Fieldwork in Malta. In Spindler 1970, 58–84.

Bowen, Elenore Smith [Laura Bohannan]. 1954. *Return to Laughter.* New York: Anchor Books.

Briggs, Charles. 1986. *Learning to Ask: A Sociolinguistic Appraisal of the Role of the Interview in Social Science Research.* New York: Cambridge University Press.

Briggs, Jean. 1970. Kapluna Daughter. In Golde 1970b, 17–44.

Carstens, Peter, Gerald Klinghardt, and Martin West, eds. 1987. *Trails in the Thirstland: The Anthropological Field Diaries of Winifred Hoernle.* Communication 14. Cape Town: Centre for African Studies, University of Cape Town.

Casagrande, Joseph B., ed. 1960. *In the Company of Man: Twenty Portraits of Anthropological Informants.* New York: Harper Torchbooks.

Cesara, Manda. 1982. *Reflections of a Woman Anthropologist: No Hiding Place.* New York: Academic Press.

Codere, Helen. 1966. Introduction. In Franz Boas, *Kwakiutl Ethnography,* xi–xxxii. Chicago: University of Chicago Press.

———. 1970. Field Work in Rwanda, 1959–1960. In Golde 1970b, 141–64.

Conklin, Harold. 1960. Maling, a Hanunoo Girl from the Philippines: A Day in Parina. In Casagrande 1960, 101–25.

Cushing, Frank Hamilton. 1882–83. My Adventures in Zuni. *Century Illustrated Monthly Magazine* 25:191–207, 500–511; 26: 28–47. [In Green 1979.]

Davis, John. 1984. Data into Text. In Ellen 1984a, 295–318.

Dentan, Robert K. 1970. Living and Working with the Semai. In Spindler 1970, 85–112.

Diamond, Norma. 1970. Fieldwork in a Complex Society: Taiwan. In Spindler 1970, 113–41.

Ellen, R. F., ed. 1984a. *Ethnographic Research: A Guide to General Conduct.* San Diego: Academic Press.

———. 1984b. Notes and Records. In Ellen 1984a, 278–93.

Emeneau, M. B. 1944. *Kota Texts.* Berkeley: University of California Publications in Linguistics.

Epstein, A. L. 1961. The Network and Urban Social Organization. *Rhodes-Livingstone Institute Journal* 29:28–62.

Evans-Pritchard, E. E. 1974. *Man and Woman among the Azande.* New York: Free Press.

Fenton, William N. 1972. Return to the Longhouse. In Kimball and Watson 1972, 102–18.

Firth, Raymond. 1936 [1963]. *We, The Tikopia: A Sociological Study of Kinship in Primitive Polynesia.* Boston: Beacon Press.

Firth, Rosemary. 1972. From Wife to Anthropologist. In Kimball and Watson 1972, 10–32.

Forge, Anthony. 1972. The Lonely Anthropologist. In Kimball and Watson 1972, 292–97.

Freeman, James. 1979. *Untouchable: An Indian Life History.* Stanford, Calif.: Stanford University Press.

Freilich, Morris, ed. 1970a. *Marginal Natives: Anthropologists at Work.* New York: Harper & Row.

———. 1970b. Mohawk Heroes and Trinidadian Peasants. In Freilich 1970a, 185–250.

Gearing, Frederick. 1970. *The Face of the Fox.* Chicago: Aldine.

Geertz, Clifford. 1973. *The Interpretation of Cultures.* New York: Basic Books.

———. 1988. *Works and Lives: The Anthropologist as Author.* Stanford, Calif.: Stanford University Press.

Golde, Peggy. 1970a. Odyssey of Encounter. In Golde, 1970b, 65–93.

———. 1970b. *Women in the Field: Anthropological Experiences.* Chicago: Aldine.

Gonzalez, Nancie L. Solien. 1970. Cakchiqueles and Caribs: The Social Context of Field Work. In Freilich 1970a, 153–84.

Goody, Jack. 1977. *The Domestication of the Savage Mind.* Cambridge: Cambridge University Press.

———. 1986. *The Logic of Writing and the Organization of Society.* Cambridge: Cambridge University Press.

———. 1987. *The Interface between the Written and the Oral.* Cambridge: Cambridge University Press.

Green, Jesse, ed. 1979. *Zuni: Selected Writings of Frank Hamilton Cushing.* Lincoln: University of Nebraska Press.

Gulick, John. 1970. Village and City Field Work in Lebanon. In Freilich 1970a, 123–52.

Gupta, Khadija A. 1979. Travails of a Woman Fieldworker: A Small Town in Uttar Pradesh. In Srinivas et al. 1979, 103–14.

Hitchcock, John T. 1966. *The Magars of Banyan Hill.* New York: Holt, Rinehart & Winston.

———. 1970. Fieldwork in Gurkha Country. In Spindler 1970, 164–93.

Holy, Ladislav. 1984. Theory, Methodology, and the Research Process. In Ellen 1984a, 13–34.

Honigmann, John J. 1970. Field Work in Two Northern Canadian Communities. In Freilich 1970a, 39–72.

Hostetler, John A., and Gertrude Enders Huntington. 1970. The Hutterites: Fieldwork in a North American Communal Society. In Spindler 1970, 194–219.

Howard, Jane. 1984. *Margaret Mead: A Life.* New York: Fawcett Crest.

Husmann, Rolf. 1983. Preface. In Jana Salat, *Reasoning as Enterprise: The Anthropology of S. F. Nadel,* 1–7. Göttingen: Herodot.

Jacobs, Melville. 1959. Folklore. In *The Anthropology of Frank Boas,* ed. Walter Goldschmidt, 119–38. San Francisco: Chandler.

Jenness, Diamond. 1928 [1959]. *The People of the Twilight*. Chicago: University of Chicago Press.

——. 1957 [1985]. *Dawn in Arctic Alaska*. Chicago: University of Chicago Press.

Keiser, R. Lincoln. 1970. Fieldwork among the Vice Lords of Chicago. In Spindler 1970, 220–37.

Kimball, Solon T. 1972. Learning a New Culture. In Kimball and Watson 1972, 182–92.

Kimball, Solon, and William Partridge. 1979. *The Craft of Community Study: Fieldwork Dialogues*. Gainesville: University Presses of Florida.

Kimball, Solon, and James B. Watson, eds. 1972. *Crossing Cultural Boundaries: The Anthropological Experience*. San Francisco: Chandler.

Kluckhohn, Clyde. 1927. *To the Foot of the Rainbow*. New York: Century.

——. 1933. *Beyond the Rainbow*. Boston: Christopher.

——. 1960. A Navaho Politician. In Casagrande 1960, 439–65.

Köbben, A. J. F. 1967. Participation and Quantification: Field Work among the Djuka (Bush Negroes of Surinam). In *Anthropologists in the Field*, ed. D. G. Jongmans and P. C. W. Gutkind, 35–55. New York: Humanities Press.

Langness, L. L., and Gelya Frank. 1981. *Lives: An Anthropological Approach to Biography*. Novato, Calif.: Chandler & Sharp.

LeClair, Edward, Jr. 1960. Problems of Large-Scale Anthropological Research. In Adams and Preiss 1960, 28–40.

Lévi-Strauss, Claude. 1955 [1974]. *Tristes Tropiques*. Trans. John and Doreen Weightman. New York: Atheneum.

Lewis, I. M. 1977. Confessions of a "Government" Anthropologist. *Anthropological Forum* 4:226–38.

Lewis, Oscar. 1951. *Life in a Mexican Village: Tepoztlan Restudied*. Urbana: University of Illinois Press.

Lowie, Robert H. 1960. My Crow Interpreter. In Casagrande 1960, 427–37.

Malinowski, Bronislaw. 1967. *A Diary in the Strict Sense of the Term*. New York: Harcourt, Brace & World.

Mandelbaum, David G. 1960. A Reformer of His People. In Casagrande 1960, 273–308.

Marshall, Gloria [Niara Sudarkasa]. 1970. In a World of Women: Field Work in a Yoruba Community. In Golde 1970b, 165–91.

Maxwell, Robert. 1970. A Comparison of Field Research in Canada and Polynesia. In Freilich 1970a, 441–84.

Maybury-Lewis, David. 1965 [1988]. *The Savage and the Innocent*. Boston: Beacon Press.

——. 1967. *Akwe-Shavante Society*. Oxford: Oxford University Press.

Mayer, A. C. 1978. *The Remembered Village:* From Memory Alone? *Contributions to Indian Sociology* 12:39–47.

Mead, Margaret. 1970. Field Work in the Pacific Islands, 1925–1967. In Golde 1970b, 291–331.

——. 1972. *Blackberry Winter: My Earlier Years*. New York: William Morrow.

——. 1977. *Letters from the Field, 1925–1975*. New York: Harper & Row.

Minocha, Aneeta A. 1979. Varied Roles in the Field: A Hospital in Delhi. In Srinivas et al. 1979, 201–15.

Mintz, Sidney. 1960 [1974]. *Worker in the Cane: A Puerto Rican Life History.* New York: Norton.

Mitchell, William. 1978. *The Bamboo Fire: An Anthropologist in New Guinea.* New York: Norton.

Murphy, Robert F., and Buell Quain. 1955. *The Trumai Indians of Central Brazil.* Seattle: University of Washington Press.

Nader, Laura. 1970. From Anguish to Exultation. In Golde 1970b, 95–116.

Norbeck, Edward. 1970. Changing Japan: Field Research. In Spindler 1970, 238–66.

Osgood, Cornelius. 1953. *Winter.* New York: Norton.

Pandey, Triloki Nath. 1979. The Anthropologist-Informant Relationship: The Navajo and Zuni in America and the Tharu in India. In Srinivas et al. 1979, 246–65.

Parsons, Elsie Clews. 1917. *Notes on Zuni.* American Anthropological Association Memoirs 19 and 20. Washington, D.C.: American Anthropological Association.

Partridge, William. 1975. Cannabis and Cultural Groups in a Colombian Municipio. In *Cannabis and Culture,* ed. Vera Rubin, 147–72. The Hague: Mouton.

Pelto, Pertti J. 1970. Research in Individualistic Societies. In Freilich 1970a, 251–92.

Powdermaker, Hortense. 1966. *Stranger and Friend: The Way of an Anthropologist.* New York: Norton.

Quinn, Naomi. 1981. Marriage Is a Do-It-Yourself Project: The Organization of Marital Goals. *Proceedings of the Third Annual Conference of the Cognitive Science Society,* 31–40. Berkeley: University of California.

———. 1982. "Commitment" in American Marriage: A Cultural Analysis. *American Ethnologist* 9: 775–98.

———. 1987. Convergent Evidence for a Cultural Model of American Marriage. In *Cultural Models in Language and Thought,* ed. Dorothy Holland and Naomi Quinn, 173–92. New York: Cambridge University Press.

Rabinow, Paul. 1977. *Reflections on Fieldwork in Morocco.* Berkeley: University of California Press.

Read, Kenneth E. 1965. *The High Valley.* New York: Scribner.

Richards, Audrey I. 1939. The Development of Field Work Methods in Social Anthropology. In *The Study of Society,* ed. F. C. Bartlett et al., 272–316. London: Routledge & Kegan Paul.

Robertson, A. F. 1978. *Community of Strangers: A Journal of Discovery in Uganda.* London: Scolar Press.

Romanucci-Ross, Lola. 1985. *Mead's Other Manus: Phenomenology of the Encounter.* South Hadley, Mass.: Bergin and Garvey.

Schapera, I. 1935. Field Methods in the Study of Modern Culture Contacts. *Africa* 8:315–28.

Shah, A. M. 1979. Studying the Present and the Past: A Village in Gujarat. In Srinivas et al. 1979, 29–37.

Spindler, George D., ed. 1970. *Being an Anthropologist: Fieldwork in Eleven Cultures*. New York: Holt, Rinehart & Winston.

Spindler, George, and Louise Spindler. 1970. Fieldwork among the Menomini. In Spindler 1970, 267–301.

Srinivas, M. N. 1987. *The Dominant Caste and Other Essays*. Bombay: Oxford University Press.

Srinivas, M. N., A. M. Shah, and E. A. Ramaswamy, eds. 1979. *The Fieldworker and the Field: Problems and Challenges in Sociological Investigation*. Delhi: Oxford University Press.

Stocking, George W., Jr. 1974. *The Shaping of American Anthropology, 1883–1911: A Franz Boas Reader*. New York: Basic Books.

Sturtevant, William C. 1959. A Technique for Ethnographic Note-Taking. *American Anthropologist* 61:677–78.

Turnbull, Colin. 1961. *The Forest People*. New York: Anchor Books.

Turner, Edith. 1987. *The Spirit and the Drum: A Memoir of Africa*. Tucson: University of Arizona Press.

Van Maanen, John. 1988. *Tales of the Field: On Writing Ethnography*. Chicago: University of Chicago Press.

Wagley, Charles. 1977. *Welcome of Tears: The Tapirape Indians of Central Brazil*. New York: Oxford University Press.

Warner, W. Lloyd, and Paul Lunt. 1941. *The Social Life of a Modern Community*. New Haven, Conn.: Yale University Press.

Watson, James B. 1972. Talking to Strangers. In Kimball and Watson 1972, 172–81.

Weidman, Hazel Hitson. 1970. On Ambivalence and the Field. In Golde 1970b, 237–63.

Werner, Dennis. 1984. *Amazon Journey: An Anthropologist's Year among Brazil's Mekranoti Indians*. New York: Simon & Schuster.

White, Leslie A. 1963. *The Ethnography and Ethnology of Franz Boas*. Austin: Texas Memorial Museum.

Whiting, Beatrice, and John Whiting. 1970. Methods for Observing and Recording Behavior. In *A Handbook of Method in Cultural Anthropology,* ed. Raoul Naroll and Ronald Cohen, 282–315. New York: Columbia University Press.

Whitten, Norman E., Jr. 1970. Network Analysis and Processes of Adaptation Among Ecuadorian and Nova Scotian Negroes. In Freilich 1970a, 339–402.

Winter, Edward. 1959. *Beyond the Mountains of the Moon: The Lives of Four Africans*. Urbana: University of Illinois Press.

Wissler, Clark. 1938. *Indian Cavalcade*. New York: Sheridan House.

Wolcott, Harry F. 1981. Home and Away: Personal Contrasts in Ethnographic Style. In *Anthropologists at Home in North America: Methods and Issues in the Study of One's Own Society,* ed. Donald A. Messerschmidt, 255–65. New York: Cambridge University Press.

Wolf, Margery. 1968. *The House of Lim*. Englewood Cliffs, N.J.: Prentice-Hall.

——. 1972. *Women and the Family in Rural Taiwan*. Stanford, Calif.: Stanford University Press.

Wolff, Kurt. 1960. The Collection and Organization of Field Materials: A Research Report. In Adams and Preiss 1960, 240–54.

Yang, Martin M. C. 1972. How *A Chinese Village* Was Written. In Kimball and Watson 1972, 63–73.

Yengoyan, Aram A. 1970. Open Networks and Native Formalism: The Mandaya and Pitjandjara Cases. In Freilich 1970a, 403–39.

Examples of Fieldnotes

Canoe magic

That [?] the magic associated with building canoes belong to Zababia — is that connects with making the canoe, [?] Twull & launching [?] same. Bala also knows the coconut magic for cooking the canoe (Mogawa).

A/. & Tsuine [?] Abala knows the [?]cabua cooking magic, not if I ([?]) [?] & flea. I I did she (I think to really be known this — the threat [?] deathraining? a concerns merely of keeping it in the dark).

29 VI 33

1. A page from Camilla Wedgwood's Manam Island fieldnotes; a July 29, 1933, entry on "Canoe magic." (Size: 7.75 by 4.75 inches.)

INDEX.

Barasi. 1-3.

Birth. 59.

Canoes. 5; 9; 11-25; 29-33; 35-7;
        42-51; 60-239; 291.

Canoe songs. 81-5.

Children. 43; 89; 282.

Death. 289.

Designs. 48.

Eating habits. 87; 96. (v also canoes)

Fishing. 3; 13;

Food. 281-5; 288.

Food Giving. 25-9; 37-9 (v. also Canoes)

Homesteads. 291.

Kinship. 33; 53; 76.

Language. 240-1. (v. also Canoes)

Marriage. 7-8; 53-5; 241-277.

Medicine. 3.

Measurements. 80.

Menstruation. 291.

2. An index page from one of Wedgwood's field notebooks.

There are two roof making groups in the village: one in
Imamura consisting of Kitagawa old man, Sakaguchi and two Kurohiji
(Chokichi's brother and Kumaichi).

Another group consists of Kaneda, Ishikawa and a Kamo man.
They are usually invited to work by regions - i.e. Imamura in that
buraku and neighboring, Oade for this region. But I heard people
say that the Oade kumi is better.

I watched a Kawaze group of children play"ishi iri". At first
a set of small squares are made like this

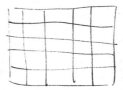

Some children vary this and make ~~vertiele~~ horizontal lines curved, or the whole
set in a circle.

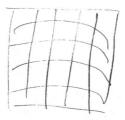 

A small stone is put in some square at either end and one
must cover the entire surface knocking the stone with a finger trick
from one square to another. As one covers the course one rubs out
lines between squares already covered, which makes it that much
harder for the next person who had to shoot longer distances.between
squares. When all lines have been rubbed out, the whole square is

3. A page from Ella Embree's Suye Mura fieldnotes. (Size: 8.5 by 11 inches.)

Sept.30.

Today is ħ5th of Aug. o.c. - jugoya ᴋᴀʏᴀx(ᴛʜᴇxfᴀɪɪxɢʀᴀx.
Flower arrangement of kaya (the fall grass) and cooked taro and
potatoes - now out (sweet?) are offered to jugoya san, although
I only know of Mrs.Koꞥda who made them and she has no worms to
look after.

Many of the worms are spinning, but some are still down and
these days people are busy with them.

After supper children began to gather, they went from house
to house collecting straw from each (and 2-3 sen from none farmers)
which they brought to the empty lot next ot us. Bunji and the two
Aiko ᵞoung men came to do the job - other young men came up later
but did not do much. The rope was woven by Bunji and Kurahei's
servant while the son held the pole which they used as support,
the kids were to turn the rope as it emerged at the other end
thus helping it to twist. When the tremendous rope was ready - done
under pretty heavy rain instead of moonlight - the men came into our
hall and one made a huge warabi while the other one made an equally
(dowa)
huge ashi naka.

Senko were offered to the jidzo san and the zori hung there. Then
the rope was coiled in ᴛʜᴇ one huge lump and ʂenko were stuck into it
here and there and children told to give an offering prayer - they
all leaned over the coil and inchanted unintelligible words in
imitation of praᵞing. Then they grabbed one end and the tug of war
began. There is no winning and loosiη g since the rope won't break
but they just pull, now one side getting stronger, now the other
pulling each other along the slippery road. Eventually ᴛʜᴇʏ the
rope became weak and when tired of the game they stop. Children
were chief participants - all girls and boᵞs turned out in their
undo outfits.

4. Another page from Embree's notes, for September 30, 1936.

RELIGION

General: (See Churches; Schools, Education and Missions; Moslems;
              History, Amade-Otosi, Long Juju-Aro; Swear Erosi; Yam Priest
              and Shrine; Wrestling; Warfare, Inheritance; Funerals; Com-
              pound and Umudi, Village and Wards, Village-group, Ogo; Ikwu,
              etc.). Here list under General only items that do not seem
              to fit well elsewhere.

Term Erosi, 3437
Miscellaneous, 5-6, D-42-43.
Three erosi in Government Station, 119.
Sacrifical materials, 247.
Three women's erosi, 299-300, 2241-42, 2455, 2284, L-96-99, 2307, 2376,
                    2377, 2438-39. See ikwu, umudi, funerals, inheri-
                    tance, Phoebe's notes.
Egbo erosi, ogbo's tree, 538.
Cross River erosi, 544-45.
Seven animals, 2436-37, 2521-22 and various.
Ogbe, 1504-11.
Aho- New Year, 973-75, 1089-90 and Phoebe's notes. Mine 2nd trip also?
Sacrifices to sheines on aho day, 975-79.
Catholic attitude toward work, L-74
Blessing, 1729
Lack of belief in erosi and in dibias, 2441; see elso Enwo's attitudes,
        Tom Ibe's, mainy regard to Ogo. Also Jane Nwachi. Also OE 94-95.
Fish in streams are erosi, 0-81, 0-83-84.
Ibia, Nyali, Nbase no Elu, Chineke - OK-57-65, OK-66-76.

Diviners and Divination
                   532,
    55, 164-68, 1054-56, 1084, 167-168, 168, 411-415, 530-34, 805, 1498-99,
    1505-09, 1512-14, 1572-74, 1521, 1571, 1837-40, 1853-54, 1966-67, 1972,
    2161-63, 2119, 2174-79, 2186, 2224-48, 1505-09, 2262, 2283-87, 2288-89,
    2296-2306, 2323-34, 2345, 2366-70, 2371-75, 2376-80, 2403-06, 2429-30,
    2436-39, 2440, 2459-66, 2468-72, 2473, 2483-84, 2475-78, 2491-92, 2494,
    2499-2506, 2509-10, 2513-15, 2523, 2534, 2524-28, 2530-31, 2532, 2533,
    2535-40, 2541-44, 2562-67, 2572-74, 2594-2603, 2607-17, 2647-55, 2656- 62,
    2830, 2737, LA-281, 0-44, OE-66-67. 1722, 0K-9-10.

obanji
    2288-89, 2307-14, 2327, 2328, 2349, 2461, 2543, 2609-17, 2647-51, 2651-55.
    See Phoebe's notes.

Ndemeja
    3328, 2376-80, 2437. See Phoebe's notes.

Illness (see above) see various other categories, especially for first trip.)
    1666, 1707, 1762-65, 1766, 1972, 2241-43, 2244-45, 2296, 2298-2300,
    2303, 2304-06, 2333, 2366-70, 2371, 2403, 2404, 2429-30, 2483-84, 2523,
    2535-39, 0-17-18, 0-81, 0-83-84, OE-66-67.

                                              Naobu.
Reincarnation (See Ikwu, especially genealogies, obanji, Diviners, etc.)
    530-34, 1389-90, L-141-42, 1498, 1500, 1571, 1572, 1769, 2283-87, 2346,
    2376-80, 2402, 2410-16, 2439, 2454, 2468-72, 2616-17, 0-38, 0-50. *510-11, 1056-7,*
                                                                    1061-63,

5. A page from Simon Ottenberg's index to his 1952–53 and 1959–60 Afikpo fieldnotes. (Size: 8.5 by 11 inches.)

VILLAGE-GROUP AGE GRADES

See also VILLAGE-GROUP

general 133-40, 1084-90, 354-60, 746, 1005-07, 1011-13, D-62-65, L-127-30,
    L-238-43, 1018-25, 921-24, 1684-90, 2279, 1449,
change in powers under British 155, more powerful in old days 719
cases where village-group grades not called 310, 317, 322, 334, 385, &tc.
village-group grades ont concerned with warfare L-132
Oni Ekara and yam planting season-shrines and activities, etc. 745-46, 2280
hori 746, 1477.
order of greeting at age grade meetings 868
village-grades, especially how they move up 354-60, 921-25, 1014-17
Esa try various cases at market 1011-13-general rules as well
ikpukeisi 1012, L-124-27, L-128-131, D-44, D-62-63, D-109, D-252, 746, 155, 921,
    149, 2279,
village-group pleaders 1421-28
oni Ekara and Amade L-118, L-120, L-121, L-124-35   D-40,
    shale 217 356, 357, 361, etc 1477, etc.
        O-20-27, 0-27-
D.O. interferes Afikpo market, 11, 25, 156,   1918, 36
Back women against ATWA and D.O. in Igwe affair 77-78, 148-49,   2025,
in Ikwozo (prepare-daed) ceremony 123-29
case in Esa court 147
Esa set day for bush burning 157, 347,
Esa set day for farming and harvest 346
Esa give ceremony to rainmaker for rain 164-67
Esa backs up decisions of Afikpo dibia society 168
ostracism of Enwo at brideprice ceremony, Mgbom 172-73, in general 303-04,
attempt to regulate bride price circumvented 307-8, 314,
part of Esa in "plant yam together" land dispute and in land cases
    in general, 342-343,
one large Mgbom grade in Clan Esa instead of two small ones 361,
ask young men as messengers, but never ask village grades 365
lay down changes in ogo initiation rulings 366-67
what grades one joins in village-group when a member of two in
    village 395
pass marriage resettlement rulings 400-01   (IN HIGH COURT)
sanction money collection to try Ibi murder case∧ 402-03
to try ikwu land case 566-67 in Esa court
elders and Afikpo people do not go Amaseri market-ruling 806
clan law violaters do not take uhichi 850
send Esa man in Ikwu dispute 860
meeting-Oji's preresentations, bride price regulations, fining those
    who side with Okpoha in dispute, 866-67
at New Yam festival and Yam priest 1010-11, (see YAM PRIEST AND SHRINE), 915-18,
omume title members do not have to pay certain fines of village-group
        grades 1035, take part in ceremonies 1094, 2348
in Afikpo-Amaseri market dispute 1104-05 and see CASES
market payment dispute 1117
in Ngodo-Amachara-Ukpa school site dispute 1113,
Esa rules a limit of foo foo for marriage feast 1126
in omume title 1129
elders and D.O. rule first ogo ceremony should occur on Saturdays 1234
attempt to settle Anofia Nkalo-Ndibe dispute D-84-85
resolve to import Ogu men to catch criminals D-232,
try to maintain Ibe Osim women priest at shrine L-25-26
In New Yam festival dispute L-19-23.
Igwe and elders 148-179
Meeting 395-404

6. Another page from Ottenberg's fieldnote index.

March 11

There is other evidence other than G's saying so, that
parts of the Bara language are lost, at least in this maloca.
He often says the 'viejos' talk thus – the right way. We the
younger people, don't, or have forgotten, etc. Is it because
this maloca is isolated and they have the most contact with
Tuyukas?
Two instances: Juanico gave me two forms for eyelash and
eyebrow; G didn't accept the one for eyebrow, said there was only
one term, I didn't tell him Juanico had told me the other. Also
Juanico gave me a term for Forehead that G didn't accept a couple
of times; accepted it yesterday (differentiating it from 'face')

April 2

More formal work with tribe-language. G said there is
no word for 'tribe' (which I knew), but mohoka can be asked,
'what people are they'. Questions are: (note difference in
interrogative pronouns:

ñiwõ nomohoko pakho kututi Estribina

ñe wadego pakho kututi ko / ñeno wadegu eahani

G said entity of mohkko was always distinguishable by a separate language, that word for them was always the same, meaning
'Bara people'/ 'people who speak Bara' and that the questions
were synonymous in that they always elicited the same answers,
referringto specific persons or groups.

note: kuturike used - "to have"

July 6

Marcelino had a quarrel with the dressed Maku Sunday
morning of the fiesta – outside in front. He was doing most
of the talking, but the other man wasn't acting subservient
or anything. Other men looked on, expressionless. Aside
from that, there was little interaction between guests and
Makus. The girl, Isiria, danced. Others looked at them.
Girls giggled that old woman's breasts were funny-looking –
one much bigger than the other. They aren't greeted or
acknowledged in any way. In this case, they are (seem to be)

Miguel's particular pets.

---

7. Three fieldnote cards from Jean Jackson's 1969–70 work among the Bara Indians of
the northwest Amazon River basin. The notes were filed by subject in baskets made for
them by the Bara. (Size: 4 by 6 inches.)

HOUSE LINE PREPARATIONS: Alwesa
13 October 78

He has been referred to recently as one ᴍᴍ of those who
wants to kill pigs this Xmas. People say he never kills
his pigs and so has alot of them saved up to kill soon.

He says now that he wanted to join Sale in killing pigs
soon but he doesnt think he can because he hasnt found the
shells he needs to pay off his wife's line -- ᴊᴍ ya tia.

ɪxxxᴘᴜɴᴅɪᴀᴇᴘ

What does he need in order to kill pigs: his list of
debts to his wife's kin:

1. Pundiaep -- he owes him one shell and K8
                  he will return this with "5": three shells and
                  K20

2. W of Pundiaep -- two pigs
                  he will return this with five shells for
                  each plus two shells as nOpae

3. F of Waekiem in Komia: he owes him K10
                  he will return to him two shells, one of
                  which is nopae
4. Z of his W Kalta living in Tambul: he owes her two pigs
                  and one shell
                  he will return K80 for one pig
                           5 shells for another pig
                           one shell for the shell
                  he has already given the nopae of one shell
5. Marup Okipuk he owes K40
          he will return two shells for this. He has already
          given the nopae of one shell

6. Pepena he owes K10
          he will return this with two shells

7. Tamalu, a ᴷagol Yakop man in Komia, W's line he owes one shell
          he will return two shells

Pigs: He killed three pigs at the recentɪx parade.
       He says he has four he can kill at the houseline
       He says no women are looking after pigs for him elsewhere
           and so he has no other mok ya ri payment to make
       (Kus, overhearing this, says "Ah, he must have about 20
           to kill, he's lying!)

8. A page from one of Rena Lederman's formal interviews in the Mendi Valley, Papua
New Guinea, October 13, 1978. (Size: 8.5 by 11 inches.)

45

Sunday, 26 June

Timbew came by a bit angry about <u>Maklen's</u> marriage arrangements (Maklen is her next-to-last D; the last is in Grade 4 w/ Andrew Ipopi in Banz). <u>Pospeya's son</u> had showed the family sufficient wealth, in a formal presentation, already — <u>Munganawe</u> (F) had been satisfied. But <u>Paki</u> had befriended a man from <u>Olmanda</u> when both were in town — the Olmanda had given Paki food & school fees, and had asked Paki to find him a wife later on. Paki had suggested Maklen — and now the Olm. is inviting the family to check out the wealth <u>he</u> wants to give them. Timbew was angry because <u>Nare</u> (M's 'Z'H, Paki's F) said he couldn't go along w/ her to look it over since Rina is sick. T. says "So what are we women to do? Munganawe won't go: he's pleased w/ Pospeya's son's wealth. <u>Waige</u> commented that he'd been asked to go too, but he refused since he's not one to talk out "What am I going to do? Stand up and say 'this isn't good enough!'?" (!)

Who <u>does</u> talk out, then? <u>Tui</u> (who's been sitting around the fire with Waige + me this morn) says two here are known for it: <u>Kiluwa</u> and <u>Walipa</u>. I suggest <u>Onge</u>, and they agree. They also added: <u>Munganawe</u>, <u>Takuna</u>, <u>Kandi</u>, and joked that it isn't a matter of being 'headmen' but just of having a "loud voice"! (A partial truth...)

Waige reported that when his ZD in Pimanda

9. Two pages from Rena Lederman's 1983 "daily log" fieldnotes in the Mendi Valley, Papua New Guinea. (Size: 7 by 9.75 inches.)

got married yesterday, she was given K1700 of nopae (ie - not counting the money given to repay the wedding pigs!). The new husband is an ADC and has been stationed all over the SHP.

More about Nande's garden: turns out that its not such a special case. M of Nande's MM is from Egari (You). Mopna gave Nande the garden. Mopna was divorced from her Bela H and returned to her F's place to live. So Nande is actually gardening in the place of her MF (not her MMM) — this is the garden of her MM too, of course, in terms of use, but its a Yansup garden (MF's group): effectivel, her M's group. Nothing unusual about that at all. She isn't gardening on lands of her MM's group (Marup) — though, in this case, she could have since its Kuma!

(Egari: You) ⊙ = △ (Kuma: Marup)

(Marup) Wokiam ○ = ▲ (Sol: Yansup)

(Kombal: Molsen) △ = ● Kurum (Yansup)   mopna ● = △ (Bela: Kondup)   ● Timben (Yansup)
(Yansup)

⦵ Nande ← GARDEN
(Molsem)

See typed pp., Poya interview for this date on Keyosem's charged affiliation.

Nande wanted Alin to hear her konaen which

G$_e$n Ankrah's mother was visiting M/M Q today. He ~~introduced~~called her as "Madam Quaynor" at the family accounting. She is the senior woman in the Q family.

2 men ~~visited~~ Mr. Q in the afternoon. One lives at Kwabenya and works at the A$_t$mic Emergy installation. The other, with a Fanti sounding name, Archie Davidson, was a primary teacher with Mr. Q in the founding of ~~Gnat in the early1950's.~~ He said then "The old men were fighting for better pay and conditions for us." He is now a sociologist with the VRA and studied at Rutgers. They were drinking schnapps.

~~A$_t$tikpo borught shorts to be fixed by an inténeratnt tailor~~ who set up his machine in front of the Q house.

T gave me data on the family and funeral affairs.

11/2 mon   ~~Mrs. Solo Q visited M/M Q in the morning.~~

Legon, notes, OT 5:30.

we met Ben and Alex at 7 pm and walked to the Adovors.

~~Alex asked Ben to buy smuggled matches "butterflies" for him at~~ the kiosk opp. Yankah becasue he says the Ghana matches are no good. He said they wouldnot sell to him becasue they thought he was a cop. ~~Ben did not get any either. Alex said becasue Ben is known they would~~ sell to him.

We walked to the Adovor's house and met Attikpo who was visiting ~~someone else there . He also used to live there. We went up and~~ Alex excused himself. Mrs. Adovor came up from the kitchen.

She said Mr. Adovor's cousin had his VW stolen today and Mr. Adovor went to help him. ~~Mr. A's brother came by and asked about the affair.~~

We discussed Ewe food which they see as identifying them as different, say from the Ashantis who eat only "fufu and ampesi," and Gas wholike kenkey and banku. ~~The Ewes they say have "so many foods."~~ They later talked about having sent Ewe food overseas tokin and friends studying.

~~Mr. A came with a friend who is from Nzodze and works for the~~ ~~VRA at Akosombo; he is visiting in A$_c$cra.~~ He works in the fisheries and studied fish farm ng in Seattle for 2 years. He told us how he used farina and peanut butter to substitute for gari and groundnut paste. ~~He said the food he missee most from US was pie, esp. lemon pie.~~ He said Accra is too fast and expensive for him.

He said you canot tell tribe of women by dress in Ghana becasue ~~the Ga and Akan and Ewe women all dress alike (also true in LOme.)~~ "Even by the face you cant tell," if there are no marks, he said.

M$_r$. A said the Adas are related to the Gas, but there has ~~been some marriage with Ewes on the border, and they go to each others~~ markets. Some of the boarder speak Ewe. He said their names are either Ewe or Ga. The Ewes he said have vert distinctibw names.

~~"Our names are very different."~~

We talked about dress differences in men's traditional clothes. The Akans dont wear jumpers, but the Gas, Ewes and Fantis do, with cloth, Mr. A said. ~~The Gas wear the long shorts. They said the stocking cap is~~ only worn by Anloga people.

The Ewes along the Volta river, eg. Sogakofe, have a very ~~difficult dialect for other Ewes to speak. Mrs. A said Adama, head of~~ ~~the opppstion speaks this dialect, from Sogakofe.~~

10. A page from Roger Sanjek's 1970 Adabraka, Ghana, fieldnotes. (Size: 8.5 by 11 inches.)

7 May 1988 - <u>Carmela George's Cleanup Day</u>

Milagros and I arrived at 10 am, as Carmela told me, but 97th
Street, the deadend, was already cleaned out, and the large
garbage pickup truck, with rotating blades that crushed
everything, was in the middle of 97th Place. I found Carmela, and
met Phil Pirozzi of Sanitation, who had three men working on the
cleanup, plus the sweeper that arrived a little later. The men
and boys on 97th place helping to load their garbage into the
truck included several Guyanese Indians in their 20s, whom CArmela
said have been here 2-3 years ['They're good.']; several families
of Hispanics, and Korean and Chinese. They were loading tv sets,
shopping carts, wood, old furniture, tree branches and pruning,
and bags and boxes of garbage. Most houses had large piles of
stuff in front, waiting for the truck. The little boys hanging on
and helping were Hispanic, except for one Chinese. They spoke a
mixture of Spanish and English together, when painting the LIRR
walls.

Carmela had put flyers at every house on Wednesday, and Police 'No
Parkin Saturday' signs [D   ] were up on the telephone poles. A
few cars were parked at the curb, but most of the curbside on the
three blocks was empty so the sweeper could clean the gutters.

The sweeper this year was smaller than the one in 1986, and there
was no spraying of the streets, only sweeping the gutters. As
before, people swept their curbs, and in some cases driveways,
into the gutter. Carmela was a whirlwind. She asked her elderly
Italian neighborh Jenny, who did not come out, if she could sweep
the sand pile near Jenny's house in their common driveway. Jenny
said don't bother, but Carmela did it anyway. She was running all
around with plastic garbage bags, getting kids to help paint off
the grafitti on the LIRR panels she had painted in the past, and
commandeering women to clean out the grassy area near the LIRR
bridge at 45th Ave and National Street. She got a Colombian woman
from 97th Place, and gave her a rake and plastic bag. She then
rang the door bell across from the grassy area, behind the bodega,
and an Indian-looking HIspanic women came down, and later did the
work with the Colombian woman..

Mareya Banks was out, in smock, helping organize and supervising
the kids doing the LIRR wall painting. Milagros helped with this,
and set up an interview appointment with Mareya. She also met a
Bolivian woman, talking with Mareya, and sweeping her sidewalk on
45th Avenue.

Carmela also had potato chips and Pepsi for the kids, which the
Colombian women gave out to them, and OTB t-shirts.

Phil said this was the only such clean up in CB4. A man in
Elmhurst does something like this, but just for his one block.
They Dept. likes this, and hopes the spirit will be contagious.
We like anything that gets the community involved. He said it
began here because the new people didn't understand how to keep
the area a nice place to live. Carmela went to them, and now they
are involved.

11. A page from Roger Sanjek's 1988 Elmhurst-Corona, Queens, New York, fieldnotes, printed from a computer word-processing program. (Size: 8.5 by 11 inches.)

PART III

Fieldnote Practice

Most good investigators are hardly aware of the precise manner in which they gather their data.

—PAUL RADIN

SIMON OTTENBERG

Thirty Years of Fieldnotes: Changing Relationships to the Text

When I was out in the field as a graduate student at Northwestern University, we were instructed by our major professor, Melville Herskovits, to send home a copy of our typed notes as our research progressed so that he could read and comment on them. I did this every few months during my first field trip to the Afikpo, an Igbo group in southeast Nigeria, in 1952–53.[1] The comments I received, I later learned, came mostly from his wife, Frances, who was not a trained anthropologist but had collaborated with her husband on much of his research and many publications. Some of the replies were useful, but many did not make sense to me. Those that did not were based upon the Herskovitses' interviews in Evanston years before with a man who came from a different Igbo area. I resented my professor's intrusions and was anxious over negative criticism. I wanted to be in the field just with my wife and not have the Herskovitses with me.[2]

I thank John Barker, Jean-Paul Dumont, Charles Keyes, Lorna Rhodes, Melford Spiro, and Pierre van den Berghe for their comments on this paper.

[1] I had already carried out a summer's field research in a Gullah community in Georgia in 1950, while a student at Northwestern, but there I had not been required to follow this procedure.

[2] On the other hand, John Messenger, a fellow student at Northwestern, enjoyed sending back a copy of his notes, felt that the responses he got were helpful, and uses the same procedure today with his students.

There are analogies between the fieldwork situation and my childhood. Herskovits was a strong man, well known in anthropology, who single-handedly ran the department. He was on every graduate student's committee; two of the three other professors in the department had been trained at Northwestern with him; and he and his wife in many ways created the image of parents toward us as student-children. (The infantilization of graduate students by their professors, whether consciously done or not, is not uncommon; in fact, some students unconsciously seek the child role with a parental professor.) The consequence is that my fieldnotes from my first research in Africa are psychologically linked to my own childhood with my father and mother. These notes were a test, an examination of my competence as a graduate student; the school of my childhood was linked to the school of professional training. I was not in this position on my second trip to the same area six years later[3] or in my research in northern Sierra Leone in 1978–80, yet Herskovits was still looking over my psychic shoulder, following that crucial experience of my "childhood" as an anthropologist. I still take notes, type them up, and send off a copy (though they go to storage now), and my notes still take much the same form: ethnographic and outwardly objective in appearance. It was a thorough job of imprinting.

I don't think my experience is atypical, whether other student anthropologists had their professors read their first research notes or not. Graduate school is a dependency situation with many aspects that may be associated with childhood. The fieldnotes inevitably connect with one's own personal experiences in childhood and maturation. They are employed in writing the dissertation, the end of formal schooling. When one starts to publish from these notes, as I soon did, the pattern is extended: journal and press reviewers become the anonymous fathers and mothers of the writer. Fieldnotes—particularly the first set but, by extension, others—are a physical manifestation of childhood experience. Whenever I draw upon them, they bring back—consciously or unconsciously—the father-son tensions, the wish for the comforting, supportive mother.[4] The notes are part of both my real childhood and my childhood as an anthropologist.

[3]Since this paper was written I returned to Afikpo for a week in 1988 (see Ottenberg 1987, 1989b).

[4]Jean-Paul Dumont (personal communication) has suggested that the notes are associated with mother and breast, with a source from which we draw anthropological nourishment in writings. On the other hand, James Clifford (personal communication) thinks that symbolically they are feces, that we are anal retentive about them, and that some of the jokes and phrases we use in speaking of our notes are anal in quality.

I wonder whether this is not true for at least some other anthropologists as well. I am not saying that we don't overcome the experience or integrate it as we reach middle age as anthropologists. Nonetheless, our notes may all have a psychological residue that influences the way we write, if not what we write. For example, it took me years to look on my notes as more than facts and to use them to create rich interpretations.

Another aspect of the field experience connects with childhood. Like all graduate students I took courses, wrote papers, and did various things at the command of my professors, albeit with some negotiation. Although a young man, I was a dependent psychologically, which I resented emotionally. But in the field I was on my own. I made decisions, within the limits of my funds, alone or in consultation with my anthropology student wife, Phoebe, also working on her dissertation project. There was a feeling of exhilaration in this, dampened somewhat by the need to "report" to Professor Herskovits. Then, during the writing of my dissertation from these notes upon my return to the United States, I lost much of the sense of freedom of the fieldwork situation. It was as if I had developed my own ego as an anthropologist and was then losing it. The notes were mine, but Herskovits was still there; there was still that childhood position and feeling. In defense, I believe that I overtreasured my notes. They early took on a much too sacred character; they became an extension of me—like an extra penis—that I planned to use for many years to come.

The early field situation resembles childhood in many respects. We are in a strange world where we are in the process of learning the language and the rules, learning how to live. Much of our previous experience seems useless, unhelpful, or downright contradictory. We are dependent upon others to guide us: pseudoparental figures such as interpreters, field guides, the persons we live with, the friends we make in the field. We are as children during the time when we are learning the culture. As we acquire knowledge and experience, we have a sense of growth, of adolescence, of maturation, much as children do.

Our fieldnotes reflect this cultural childhood. They are written attempts to impose order on the external world of our research as well as on our personal lives in the field, to grow up through understanding the culture we are studying, to perceive the realities of the interests and motivations of those who interact with us in the field. Our own increasing maturation and understanding is reflected in the changing nature of the notes as the field research progresses. Mine are documents of my own anthropological maturation at Afikpo; thus their nature changes according to the date when they were written. In using them to write for publication, of course, this fact must be taken into account.

Similar experiences recur in second and subsequent field trips to differing peoples, although now one has a sense from past experience of the pacing of maturation in the new culture that one lacked on the first trip. And one is freed from one's teachers. In later fieldwork elsewhere I had a clearer awareness of my own transferences, of my reactions to certain persons I was studying and to their feelings toward me. Yet there was still a sense of childhood association and of reliving adolescence in learning another culture. It may be that our anthropological tendency to identify with the group we study, a secondary ethnic identification (and I had it for many years with the Igbo), is a consequence of this maturation process in another culture, a process that duplicates to some extent our childhood experience. This strong identification with our "tribe" often influences our anthropological reasoning in writing for publication. Our anthropologist's ego, through our research and fieldnotes, becomes overbound with the group we study. We cannot see the anthropological forest for our tribe.

Death, Immortality and Success

At the other end of the spectrum is the question of death, immortality, and the fate of my notes. For many years—in fact, almost from the first—I have thought of my fieldnotes as invaluable documents. It was unlikely at the time that anyone else would go to Afikpo, and later it became clear that so much has changed there that even if others were to do research there now, they would have trouble duplicating the information I have. So I think about where I will leave my notes, and I have chosen two places that will take them and where they will be available for scholars.

I have had a related idea that it is important to publish the information on the Afikpo as a record of a people. I am aware that they are an obscure Igbo group, not at the center of things in Igboland and certainly not in Nigeria as a whole. Nevertheless, I have seen my writing as valuable, a record for Nigerians and the Afikpo as well as for professional anthropologists and students everywhere. I came to delight in making publications available for the Afikpo to read.

But now I think that my wish to preserve my notes and to make a public record from them through publication masks a deeper motivation. I sense in myself the desire for personal immortality, a denial of my own eventual death. Lacking children of my own, I want my notes and publications to live on as surrogate descendants. I sometimes fantasize about persons using my notes after my death and even think of providing an explanatory guide to them. It may be not so much the Afikpo that I want to live forever through my notes as Ottenberg. Afikpo has become a projection of myself, my fieldnotes inextricably a part of the process. The insistence of my professor that I send home a set of notes—a procedure that I have carried out ever since, like an unthinking habit inculcated in childhood—helped to ensure my immortality by avoiding loss of the notes and allowing them to be written up and published. My notes connect with death and immortality as well as with childhood.

To continue in this personal vein, when I was working at Afikpo, persons there frequently demanded money or assistance in exchange for helping me. I took it to be their style, which in part it was. But they pointed out that I was going to go back home and write a book about them, and they believed that I would become famous. A book was a big item in their largely nonliterate world. On the first research trip I protested that I was only a student; on the second, that I was merely a young teacher. But they were right. Relative to their status and income, I did well. I am somewhat known in my field; I have a comfortable job and a fair salary. Like the people I studied, I live in a highly competitive society that stresses upward mobility and personal success. My fieldnotes symbolize to me a crucial aspect of my success, an absolutely necessary part of my personal progress as an individual through life: they are the fundamental source of the publications that have given me tenure and a modicum of recognition as a teacher and university professor.

My fieldnotes, then, have very strong psychological referents for me: childhood, death and immortality, and personal success. They are a key element in my personal life. They stand for field experience as well—that seemingly mystical experience, as outsiders see it. As a personal record of adventure, they are very much a part of me. I believe that one reason it was so rare for anthropologists to comment publicly on their field research until the 1970s, and on their notes until even more recently, is the very internalized and personal quality of research. I believe that this is changing now, not only because of growing criticism within and beyond anthropology as to how research is conducted but because the more problem-oriented nature of fieldwork today and the move toward field experiences in the West make for different sorts of personal identification with the people that we study, and thus with our fieldnotes. The "my tribe" or "my people" syndrome is disappearing.

The very personal nature of fieldnotes and their association with our egos suggest that we will have toward them strong feelings—endearment, rejection, hostility, preciousness, or whatever—and that the writing-up process may require some wrestling with personal emotions of these sorts. One reason we write up so very little from our total fieldnotes is the considerable ego strength needed to do so; the notes are, after all, very autobiographical, however that aspect is disguised.

Headnotes

There is another set of notes, however, that anthropologists might consider to be incorporeal property. These are the notes in my mind, the memories of my field research. I call them my headnotes. As I collected my written notes, there were many more impressions, scenes, experiences than I wrote down or could possibly have recorded. Indeed, I did not keep a diary and only occasionally incorporated diary-type material into my fieldnotes, a fact that I very much regret today. But we were brought up in a positivistic age where personal impressions were seen as less important than the "facts out there," which had a sense of reality that some anthropologists find misleading today. Since I do not have a diary to jog my memory of personal experience, my fieldnotes seem distressingly "objective." This is, of course, an illusion.

But the notes are also in my head. I remember many things, and some I include when I write even though I cannot find them in my fieldnotes, for I am certain that they are correct and not fantasy. I remember a great deal of haggling over payments for information, but my notes reveal little of this or of the anger that it brought me. Nor do my notes reflect the depression occasioned by my linguistic failures. My written notes repressed important aspects of field research. But my headnotes are also subject to distortion, forgetting, elaboration, and I have developed stereotypes of the people I study as a consequence of using this mental material over the years: Ottenberg's

Afikpo are essentially a highly democratic people; they are more richly metaphoric than we Americans are; they are extremely talkative and demanding of others (including me); they are entrepreneurial. Some of these features may be true or not, but they provide a satisfactory image for me, as if I have completed the jigsaw puzzle that is Afikpo culture and society and can see clearly what they are like. I also have certain stories that I have undoubtedly elaborated on, extended, made richer through the telling of them to students, colleagues, and friends over the years: the time that I went to a diviner to discover why I had not had mail from my mother in some months; the proverb that my carver friend repeated to me when he discovered that I had shown his masks to my wife even though he had instructed me not to do so. In short, the processes of reflecting, ordering, suppressing, and connecting go on not only in the process of writing from notes but in teaching, in reading anthropology, and throughout my everyday life experience, when I sometimes compare my lifeway with that of the Afikpo. And the published record that draws upon my headnotes and my written notes is, in a sense, a sort of storytelling, much as Bennett and Feldman (1981) argue that storytelling goes on in American courts. It is a construction of reality out of my two sets of notes.

Except for some pre-research impressions through reading, my views of Afikpo culture developed in the field. I began early to create conceptions that bordered on stereotypes. I was fortunate to have my anthropological wife with me. We have different views of Afikpo culture, partly deriving from the fact that I worked extensively with males and she with females, and each sex there had some differing views as well as sharing others. Partly it was also because of our personal natures. She saw more deviltry there than I did, and I thought that she was too suspicious of people's motivations. I was too amiable about conflict and deviousness on the part of some persons there. We continued to correct each other and to argue these points as we published jointly or separately until the mid-1960s, when we divorced. We have had little anthropological cooperation since, and from then on I have had few checks to my headnotes of this kind. I go on my way convinced of their accuracy.

As I matured and began to develop some small influence in the anthropology circle at my university, my headnotes began to change. I came to see the Afikpo as not so democratic: weren't there some autocratic leaders who stood above democracy? As I went through several marriages with not always shining success, I began to reflect differently on Afikpo marriages and on the fate of mates in their society. As anthropological theory has changed, so has the way I look at both my headnotes and my written notes. In short, as my own life unwinds, I naturally see and reflect upon Afikpo life differently. I am constantly reinterpreting Afikpo, ever looking at my fieldnotes in different ways. There is no constancy except their yellowing pages as physical objects.

Yet the words in my written notes stay the same. Except for a few additions written several years ago, when I had a chance to discuss some elements of the culture with an Afikpo student at my university, the notes have not changed. But my interpretations of them have as my headnotes have altered. My headnotes and my written notes are in constant dialogue, and in this sense the field experience does not stop. Things that I once read in my fieldnotes in one way, I now read in another. Evidence that I thought excellent, I now question. I don't believe that I am more objective now than then, only that my interpretations are more accurate; that I really "see" Afikpo now in my middle-aged maturation; that I can reflect now as a sage, whereas my youthful interpretations were less intelligent, more hesitant. Through more than thirty years of using these notes, I have been working with many texts and many interpretations.

Writing Up in the Field and at Home

I have twice written articles in the field, one with my wife during our second stay in Afikpo in 1959–60 (Ottenberg and Ottenberg 1962), and one while I worked alone in Sierra Leone (Ottenberg 1983). In writing in the field I found that I was wrestling with inconsistencies in my notes and tried to untangle these by going out to do more research. But this experience too left puzzles. What I wrote somehow still did not express the irregularities of the culture; the publications became too regular, too ordered. It has been more comfortable to deal with inconsistencies and disorder while writing in America! Here they don't seem as penetrating, as disturbing.

Lani Sanjek has suggested to me, I believe correctly, that one reason it is difficult to write in the field is that we have personal contacts there; we need distancing from them before we can write. This again suggests the latent emotional quality of collecting field data as against its supposed objective nature. I am reminded of the late Dr. R. E. Bradbury, who studied Benin culture but who lived in Nigeria so close to the Edo for many years that while there he could not fully write up his work. Unfortunately, he died before much of his very important research was ever published.

I suspect the fact is that most of the cultures we study are much less consistent, have much greater irregularities than we admit to ourselves in our drive to conceptualize them, to order and to "invent" them (Wagner 1981). But whether in the field or out, the fieldnotes represent disorder and irregularity, in contrast to the publications growing from them and to the headnotes. There is a constant tension, then, between fieldnotes and headnotes, perhaps reflecting a view of the fieldnotes as a physical symbol of childhood growth and the headnotes as the maturing, increasingly independent adult ego of the anthropologist. At the very least, there is a continuing dialogue between the two.

As soon as I left the field the first time, and again the second, I was no longer in contact with Afikpo except for an occasional letter. The dialogue among my written notes, my headnotes, my wife's views and notes, and the views of the people I was studying was replaced by another dialogue in which the African was missing and my professors and fellow students appeared. It became easier, away from the field, to put aside that inconsistent datum in my fieldnotes, to dismiss certain data as obviously in error in my drive for order and consistency. Deriving from my growing stereotypic vision of Afikpo, my publications create the illusion of cultural consistency. In this sense my headnotes have come to dominate my written notes. In the dialogue between the two, the written form is losing out to my head.

I believe that the headnotes are always more important than the written notes. Only after their author is dead do written notes become primary, for then the headnotes are gone. Headnotes are the driving force, albeit subject to correction by the fieldnotes. The written notes have a sacred quality that is also an illusion. The process of employing fieldnotes should make them an adjunct to the more primary headnotes, which lead the written form, even though for living anthropologists, writing up headnotes *without* written notes—as when the latter are lost—presents immense difficulties. Only a few have attempted it. For most of us, both are required. But does not the primacy of headnotes as the driving force over the written form suggest that we are closer to the nonliterate people we study than we are willing to admit?

There is a paradox, then. We need to be away from the people being studied in order to write. This is a pattern that most of us follow, reinforced by the relatively short time most of us can financially afford to remain in the field and by other necessities, such as work. Yet there is need to be with the people we study in order to check our writing. Being away allows for the possibility of increasing distortion in our headnotes and thus in our interpretation of the written notes, though it provides us a fine chance to order our data. Writing in the field creates conflicts of time and energy, as against doing field research, and a bombardment of data which makes it hard for us to see order and arrangement without falsifying. I note that most of us have been trained not to write for publication in the field but to prepare written notes there and to do our formal writing away from the field. Perhaps the ideal solution is to have one or two extensive field periods in one place and then return to it for short periods of time over the years, allowing us to check on ethnographic material. But this has not been a typical model for anthropology.

Scratch Notes

My fieldnotes themselves are based upon "scratch" notes taken in longhand with a pen on small pads of paper and then typed up in my "free time"—often in the late evening when I was quite fatigued. The handwritten notes are brief sentences, phrases, words, sometimes quotes—a shorthand that I enlarged upon in typing them up, adding what I remembered. Obviously, selectivity was involved in this typing process. I forgot or repressed some things and distorted others. I was aware of it at the time and tried to avoid it, but I don't believe I fully succeeded. So my handwritten notes are my original written text, and my typed notes are a reinterpretation of the first interpretation of what was in my head when I produced my handwritten notes. My dissertation was a third, my published work a fourth. For many years I kept my handwritten notes and occasionally referred to them when something was obscure in my typed notes. Because I usually discovered that it was also obscure in the handwritten version, I finally abandoned this practice and threw the scratch notes away. I am sorry now. Eliminating the handwritten ones has reified the typed form. The hand notes would make an interesting comparison with my typed notes.

Organizing Data

Many things that my written notes left out or minimized still exist in fuzzy form in my head. These include the details of endless negotiations over rewards for help given, problems of learning the language, critical comments about my research abilities, and the details of my disagreements with my wife over interpretations of our data. Such omissions protect the ego of the researcher but make for poor, non-reflective notes.

I find that my data on any specific topic are scattered about in my written notes. I come across key passages here and there, some comments I don't easily understand today, some contradictory data, maybe a few helpful photographs that have a reality my notes lack (I employed photographs a great deal in my book on Afikpo masquerades; see Ottenberg 1975). I begin with a focus for my writing and then organize the key categories in my data, with other categories growing out of my ordering of the notes. My fieldnotes tend to be nonreflective and noninterpretive, with simple analyses at best—an observation or two that I did not get from other persons. With little overt interpretation or analysis in my notes to draw upon, except for some informant views and understandings, what I do is to create my interpretations out of (1) existing ones that I have carried in my head from fieldwork days or earlier, (2) my mind's reactions and reflections on the data, and (3) social science ideas prevalent at the time I am writing.

Out of these elements I construct an organization of the data—that is, an ethnography, which is already interpretive—and then an interpretation of this, which I see as my final analysis. The first step, the organization, helps me spot contradictions in data and try to resolve them, or eliminate them by discarding some information. Otherwise, I tend to treat the data as factually correct or as the evident interpretation of informants. I generally feel that my descriptive account of the data is objective, and this allows the interpretation to come second. To me, all this has a comforting positivist feel to it. Of course, even these data constitute the endpoint of a complex process of selectivity in fieldwork on my part and on the part of my informants. And I am aware that even with discarding and reinterpreting, there are still gaps. How do I recognize a gap? Clearly, because I have some scheme, some order in mind. I may search my notes again for data to fill the gap, and occasionally I succeed in finding some. But generally I do not, and I have to leave questions unanswered or make interpretations that are unsure. This became particularly frustrating after the second field trip, when I realized that I had still not filled in all the gaps, for new ideas concerning necessary data arose in the writing process even then.

I am a compulsive collector. When I was doing research in the field, I collected fieldnotes; now it is mostly ethnographic and art objects. I have always had the need to collect lots and lots of notes, perhaps originally because I wanted to show the Herskovitses that I was a dutiful anthropological son, but also because it is my nature. In both Afikpo field trips I took pride in my massive collection of notes on a wide range of topics. I felt I might employ them all some day but had no idea at the time how to do so. Unlike my headnotes, my written notes have little obvious order; they were typed and filed day by day and paged as typed. They are a thicket of ethnography.

In order to begin to make sense of my notes, in the field I kept an index on small cards. This gave me a rough idea of how many pages of material I had on any topic but no notion as to its quality. My categories of indexing altered during the course of the first field trip, and though I made adjustments to the index as I went along, it had problems. After leaving the field I reworked it entirely. I followed a similar procedure on my second Afikpo trip, finally integrating the two indexes completely.

The index reflects my need to collect fieldnotes extensively, whatever other purpose it serves. It is now the heart of my written notes, though as my ideas as to what and how to write about Afikpo changed, its categories were not always appropriate. But the index is a vital, time-saving part of my notes. It reflects my substantive anthropological categories and subcategories—family, descent, association groups, leadership—rather than highly theoretical ones. The job of developing the index was long and time-consuming, since many data fit many categories, but it has paid off in the writing-up stage. The index has a positivistic quality; it is the key to locating the "facts," not ideas.

I defend my compulsion to collect ethnographic data. I believe it is done less by anthropologists today than by those of my generation, which was not so much concerned with theory. For me, this compulsion has been coupled with a second one—to write a great deal and thus turn notes into lots of publications. So, I have published four books on Afikpo (Ottenberg 1968, 1971, 1975, 1989a), plus numerous articles. Except those of recent years, my publications are heavy in ethnography, and much of the theory is implied, covert, or shyly presented. This suggests a hypothesis: those who produce ethno-graphic, nontheoretically oriented notes will produce ethnographic writings; those who produce problem-oriented or theoretically di-rected notes will produce like writings. The notes are signs of the nature of the scholar.

Colonialism

Nigeria became independent on October 1, 1960. Most of my fieldnotes on Afikpo were obtained before that date. They are colo-nialist documents, and I am a colonialist anthropologist, I am told by some of my colleagues nowadays! I thought not. Imbued with the spirit of cultural relativism, so carefully and thoroughly nourished by Professor Herskovits at Northwestern, I went to the field to "under-stand" another people and to write about them. I hoped to bring some sensible comprehension of them and their way of life to a largely nonunderstanding Western world, some appreciation of the values of cultural differences, some nonracist, nonprimitive views of Africans. That I have succeeded only in bringing such views to the attention of students and some of my colleagues—who, by and large, already agree with them—is beside the point. I went to the field holding these views and also a considerable suspicion of colonialism. It is evident that through my notes I "captured" and took away the Afikpo, a "subtribe" of the Igbo. They became mine, "my people." Anthropo-logical colonialism? Yes, but also personal possessiveness.

But of course, I was inevitably trapped in the colonial web—in social relationships with the British colonial officials; in African per-ceptions of myself and my wife as essentially British in culture; in a research focus on traditional politics rather than on the colonial world as part of that politics; in seeking to study the "pure" native rather than the "detribalized" townsmen, as colonial officials referred to them; in a failure to understand fully the economic consequences of colonialism. I also shared the naive optimism of most of my Africanist colleagues, but not of colonial officials, that independence for African countries would have a smooth course and that post-independence governments would be successful and largely democratic. We thought that colonial-ism had provided a start in the right direction which would continue with independence.

I have no shame or remorse for having held these values in the past. I was a product of my times. Those scholars today who are critical of the colonial mentality of that time are just as likely to be blind to the current political realities in which they are entrapped and for which they will be condemned in twenty or thirty years. The more difficult problem is perception of the current world one lives in; the past seems much easier to understand from within the framework of the present. But how do we get around the errors of misperception of our world today and their influence on our research, on the nature of our notes and on our interpretations of them?

My notes are colonial documents, reflecting attitudes of that time; they are archives that I have to translate in terms of present values, standards, and views for my writing based on them. My headnotes, however distorted and reinterpreted through time, are mental archival resources. Historical scholars working with archives do not usually employ materials that they themselves have written! They have no headnotes coeval with the documents, only those they begin to develop as their heads carry out dialogue with the archives and those arising through previous experience and conceptions. But these archives are mine. They include the little government archival material that I was able to obtain, but this is supplementary material at best. The advantage of using one's own archives is that one can better understand the circumstances in which they were written, despite the distortions in the head. The disadvantage is that one is terribly inclined not to be too critical of one's own archives. They are too much a part of one's person, one's ego, not only because of the hard work and struggle to obtain them but also because, as I have indicated, they may relate to childhood identity, the striving for success, and the wish for immortality.

Fieldnotes as Archives

Only recently have anthropologists had much interest both in using archives in their research and writing and in viewing their own fieldnotes as archives. There is also concern now about the ultimate preservation of fieldnotes. Our archives have not yet generally assumed commercial value except occasionally for tax purposes in inheritance matters. The "commodifaction of everything" (Wallerstein 1983: 16–17), so characteristic of capitalist society, has little touched our fieldnotes yet; they are not being auctioned off at Sotheby's or Christies. In fact, when I was younger, I would have felt uncomfortable at the thought of someone else using my notes, whether I was alive or dead—they are so much a private thing, so much an aspect of personal field experience, so much a private language, so much a part of my ego, my childhood, and my personal maturity. But now I have shown them to graduate students preparing to go to the field; a student of mine in ethnomusicology read my 1978–80 notes on the Limba of northern Sierra Leone before doing field research there, and even took a copy with him.

The private nature of our largely "loner" research (anthropologists rarely do fieldwork in groups) and the idea that unless you thoroughly experience the culture yourself you cannot know it make sharing notes with others difficult. Only occasionally has someone edited for publication the fieldwork of a deceased anthropologist (see Pehrson 1966; Bradbury 1973). Written notes are a private language, a special language for interacting with the headnotes. They are not intended for publication. Yet now, along with photographs, letters from the field, and material objects collected during research, they have become of value as archives.

I have to bring the critical eye of a postcolonial anthropologist to my colonialist archival notes. It is difficult. When I was doing my fieldwork and writing, there was little criticism on the part of other social scientists of my kind of liberal political leaning; now, in anthropology there is. When I was doing my field research, very few of the people I was studying could read or write; now many can, and they have read what I have written about Afikpo. Some are pleased to have this obscure corner of Africa "on the map"; some are happy to see their own names or photographs in print. Some are critical of my interpretations or my data; others feel that they are accurate. Some Igbo scholars (not from Afikpo) have cited my published work, and I am now in a dialogue with them. Their interpretations of their notes are matched to my interpretations of my notes. But when I was doing field research, there was no such dialogue with Igbo once I had left the field. There was only the silence of the "native," characteristic of the anthropological research and writings of the colonial period.

I find that I have had to struggle with these issues as I employ my fieldnotes and my headnotes in my writing. I have had to deal with the overconfidence that silence from the "native" brings, and later with the critical dialogue of Igbo anthropologists over my work. I can refer in my publications to the specific time I am writing about and make the usual anthropological apologies about the "ethnographic present" in which I frame my materials. This is, of course, subject to criticism today for its unrealism. I can write as a historian, citing my own notes and memories as documents. In fact, all anthropological writing is history, for even as one leaves the field, the culture is already changing, and by the time of publication it is not the same. My problem has become ever more severe; what I am writing is ever more historical as the origin point of my fieldnotes recedes in time. I cannot go back and check my data; there has been too much change in Afikpo. I have virtually the only data that exist in the world on Afikpo except for some government documents that survived the Nigerian civil war. Unless the Afikpo write their own memories of the past—which they have not done, but which I would encourage—there remains only my interpretation of their past. I consider this an immense responsibility. I do not denigrate my Afikpo fieldnotes because of the colonialist milieu in which they were written, but they do remain the same, while my headnotes alter through my own exposure to new ideas and new politics.

Anthropological Theory

What is true of politics is true also of anthropological theory. When I gathered my Afikpo fieldnotes, they related to the major contemporary theories in anthropology. In America there were the competing concepts of culture of Herskovits, Kroeber, Kluckhohn, Boas, and others. Ideas of centrality in cultural features were predominant—patterns of culture, ethos, value orientations, and Herskovits's cultural focus, which I and all his students tried to employ in the field. There was a holistic attitude toward field data as there was in these analytical approaches. Ideas of cultural relativism abounded and were openly debated. And there was British social anthropology, in which I was very poorly trained—though I learned much of value from this approach on my own and with the help of personal contacts with Meyer Fortes and with students and faculty at the University of Chicago before my second Afikpo research trip. It was from these encounters that I was able to work out the complex double Afikpo unilineal descent system later on (Ottenberg 1968).

In both American and British anthropology there was the view of the tribe as a separate, distinctive group. There were crude theories of culture contact, culture change, and acculturation. There was little in the way of historical orientation, little Marxism, little study of aggression and militarism, little symbolic analysis; there were no conscious emic and etic perceptions as yet. Despite the presence of influential women in the profession, anthropology was male-oriented in problem and research. I did my Afikpo fieldwork at the end of the age of positivism in anthropology. Where are all the theories today that existed then (and some seemed quite exciting to me at the time)? They are gone, dead as a doornail. Positivism is largely gone, swallowed in hermeneutics and the text, in the replacement of the biological analogy and metaphor in anthropology with humanistic ones: the trope, symbol, and the text. My fieldnotes represent dead traditions.

I have considered that it might be better simply to put aside these early fieldnotes: to let other scholars, when I am dead, puzzle over what the informants were like whose names appear in the interviews; to let others work out the obscurities of certain details in the text without knowing whether these matters were really obscure to me or not. Leaving my notes with the possibility that no one will ever be interested in looking at them at all—the ultimate death! Still, I could go on to other field research based on the newer theories and ideas in anthropology, with the current criticisms of the politics and "colonialist mentalities" of earlier anthropologists in mind. In fact, I have done so with my own research into aesthetics and symbolism among the Limba of northern Sierra Leone in 1978–80.

But even after that trip I went back to my fieldnotes and headnotes to write one more book on Afikpo, on the life of boys from birth through initiation (Ottenberg 1989a). I see my notes as so much a part of my childhood and life in anthropology that it is hard to grow up. This is personal idiosyncrasy, not necessarily common to other anthropologists, though I doubt that it is rare. The writing of this last major work of the Afikpo, which itself connects with childhood, is my most personal anthropological document of all; I used my notes, both written and in my head, to explore my own past through the childhood of Afikpo persons. The two became intertwined. I used the notes as text for understanding both myself as a child and the Afikpo boys—their initiations, their development through childhood. But only the Afikpo side comes out directly in the writing. So instead of putting aside my colonialist notes with their old-fashioned theory, I have employed them in order to understand myself, including my Afikpo anthropological childhood. My earlier writings were also self-serving but more in the interest of personal advancement and success than of self-understanding. I am not much worried about success now; I don't expect to become more or less than I am.

I can be anthropologically cynical about all of this. If hermeneutics and the study of the text tell us that textual analysis is all interpretation, and that perhaps the best we can do is to give some idea of our biases and our own rules of interpretation, or try to follow some more or less standardized rules of interpretation (Ricoeur 1971), why shouldn't I make use of my own colonial era archives? So I go ahead.

The fact is that cultural relativism has been replaced by textual relativism. We have moved from ideas of the relativism of the cultures of the people we study to concepts of the relativity of interpretation and the interpreter. That is possible because we have moved from employing scientific metaphors, particularly those relating to organic qualities (organic solidarity, society as a metaphor for a living animal) to using humanistic metaphors drawn largely from literature, literary criticism, history, and drama (symbols, the text, performance). Fieldnotes have gone from being viewed as scientific data to being seen as interpretive text in the years that I have been writing up my Afikpo research. Anthropology has shifted from questions of the accuracy of the data in the notes to matters of how one interprets them as text. Now everything is interpretation: culture is a text to be interpreted: fieldnotes are a text; we are in a world of hermeneutics, symbolic and metaphoric analysis; and there is a strong turn to examining the self as anthropologist, as recent writing about fieldwork indicates (Dumont 1978; Wagner 1981). Curiously, all this allows me to keep writing. I consider my fieldnotes as text, where a positivist might object that my data are outmoded and not systematic. My positivist notes have been saved by the concept of the text. An ironic, unexpected twist!

Despite my own changing interpretations of my headnotes and written notes, I believe they have some consistencies that anchor them through time, and these are probably rooted in my particular personality. On the negative side they include poor linguistic skills, an uneasy relationship to the oral arts in contrast to visual arts, a tendency to underemphasize conflict and aggression, and a failure to take as seriously as I might the obvious meanings of informants' statements. On the positive side there is a considerable sensitivity to status and role differences and to their meanings for the persons I study, a great delight in participation in their culture, and a strong need to check data against the views of others. Such consistencies as these must be reflected in many of my publications, whatever my changing interpretations of my own mental and written texts.

Despite the demise of positivism in much of anthropology, especially in symbolism and art, the fields that interest me to a large extent today, I am left with a nagging residue of positivistic feeling. Is this the childhood that I can never shake? Or is something more? It is hard to tell. But I have found that some of my data, collected with other theories in mind and during a colonial period, can nonetheless be reinterpreted in the present political world and in terms of current theory. Not as well as fresh data, perhaps, the results not as original—but possibilities exist. I would argue that despite the ridicule of past scholarship which marks much of social and cultural anthropology today, we can—because we study the past—make use of our own scholarly past if we are sensitive to the nature of our anthropological texts, their complexities and their limitations. I have been able to publish enough material from my compulsive fieldnote-taking to believe that there is a certain minimal sanctity to a collection of field data. It *does* have unexpected uses; it *is* an unknown mine for interpretation. In fact, I have probably used only half of my written notes, if that much. It is the fate of most notes to remain silent forever, like the native before literacy.

Realizing how much of what we write is not really objective but interpretive leads us to a better understanding of how we do fieldwork, which should therefore come to be carried out more fruitfully than in the past. The approach provides us rich insights into the mental processes of analyzing our data and writing them up. But it is also part of present Western society's preoccupation with the self, a narcissism in which the "native" becomes secondary, while concern with our anthropological and personal processes becomes primary. Those of us who become so textually involved—unlike Marxists, World System theorists, development anthropologists, ecologists, and ethnoscientists—can avoid some salient facts about the people we study.

For example, physical aggression and militarism were widespread in Third World areas in the precolonial period. Their decline occurred in colonial times following the initial, sometimes brutal, aggression of the colonialists. During this colonial time much of anthropology that was published was without reference to militarism, despotism, and aggression; our fieldnotes reflect the rather amiable view of the native world that many of us held. But in our neocolonial times, aggression and militarism and autocracy are considerably on the increase again in the Third World, involving both the peoples there and the Great Powers. Food shortages are widespread; Western medicine has not brought a desirable standard of health; Third World countries rarely control major aspects of their economies, and their cities are in chaos. Meanwhile, we talk of the decline of positivism and of ourselves as only interpretive animals, although some are quite skilled.

I suggest that our turn to the anthropology of ourselves, of our own anthropological processes, to reflexivity, to the text, is partly an avoidance of these unhappy issues, a defense mechanism against our own disappointment with the present situation of many of the peoples that we have traditionally studied. It is related to our sense of an inability to control these conditions. Either we react to them by moving toward development theories, Marxism, ethnoscience, ecology, and so on, where we believe that we see realities (though ideologies may obscure them), in which case our field notes are generally said by their makers to reflect objectivity, positivism, and the like; or we withdraw into the examination of ourselves as anthropologists through a strong concern with symbolism, structuralism, deconstruction, and the like, a withdrawal from facing the realities of the condition of the people we study. Insofar as we take this second course, will we be revealed in the fieldnotes we collect as any less blind than the colonialist anthropologist who studied the native outside the context of the colonial situation? To me the challenge for the textual, reflexive view is to discover how can it be, and how should it be, related to the realities of the Third World today. All of this is linked very closely to the nature of our fieldnotes—how they are collected and how they are used.

Fortunately, our field is self-oriented nowadays not only with regard to the anthropologists and their own experience but also in terms of the selves of the individuals we study, particularly through an interest in the person and a phenomenological approach (Riesman 1986). This important aspect is largely absent in my notes and in the fieldwork and writing of my generation. Anthropologists who examine their own selves may also be led to the selves of those they study. Insofar as we connect the two kinds of self-studies, I think this is highly desirable. Insofar as we focus mainly on our own selves, I think it is self-defeating. Riesman (1986: 110), citing Jules-Rosette's study (1975), indicates that "it makes eminent sense to study oneself in order to know the other." And Riesman (1986: 112–13) writes that we study other selves in order to find meaning in our own lives. It seems more important to anthropology to be conscious of this process now than when I did my own Afikpo fieldwork.

We are on a moving escalator with our fieldnotes. They change during the process of field research as we mature in the field. They are in a changing relationship to the native as well as to our headnotes. As our social milieu alters through our lifetime maturation, our relationship to our notes alters. As the political and intellectual climate of our scholarly field changes, our relationships to and uses of our fieldnotes change.

Positivism allowed the illusion of the permanence of fieldnotes. Now we see how relative the text is to the situation at hand. But paradoxically, I hope that we can ultimately handle this moving escalator, this continual change in relationships to the fieldnotes, in a more objective manner than we have done before.

REFERENCES

Bennett, W. Lance, and Martha S. Feldman. 1981. *Reconstructing Reality in the Courtroom.* New Brunswick, N.J.: Rutgers University Press.

Bradbury, R. E. 1973. *Benin Studies.* Ed. Peter Morton Williams. London: Oxford University Press for the International African Institute.

Dumont, Jean-Paul. 1978. *The Headman and I.* Austin: University of Texas Press.

Jules-Rosette, Bennetta. 1975. *African Apostles: Ritual Conversion in the Church of John Maranke.* Ithaca: Cornell University Press.

Ottenberg, Simon. 1968. *Double Descent in an African Society: The Afikpo-Village Group.* American Ethnological Society, Monograph 47. Seattle: University of Washington Press.

———. 1971. *Leadership and Authority in an African Society: The Afikpo-Village Group.* American Ethnological Society, Monograph 52. Seattle: University of Washington Press.

———. 1975. *The Masked Rituals of Afikpo: The Context of an African Art.* Seattle: University of Washington Press.

———. 1983. Artistic and Sex Roles in a Limba Chiefdom. In *Female and Male in West Africa,* ed. Christine Oppong, 76–90. London: Allen & Unwin.

———. 1987. Return to the Field: Anthropological Déja Vu. *Cambridge Anthropology* 92 (3): 16–31.

———. 1989a. *Boyhood Rituals in an African Society: An Interpretation.* Seattle: University of Washington Press.

———. 1989b. "We Are Becoming Art Minded": Afikpo Arts 1988. *African Arts* 22 (4): 58–67, 88.

Ottenberg, Simon, and Phoebe Ottenberg. 1962. Afikpo Markets, 1900–1960. In *Markets in Africa,* ed. Paul Bohannan and George Dalton, 117–69. Evanston, Ill.: Northwestern University Press.

Pehrson, Robert N. 1966. *The Social Organization of the Marri Baluch.* Comp. and ed. Fredrik Barth. Chicago: Aldine.

Ricoeur, Paul. 1971. The Model of the Text: Meaningful Action Considered as a Text. *Social Research* 38:529–62.

Riesman, Paul. 1986. The Person and the Life Cycle in African Social Life and Thought. *African Studies Review* 29 (2): 71–138.

Wagner, Roy. 1981. *The Invention of Culture.* Rev. ed. Chicago: University of Chicago Press.

Wallerstein, Immanuel. 1983. *The Capitalist World Economy.* Cambridge: Cambridge University Press.

ALLEN JOHNSON
ORNA R. JOHNSON

Quality into Quantity:
On the Measurement Potential
of Ethnographic Fieldnotes

Anthropology straddles the border between the sciences and the humanities (Bennett 1976; A. Johnson 1978: 60–74; Schweder 1986; Service 1985). This is an awkward stance to maintain, and some anthropologists resolve the tension by moving resolutely to one side or the other. But most anthropologists accept the situation because we want a *science* of humankind capable of studying whole persons within a framework of humanistic values. Nonetheless, this border-straddling entails no end of contradictions, and nowhere are these more evident than in ethnographic fieldnotes, perhaps our single most crucial repository of knowledge. Fieldnotes provide scientific data to the extent that they contain intersubjectively reliable descriptions of beliefs and behavior of individuals in other cultures; and they are humanistic documents to the extent that they enhance our *understanding* of behavior and beliefs by illuminating their meaning within a cultural context of related meanings. What makes joining the scientific and humanistic traditions in anthropology so challenging a task is that like oil and water the two do not mix well: every step toward scientific reliability seems inevitably to be a step away from humanistic intimacy, and the achievement of many-layered humanistic interpretation seems possible only at the expense of scientific precision.

Ethnographic fieldnotes, serving these incompatible masters simultaneously, cannot always be faithful to both. Let us begin by examining their shortcomings from the standpoint of scientific research.

First, they are usually prose texts that record observations or impressions and are intended to describe diverse events, recollections, thoughts, and feelings. Although the notekeeper may have various schemata in mind for future organization and reduction of the contents of the fieldnotes, there is no obvious coding scheme or scale at hand allowing for immediate quantification, or even for simple grouping into analytic categories.

Second, the looseness of most qualitative research designs results in a labor-intensive, vacuum-cleaner-like comprehensiveness that generates enormous numbers of data, even if data on any specific point may be skimpy. Furthermore, the voluminous data generally require many hours of analysis for each hour spent in collecting them.

Third, when fieldwork consists of the usual participant-observation in a small community of individuals who come to be well known to the ethnographer in the course of long-term research, the observations recorded in the fieldnotes repeatedly describe the same persons over time, violating the standard of "independence of observations" demanded by proper sampling procedures in quantitative social research. Since observations are biased toward, indeed usually limited to, members of a single community, the research findings cannot be generalized to a larger population, such as a region or a community type. This leads to the familiar criticism that anthropological research in a small community really contributes only one case to our cross-cultural store of knowledge. In the view of a social science statistician, those hundreds or thousands of pages of fieldnotes we collect in a year or more of fieldwork amount to a *single observation,* however rich and complex!

It should not be surprising, therefore, that ethnographic fieldnotes are so often considered to be "soft," nonquantifiable data, useful for providing background information and illustrative case materials but incapable of providing numerical descriptions. But now let us consider the difficulties from the humanistic side. Say we do restrict our fieldnotes to data based on proper sampling and measurement. Then the following criticisms apply.

First, number-crunching behavioral scientists, by sampling randomly and maintaining independence of observations, never get to know their research subjects. This raises several related problems:

Subjects who do not personally know the researcher are likely to hide or distort information because they do not trust the researcher or the ultimate purposes of the research, and there is no reason to believe that fieldworkers who are not trusted will ever discover that they have given inaccurate information.

When subjects are studied at only one point in time (the moment of the interview), the direct experience of people's lives as continuous through time, with wide-ranging connections to other persons and past and future events, is lost. Questionnaires can attempt to correct this defect, especially if constructed late in the fieldwork, but responses to questionnaires are no substitute for the rich contextualization provided by an experienced ethnographic fieldworker who has witnessed community members' behavior day in and day out, through ordinary and extraordinary events.

There are consequently few checks on the validity, as opposed to reliability, of quantified survey data. That is, survey methods may produce reliable results in the sense that a second researcher may be able to replicate the results of a first by following the same research methods. But the question of validity remains: are the results true as descriptions of community members' thoughts and actions? Recent studies suggest that survey research methods, no matter how reliable, give poor measures of actual behavior and in that sense are invalid (Bernard et al. 1984). It is an axiom of qualitative research that if we are to develop authentic descriptions of individual behavior and beliefs, we must accompany the subject into the several significant settings that evoke the many facets of the whole person. We must know our subjects well, and be well known to them, if we are to obtain the most valid information about them.

The second criticism is that the tight, deductive research designs of the behavioral scientist are necessarily reductionistic. They focus research efforts on the small number of variables that have been determined to be of theoretical relevance. In this, such designs try to mirror the ideals of laboratory science, where all but two variables (one "dependent" and the other "independent," so that unilinear causality is assumed from the outset) are held constant in the artificial environment of the laboratory. Again, field experience teaches us that theory rarely identifies in advance all the variables that will determine or explain any given behavior. Anthropologists generally agree that most human behavior is overdetermined, serving multiple purposes or reflecting multiple meanings simultaneously. A researcher's proper stance is not to limit theoretical possibilities in advance but to be open to many complementary perspectives simultaneously.

It is through this maze of contradictions between scientific and humanistic criteria of what "good field research" is that the anthropological fieldworker must find a path. That this is not a new problem either for anthropology (Bennett 1976: 4–5; Service 1985) or for the larger community of scholars (Snow 1959) is somewhat reassuring; it suggests at the very least that no easy solutions for it exist. But the temptation is always there to find quick relief from the contradictions by embracing one side or the other of the dichotomy.

For example, those who emphasize the humanist goal of studying systems or structures of meaning tend to view quantitative research methods and data (identified with the scientific wing of anthropology) as hardly relevant to a modern, interpretive, critical discipline (Marcus and Fischer 1986; Sahlins 1976; Schweder 1986). They see positive science as having occupied a comparatively brief moment in anthropology which we have moved beyond with the hermeneutic and reflexive methodologies now available to us. Science, in the usual sense of the word, has been not so much criticized as passed by, although Sahlins (1976) reveals a deeper antipathy than most by seeing scientific research as culturally bound to "bourgeois" industrial technology and class exploitation.

But rather than disappearing, as some interpretive anthropologists might wish, the scientific wing has persisted in a kind of parallel development, as indifferent to the achievements of interpretive anthropology as the interpretive wing has been to developments in scientific theory and method in anthropology. Such mutual indifference most likely derives from the habit of "talking past" one another that commonly characterizes people working from fundamentally different assumptions as to what is worth knowing about in the universe (Snow 1959).

Counting on Fieldnotes

Curiously, neither camp has much specifically to say about fieldnotes, at least not about the broad-ranging notes that are the main focus of our discussion here. One thing all anthropologists seem to share is a certain shyness about their fieldnotes. We are hopeful that this volume will help reverse this public neglect. We suspect that both humanistic and scientific anthropologists keep their notebooks in roughly comparable ways: that is, as relatively uncensored and unstructured repositories for events, experiences, and musings that have struck the researcher throughout the day. Open discussion of our fieldnotes—what they are, how they came to be, and what has become of them—might reveal more similarities between varieties of anthropologists, illuminating the bases that unite us as a profession rather than splitting us into feuding clans (Goldschmidt 1986). At the very least, a more open attitude toward discussing anthropological fieldnotes will expose crucial epistemological questions that both camps now tend to avoid: the scientists by minimizing the use of qualitative data in their research papers, the humanists by asserting that ethnography is really just fiction anyway (Schweder 1986).

In any case, the humanistic wing of anthropology appears to have rejected all forms of quantification, and qualitative fieldnotes are generally taken to be part of the nonquantitative side of anthropology. We argue here that such dichotomizing is too extreme, that qualitative fieldnotes can be collected in such a way that some degree of quantification is possible, even though it may not conform to the standards demanded by statistical methodology. We hope it will be obvious that we do not view such efforts at quantification either as anti-scientific (just because they do not meet the most rigorous criteria of statistics) or as antihumanistic (just because they propose to quantify aspects of human behavior and belief). Qualitative data can be transformed into quantitative data without abandoning an integrative position between science and the humanities.

By "fieldnotes" we mean mainly the information collected during participant-observation within a face-to-face community over a long term of research. The fieldworker usually has many notebooks or files: some may be in the form of questionnaires or surveys that lend themselves easily to quantification; others may be devoted to particular qualitative tasks such as collecting folktales, life histories, or taxonomies. But in the midst of these special-purpose files there is usually one general-purpose notebook in which the fieldworker records "random" observations, bits of conversation, and instances of events or ideas that are subsidiary to the main fieldwork goals yet somehow interesting or suggestive of unanticipated new directions for the research. This file, which we call "the notebook," is such a hodgepodge of haphazard information, collected without any discernible method other than our being there and taking notes, that it has never seemed to offer much possibility for systematic quantitative analysis. Yet there are ways to reduce the haphazard aspect in favor of more order and completeness, and this can be done quite efficiently with relatively little additional effort in the field.

The problem is not that there is nothing to count in such a notebook. We could always count the number of times the word "maize" appears, for example, or the difference in the average length of entries on Sundays as opposed to those on other days of the week. The rapidly growing technology of text processing actually makes such counting very easy, once the fieldnotes have been entered into a database-management system (we briefly discuss below an example of appropriate computer software).

The difficulty lies rather in establishing that such counting has value. There are many reasons why an ethnographer might enter the word "maize" in a notebook: the grain could be in season or not in season; it could be a major crop or completely absent; it could be served for dinner, given to livestock, or offered to the harvest deity. A count of the frequency of "maize" in the notebook would be quantitative but practically useless. In order to interpret a count of occurrences in fieldnotes, we would have to believe that the fieldnotes were an adequate sample of meaningful observations of a universe that we want to know about.

The question we need to address, therefore, is how a notebook can become a meaningful sample of cultural events. It can, if certain procedures are followed. First, our notebook can be a representative sample of events occurring in the lives of the members of our research community if we are unbiased in our exposure to all members of the community. Second, our notebook can be a representative sample of those events to the extent that we are alert to and willing to record without bias all aspects of our subjects' lives. Third, our notebook can generate meaningful counts of events if we classify its contents in theoretically appropriate ways before counting them. We now elaborate on these answers, with examples.

Whatever Happened to Holism?

Whereas the third answer refers to a measurement problem (and will be addressed shortly), the first two answers refer to sampling problems. As it happens, the more closely we approach these two solutions, the more we embrace the anthropological ideal of "holism" as a research strategy. This should be a congenial idea to anthropologists. Yet while continuing to proclaim holism as an identifying symbol of our discipline, anthropologists are in fact becoming less and less holistic in both theory and research methodology.

Holism has a number of specific meanings in anthropology, not all of which are compatible (Johnson 1987). Here we focus on the enduring core meaning of holism for anthropology: that culture is an integrated whole and that individuals can be understood only within the context of that whole. In order to study this context, it is necessary to adopt approaches specific to many other disciplines: biology, prehistory and history, language, the several social sciences, art, literature, and so on. Anthropologists criticize disciplines in which single aspects of culture, such as economy or mythology, are isolated and analyzed for committing the reductionistic error of mistaking the part for the whole.

Holism is not merely an idea or technique but a basic commitment, a component of identity fundamental to anthropology among the sciences and the humanities. Anthropological fieldwork is historically holistic, and fieldwork notebooks are the key repositories of holistic information. Whether originating in scientific or humanistic concerns, and no matter how sharp the initial problem focus, the best anthropological fieldwork is holistic, if for no other reason than that our subjects' lives constantly present us with occurrences that are more or less tangential to our research focuses yet obviously important to them. To exclude such occurrences from our fieldnotes would be tantamount to turning away from the people as guides to their cultures as they live them; it would raise the question whether any truly anthropological research was being done.

In the second half of the twentieth century, however, there has been a de facto shift away from holism in anthropology (though we suspect that fieldnotes remain more holistic than published ethnography). Considering the significance of this change, there has been surprisingly little discussion and certainly no outcry. Introductory textbooks still routinely mention the breadth of anthropology, usually in the first few pages. Yet even the term "holism" seldom appears in print today; of a dozen recent textbooks on our shelves, only one actually uses the word (Ember and Ember 1985: 3). The fullest discussion of holism we have noted is in an out-of-print textbook (Friedl 1976), where a full page is devoted to the subject. Anthropologists appear to have reached a point of thinking that though holism sets anthropology apart from other social sciences, it is no longer feasible to do holistic research or to train our students to do it. The Embers acknowledge that anthropologists are becoming more specialized than in the past but add, optimistically in our view, that the "discipline . . . retains its holistic orientation" (1985: 3). We wonder. If individual anthropologists are losing their commitment to holism in practice, just where does that holistic orientation reside?

To some, the drift away from holism is the result of the growing commitment of anthropology to a scientific methodology. A scientific research design narrows the focus to a fraction of the whole:

> Anthropology as a discipline [has undergone a] sharpening of problems and a decreased emphasis on the holistic approach as a fundamental goal of all field work. This in turn has led to more detailed and systematic research on limited sectors of a culture or on a number of cultures, using a comparative approach. . . . More limited problems demand more rigorous and systematic research techniques and methodological strategies [Naroll and Cohen 1970: 4]

Viewed from the standpoint of the scientific paradigm, holism is a vague and confusing notion, ultimately indefensible (Phillips 1976).

This would appear to leave the guardianship of holism in the humanist wing of anthropology, but the humanists have lost track of holism just as much as the scientists have. Roger Keesing anticipated the developments of the past decade when he embraced the definition of culture as ideational system, distinct from social system, biological system, ecosystem, and so on. Although he hoped that anthropologists would continue, holistically, to examine human beings in the context of all these systems together, he seemed to sense that they might not: "To study cultures as ideational systems without mapping the complex cybernetic circuits that link them to social systems, to ecosystems, and to the psychology and biology of individuals would turn cultural analysis into an arcane pursuit isolated from surrounding disciplines" (1974: 91).

Significant examples of interpretive theorizing (as distinct from ethnography) have since ranged from radical denial of the relevance of biology, ecology, and society (Sahlins 1976) to seeming indifference (Marcus and Fischer 1986). We stress that these events have tended to occur at the level of abstract theory. Moving the contested ground to include fieldwork and fieldnotes, which concern all ethnographers, might help clarify what is most at stake in current theoretical debates.

We surmise that what has happened in anthropology since 1950 is a huge growth in the number of anthropologists, leading to a rapid elaboration of subfields and specialties. This kind of niche specialization is common to all ecological communities as they become more crowded with competitors; it is actually a way to minimize competition (see Goldschmidt 1986). Departments of anthropology do seek to hire general-purpose anthropologists on occasion, but the dominant trend is to advertise for specialists to fill gaps on the departmental team. For the individual anthropologist, especially the young professional trying to find a place in the job market, acquiring a specialized, focused expertise is the best way to be unique and noticeable in the throng of job applicants. The inevitable outcome of such proliferation is that each of us individually is less fully informed about anthropology as a whole than were our founding ancestors.

This new expertise changes fieldwork in several ways. First, tying fieldwork plans to a focused research design builds in a lack of holism from the start. In our own experience, graduate students' research proposals are ever more narrow, often limited entirely nowadays to discussion of a single research question: What is the medical belief system of the "X"? How has recent economic change affected social stratification? Aside from the obligatory sentence claiming that the research method will be participant-observation, no real attention is devoted to holism. In fact, it is our impression that a firmly stated commitment to do holistic research would hurt rather than help a proposal during the funding review process.

Second, being a specialist, the modern fieldworker may feel obligated to pay scant attention to events or statements that fall outside the scope of the research design. "After all," we appear to be saying, "you cannot study everything (as old-fashioned anthropologists believed they could), so why try?" These changes in the professional strategies of anthropologists amount to a license to bias their research in the direction of their specialties.

Third, and partly as a result of the first two changes, fieldwork notebooks may themselves have become less wide-ranging and, probably, less voluminous. The evidence, of course, is by its nature closed to us, but we hazard that although holism survives in anthropology mainly in its practitioners' notebooks, even there its vigor is steadily diminishing.

We accept these developments as desirable to many and probably inevitable, but we do not willingly accept all the consequences that they imply. We prefer to think of anthropological fieldwork as having two aspects. One is the special focus of the researcher, where the best in modern techniques of description and analysis may be brought to bear; the other is comprehensive, holistic, general-purpose description. The first aspect may be thought of as pertaining to the interests of the researcher; the second, to the interests of anthropology as a whole. Each of us needs to be reminded from time to time that his or her immediate professional interests do not alone justify anthropological fieldwork. We share a common responsibility to provide data on the context that surrounds our particular research focus so that our colleagues have a chance to criticize and expand our analyses, using the holistic data we have collected. The payoff to the individual researcher is also there: collecting holistic data helps us to expand our own analyses, as others comment on our work and as our professional careers mature.

Holistic Field Methods

The modern move away from holism has lessened the importance of the most holistic of fieldwork documents, the notebook. Yet for both scientific and humanistic purposes, the notebook has the most underutilized potential. All of us can and should put more into our notebooks and make more use of them. It is possible to develop strategies in the field that increase the representativeness of the notebook as a sample of community life.

We discovered this indirectly in the course of our research on time allocation in a Machiguenga community (Johnson and Johnson 1987). The time allocation study originated in ecological concerns, as one method for estimating labor time in all areas of Machiguenga life (see A. Johnson 1975). It seemed important, therefore, neither to decide in advance which activities would ultimately be analyzed as "work" nor to assume in advance that only some kinds of individuals would be doing "work." We therefore selected a sampling procedure that included all community members, all kinds of activity, and all observable times of day. We realized later that we were overcoming two sources of bias in fieldnote-taking that had not really concerned us before.

Bias in the Locus of Description

Any biases affecting when and where we make the observations that enter our fieldnotes will naturally be reflected in the data we extract later from those notes. Unless steps are taken to avoid them, such biases are inevitable, simply because we tend to be creatures of habit: to follow predictable routines that have us in set places at set times; to seek out certain congenial community members and avoid those with whom some tension exists; to stay indoors in inclement weather. As a result, our fieldnotes will be filled with observations and opinions of our next-door neighbors and best friends; few observations will be made before, say, eight o'clock in the morning; evening observations will tend to focus on special events such as religious observances; and fair-weather settings will be overrepresented.

We cannot eliminate such biases, since routine is as necessary to fieldworkers as to any other human beings, but we can be aware that they are constantly shaping our fieldnotes and take steps to alleviate them. For example, it is neither difficult nor time-consuming to introduce elements of randomness into field routine. One method now in common use is to make random behavioral observations as part of a time allocation study (Gross 1984). Using the method of spot checks of randomly selected individuals at randomly selected times of day (A. Johnson 1975), the fieldworker will, with some predetermined frequency—such as once per day or three times per week, depending on the other goals of fieldwork—pay a random visit to some individual or household (it could be anyone) at a random moment (these may be selected ahead of time using a table of random numbers). The effect of this procedure is to move the fieldworker widely and unpredictably through the scene of fieldwork. All times of day (it is not usually feasible to make these observations at night) will be represented equally, and all members of the community will be included in the observations.

This is an advantage to any anthropologist, without regard to theoretical preference. Although time allocation research originated in studies of human ecology and socialization, the benefits of the fieldworker's wide-ranging presence in the research community are not restricted to scientific ones. The opportunity to meet, talk to, and observe the whole range of members of our community, in all the settings to which we can gain admittance, is desirable for the humanistically oriented as well. It increases the number of opinions we are exposed to, and the number of opportunities to see how cultural meanings are expressed in verbal or physical behavior. In a phrase, it is context-building, for humanist and scientist alike.

The randomness of observations during a time allocation study is the basis on which a statistically valid picture of community behavior may be constructed. The results of such randomized observations are often surprising and counterintuitive. For example, in our research with the Machiguenga, we noticed on innumerable occasions that people were sitting indoors during the rains, and we reached the plausible conclusion that they worked harder during the dry season. But time allocation data showed that people actually worked more hours per day during the wet season, and this made sense when we recognized that the labor-intensive activities of cultivation are concentrated in the wet season.

Similarly, casual observation gave us the impression that the Machiguenga have a separation of work between the sexes. Yet the time allocation data showed that although men and women do perform different tasks, a husband and wife spend much time together, keeping each other company while performing complementary tasks (Johnson and Johnson 1975). We also discovered a further division of labor in polygynous households. Younger wives with one or two young children spend more time away from the house with their husbands, whereas senior co-wives stay home and direct the labor of their maturing children (O. Johnson 1975).

Such misleading impressions and overlooked patterns can be very difficult to discern by fieldworkers who, after all, can claim to have "seen" the behavior in question with their own eyes. And the misinformation, in the absence of methodological checks, will persist to confound future efforts at analysis.

In a similar though less rigorous way, when observations made during random visits find their way into notebooks, a measure of serendipity is added to the fieldwork. Fieldnotes become more representative of the entire life of the community. Our random visits forced us out sometimes early in the day, sometimes during rainy periods. Otherwise, we would nearly always have spent the hour between six and seven in the morning in our own rituals of waking and eating, and we would have missed many opportunities to observe how the Machiguenga spend the early morning hours: the foods they eat, how often they are already out in quest of wild food, how much visiting goes on, who is asleep and who already busy, and so forth. Similarly, we observed the great variety of rainy-day activities, from manufactures to indoor games and storytelling, that the Machiguenga engage in. In visiting homes we might find unexpected visitors, or quantities of certain foods such as game or bananas, which otherwise we would have missed completely. The serendipity of exposure to unexpected information through random visits is one of the most useful side benefits of the procedure (Hames 1979).

Bias in the Content of Description

Anthropologists have often thought of themselves as arriving in the field unbiased by preconceptions, allowing the people and their culture to lead them to develop relevant research questions (e.g., Wolf and Hansen 1972: 76). But this is something of a conceit of ours, for no one—certainly not a well-trained cultural anthropologist—arrives in the field naive and free of bias. Increasingly, we arrive with well-formulated research designs focused on so restricted a set of research questions that a sufficient abundance and detail of data can be collected within the relatively short space of a year or so in the field.

As we wondered above, "Whatever happened to holism?" Prior to 1960 a significant number of ethnographies were broad-ranging and holistic in their descriptions, with remarkably similar tables of contents, listing geography, history, language, physical type, economy, social organization, politics, religion and world view, and, often, a chapter on recent cultural change. Now, virtually the only form in which such comprehensive accounts are still published is the abbreviated case study for teaching purposes. The typical new-style ethnography may have a "setting" chapter in which the ethnography of the community is summarized in a few pages, but the remainder of the work is devoted to some focal issue, such as the prestige economy (Cancian 1965) or the healing system (Katz 1976).

The ethnographic summary outlined in the Royal Anthropological Institute's *Notes and Queries on Anthropology* (Seligman 1951) was required reading for a generation of anthropologists but is rarely cited anymore. Instead, a sort of legitimized bias is restricting the scope not only of special fieldnotes but also of general-purpose notebooks, if for no other reason than the "selective forgetting" that afflicts all researchers when they attempt to describe events that do not fit their notions of what "ought" to have happened or what is "relevant" (Bernard et al. 1984).

Whether one's research proceeds from humanistic or from scientific concerns, we hold that the time has come to rethink the balance we are achieving in ethnographic fieldwork between old-fashioned holism (with its lack of deductive theory) and modern specialization (with its corresponding lack of comprehensiveness). Researchers should arrive in the field with both special problems to focus upon *and* a holistic checklist to remind them of what else to notice while keeping field-notes. *Notes and Queries* is still a valuable resource and ought to be included in graduate student reading requirements. The appendix to this essay presents the topics (but not the actual questions) from a cultural summary checklist that we have used in our time-allocation research. It is a reduction from the more than 800 variables that White et al. (1983) have compiled from a large number of cross-cultural studies published over the years.

We recommend that frequently, perhaps once a day, this or some similar checklist be used as a mnemonic aid while notes are written up. If, as we write, we run our eyes down the list and ask, "Did I learn anything new about that topic today?" we will be more likely to remember events outside the boundaries of our research design and to include them in our notebooks. A checklist like this is useful because it reflects the concerns of many diverse anthropologists across decades of research; reviewing it reminds the fieldworker of the questions that have persistently interested the discipline at large.

Our checklist is likely to seem too general in some areas (especially those in which we are experts) and too detailed in others (those that hold little interest for us as research topics). But this would be true of any checklist, for its purpose is not to match the research interests of the fieldworker but to indicate what a general-purpose summary of the culture, useful to the larger community of scholars, might look like. Anthropology is unusual among disciplines in the uniqueness of each researcher's field site. Others cannot verify our findings or look for new ones simply by reconstructing the circumstances of our re-search, as laboratory scientists do. We should not let excessive individ-ualism, an American culture trait (though not exclusively American), overpower the place we each occupy in the historical stream of anthro-pology and the responsibilities it entails.

Processing Holistic Fieldnotes

So far we have considered the problem of keeping a fieldwork notebook that will be minimally biased by the natural tendency of fieldworkers to focus on particular individuals or neighborhoods and on the topics closest to the researchers' main interests. The question remains whether the resulting fieldnotes can be processed later in such a way as to produce useful quantitative data. We may examine three objections to such processing. The first involves the question of whether such data meet statistical criteria; the second, whether it is possible to identify units worth counting in such data; and the third, whether it is feasible to do so, considering the costs in labor time involved.

Whether these data will meet statistical standards is a somewhat loaded question, for anthropologists (not to mention other social scientists) often exaggerate the value and power of statistical tests of significance. Let us say we are presented with a table of numbers showing that the women in a peasant community work longer hours per day than the men, with the familiar annotation "$p < .05$." The following points are relevant (see A. Johnson 1978: 42–60 for the full argument).

To begin with, the "$p < .05$" does not tell us that the difference between men's and women's labor is meaningful or important, only that the chances are less than 5 in 100 that the sex differences found in the *sample* that we measured are greatly different from the sex differences we *would* find if we measured everyone in the larger *population* from which the sample was drawn. We still must decide whether the difference is large enough to be theoretically significant, and statistics offer no aid at all in this crucial matter. It is misleading, therefore, to present tests of statistical significance as though they establish the theoretical significance of a finding.

Next, if we have measured labor time for all community members, then our "sample" is the same as our "population," and statistical tests of significance are meaningless. When reports of research provide statistical tests of significance in such cases, they are using a spurious statistical significance, again in an effort to bolster the impression that the data have theoretical significance.

Finally, if we have taken our measurements on a sample of men and women that was not drawn randomly from the population—such as an "opportunity sample" of individuals available to the fieldworker— then statistical tests of significance do not apply, because such tests concern only relationships between populations of objects and samples drawn *at random* from them. Using tests in these cases is again an effort to make some theoretical argument seem more plausible by adding statistics.

Clearly, statistics are often used inappropriately by sociocultural anthropologists. This is due partly to misunderstanding about rigorous sampling requirements, partly to confusion between statistical and theoretical significance, and partly to the real difficulties that anthropological fieldwork places in the way of rigorous sampling procedures. Yet anthropologists still want to use statistics like their prestigious, quantitative sibling disciplines.

Overdependence on inappropriate statistics has obscured the benefits of quantification that exist apart from statistics. For one, simply counting cases allows greater precision in specifying the patterns that ethnographers usually express in such phrases as "most men" or "few households." Instead of concluding, for example, that meat is rarely served except on high holidays or in wealthy households, we should prefer to report that of twenty cases where we observed meat being served at meals, fourteen were on high holidays and the other six occurred in the two wealthiest households. Random sampling and significance tests, when appropriate, might enhance the plausibility of such a finding, but the quantification itself stands as an improvement over vague wording.

Counting also keeps in view the "negative cases" that contradict our intuitions and help keep us "honest" in light of the universal tendency to forget selectively the instances of behavior that do not conform to our developing models of community life. Furthermore, counting cases contributes to the clarity of operational definitions of theoretically relevant categories. If we are to count meat-eating events, as in the foregoing example, we must be clear about what is to be included as "meat" (do eggs count?), "high holidays" (does Independence Day count?), and "wealthy households" (how wealthy is "wealthy?").

In short, data in notebooks need not satisfy the rigorous requirements of statistical tests in order to be counted and thus rendered more useful. Much use of statistics in anthropology is flawed in any case. If we make fieldnotes representative in the two senses discussed earlier—so that all members of the community and all kinds of behavior have a more or less equal chance of being represented—then we may be fairly confident that counting cases from fieldnotes is an improvement over vague, impressionistic generalities that obscure negative cases.

The second objection asks whether it is possible to identify units worth counting in notebooks. We saw earlier that simply counting frequencies of words led nowhere. But the answer to that objection is already at hand in the indexing that we all do on such fieldnotes as a first step in "working them up." Whatever the specific method of indexing may be (see Ottenberg, this volume), the function is to label the contents of the fieldnotes according to theoretically relevant categories. Thus, "maize" as a major crop might be indexed under "Economy," whereas "maize" as an offering to the harvest deities might be indexed under "Supernatural." This done, we are now counting not haphazard appearances of the word but theoretically meaningful events in which maize played a role. It might be of interest, for example, to know what proportion of instances indexed as "Supernatural" involved offerings of food, and what proportion of those were offerings of maize.

This leads to the third objection, whether it is feasible to make these counts, considering the labor costs involved. Levine (1985) has shown in some detail how proper coding and indexing of fieldnotes enhances both quantitative frequency analysis and selection of text materials for qualitative analysis. In the past, however, indexed fieldnotes could be counted only by manual inspection, even when indexing was done with mechanical card-sort methods. And if we subsequently wished to revise our coding scheme as our understanding changed, we were faced with a major investment of time in redoing the index. But today the labor costs of searching through indexed fieldnotes have been radically reduced by the advent of computer database management systems. By allowing us to enter our ethnographic fieldnotes as texts by word processing and then to index them just as we would have done in the past by hand, database programs make it possible to leave all the tedious searching, cross-referencing, and even some of the re-indexing to be done by computer.

Figure 1 gives two examples of sorted output from computerized journal notes. The computer program used, called the *Ethnograph* (Seidel 1985), accepts fieldnotes that have been entered into a word-processing program, permits these notes to be indexed by bracketing sections of text and labeling them, and then offers an array of searches that can be done on the indexed notes. In this example, notebook entries from our fieldwork among the Machiguenga in 1972–73 were entered into the *Ethnograph*. Figure 1a shows an example from a search for all entries indexed as AGRIC (agriculture) for the month of January 1973. The entry is interrupted before the last line because that part of the notes was also coded ENV (environment). Our personal computer needed less than five minutes to search for and print all entries coded AGRIC for the month of January.

Figure 1b is an example of an entry that is indexed under two

SORTED OUTPUT FOR FILE JANUARY   Page 5
SORT VARIABLE: AGRIC   1a

JANUARY   + TRIAL RUN

E: ⋆–US
E: $–DAY15
E: #–JANUARY

C: %–AGRIC

SV: AGRIC

		#	$	%	⋆	@	^
this morning's interviews. Everyone	299	:	:	–%–⋆			
seems to cut the corn stalks and pile them	300	:	:	%			
at the edges of the fields. This surprises	301	:	:	%			
me since the stalks left to rot would, one	302	:	:	%			
might assume, provide some nutrients for	303	:	:	%			
future years and slow erosion somewhat	304	:	:	%			
(fear of	305	:	:	%			
!–ENV							
snakes?). Temp 5:42 26.	306	:–$–%					

JANUARY   + TRIAL RUN   1b

E: %–US
E: #–DAY22

C: $–AGRIC $–SUPERNAT

SV: SUPERNAT

		#	$	%	⋆	@	^
Roberto. He says that you should plant	567	:–$–%					
tsota in the full moon, and maize in the	568	:	$				
new moon (imarani kashiri and itiomi-	569	:	$				
ani kashiri, respectively). Also, he said	570	:	$				
one should not go into a corn field on a	571	:	$				
hot day. I have the greatest difficulty, de-	572	:	$				
spite his excellence as an informant, in	573	:	$				
getting him to talk about taboos of any	574	:	$				
sort.	575	:–$					

Figure 1. Sorted output of *Ethnograph* program: 1a is a section of
fieldnotes from January 15, 1973, concerning agriculture (AGRIC);
1b is an example from January 22, 1973, coded both AGRIC and
SUPERNAT (supernatural).

headings, AGRIC and SUPERNAT (supernatural). The *Ethnograph* allows complex searches, combining index categories using logical operators. In this case, the search is for "AGRIC & SUPERNAT," and the printed output includes all entries that are indexed under both headings. The *Ethnograph* is a flexible, powerful text database management system that simply computerizes a standard procedure for indexing fieldnotes. It is easy to use because the procedure is natural and familiar, and it is a tremendous time-saver. Since we can only expect the performance of such programs to improve in the future, we can be confident that if the other two objections to counting from fieldnotes have been met, the labor costs will be relatively minor.

Conclusions

In sum, we have argued three main points.

First, counting cases is a way of improving both the precision and the completeness of ethnographic descriptions. This is obviously of interest to one who is scientifically oriented, but it should also attract the humanist. After all, the things we are counting (assembling might be a better word) are extracts from the qualitative record (observations, speculations, snatches of conversations) which hold clues to the complex puzzle the ethnographer is trying to piece together.

Since counting from ethnographic fieldnotes may raise serious sampling issues and does not allow statistical tests of significance to be performed, a little self-observation will show that many anthropologists use statistics inappropriately: either the data were not collected randomly or else the data refer to a whole population rather than to a sample of a population. There are times when numerical data can and should stand alone, without the possibly false enhancement of statistics.

Second, the possibilities for counting cases from fieldnotes are infinitely greater now than before, owing to the new generation of text management computer software. Tabulations that had to be done tediously by hand can now be left to the computer, freeing the researcher to focus on the meaning of the numbers and the possible sources of bias that might be affecting them.

Third, although ethnographic fieldwork has been and is inevitably biased—in the past by the implicit assumptions and the goals of the researcher; today by explicit, theoretically focused research designs—

it is possible to introduce relatively inexpensive procedures to make fieldnotes more representative of the entire social and cultural life of a community. Broadly, we need two kinds of techniques: randomizing methods, such as the spot checks used in time-allocation studies, which place the observing fieldworker at representative times and places throughout the research, avoiding the bias introduced by routine and a host of personal attitudes and habits on the part of the researcher; and a holistic checklist to remind the fieldworker of events seen or experienced during the day but otherwise likely to be forgotten in the necessary preoccupation with the special topics of the research design. Following these recommendations should not occupy so much field time as to distort the fieldwork greatly away from the central research questions or problems. Rather, these techniques should allow the researcher to balance special interests with the broader concerns of anthropology as a discipline, which requires that special topics be set in a holistic ethnographic context and that fieldworkers bring back to the discipline information about cultural practices in their communities that may be compared with life in other communities.

The payoff for the researcher will include, in addition to the satisfaction of doing broadly useful and relevant field research, a new level of quantification achieved by using fieldnotes as approximately representative samples of community life, from which instances may be counted and tabulated to strengthen arguments and interpretations.

APPENDIX: SUMMARY OF CULTURAL CONTEXT CHECKLIST

This appendix presents only the topic headings for the Cultural Context Checklist. For the detailed checklist, please write the authors at the UCLA Time Allocation Project, Department of Anthropology, University of California, Los Angeles, CA 90024.

1.   Geography and Environment

1.1 Geography
    1.1.1   region
    1.1.2   immediate location
    1.1.3   accessibility
    1.1.4   means of transportation used by community members
    1.1.5   population density
    1.1.6   natural resources

1.2 Environment
    1.2.1   map

1.2.2   location of study community
1.2.3   altitude of study community
1.2.4   relief of local environment
1.2.5   topography
1.2.6   dominant regional biomes
1.2.7   % cover by environment types
1.2.8   locally recognized (emic) environments

1.3 Climate
1.3.1   amount of precipitation
1.3.2   seasonality of precipitation
1.3.3   temperature
1.3.4   seasonality of temperature

2.   Subsistence and Economics

2.1 Predominant Types of Subsistence
2.1.1   crops and agricultural practices
2.1.2   ten most important crops
2.1.3   domestic animals
2.1.4   five major domestic animals
2.1.5   fish and fishing techniques
2.1.6   game and hunting techniques
2.1.7   food gathered
2.1.8   seasonal availability of food

2.2 Food Storage
2.2.1   list foods stored, length of time, and locus

2.3 Building and Construction
2.3.1   type of building materials
2.3.2   type of structures

2.4 Money and Credit
2.4.1   forms of currency
2.4.2   type of credit

2.5 Markets
2.5.1   characteristics of major exchange places

2.6 Trade
2.6.1   imports
2.6.2   3 major imports
2.6.3   exports

2.7 Political and Economic Incorporation
2.7.1   levels of effective political incorporation
2.7.2   wage labor activities
2.7.3   wage labor locations
2.7.4   forms of economic organization
2.7.5   payment of rent by community members
2.7.6   types of taxes paid by community members

3.   Social Structure

3.1 Settlement Patterns
     3.1.1   fixity of settlement
     3.1.2   spatial distribution
     3.1.3   size of community

3.2 Household Form
     3.2.1   household composition

3.3 Marriage
     3.3.1   marriage practices
     3.3.2   marriage arrangement for male
     3.3.3   marriage arrangement for female
     3.3.4   marriage payment
     3.3.5   attitudes toward divorce
     3.3.6   frequency of divorce
     3.3.7   grounds for divorce by male
     3.3.8   grounds for divorce by female

3.4 Postmarital Residence
     3.4.1   residence practice

3.5 Kinship and Descent
     3.5.1   kin terminology
     3.5.2   descent rule
     3.5.3   descent groups
     3.5.4   functions of descent group

3.6 Non-Kin Organizations
     3.6.1   non-kin organizations present for males and females

3.7 Ceremonies Affirming Solidarity or Status
     3.7.1   prominent community ceremonials
     3.7.2   ceremonial elements

4.   Political Organization

4.1 Political History
     4.1.1   political autonomy since 1950
     4.1.2   past trend in conquering and colonization before 1950
     4.1.3   history of being conquered or colonized by other societies before 1950
     4.1.4   dominant contacts
     4.1.5   effects of contact

4.2 Community Leadership
     4.2.1   type of leader
     4.2.2   selection of leader

4.3 Stratification
     4.3.1   type of stratification
     4.3.2   land tenure
     4.3.3   land transfer rules

4.4 Law and Order
    4.4.1 instituting of societal rules
    4.4.2 mechanisms to enforce social rules
    4.4.3 dispute settlement
    4.4.4 forms of punishment
    4.4.5 personnel who enforce penalties
    4.4.6 prevalence of deviant behavior in the community

4.5 Warfare
    4.5.1 history of warfare
    4.5.2 type and scale of warfare
    4.5.3 what is/was the frequency of warfare for the average adult?
    4.5.4 what is/was the death rate due to warfare?
    4.5.5 what are/were the gains from warfare?
    4.5.6 what is/was the aftermath of combat?

5. Family Life

5.1 Reproduction
    5.1.1 menstruation
    5.1.2 conception
    5.1.3 pregnancy
    5.1.4 childbirth
    5.1.5 abortion and infanticide
    5.1.6 infant and childhood mortality
    5.1.7 major etic causes of infant/child mortality
    5.1.8 sources of variation in child mortality

5.2 Childhood
    5.2.1 ceremonies performed during infancy and childhood
    5.2.2 infant carrying practices
    5.2.3 sleeping proximity to child
    5.2.4 weaning
    5.2.5 emotional role of father during infancy
    5.2.6 emotional role of father during early childhood
    5.2.7 normal extent of aggressive behavior in early childhood
    5.2.8 punitive behavior toward children
    5.2.9 general permissive behavior of parents
    5.2.10 affective behavior of parents
    5.2.11 evaluation of children by society
    5.2.12 age and sex associations

5.3 Domestic Relations
    5.3.1 husband-wife eating arrangements
    5.3.2 wife beating
    5.3.3 female production
    5.3.4 female control over production and wealth
    5.3.5 female influence
    5.3.6 male solidarity groups
    5.3.7 female solidarity groups

5.4 Sexuality
    5.4.1 talk about sex
    5.4.2 sex seen as dangerous
    5.4.3 premarital sex
    5.4.4 extramarital sex
    5.4.5 homosexuality

6.   Welfare, Illness, and Death

6.1 Social Welfare
    6.1.1 social problems
    6.1.2 social services

6.2 Illness
    6.2.1 common types of diseases
    6.2.2 rank most important diseases
    6.2.3 believed sources of illness
    6.2.4 medical personnel

6.3 Death
    6.3.1 conception of death
    6.3.2 funeral practices
    6.3.3 mourning

7.   Recreation

7.1 Leisure
    7.1.1 leisure activities
    7.1.2 games
    7.1.3 sports

7.2 Arts
    7.2.1 decorative art
    7.2.2 music
    7.2.3 dance
    7.2.4 drama
    7.2.5 oratory
    7.2.6 literature

8.   Religion and Cosmology

8.1 Religious Beliefs
    8.1.1 prominent religion(s) in community
    8.1.2 degree of faith
    8.1.3 general character of the cosmology

8.2 Ecclesiastical Organization
    8.2.1 spiritual personnel
    8.2.2 levels of worship
    8.2.3 locus of religious education
    8.2.4 types of rituals
    8.2.5 religious artifacts

REFERENCES

Bennett, John W. 1976. *The Ecological Transition*. New York: Pergamon Press.

Bernard, H. Russell, Peter Killworth, David Kronenfeld, and Lee Sailer. 1984. The Problem of Informant Accuracy. *Annual Review of Anthropology* 13:495–517.

Cancian, Frank. 1965. *Economics and Prestige in a Maya Community*. Stanford, Calif.: Stanford University Press.

Ember, Carol, and Melvin Ember. 1985. *Cultural Anthropology*. 4th ed. Englewood Cliffs, N.J.: Prentice-Hall.

Friedl, John. 1976. *Cultural Anthropology*. New York: Harper & Row.

Goldschmidt, Walter. 1986. Clan Fission among the Ygoloporthna: A Study in Dysfunction. *American Anthropologist* 88:172–75.

Gross, Daniel. 1984. Time Allocation: A Tool for Cultural Analysis. *Annual Review of Anthropology* 13:519–58.

Hames, Raymond. 1979. A Comparison of the Efficiencies of the Shotgun and the Bow in Neotropical Forest Hunting. *Human Ecology* 7 (3): 219–52.

Johnson, Allen. 1975. Time Allocation in a Machiguenga Community. *Ethnology* 14:301–10.

———. 1978. *Quantification in Cultural Anthropology: An Introduction to Research Design*. Stanford, Calif.: Stanford University Press.

———. 1987. The Death of Ethnography: Has Anthropology Betrayed Its Mission? *The Sciences* 27 (2): 24–31.

Johnson, Allen, and Orna R. Johnson. 1987. Time Allocation among the Machiguenga of Shimaa. In *Cross-Cultural Studies in Time-Allocation*, vol. 1, New Haven, Conn.: Human Relations Area Files.

Johnson, Orna R. 1975. Shifting Hierarchies in Polygynous Households among the Machiguenga of the Peruvian Amazon. Paper presented at the 74th annual meeting of the American Anthropological Association, San Francisco.

Johnson, Orna R., and Allen Johnson. 1975. Male/Female Relations and the Organization of Work in a Machiguenga Community. *American Ethnologist* 2:634–48.

Katz, Richard. 1982. *Boiling Energy: Community Healing among the Kalahari !Kung*. Cambridge, Mass.: Harvard University Press.

Keesing, Roger. 1974. Theories of Culture. *Annual Review of Anthropology* 3:73–97.

Levine, Harold. 1985. Principles of Data Storage and Retrieval for Use in Qualitative Evaluations. *Educational Evaluation and Policy Analysis* 7:169–86.

Marcus, George E., and Michael M. J. Fischer. 1986. *Anthropology as Cultural Critique: An Experimental Moment in the Human Sciences*. Chicago: University of Chicago Press.

Naroll, Raoul, and Ronald Cohen, eds. 1970. *A Handbook of Method in Cultural Anthropology*. New York: Columbia University Press.

Phillips, D. C. 1976. *Holistic Thought in Social Science*. Stanford, Calif.: Stanford University Press.

Sahlins, Marshall. 1976. *Culture and Practical Reason.* Chicago: University of Chicago Press.

Schweder, Richard. 1986. Storytelling among the Anthropologists. *New York Times Book Review,* September 21, pp. 1, 38–39.

Seidel, John V. 1985. *The Ethnograph.* Version 2.0. Computer software. Littleton, Colo.: Qualia Research Associates (611 E. Nichols Drive; 303/795-5378).

Seligman, Brenda Z., ed. 1951. *Notes and Queries on Anthropology.* 6th ed. London: Routledge & Kegan Paul.

Service, Elman. 1985. *A Century of Controversy.* New York: Academic Press.

Snow, C. P. 1959. *The Two Cultures and the Scientific Revolution.* New York: Cambridge University Press.

White, Douglas, Michael Burton, and Lilyan Brudner-White. 1983. *MECCA Codebooks: Murdock and White's Standard Cross-Cultural Sample.* Project MECCA (Maximum Extensibility for Cross-Cultural Research). Irvine: University of California School of Social Sciences.

Wolf, Eric, and Edward Hansen. 1972. *The Human Condition in Latin America.* New York: Oxford University Press.

ROGER SANJEK

The Secret Life of Fieldnotes

It would be futile to posit a "typical" anthropological mix of scratch notes, fieldnotes proper, records, texts, and other fieldwork writings. Yet there is far less of the totally individualistic, I-did-it-my-way, a-thousand-flowers-blooming, endless sinking-or-swimming that anthropologists tend to allege about fieldwork conduct. If we ask how anthropologists have transcribed, inscribed, and described, we see patterns, but we also see change over one hundred years of fieldwork. The answer to the question of what fieldnote practice is must be a historical one.

The sources for this history, at present, are not fieldnotes themselves. As James Clifford (this volume) points out, "Most of the actual practice and advice is unrecorded or inaccessible." A few anthropologists, we have seen, have given extracts or snippets of fieldnotes in various ethnographic, personal, and didactic writings. Yet the purposes for these offerings have not been historical record, nor is the record sufficient. Few anthropologists have seen fieldnotes before doing fieldwork. Unless it was some secret London School of Economics (LSE) rite, Jeremy Boissevain's obeisance at the Malinowski icon was unusual: "The only 'anthropologist's field notebook' I was actually able to touch and look at, and this only after many unsuccessful requests, was one of Malinowski's old field notebooks from the Department's museum" (1970: 79).

"While historians of the discipline have approached aspects of its development," Stocking writes, "there is as yet no general historical account of the modern anthropological fieldwork tradition" (1983b: 9). But sources for a conjectural history of fieldnotes there are—in the stream of personal accounts of fieldwork that began with Cushing, in the more reportorial collections of essays and accounts, in prefaces and appendixes to ethnographies, in methodologically aimed volumes and essays, in some historical studies of anthropology, and in the letters and diaries of Cushing, Boas, Malinowski, and Mead. While most of this literature is not directed to fieldnote practice, bits and pieces here and there afford material for a provisional outline.

A full history of fieldnotes would have to consider the notes inspired by the nineteenth-century ethnographic fact-gathering guides which were designed for travelers, missionaries, and administrators by Joseph-Marie Degérando, Lewis Henry Morgan, James Frazer, and anthropologists from the British Association for the Advancement of Science and the Smithsonian Institution (Evans-Pritchard 1951: 70; Pelto and Pelto 1973; Urry 1973, 1984a), but these are beyond our consideration here. We turn first to five founding figures of fieldwork-based anthropology: Frank Hamilton Cushing (b. 1857), Franz Boas (b. 1858), W. H. R. Rivers (b. 1864), Bronislaw Malinowski (b. 1884), and Margaret Mead (b. 1901). Fieldnotes figure pointedly in writings by and about them, more so than for their less innovative or controversial contemporaries. Others will have to uncover the fieldnote practices of such late nineteenth-century fieldworkers as James Mooney and George A. Dorsey among native American groups, and Alfred Cort Haddon among the Torres Straits Melanesians and Aran Islands Irish (Hinsley 1981; Urry 1984b), or A. R. Radcliffe-Brown, Alfred Kroeber, Robert Lowie, and other early twentieth-century anthropologists.

Mead continued her fieldwork and her writings on fieldnotes after her jam-packed Samoa, New Guinea, and Bali years in the 1920s and 1930s. No figure as significant as Mead, however, enters our overview of fieldnotes from the 1930s through the 1980s. For these decades, rather than seeking the example of a few towering figures, we turn to a survey of professional practice. We face the practical problem that perhaps "people who publish autobiographical accounts of their own fieldwork are somehow different from the average ethnographer" (Pelto and Pelto 1973: 247). Average or not, nuggets of candor are what we have, from the fieldwork literature and from the contributors to this volume. When future historians of anthropology examine the real thing in archives—or break into the LSE vault—this first sketch of fieldnote history may be a contribution to their headnotes.

Frank Cushing

In 1879, twenty-two-year-old Frank Hamilton Cushing arrived at Zuni Pueblo, having traveled by railroad from Washington, D.C., to Las Vegas and by muleback from there. He was posted by Smithsonian Institution secretary Spencer F. Baird as part of an expedition of the new Bureau of American Ethnology (BAE), founded earlier that year. "I want you to find out all you can about some typical tribe of Pueblo Indians," Baird told him. "You will probably be gone three months" (Cushing 1882–83; Green 1979: 46). Cushing stayed four and a half years, making one trip east in 1882 in the company of five of his Zuni hosts and publishing his personal account that brought him notoriety, "My Adventures in Zuni," in 1882 and 1883.

At first, Cushing expressed anxiety over the task of salvaging a disappearing way of life, a disappearance to be hastened by the arrival of the railroad in 1880 (Green 1979: 135–36). Yet he soon assumed a style of participant-observation far different from that of his Smithsonian colleagues and closely watched from Washington (Cushing 1882–83; Hinsley 1981: 193–200). He learned to speak Zuni, and in 1881 he was inducted as "Son of the Parrots" into a Zuni clan and then into the Bow priesthood. "I would be willing to devote, say, a year or two more to it," he wrote Baird that year, "to study for a period almost as great, from the *inside,* the life of the Zunis, as I have from the outside" (Green 1979: 150). Publications on Zuni religion, myth, agriculture, food, and crafts would follow.

If "Cushing had few models for his fieldwork" (Hinsley 1983: 56), he certainly had few also for his fieldnote practice, at least at first. The *what* to record was laid down by the BAE director John Wesley Powell. Extensive documentation was called for, so that "by following Powell's lead, Cushing gained information not only on art and technology but also on language and conceptual categories. . . . Powell was so successful in requiring uniformity in the notes taken on collecting trips that the field lists of Matilda Coxe Stevenson at Zia in the 1890s and at Taos in the early 1900s are remarkably similar to those made by Cushing at Zuni in 1879 and 1880" (Parezo 1985: 765–66).

Cushing's assignments from Powell included an 1881 census that amounted to 210 pages and, presumably, most of the other items listed in his 1885 "Schedule of Zuni Material Collected by Frank Hamilton Cushing and Turned In to BAE." Among these were records on 1,619 cards of the members, landholdings, and houses of each clan; a census of the "Esoteric Societies, giving also ranks and titles of Priests"; and "notes" on dance organizations, chiefs, ceremonials, and judicial councils (Green 1979: 148, 151–52).

The *how* of taking fieldnotes is a more complex story. The anthropological standard of the time was transcription with a key informant; in subsequent years BAE anthropologists would even bring Dakota, Omaha, Ponca, Quapaw, and Winnebago informants to Washington to depose texts (Hinsley 1981: 174, 187). On his arrival at the pueblo Cushing spoke no Zuni or Spanish, and his hosts no English. Through a Mexican Spanish interpreter, the BAE party conveyed to the Zuni their mission to collect and document artifacts (Green 1979: 59). Cushing played an active role in this work, but his principal assignment was as "ethnologist." He was instructed by Powell to remain after the collecting party left Zuni and to study the pueblo's art, language, mythology, and sociology (Parezo 1985: 766).

Even while the BAE group was camped nearby, Cushing began observation within Zuni, openly sketching and writing fieldnotes. Zuni disapproval ensued, but Cushing persevered.

> When I took my station on a house-top, sketch-books and colors in hand, I was surprised to see frowns and hear explosive, angry expostulations in every direction. As the day wore on this indignation increased, until at last an old, bush-headed hag approached me, and scowling into my face made a grab at my book and pantomimically tore it to pieces. . . . The sketching and note-taking were essential to my work. I was determined not to give them up. [Cushing 1882–83; Green 1979: 60–61]

Without invitation, Cushing next moved into the house of the "governor," a high-ranking Zuni. He was under constant surveillance, but his writing—into the night—continued (Cushing 1882–83; Green 1979: 67). He soon concluded that his approach to fieldwork was something new. He wrote Baird in October 1879: "My *method* must succeed. I live among the Indians, I eat their food, and sleep in their houses. . . . On account of this, thank God, my notes will contain much that those of all other explorers have failed to communicate" (Green 1979: 136–37). Cushing was also learning Zuni. After ten months' residence he reported to Washington in 1880: "My reward is that today . . . I speak a strangely complicated tongue, not perfectly but fluently and easily" (Hinsley 1983: 57).

It is not clear whether the notes Cushing took openly as he moved about Zuni were narrative descriptions or scratch notes to be turned into descriptive fieldnotes during the evening work he mentions in both "My Adventures in Zuni" and a letter to Baird (Green 1979: 67, 138). The "notes" produced in the evening sessions may well have included the narrative reports to Baird and the BAE, among them the "sixty-eight closely written pages" lost in the mail to Baird early in 1881 (Green 1979: 146; Parezo 1985: 767), an 1884 draft report (Pandey 1972: 325n; Green 1979: 27), and the documents listed in his 1885 "Schedule of Zuni Material." At least some of the evening sessions were devoted to working on descriptive accounts of data acquired through interaction with informants, though how scratch notes, transcribed texts, or memory figured in this we do not know. In 1881, while working by day on the census for Powell, he wrote Baird:

> By night I am as busy with my more proper pursuits. I am making more rapid progress in the study of the *inner life* of these wonderful savages during the past few days than ever before. . . . I have not until within a week secured anything like a complete vocabulary of their consanguinity terms, or any conception of their *true* belief in immortality. [Green 1979: 148]

Later that year he wrote Baird again that the priests of the Bow Society "have required me already to write carefully" ten prayers and songs "embodied in ancient and obsolete language" (Green 1979: 149).

Whether Cushing wrote any additional fieldnotes beyond the unpublished "notes" listed on the 1885 "Schedule" and now at the Southwest Museum is a matter of controversy. In 1956 Edmund Wilson contended that Cushing destroyed his fieldnotes on "the secrets that he had learned in his capacity as a priest" (qtd. in Pandey 1972: 326). While it is "hard to rule out the possibility that Cushing destroyed some of his notes," Pandey writes, he also relates that "there are some prayers and other esoteric texts in the Cushing Papers which the Southwest Museum bought a few years ago" (1972: 326n).

In January 1884 Cushing was recalled to Washington, following an affair in which his advocacy for Zuni land claims antagonized an influential senator and 1884 Republican vice-presidential candidate (Gronewald 1972: 46; Pandey 1972: 325–26). He remained there for two years, writing only one article on Zuni. In 1886, with the backing of Boston philanthropist Mary Hemenway, he returned to the Southwest to direct a program of archaeological and allied research. He was replaced as director by Jesse Walter Fewkes in 1889. Although Cushing accused Fewkes of seizing some 1,000 pages of his notes, apparently neither Cushing nor Fewkes produced much at all in the way of fieldnotes from this work. Frederick Webb Hodge, Cushing's brother-in-law, who prepared his posthumous Zuni publications and was also a member of the Hemenway project, recalled years later that Cushing took no fieldnotes and expected to rely upon his memory and annotations on maps for the later writing he never completed (Green 1979: 13–14, 28–31; Hinsley 1981: 200–204; Hinsley 1983: 60–66).

Cushing returned to the BAE for a few years of productive Zuni ethnographic writing in the early 1890s and attempted another (aborted) archaeological project, in Florida, later in the decade.

In 1885 James Mooney, another young BAE ethnographer who would be more prolific if less controversial than Cushing, received the advice of Washington Mathews, an ethnographer of the Navajo and a friend and defender of Cushing. "Mathews offered Mooney four points of guidance for field work: learn the language; be authoritative but sympathetic; record everything precisely; and avoid preconceptions" (Hinsley 1981: 210).

To these Cushing had added the ingredient of participant-observation (Pandey 1972: 322n). Whatever was thus gained in descriptive fieldnote practice by Cushing at Zuni, however, was a false start for anthropology. He died in 1899 at age forty-two.

But perhaps little was lost.

In Cushing's lifetime, the impression was strong among his colleagues that he was withholding a great deal of information to be written up in the future. Cushing himself contributed to this belief by mentioning in almost every piece he wrote for scholarly journals that the present effort was a sort of preliminary jotting down, to be followed later by further detail from his large store of materials. . . . There can be no doubt [however] that much of his knowledge was never written down. [Gronewold 1972: 37, 44]

Franz Boas

While Cushing was in his final year at Zuni, twenty-five-year-old Franz Boas began his 1883–84 field research among the Baffin Island Eskimo. Like Cushing, Boas studied a living culture; and like Cushing, Boas produced ethnographic writings (Boas 1888), a published personal account (in Stocking 1974a: 44–55; cf. White 1963: 17), and letters (Cole 1983) from which we may assess his fieldnote practice. Because his geographical objectives led him to travel 3,000 miles during his research, however, he did not gain the intimate, situated cultural knowledge that Cushing came to value. Nonetheless, Boas's Arctic fieldwork came much closer to participant-observation than did the Indian studies on the Canadian northwest coast for which he is more famous.

The letters, actually one 500-page document added to incrementally over fifteen months, were delivered to Marie Krackowizer (later Boas) only after the Arctic sojourn. They were written in pencil on notepads roughly three and a half by seven inches in size, as presumably was the chronological fieldnote "journal" Boas also kept (Cole 1983: 16–17). Some of the letters duplicated fieldnote entries, but the "letter-diary" (as Cole labels it) clearly also functioned as a personal diary. For us, its abridged, published version provides a window through which to view Boas's first ethnographic experience.

As would be regular practice in his later fieldwork, Boas interviewed informants about topics of his own priority. "I am . . . busy with questioning the natives who are giving me information on all parts of their homeland." But the exigencies of working in a living culture also brought information not sought directly: "Evenings my good friends came to tell me something or sing to me. Whether I wished to or not I had to write down what they told me." Boas also observed an ongoing way of life: "Signa builds the iglu in four and a half hours"; "Today I hunted just as an Eskimo, with a spear and all that goes with it. I sat beside the water just as patiently as they do. . . . Oxaitung was the only one who caught anything, two seals. . . . Metik was here this evening and told an endlessly long story" (Cole 1983: 24, 25, 28, 40).

There is one indication in the letters that Boas took notes while observing and listening, but this was no doubt indoors. During much of his fieldwork the weather did not permit outdoor notetaking; even indoor writing time was limited: "Now that we have been in the iglu for four hours, it is warm enough to write." It was in the evenings that he "organized" his notes. In the six-week summer period spent waiting for a ship home, Cole tells us, Boas "settled down to work on his ethnographic material" (Cole 1983: 44, 28, 48, 49).

Boas's ethnography *The Central Eskimo,* published in the BAE's 1888 annual report, reflects his fieldwork well. It covers Eskimo geographical distribution, subsistence, material culture, observable "customs," and songs and traditions. There is balance between what he heard and what he saw.

The songs and traditions make up less than one-eighth of the report; the circumstances of their recording are unclear. Boas's personal account of his fieldwork, "A Year among the Eskimo" (Stocking 1974a: 44–55), suggests that he recorded tales during performances rather than with an informant apart from this social context.

> The Eskimo . . . have an enormous stock of folk-lore, of which I succeeded in collecting a considerable amount. The scene when traditions are told is extremely interesting, and I welcomed such occasions. . . . The man who relates the tradition strips off his outer jacket and sits down in the rear of the hut facing the wall. He pulls up his hood, puts on his mittens, and prepares himself by a brief song. The audience stand or squat on the floor of the huts, and now the lamps are lowered, a dim light only filling the small room. I shall tell here one of the most characteristic of these stories, as I heard it in a village on Davis Strait. [Stocking 1974a: 53]

Whether Boas "welcomed such occasions" or "wrote down what they told me whether I wished to or not," it is not clear that his mastery of Eskimo permitted him to transcribe spoken performances. When he arrived in Kikkerton in September 1883, he found that "almost all the Eskimo understand English and I can deal with them very well." On December 23, when he had moved north to Anarnitung, he wrote: "The Eskimo are now sitting around me, telling one another old tales. Too bad I cannot understand them." Yet in one-to-one interview situations, he tried to use Eskimo. Still at Anarnitung, December 30: "Yesterday evening I had a long conversation with an old woman, who came here from far in the north. . . . I am gradually learning to make myself understood somewhat by the Eskimo and to understand them. The language is dreadfully difficult." A month and a half later, on February 16, 1884, his Eskimo had improved, but he could still not record texts. "I listened to stories and wrote down words. My glossary is really growing." Later the same day, he also wrote of hearing "all kinds of stories" told in "pidgin English used by the Eskimo who know English words" (Cole 1983: 21, 33, 34, 41, 42).

On May 18 Boas reached the Davis Strait, where he remained until leaving Baffin Island in August. He brought no Kikkerton Eskimo companions, and the letters do not state whether the Davis Strait Eskimo also spoke English. Perhaps Boas's Eskimo was now sufficient to record the tale as spoken; perhaps the unpublished journal reveals other circumstances of its recording. In any event, the Davis Strait folktale is presented in English narrative form, not in the literal word-for-word translation that would mark his northwest coast publications.

Boas on the Northwest Coast

Boas's four and a half decades of northwest coast research began in Berlin in 1885, the year after he left the Arctic. There he interviewed several Bella Coola Indians, part of a traveling "exhibition," and wrote four short articles that were published in 1886 (Boas 1966: 3–4; Knight 1978: 45–46; White 1963: 18). In September 1886 he arrived on Vancouver Island for his first three-month field trip. In all, Boas would return twelve times, for a total of twenty-nine months. His major fieldwork, from 1886 to 1900, was conducted between the ages of twenty-eight and forty-two, in eight trips of two to four months each. He returned again in 1914 for three weeks, three times in the 1920s for a total of three months, and for three months in 1930–31 at the age of seventy-two. Of equal importance to this fieldwork was his work and correspondence with local northwest coast collaborators—particularly George Hunt, Henry Tate, and James Teit—which extended from Boas's first meeting with Hunt in 1888 through their last work session in 1931 (Rohner 1969: 90–91, 300).

The resulting published work is enormous: 10,000 pages, half in 175 publications on the Kwakiutl and half on other groups (Codere 1959: 61, 1966: xix; Rohner and Rohner 1969: xxiii). Boas prepared material for publication until his death in 1942; his *Kwakiutl Tales* (*Part 2*) appeared in 1943. Some of his unpublished writing was incorporated by Codere into *Kwakiutl Ethnography* (Boas 1966). He also left unpublished letters, diaries, and fieldnotes. An 1888 field journal and letters to his family written from the northwest coast between 1886 and 1931 have been translated from German to English and compiled in a volume that is revealing of Boas's fieldwork and fieldnote practice (Rohner 1969).

The 1886–1900 research involved two goals: first, survey work to determine variation and relationships in the language, physical characteristics, and social customs of the Indian groups; second, "a presentation of the culture as it appears to the Indian himself," for which the Kwakiutl were the focus of attention (Boas 1966: 1–6; cf. Richards 1939: 280–81). Boas had achieved considerable progress in the first goal by the mid-1890s, as summarized in his report to the British Association for the Advancement of Science (Stocking 1974a: 88–107; see also Boas 1966: 7–14).

In the survey work it had been important to document myths and tales because Boas saw a comparison of their elements and motifs as an index to historical relationships (Jacobs 1959; Rohner 1969: 29, 38, 54–55, 63). Yet these traditional narratives were also crucial for Boas's shift during this period from distributional concerns to focused Kwakiutl ethnography (Codere in Boas 1966: 299n; Rohner 1969: 215–16). Myth, he came to see, was "adapted and changed in form according to the genius of the people who borrowed it" (Stocking 1974b: 96). By 1900 his second goal was accomplished. Toward the end of a summer of fieldwork in Kwakiutl art, language, and plant uses, Boas wrote: "I can now prepare a description of the way of life of this tribe, and perhaps have it printed next year. . . . Then, I think, I will have finally finished with this tribe" (Rohner 1969: 262).

"A description of the way of life of this tribe" for Boas did not mean what he had observed of ongoing Kwakiutl behavior during 1886–1900. The balance achieved in his Eskimo ethnography between what he heard and what he saw now tilted steeply toward what he heard or, better, what he asked to hear. "Like most anthropologists of this period, Boas directed his study to the past rather than the present" (Stocking 1974a: 86). But it was a past from which one hundred years of Western contact was filtered out.

An international maritime fur trade had flourished on the northwest coast between 1785 and 1825. In the 1820s, land-based trading posts were established, and the Hudson's Bay Company "effectively became the colonial government" of British Columbia until the 1850s. Vast changes occurred among the Indian societies with the advent of firearms, fortifications, political destabilization and realignments, and, later, epidemics and depopulation. British naval patrols from 1848

shelled native settlements: "Two separate naval expeditions were sent
to bombard the Kwakiutl villages in the Fort Rupert area in 1850–1851
after the murder of three British sailors who had jumped ship." In 1858
the British Columbia gold rush began, and the white population of
less than eight hundred increased by more than 1,000 percent. Chinese, Hawaiians, Black Americans, Chileans, and Japanese appeared
on the scene. Indians remained the majority, however, until the mid-
1880s, when completion of the Canadian Pacific railroad brought
a wave of European immigrants—and young anthropologist Franz
Boas (Knight 1978: 219–44, 301).

The Kwakiutl were one of the more traditional Indian groups, and
this attracted Boas (Rohner 1969: 13). But they had not escaped the
massive transformations around them. By World War I,

> some Kwakiutl groups had a forty to fifty year history as coal miners,
> handloggers, commercial fishermen, and entrepreneurs. . . . The[ir]
> parents and grandparents . . . travelled to the canneries, sawmills,
> hopyards, and cities of Puget Sound and the Fraser Valley for seasonal
> jobs from at least the 1870s. A largely Kwakiutl-operated sawmill and
> cannery functioned at Alert Bay from the early 1880s. Kwakiutl men
> and women had worked as seamen on coastal vessels, as sealers winter-
> ing over in Japanese cities, and had attended Fairs and Expositions in
> Chicago, St. Louis, New York and other cities. [Knight 1978: 50]

None of this escaped Boas, as his letters reveal. They note de-
nominational and ecstatic Christian churches, missionary influence,
Indian mixed farming, migrant farmwork, sawmills, work camps,
salmon canneries, racial mixing, a European-style wedding ceremony,
celebration of Dominion Day, and an 1890 reunion with the Bella
Coola—now cannery workers and migrant laborers—he had met in
Berlin (Rohner 1969: 21, 22, 76, 86, 92–94, 96, 99–100, 127–32, 140,
158, 165). A vivid account in 1900 of the Alert Bay salmon cannery,
with its Chinese/Indian division of labor, is a gem of ethnographic
description (Rohner 1969: 251–53). But all this is in letters, not in
fieldnotes. What went into his fieldnotes?

Texts, with few exceptions. The recording of texts with the help of
bilingual key informants was a common ethnographic procedure in
the late nineteenth century (Jacobs 1959: 119; Rohner and Rohner
1969: xxviii), but Boas "made them the keystone of an ethnographic
style" (Stocking 1974a: 85). As his pool of informants, always paid,
narrowed from anybody he could find on his earlier trips to a few key

informants in later work, so his procedures of "transcription," as he called it from 1886 (Rohner 1969: 63, 71) also changed. Although his Columbia University students attest that he gave them little methodological advice, did not discuss methods in his "Methods" course, which was about theory (Mead 1959a; cf. Boas 1938), and "left no explicit statement of his field technique" (Smith 1959: 53), his letters do shed light on his fieldnote practice.

On his first trip in 1886 he moved from community to community, contacting local whites to help locate "his Indian" for the next day or so. He then spent long hours transcribing, either in English or, as he preferred, in an Indian language, followed by his informant's translation into English. These transcriptions were then reread and recopied at night. Boas wrote several times of falling behind in his "copying," and he noted in his letters the progress of "my manuscript" from 160 to 212 to eventually 326 pages, with some material saved to be "worked over" in New York. He intended to publish these recopied transcriptions first as journal articles and then as a book. On this trip he secured texts in Bella Coola, Comox, and three other Indian languages (Rohner 1969: 19–77).

On later trips his methods were similar, although by 1890 he could use the Chinook lingua franca for work with some non-English-speaking Indians, and he would occasionally transcribe first in English and then have his informant translate back into the Indian language (Rohner 1969: 117, 166). In 1900 he spent time with informants revising Kwakiutl texts he had recorded earlier. A page from his Kwakiutl fieldnotes, reproduced in *Kwakiutl Ethnography* (Boas 1966: vi), shows the results: lines of Kwakwala and English alternate in neat handwriting on lined paper. In 1900 Boas recorded fieldnotes on Kwakiutl art (Rohner 1969: 246–47), but certainly the bulk of his fieldnotes consists of texts, plus his separate notes on Indian material objects, and human and skeletal measurements.

Boas and Hunt

The major change in Boas's text transcription methods came with his collaboration with George Hunt, just three years older than Boas (Codere 1966: xxix). Of a Kwakiutl-*Metis* Fort Rupert family, Hunt was employed as an interpreter for the government Indian Reserve Commission in 1879 and had begun work on Kwakiutl traditions on his own before meeting Boas (Knight 1978: 52, 275). They met on

Boas's second trip, in 1888, for one morning's work; Hunt was then working as a court interpreter (Rohner 1969: 91). He is not mentioned in the 1889 or 1890 letters, and no letters from 1891 are included in Rohner's compilation. In 1893, while curating a Vancouver Island exhibit at the Chicago World's Fair, Boas again met his "former interpreter," so it is likely they had by then had more than one morning's contact. In Chicago, Boas taught Hunt to write Kwakiutl texts in the manner Boas had himself devised (Boas 1966: 4–5; Codere 1966: xv, xxviii).

In 1894 Boas returned to the northwest coast for his only fall-winter trip since his first in 1886; all the others were in summer months. He met Hunt in Fort Rupert, and they worked closely together, especially during the Winter Ceremonial activities. It was a tense relationship, Boas's letters reveal: "He knows exactly how I depend upon him" (Rohner 1969: 183). In 1894 Hunt also began sending Boas texts by mail, and their correspondence continued until Hunt's death in 1933; over these years Hunt supplied Boas with two-thirds of his published Kwakiutl data (Rohner and Rohner 1969: xxiii, xxviii; White 1963: 30–33). On his 1897 field trip Boas reviewed Kwakiutl texts with Hunt, including ones he had sent to Boas in New York (Rohner 1969: 211–19).

On Boas's 1900 trip, when Hunt and his family were working in the canneries (summer employment for many Kwakiutl), the two men worked together on Kwakiutl text revisions in the evenings and for a few days at the end of the season (Rohner 1969: 246–62). Boas now felt comfortable having Hunt continue locally on his own: "I hope George Hunt will be able to do by himself many things which yet have to be done. I revised much of what he had done and can see that he does everything properly and that he does not pull my leg. I find him quite dependable, more than I had thought" (Rohner 1969: 261). Hunt would visit New York in 1901 and 1903 (White 1963: 33), and Boas would meet him again in Fort Rupert in the 1920s and in 1930.

As Hunt's texts came in, the Kwakiutl volumes came out (White 1963: 23–33). The first, *The Social Organization and Secret Societies of the Kwakiutl Indians* (428 pages), published in 1897, was based upon Hunt's work, as the preface acknowledged. The two volumes of *Kwakiutl Texts* (795 pages) published in 1905 and 1906 were also Boas's editions of materials Hunt had collected between 1895 and 1903. Boas next turned to his own fieldwork materials and published in 1909 *The Kwakiutl of Vancouver Island* (222 pages on crafts, art, food, and technology, including many texts) and in 1910 *Kwakiutl Tales* (495 pages), his own texts and translations. Three more volumes of Hunt texts and translations appeared in 1921, 1925, and 1930: *Ethnology of the Kwakiutl* (1,418 pages), *Contributions to the Ethnology of the Kwakiutl* (357 pages), and *The Religion of the Kwakiutl Indians* (572 pages). Boas's final two volumes were again his own work: a second collection of *Kwakiutl Tales* (458 pages) was published in English translations in 1935 and in Kwakwala in 1943. Evidently Boas placed a higher publishing priority on Hunt's work than his own.

If texts are a type of fieldnotes, then most of these Kwakiutl volumes consist of edited fieldnotes. They are presented with few synthesizing passages: "Boas's conclusions on . . . various aspects of Kwakiutl culture are austerely restricted to those he can base on documentation he can share with the reader" (Codere 1966: xx, xxiii). The corpus is loosely organized; the Boas volumes separate technology from folktales, but the Hunt-derived volumes, published as material arrived, mix together a variety of topics (Codere 1966: xxx; White 1963: 24–30). *Kwakiutl Ethnography* (Boas 1966), the posthumous volume edited by Helen Codere, is much the same, not "the summary, synthesizing volume on the Kwakiutl" that Boas had planned to write (Mead 1972: 183). It is based on manuscripts that covered several topics and were left with no chapter outline; Codere (1966) added sections from earlier Boas publications to give it coherence.

The Kwakiutl texts are depositions transcribed by Boas or Hunt as recited to them by informants; others, based on his own reminiscence, were composed by Hunt directly. They concern techniques no longer practiced; memories of events and customary behavior; narrations of ceremonies and speeches recalled for the ethnographer's transcription (Boas 1966). They are not verbatim records of ongoing social performances. "He never intensively considered style in oral literature. . . . Boas . . . appear[s] to have lost sight of audience and community as loci of many of the factors which determine style" (Jacobs 1959: 134–35). Boas did not attempt to study oratory until his 1930 field trip and found then that he could not record it; his Kwakwala ability was sufficient for seated informant narrative but not for natural conversation or formal speeches (Rohner 1969: 290–97; cf. Boas 1966: 352–54).

Perhaps because Hunt produced such a harvest of texts, Boas did not follow the stricture of cross-informant checking which he urged upon others (Rohner and Rohner 1969: xxi). In Boas's Tsimshian textual work with Henry Tate, even more rules were broken; tales were

written by Tate first in English and then in Tsimshian, and some even
appear to be based upon texts Boas himself recorded before meeting
Tate (Maud 1989).

It is difficult to sustain the argument that Boas's texts "present
Kwakiutl culture as it appears to the Indian himself," or that they are
"a solution to the problem of acquiring ethnographic data as free as
possible from the certain self-contamination of the data by the ethnographer" (Codere 1966: xv). In pursuing his goals on the northwest
coast from 1886 to 1900, Boas was selective and worked from his own
list of priorities (Smith 1959: 55). In an 1888 letter he wrote: "Tomorrow I shall have reached the point where I shall have no more questions and will have to allow myself to be guided by the Indian. This is
usually the point at which a brief survey becomes unprofitable" (Rohner 1969: 103). Hunt's texts also were produced in response to questions from Boas (Boas 1966: 35).

Back to Participant-Observation

The one exception to the textual method is Boas's remarkable participant-observer account of the 1894 Fort Rupert Winter Ceremonial
(Boas 1966: 179–241). Boas earlier published text-based passages from
Hunt on this ritual cycle, including one on the 1895–96 Winter Ceremonial, in his first major Kwakiutl volume in 1897 and another in
1930, both reprinted in part in *Kwakiutl Ethnography* (Boas 1966: 242–
98). These are flat and dry compared to the vivid description of the
November 3–December 15 events that Boas witnessed in 1894.

> November 19. . . . In the fourth song the word "raven" occurred. As
> soon as it was heard, one of the Cannibal dancers of the Koskimo
> became excited. He jumped up, crying, "*hap, hap, hap,*" trembling all
> over. His attendants rushed up to him, the people beat time violently,
> and the drummer beat the drum, while the Cannibal dancer tried to rush
> up to the people and to bite them. But he was held back by his six
> attendants. Slowly he moved to the rear of the house, where he went
> once to the left, once to the right; then he continued his course around
> the fire. When he came to the door, he went out, followed by his
> attendants. The Koskimo called four times, "*yu!*" [Boas 1966: 186]

Boas includes a section in which Kwakiutl masqueraded as white
policemen and a judge, and an allusion during a performance to fear
and defiance of the police (Boas 1966: 196, 234–35). By this time these

performances had been outlawed (Codere 1966: xxviii; Knight 1978: 268). Presented in dated installments, the account reads like fieldnotes.

I doubt that Boas knew exactly what to make of these notes. They cover only part of the Winter Ceremonial period and have none of the finality in tone of presentation that the text-based, "full" accounts do. They account for half of the unpublished "Kwakiutl Ethnography" manuscripts that Boas left, and appeared only in 1966.

Boas's field letters, published three years later, reveal the circumstances of recording the 1894 Winter Ceremonial sequence. The first day's feast was paid for by Boas: $14.50 for a round of hardtack and molasses for 250 Indians. This netted him a set of reciprocal invitations. To keep up, he was forced to take "stenographic notes"—scratch notes—which he went over with Hunt following each event. Hunt was also employed to recall speeches for transcription; on December 1, when Hunt was not with him, Boas wrote, "I did not know what was going on" (Rohner 1969: 177–89). The pace was taxing. At his busiest, on November 23, Boas produced a 10,000-word description of the day's events (Boas 1966: 201–17).

But the opportunity to see Kwakiutl ceremony in performance did not thrill Boas as one might expect. "There is never a quiet moment here. I will be glad when this is all over," he wrote November 28. On his last day he lamented, "Today is packing day. I have not done much, though." And on board the steamer: "My stay in Fort Rupert was not at all agreeable, although I saw and learned a great deal" (Boas 1966: 186–90). Without his accustomed text transcription practices to rely on, participant-observation left Boas unsettled and agitated. At home, he returned to the Hunt texts and the "emotional release" he enjoyed in editing them (Jacobs 1959: 120). The 1894 fieldnotes remained unpublished during his lifetime, nor did he return again in fall or winter months to witness Kwakiutl ceremonial activities until 1930, when he filmed them—and unfortunately lost the film (Boas 1966: 171). His one other winter trip, for a month in 1923, was spent working on Kwakiutl texts with Hunt in Bella Bella, not at Fort Rupert (Rohner 1969: 277–87). "Participant observation was much less possible for him than for most of his students" (Jacobs 1959: 127).

Boas's texts represent his attempt to salvage the culture of the northwest coast from the acculturative pressures he noted in his letters and, on occasion, in his published general statements (Rohner 1969: 13). The exigencies of the situation could be severe; only three Kathlamet speakers, for example, remained when Boas collected texts in that language (Stocking 1974a: 116). But the cultural life he recorded was in reality that of the earlier nineteenth century, and a product of three generations of fur trade transformations (Knight 1978: 218). Boas himself was aware of the shaky foundations of his enterprise. "It must be remembered that these events occurred about 1870 or 1874, and that they were told between 1900 and 1925—time enough to allow the imagination free play with the actual occurrence," he wrote of Hunt's texts on Kwakiutl shamans (Boas 1966: 125).

The major loss for anthropology, which Boas would influence enormously in the early decades of the twentieth century, was that the salvage enterprise "led to a distorted notion of the separation of culture from society, practice from person" (Gruber 1970: 1297). Participant-observation led to descriptive fieldnotes on Signa building an iglu and Oxaitung catching seals among the Central Eskimo. That course would lead to police masquerades in Winter Ceremonials and Indians at work in canneries among the Kwakiutl. Boas chose to transcribe and edit texts instead.

W. H. R. Rivers

While Boas was shaping the development of anthropology in the United States in the first two decades of the twentieth century, in England his counterpart was W. H. R. Rivers, the most influential figure in British anthropology until his death in 1922 (Fortes 1957: 158; Stocking 1984a: 138). As Alfred Cort Haddon in the 1890s had moved the center of gravity in professional British anthropology from armchair theorizing to field surveys, so Rivers moved it further, from survey to intensive fieldwork (Stocking 1983a; Urry 1984b). The list of anthropologists whose careers he influenced, both in and out of "the Cambridge school," includes a generation of pre– and post–World War I fieldworkers now largely unread, with the exceptions of Radcliffe-Brown and Malinowski (Langham 1981: 171–77, 202–300; Slobodin 1978: 40–41, 48; Stocking 1983a: 80–85; Urry 1984a: 47–48).

Already widely traveled, and with professional accomplishments in neurophysiology and psychology, William Halse Rivers Rivers signed on with Haddon's Cambridge Anthropological Expedition to Torres Straits in 1898 at age thirty-four (Slobodin 1978: 1–26; Stocking 1983a: 75–77). As a psychologist, Rivers was responsible for tests of color and spatial perception, and his results were included in the second of the expedition's six published volumes. But more important for the development of anthropological field research was his work on genealogies among the Torres Straits Melanesians.

While other members of the team traveled to the Papua coast of New Guinea and to Sarawak, Rivers remained continuously on Mer Island from May to September 1898; he then traveled with four others to Mabuiag Island for five more weeks of research. The fieldwork was not participant-observation; it was conducted in pidgin English and drew heavily upon information from local white residents (Stocking 1983a: 77). Through formal interviews with Mer and Mabuiag islanders Rivers secured the data on kinship, naming, marriage, and social organization included in Volumes 5 (1904) and 6 (1908) of the expedition's reports. This material was obtained through the genealogical method that Rivers "perfected" on Mabuiag (Slobodin 1978: 25–26).

Rivers published the first account of his method in the *Journal of the Royal Anthropological Institute* in 1900. His "Genealogical Method of Anthropological Inquiry" (1910) was written after further use of the approach in his 1901–2 Indian and 1907–8 Pacific field research. In it he states explicitly how genealogical records are to be transcribed in fieldwork.

> In collecting the pedigrees the descendants in both the male and female lines are obtained, but in writing them out . . . it is well to record on one sheet only the descendants in one line with cross-references to other sheets for the descendants in the other line. . . . I have found it convenient to record the names of males in capital letters and those of females in ordinary type, and I always put the name of the husband to the left of that of the wife. In polygynous or polyandrous marriages I include the names of the wives or husbands in square brackets. [Rivers 1910: 98–99]

For each individual in the genealogy, information should be listed on localities of residence and origin, totem, clan membership, adoption, and "any other facts about each person which may possibly have any social significance." Genealogies should be taken from at least three persons in a community, with experts in such knowledge sought out and young men avoided as informants. Kin terms used for non-kin should also be asked about following the genealogical interrogation (1910: 99–102).

When the overlapping genealogies of all members of a community are collected, a "register of marriages," past and present, results. Rules regulating marriages may be formulated, whether or not such rules exist in the culture studied; conflict between established cultural rules and practice may also be analyzed. In addition, genealogical data can be used to study inheritance, migration, ritual roles and obligations, demography, heredity and other topics (Rivers 1910: 103–7; see Hackenberg 1973: 293–96). With Rivers's formulation, genealogies as a form of fieldnote record became a fixture in anthropological research.

"Intensive" Fieldwork

Three years after the Torres Straits expedition, Rivers arrived in south India in 1901 for a survey of the five "tribes" living in the Nilgiri Hills. He began with the comparatively well-documented Toda and recorded the genealogies of all seventy-two families, which he included in his 800-page monograph of 1906. The analyses of his method's results constitute in David Schneider's view "the first careful field studies of kinship" (1968: 15; cf. Fortes 1957: 158). But Rivers's efforts came to include religion as much as social organization. Unlike the Torres Straits, where "ceremonial had disappeared, and the only record of it to be obtained was that derived from the memories of the oldest inhabitants," Toda ritual and religious life was in full bloom around him. With more than enough to occupy his stay of about five months, Rivers abandoned his survey for intensive study (Rivers 1906: 1–4; Slobodin 1978: 28–30; Stocking 1983a: 89; Walker 1986: 1–9).

The Toda is revealing of Rivers's fieldwork practice (1906: 2–3, 7–14, 462–66). He worked with three assistants. Two, a forest ranger and a catechist, were primarily interpreters, though one of them later sent his own fieldnotes on Toda ethnography to Rivers. The third, himself a Toda, secured informants for interviews and provided Rivers with oral reports of rituals at which he had been present. In his first few weeks, Rivers spoke freely with Toda "in public" about "aspects of social life and religion," questioning bystanders and participants in ongoing activities. Finding that many matters could not be pursued in this way, however, he turned to afternoon "private interviews" with one or two informants on religion and genealogy. In his morning sessions, open to "anyone who chose to come," Rivers conducted psychological tests and gathered ethnographic leads to be followed in his afternoon work.

His genealogical method was complicated by the Toda taboo on speaking the names of dead ancestors. The data for each family were obtained from members of other families and cross-checked with

several informants, as were his findings on ritual. As they were acquired, the genealogical records were also utilized during the formal
interviews.

> An account of a Toda funeral, for instance, with its many *dramatis
> personae* would probably have baffled my powers of comprehension if I
> had not had my book of genealogies for reference. I always worked
> with this book by my side whenever I was investigating any ceremonial
> in which the social side of life was concerned. I asked for a description of
> some ceremony recently performed of which the memories were fresh.
> The chief actors in the ceremony were always mentioned by name; and
> whenever a name occurred, I looked up the clan and family of the
> person in question and noticed his relationship to other persons who
> had taken part in the ceremony (Rivers 1906: 466).

Rivers's "notebooks" came to include many Toda words, and he
quoted a sentence from his fieldnotes to establish this point (1906: 9).
His fieldnotes included both cultural prescriptions and case accounts
obtained in his interviews, and some information from observations
and questions answered at rituals and sacred sites. From what Rivers
wrote about his "method of indirect corroboration," it is likely that his
fieldnotes were organized chronologically rather than topically: "The
whole of Toda ceremonial and social life forms such an intricate web of
closely related practices that I rarely set out to investigate some one
aspect of the life of the people without obtaining information bearing
on many other wholly different aspects" (Rivers 1906: 10–11).

Notes and Queries

In 1907, after Volume 4 of the Torres Straits report and *The Toda* had
been published, the British Association for the Advancement of Science formed a committee, including Rivers, for a fourth edition of
Notes and Queries on Anthropology. This guidebook for ethnographic
fact-finding by travelers and local amateurs had first appeared in 1874
(Richards 1939: 273); the new edition, in which Rivers took a leading
role, would be used by professional fieldworkers (among them Malinowski) as well. Appearing in 1912, it epitomized the methodological
lessons Rivers had learned in the Nilgiri Hills (Langham 1981: 199,
274, 297, 327; Slobodin 1978: 46–47; Stocking 1983a: 89–93; Urry
1973). A precise statement of what Rivers meant by "intensive" fieldwork followed in 1913.

A typical piece of intensive work is one in which the worker lives for a
year or more among a community of perhaps four or five hundred
people and studies every detail of their life and culture; in which he
comes to know every member of the community personally, in which
he is not content with generalized information, but studies every feature
of life and custom in concrete detail and by means of the vernacular
language. . . . It is only by such work that it is possible to discover the
incomplete and even misleading character of much of the vast mass of
survey work which forms the existing material of anthropology. [qtd.
in Kuper 1973: 20]

But it was others who would apply Rivers's dicta. In 1907–8 he
spent a year in survey work throughout Polynesia and Melanesia
(Richards 1939: 277, 299; Slobodin 1978: 40–43). He was now more
"committed to the idea that the elemental social structure of any group
would be systematically revealed in its kinship terminology" (Stocking 1983a: 86) than he was to doing intensive holistic research himself.
His interest in rules versus the discrepancies of individual cases was
abandoned as he converted to historical and diffusionist causes. In 1914
he wrote: "One who applies a given term of relationship to another
person has to behave towards that person in certain definite ways. He
has to perform certain duties towards him, and enjoys certain privileges (Rivers 1914: 45). The results of his retreat from the textures of
"intensive" fieldwork to the flatness of genealogical surveys were
presented in his controversial *History of Melanesian Society* in 1914.

During the World War I years Rivers's wartime medical work re-
kindled his psychological interests. In the period up to his death,
anthropology was only one interest among many, including psychiatry, the study of dreams, and a 1921 Labour Party parliamen-
tary candidacy—later assumed (unsuccessfully) by H. G. Wells when
Rivers, then president of the Royal Anthropological Institute, died
five months before the November 1922 election (Slobodin 1978: 58–
85).

Bronislaw Malinowski

Malinowski was born in Poland in 1884, the year Cushing was
recalled from Zuni to Washington and Boas concluded his Eskimo
fieldwork. He is viewed by his students and students' students as "the
founder of the profession of social anthropology in Britain" (Kuper

1973: 13; cf. Evans-Pritchard 1951: 93). Unlike Cushing, Boas, or Rivers, however, his fieldwork was in fact preceded by professional training in anthropology. Already inoculated to the subject by Sir James Frazer's *Golden Bough,* and at work on library research that would lead to a book on the Australian Aboriginal family in 1913, Malinowski arrived for postgraduate study at the London School of Economics in 1910. He studied with Edward Westermarck, who had conducted fieldwork using the local language (Arabic) in Morocco, and C. G. Seligman, veteran of the Torres Straits expedition and survey ethnographer of New Guinea Papuans, Sri Lanka Veddas, and, later, "pagan tribes" of the Sudan. He also read and met the Cambridge anthropologists Haddon and Rivers (Firth 1967, 1981; Kuper 1973).

In September 1914, at age thirty, Malinowski arrived in New Guinea and spent six months on the southeast coast, most of this time among the Mailu. A 210-page report on Mailu was rapidly completed before he began his first year of fieldwork among the 1,300 Trobriand Islanders in June 1915. He left in May 1916 to spend the next sixteen months in Australia. With the help of his future wife Elsie Masson, herself author of a 1915 book on Australia's Northern Territory and knowledgeable about Aborigines, he sorted through his fieldnotes and drafted the long essay "Baloma; The Spirits of the Dead in the Trobriand Islands" (1916). In October 1917 he returned to the Trobriands for a second year of fieldwork. His first Trobriand book, *Argonauts of the Western Pacific*—again written with Elsie's assistance—was published in 1922, the year of Rivers's death. A teaching career at the London School of Economics in the 1920s and 1930s, the training of virtually all the next generation of British anthropologists, and a stream of Trobriand publications culminating in *Coral Gardens and Their Magic* in 1935, would follow (Firth 1967; Kaberry 1957; Kuper 1973; Richards 1939: 293n; Stocking 1983a; Wayne 1985).

In 1967, long after his death in 1942, Malinowski's diaries were published, covering all his 1914–15 (Mailu) fieldwork and most of his second Trobriand year, 1917–18. Controversial for many reasons, they are valuable for many others (Geertz 1988; Stocking 1974b; Wayne 1985). With the methodological passages of *Argonauts* and *Coral Gardens,* they open up Malinowski's fieldwork practices and permit us to evaluate his distinct contributions from the viewpoint of what went into and how he used his fieldnotes.

The first scene of fieldnote writing, just two days after Malinowski's September 1914 arrival in New Guinea, is in a Motu village near

Port Moresby. At the home of Ahuia Ova, who had been an informant for Seligman,

> the old men had gathered to give me information. They squatted in a row along the wall. . . . The bamboo pipe circulated rapidly. A little intimidated by this conclave, I sat down at the table and opened a book. Got information concerning *iduhu* [Motu social groups], genealogy, asked about the village chief, etc. At sundown the old men left. [Malinowski 1967: 10]

After a week of work with Ahuia, including visits to gardens and homes, Malinowski identified "two basic defects" of this work: "(1) I have rather little to do with the savages on the spot, do not observe them enough, and (2) I do not speak their language. . . . although I am trying to learn Motu" (1967: 13). Correcting these two defects would lie at the core of his Trobriand successes, forming one of Malinowski's two principal contributions to anthropology.

In mid-October of 1914 Malinowski arrived in Mailu. His work there was conducted in silent dialogue with Seligman and Rivers. There are diary references to "Seligman"—his survey volume *The Melanesians of British New Guinea* (1910)—being used to prime Malinowski for visits to the village or inspire his writing (1967: 67, 90; for Trobriands, see 113–14). More telling, and more frequent, are references to "Rivers" and to *Notes and Queries,* the 1912 edition in which Rivers's fullest vision of anthropological fieldwork was adumbrated. Malinowski read "Rivers"—perhaps *The History of Melanesian Society* published in 1914—on the ship to New Guinea, and certainly *Notes and Queries* during his Mailu fieldwork (1967: 5, 30, 64–67; for Trobriands, see 280). Again this reading affected his fieldnotes, as may have conversation with Haddon, to whom he showed his notes when Haddon visited Mailu in November 1914 (1967: 36).

Malinowski also made diary entries about "synthesizing," "working on," "looking over," and "rearranging" his Mailu fieldnotes (1967: 30, 40, 67). Although this fieldwork resulted in a *Notes and Queries*–directed ethnography (Kaberry 1957: 80; Stocking 1983a: 96), the reviewing of his fieldnotes *in the field* prefigures the second principal contribution to anthropology that his Trobriand work would make.

The importance to Malinowski's research of analyzing fieldnotes *in the field* is evident in many references in the 1917–18 Trobriand diary (1967: 133, 146, 153, 155, 159–61, 188, 217, 249, 289, 292). For example, January 18, 1918: "Decided to spend the day reviewing my notes and listing problems. This went slowly at first, then specific problems emerged" (1967: 188). The diaries also indicate how removed from verandah survey or "old men in a hut" transcription (Richards 1939: 298n; Stocking 1983a: 95–96) was the process by which data entered the notebooks. Interviews with seated informants were still used to fill in such details as the terminology of gardening or sailing canoe parts (1967: 184–85; cf. Nadel 1939: 318; Richards 1939: 300), but discoveries were made by participating and observing. December 20, 1917:

> At 10:30 they decided to go for a *poulo* [fishing expedition] and I set out with them. *Megwa* [magic] in the house of Yosala Gawa. . . . Rode in a boat. Many observations. I learn a great deal. . . . I observe tabu. Technology of the hunt, which would have required weeks of research. Opened-up horizons filled me with joy. [1967: 158]

Fieldnotes were written not on the spot but from memory over the next two days (1967: 159–61; cf. 267 on taro garden observations and fieldnotes). A few references to "copying" and "loose notes," however, suggest that he may also have made scratch notes on occasion (1967: 255, 270–71).[1]

Malinowski's published portrayals of his fieldwork methods—heroically in *Argonauts* (1922: 2–25), mock-humbly but more revealingly in *Coral Gardens* (1935, vol. 1: 317–40, 452–82)—represent much that was common to the post-Rivers generation, if not also to Rivers (Stocking 1983a: 105, 110–111). By appropriating too much, they obscure Malinowski's signal contributions. If he did so more fully and consistently, he was by no means the first to live among the natives, observe ongoing rituals, collect concrete cases, induce patterns from data, write chronological fieldnotes, record native views, speak the native language, or produce a corpus of texts (Malinowski 1922: 2–25); Cushing, Boas, Rivers, and others, collectively, had done all these things. But in doing them all himself, plus using the native language to put "speech in action" (Richards 1939: 302) into his fieldnotes and creating positive feedback between his fieldnotes and his fieldwork, Malinowski did achieve something novel.

[1] In his 1940 Mexico fieldwork Malinowski recorded notes directly in the marketplace (Malinowski and de la Fuente 1982: 64).

Speech in Action

In *Man and Culture* (Firth 1957), the collective evaluation of Malinowski by his students, Edmund Leach asked, "What was Malinowski's really fundamental contribution?" His answer was "in two things: . . . the severely curtailed use of the professional informant, and . . . the *theoretical* assumption that the total field of data under the observation of the field-worker must somehow fit together and make sense" (Leach 1957: 120). Leach's second point, embodied in Malinowski's functionalism, arose for Malinowski, I suggest, because of the kind of fieldnotes he recorded in the Trobriands but not in Mailu. This was dependent upon the ability to speak the language comfortably, which he achieved during the first six months of his second Trobriand year (Malinowski 1935, vol. 1: 453; vol. 2: ix). But language was a means, not an end. Leach's first point is correct in that Malinowski moved away from the question-and-answer use of the seated informant. Rather than "curtailing" the role of the informant, however, Malinowski radically expanded and redefined it.

To encounter the informant or, in the parlance of later social anthropology, the actor, Malinowski embarked on "a new method of collecting evidence" (1926: 146). The anthropologist

> must go out into the villages, and see the natives at work in gardens, on the beach, in the jungle; he must sail with them to distant sandbanks and to foreign tribes, and observe them in fishing, trading and ceremonial overseas expeditions. Information must come to him full-flavored from his own observations of native life, and not be squeezed out of reluctant informants as a trickle of talk. [1926: 147; cf. 1922: 6–8]

As Malinowski did this, "his first line of evidence was always first-hand observation" (Leach 1957: 120). "What is significant is the emphasis on *practice* . . . as the 'reality' of social life, as against . . . the merely verbal formulation" (Fortes 1957: 160; cf. Ortner 1984). So observations of fishing and taro gardening, as his diary shows, went into his fieldnotes. But just as significantly, he opened up the "trickle of talk" to a flow. As he observed, he also listened.

For Malinowski, to "speak the language" meant "to think the culture." He could point to local whites who could do the first but not the second (1916: 272–73; cf. 1922: 5–6). What made the difference was the situations of speech in which Malinowski placed himself. "Lan-

guage," he argued, "exists only in actual use within the context of real
utterance" (1935, vol. 2: v). As he "put aside camera, note book and
pencil . . . to join in himself in what [was] going on," he would "sit
down and listen and share in their conversations" (1922: 21). The
"imponderabilia of actual life and of typical behavior" he recorded
included observed action *and* heard speech. Both went into fieldnotes
"put down more and more in Kiriwinian, till at last I found myself
writing exclusively in that language, rapidly taking notes, word for
word, at each statement" (1922: 23–24). Malinowski did record texts
in interview sessions with individual informants (1922: 24; 1967: 161,
270), but texts were also elicited in conversations at the site of action
and written as fieldnotes later, to be checked with the informant as
necessary (1935, vol. 2: 4–6, 23–25; Stocking 1983a: 102).

It was Malinowski's student Audrey Richards (1939: 302) who called
the approach "speech in action": "Besides questioning his informants,
the anthropologist listens to speech between natives in the natural
context of daily life. . . . [This provides] information unlikely to be
given in direct answer to a question, but sometimes vouchsafed during
the performance of an associated act, or overheard in casual conversation." Recording such data, as a discovery procedure, was essential to
Malinowski's effort "to grasp the native's point of view, his relations to
life, to realize *his* vision of *his* world" (1922: 25). It is also at the heart of
what anthropologists mean today when they speak of participant-
observation, which is in large measure situated listening à la Malinowski.

The observed and heard, Malinowski wrote, "can and ought to be
scientifically formulated and recorded" (1922: 19). It is from such
"richly documented" fieldnotes, as opposed to the "schematic" notes
of Rivers (Stocking [1983a: 99] has examined both), that I suggest
Malinowski's functional approach arose. At its least elaborated and
most powerful, it is the "consideration of the same data consecutively
from a number of points of view, such as the environmental, the
structural, the normative, the technological, the dogmatic" (Richards
1957: 26). Thus Malinowski could view the same fieldnote description—of a garden ritual, say—in its economic, political, legal, magical, educational, mythical, and other aspects.

Fieldnote entries of the matured Malinowskian approach were never
discretely about magic, or fishing, or social control, or the family.
"The mass of gears all turning and grinding on each other," as Ralph
Linton put it (qtd. in Piddington 1957: 51), traveled from observed and

heard social reality into fieldnotes, and into functionalist ethnography. To his students it was an inspired, and productive vision (Fortes 1957: 164; Kaberry 1957: 81–82; Kuper 1984: 198–99; Powdermaker 1966: 38; Richards 1957: 19, 25, 26). Not a general theory, Malinowski's functionalism was "a theory of ethnographic field-work" (Leach 1957: 119; cf. Beattie 1965: 6).

Fieldnotes-Fieldwork Interaction

Cross-cutting the several functionally integrated aspects of individual Trobriand events and conversations was Malinowski's concept of institution, better exemplified in his monographs than defined in theoretical writings. In *Argonauts,* the *kula* trading institution is shown in its technological, social, political, economic, and magical components. In *Coral Gardens,* analysis of the institution of horticulture leads to consideration of "the family and kinship system, political organization, land tenure, technical processes, religious and magic beliefs, and the language of magic used in gardening" (Richards 1957: 27–28). In the ethnographies, institutions also "grind on each other."

What connects the ethnography and the events is the fieldnotes. Each fieldnote entry relates to several institutions; each institutional ethnography draws on the same body of fieldnotes and analyzes the "functional" relations the focal institution has to others. But how did the fieldnotes come to have the richness that made all this possible? The point that investigating one aspect of social life led to another had already been made, as we have seen, by Rivers in *The Toda* (cf. Kaberry 1957: 76n). Malinowski could have controlled and screened this out, as he undoubtedly did in writing his topical Mailu monograph. Instead, he chose to maximize the multiple-aspect nature of Trobriand events and conversations in his fieldnotes.

Malinowski had apparently begun his note-taking with topical files (Richards 1957: 25), but in *Argonauts* he advocated chronological fieldnotes, "an ethnographic diary, carried on systematically throughout the course of one's work" (1922: 21). At some point he had concluded that pre-indexed fieldnotes were inadequate for the social reality he was seeking to record. I have suggested that recording "speech in action" as much as "going out into the village" was involved in this change. Next, the frequent "working on" and "rearranging" of his fieldnotes became a new form of mental indexing. It also identified gaps and problems.

So did the charts he developed to list, sort, summarize, and present fieldnote data (1916: 212; 1922: 14–16; 1935, vol. 1: 328–29, 339), which made a deep impression on his students (Kuper 1984: 198–99; Richards 1957: 25). Malinowski began this charting from his fieldnotes during the first Trobriands field trip (1935, vol. 1: 463, 466). He also used the months in Australia between his two Trobriand fieldwork periods to analyze his notes (1935, vol. 1: 328, 467). During this time he wrote "Baloma," which systematically exhausts data available in his first year's fieldnotes. He also wrote "an outline" of the *kula,* to be redrafted several times during his second fieldwork year (1922: 13).

In the Trobriands, Malinowski came to realize that a fieldwork-fieldnote dialectic was an integral part of the doing of fieldwork.

> In the field I always found it an invaluable device to map out the facts already obtained, to consider how they were related to each other and to proceed with the investigation of the bigger, more widely integrated type of facts thus arrived at. [1935, vol. 1: 457]

> The greatest source of all the inadequacies and gaps in my own field-work has resulted from the dire methodological fallacy: get as many "facts" as you can while in the field, and let the construction and organisation of your evidence wait till you write up your material. [1935, vol. 1: 467]

Audrey Richards's dictum "Spend one week analysing material to every three spent in observation" (1939: 308) may well have come from her teacher.

Malinowski also concluded that ethnography, as fieldwork process and as written product, was something to be constructed, not merely conducted and reported (Leach 1957: 134).

> While making his observations the field-worker must constantly con-struct: he must place isolated data in relation to one another and study the manner in which they integrate. . . . The principals of social organi-zation, of legal constitution, of economics and religion have to be constructed by the observer out of a multitude of manifestations of varying significance and relevance. . . . He must constantly switch over from observation and accumulated evidence to theoretical moulding, and then back to collecting data again. [Malinowski 1935, vol. 1: 317, 321]

The achievements were evident in Malinowski's ethnographies, which live on despite "needs" and other later theoretical developments (Firth 1957). Yet the sheer artistry of it all did not escape Audrey Richards, as devoted a Malinowskian as there would be (Gladstone 1986; Richards 1957; Wayne 1985). In her positive assessment of "speech in action," identified as Malinowski's contribution, Richards wrote: "To decide which remarks are 'typical' or 'atypical' in any given situation . . . the anthropologist must rely in the last analysis on his own judgment, matured during months of listening to similar conversations. . . . It is here that anthropologists need to assess far more accurately than they have done their selective interests and powers of memory" (1939: 302–3).

The assessment is not over. Malinowski's fieldnotes embody both the greatest strengths and greatest vulnerabilities of ethnographic fieldwork.

Margaret Mead

Malinowski's fieldwork practice, even acknowledging its distinctive features, presents many continuities with that of Seligman, Rivers, and their students, more than the hallowed British social anthropology Trobriand origin myth (Holy 1984: 15–16; Kuper 1973) would suggest. On the contrary, Margaret Mead's identification as a Boasian, which she certainly was, does not do justice to the radical break her fieldwork practice made with that of Boas and the cohort of students he trained before she began her work with him in 1923.

From 1900, when Boas completed his major northwest coast fieldwork, up to the 1920s, it was his approaches to cultural distributions, material culture, salvage ethnography, and texts that his students such as Alfred Kroeber, Clark Wissler, Robert Lowie, and Edward Sapir carried to the field (DeMallie 1982). Even Ruth Benedict, whose later concern with configurations and holism is well known, was a fieldworker in the Boas mold. After her first exposure to anthropology in 1919, Benedict came to Columbia in 1921 to study with Boas, just two years before Mead. "In her work with North American Indians," contemporaneous with Mead's fieldwork in the 1920s and 1930s, "she always had to work through interpreters and to seek out the particularly knowledgeable individual who was also amenable to the task of sitting and dictating while, with flying pencil and aching arm, she wrote down verbatim hundreds of pages of translated tales (Mead 1959b: 202–3; cf. 287, 301–2; 1974: 29–30).

If Benedict's fieldnotes were like those of Boas, Mead's were not.
Her first fieldwork, for nine months in 1925–26, was in Samoa, a
living culture far removed from the Native American memory cultures that the senior Boas students labored to transcribe. Mead's pre-
fieldwork doctoral thesis had been a library study of Polynesian cultural variability; her familiarity with the extensive literature on Samoa
made it possible to focus on the problem Boas selected, the cultural
expression of female adolescence (Howard 1984: 62–64; Mead 1969;
Mead 1972: 126–29, 138; Weiner 1983). With little preparation for
doing fieldwork from either Boas or close friend Benedict, Mead, as
she tells it (1977: 5), independently invented participant-observation.
"There were no precedents," she said:

> I learned to eat and enjoy Samoan food. . . . I could wander freely about
> the village or go on fishing trips or stop at a house where a woman was
> weaving. Gradually I built up a census of the whole village. [Mead 1972:
> 151]

> My material comes not from half a dozen informants but from scores of
> individuals. With the exception of two informants, all work was done
> in the native language. . . . Very little of it was therefore gathered in
> formal interviews but was rather deviously extracted from the directed
> conversations of social groups, or at formal receptions which the chiefs
> of a village accorded me on account of my rank in the native social
> organization. . . . This concentration upon a small community and
> detailed observation of daily life provided me with a kind of field
> material rarely accessible to the field ethnographer. [Mead 1930a: 5]

Shades of Malinowski? Probably not. Mead apparently had not read
Argonauts of the Western Pacific (Malinowski 1922) and its famous first
chapter on his fieldwork methods, before arriving in Samoa. Another
student had presented the work in a seminar she attended, but the
session had focused on the *kula* trade, not fieldwork methods (Mead
1969: xv, 1972: 159). She had read a 1923 paper by Malinowski,
published in 1927 as *The Father in Primitive Psychology,* which Boas
recalled to her attention in a letter he wrote her just before her Samoan
research began (Mead 1959b: 289–90). This essay, however, says nothing about Malinowski's methods; her later statement that she "did not
know how he had used the Trobriand language" is credible (Mead
1972: 139). Her utilization of "speech in action" in Samoa must be
accepted as uninfluenced by Malinowski.

But what Malinowski thought of this, or when Mead finally did read *Argonauts,* is not revealed in her autobiographical writings or Howard's (1984) biography. Ruth Benedict wrote Mead in Samoa about Malinowski's cordial visit at Columbia in the spring of 1926 (Mead 1959b: 304–6), but this letter reports none of the disparaging remarks about her ongoing fieldwork that Mead asserts he made at that time (Mead 1972: 160). When she met Reo Fortune in the summer of 1926 on her return from Samoa, he was favorably impressed with Malinowski's work though antipathetic to him personally; he would refer to *Argonauts* constantly in his Dobu fieldwork during the first half of 1928 (Mead 1972: 159), but his animosity toward Malinowski would increase during the years of his marriage to Mead, which ended in 1934.

In summer 1928, when her *Coming of Age in Samoa* was published, Mead wrote Malinowski a flattering letter, and asked for his criticism of the book (Howard 1984: 99). She does not reveal if or how he responded, but by spring 1929, as Raymond Firth remembered, both Mead and Fortune were convinced that "Malinowski had no ideas" (Howard 1984: 113). That same spring Frederica de Laguna, a Boas student, attended Malinowski's London seminar and encountered his "violent hatred of Dr. Boas" and low opinion of Boas's training of students (de Laguna 1977: 23).

The Malinowski-Mead antagonism widened in 1931 when Malinowski apparently encouraged one of his students to write a negative review of Mead's second book, *Growing Up in New Guinea* (see Mead 1972: 160, 193; 1977: 101). This stone may have been an attempt to hit more than one bird, for Malinowski's rival A. R. Radcliffe-Brown had selected the site for Mead's and his student Fortune's Manus fieldwork, which her book reported on (Howard 1984: 99, 102; Mead 1978: 102). Mead responded to the review's dig that she did not understand the Manus kinship system with her monograph *Kinship in the Admiralty Islands* (1934), written in consultation with Radcliffe-Brown while he taught summer school at Columbia in 1931 (Howard 1984: 127; Mead 1972: 163). And her "More Comprehensive Field Methods" contains disparaging characterizations of Malinowski's Trobriands research in relation to her own (1933: 6–7, 9).

Yet early in 1936, perhaps after reading Malinowski's *Coral Gardens and Their Magic* (1935), Mead wrote Fortune, "I am convinced all over again that Malinowski was perhaps the most thorough field worker

God ever made" (Howard 1984: 176). Then, later that year, Malinowski's introduction to Firth's *We, the Tikopia* pooh-poohed Mead's
1935 book *Sex and Temperament in Three Primitive Societies,* along with
the work of Gregory Bateson (who would be her third husband) and of
Benedict (Firth 1936: vii–viii). This must have done it. Mead's later
comments on Malinowski, whom she finally met in 1939, reverted to
testiness and a sharp differentiation of their approaches to fieldwork
(Howard 1984: 319; Mead 1940: 334, 1972: 209).

In fact, their fieldwork practices had much in common, as both of
them must have known (and Mead did admit once; see 1939: 190).
Only ego and ambition prevented either from acknowledging this,
though Malinowski may have been justifiably annoyed that Mead's
announcement of her own fieldwork innovations (1928: 259–65) did
not credit his work of a decade earlier.

Certainly others knew. In 1939 the Malinowskian Audrey Richards
listed *Coming of Age in Samoa,* along with Malinowski's own monographs and those of his students, as an example of "functional analysis"
(1939: 285–86). Firth, following his teacher's dismissal of Mead just a
few pages before, spoke approvingly of her work on kinship (1936:
xvi). But Mead, having broken with Boasian practice and spurned by
Malinowski, eventually constructed an anthropologized family lineage for her approach, tracing it to her grandmother's "notes . . .
during a visit to Philadelphia," her mother's "notebooks" on young
Margaret and her brother and "fieldwork" as a social worker among
immigrants, and her father's "field trips" while teaching about small
business at the University of Pennsylvania (1972: 46, 64, 257, 261;
1977: 8).

Despite the similarities in approach, Mead's fieldwork in Samoa *was*
different from Malinowski's in one major way. It was focused upon a
problem, whereas Malinowski had been concerned to study "the total-
ity of all social, cultural and psychological aspects of the community"
(1922: xvi). Malinowski was funded through six years of field research
and analysis (1922: xix), but only later did he conceive his "institutional" studies of trading, law, myth, the family, and horticulture.
Mead, once assigned her topic by Boas, applied to the National Research Council for a nine-month fellowship to study "the relative
strength of biological puberty and cultural pattern" (Howard 1984:
54). She did not later sift through her fieldnotes with an organizing
topic; she had one from the beginning, and her fieldnote practice
reflected the fact.

Mead's Early Fieldwork

Mead spent six months studying sixty-eight girls between the ages of nine and twenty, all residents in three contiguous villages on the Samoan island of Tau. She observed interaction and listened to conversations among these girls, and between them and younger and older residents of the villages. As these data entered her fieldnotes, she also kept records on each girl's sexual maturation and experience, education, "judgments on individuals in the village," performance on various psychological tests, and practice and knowledge of adult cultural routines and norms. These data were backgrounded by a study of the household composition and social roles of all 600 residents of the three villages (Mead 1928: 259–65, 282–94).

In addition, and against Boas's advice, Mead recorded data on Samoan political and ceremonial structure and other topics. This investigation was lower in priority than her funded research topic, and much of it was done in visits and interviews in villages other than the three where she studied the young girls (1928: 259, 262; 1969: xiii–xiv, xviii). As much social anthropology as Boasian ethnology, this work was published in her *Social Organization of Manu'a* (1930a). General investigations of the culture, albeit with improved methods, came first for Malinowski, and functional studies of separate institutions second. Mead worked in the opposite way: the problem structured the research, and "getting the whole configuration of the culture down correctly" was "bootlegged" in (Mead 1972: 144).

Bootlegging was not necessary when Mead and Fortune went to Manus for eight months in 1928–29. Fortune conducted the "investigation of the general culture," which, unlike that of Samoa, was little known (Mead 1932a: 102), while Mead, with Social Science Research Council funding, again conducted problem-focused research. Mead felt that her Samoan experience did not support assertions in the work of Freud, Piaget, and Levy-Bruhl that the "animistic" thinking of Western children and neurotics was similar to that of "primitive peoples." In Melanesia, conventionally viewed as animism-ridden, the question that framed her proposal was "If 'primitive' adults think like civilized children and neurotics, how do primitive children think?" (Mead 1930b: 289–90; 1962: 123–24; 1978: 97–102).

The two anthropologists settled among the 210 villagers of Peri. They were equipped with

> materials which had been carefully planned by Professor Radcliffe-

Brown for the use of students working in connection with the Australian National Research Council. These included a special type of large-paged book which could be used in developing the ramifications of a genealogy so that they worked out in both directions from the center; linguistic slips in three colors about five inches by two, notched to receive a rubber band so that they could be bound; and a serviceable type of reporter's notebook. [Mead 1940: 326; see also Powdermaker 1966: 66][2]

Mead focused on forty-one children between the ages of two and twelve. Her fieldnotes included observations of

a group of children, or of a child and an adult, or a group of children and adults, etc., in some ordinary social situation. . . . I handled this material in the form of running notes, with time records in two-minute intervals for certain types of play groups. It included questions from children to adults, children's responses to adult commands, explanations, etc., children's subterfuges, children's responses to situations of emotional stress, such as quarrels, severe illnesses, accident, fear displayed by adults, strangers in the village; birth and death; children's responses to storm, cyclone, animals, fish, birds, shadows, reflections, scenes between pairs of age-mates, between elder and younger children, between fathers and children, between mothers and children, between children and infants. [Mead 1932a: 104]

She also amassed records: psychological test results, the remarkable "Views of the Village as Seen by Two Children, Aged Five and Eleven," and some 32,000 pencil drawings by the children (Mead 1930b: 290–91, 332–59; 1932a; 1956: 490).[3]

Mead wrote scratch notes in her notebook and even typed notes directly in front of the children (1932a: 103). In addition to her chronological, typed "running notes," of which a January 1929 example is given in *New Lives for Old* (1956: 482–83), Mead filed dyadic and

[2]Nancy Lutkehaus commented to me that when she looked at Margaret Mead's fieldnotes at the National Archives, she was struck that some of Mead's notes from the early 1930s were written in the same type of notebook that Wedgwood had used. Like Mead and Powdermaker (and no doubt Bateson, Firth, Hart, Warner, and others), Wedgwood was equipped for fieldwork by quartermaster A. R. Radcliffe-Brown.

[3]"The evidence of observation was confirmed by the evidence from the drawings. There were no animals acting like human beings, no composite animal-human figures, no personified natural phenomena or humanized inanimate objects in the entire set of drawings. . . . The Manus child is less spontaneously animistic and less traditionally animistic than the Manus adult" (Mead 1932a: 110, 115).

small-group observations, recorded on hundreds of handwritten slips, under "fathers and children," "older and younger children," "interpretation of failure," "imaginative play," and other headings (1956: 483, 489; 1940: 326). She also organized some pages in her fieldnotes according to topic, with extracts from informant interviews on, for example, "*palits* [ghosts] and Social organization" (1956: 491). Fortune's fieldnotes concentrated on illness episodes, quarrels, and rituals, with a full record of such events in Peri over four months; each of these accounts—some events were recorded by Mead as well—ran up to six pages. Fortune also transcribed seance texts as recalled by his informant Pokanau after performances (Mead 1933: 11; 1956: 482–85; 1972: 174).

Both ethnographers were deliberately recording "a great number of minute and consecutive observations" so that "the inexplicit, the unformalized, the uninstitutionalized" patterns of Manus life would emerge, those not recoverable in interviews or directly deducible from single instances. Fieldnotes should be used to generate ethnographic realities articulated behaviorally, not verbally: "Only from the records of individual visions, from a running record of the lives of individuals, can an adequate picture of the structure of religion"—or child socialization and maturation, or kin term usage, or Manus trade—be formulated, Mead would argue (1933).

Mead's 1930 summer fieldwork on an Omaha Indian reservation was "depressing" compared to the "living cultures" of Samoa and New Guinea. Her mission, which she did not reveal to the Omaha, was to study women, while Fortune worked openly on the more conventional ethnological topics of visions and secret societies (Howard 1984: 122–25; Mead 1965, 1972: 189–92). Little direct observation entered her fieldnotes.

> In a compact New Guinea village, one could see what was happening and later one could interview the participants about the details of an event. In contrast, among the Antlers [Omaha], who lived scattered over a large reservation, we could observe very few actual events and instead had to depend on accounts given us by others. [Mead 1965: xiii]

Even so, interviews with seated informants were not the method Mead used. She familiarized herself as much as possible with reservation residents and then relied upon conversations, particularly with key informants, to provide data for later fieldnote entry. "The Indians . . . believed that I was merely killing time in idle conversation or attendance at ceremonies. For the most part, no notes were taken in the informants' presence but conversations were written up immediately afterwards." The conversations, "speech in action," were nevertheless steered and directed by Mead's interests in domestic life and interpersonal relations:

> [The] special informants, with whom I grew more intimate than with the majority of the Antler women . . . I used to illuminate the problems which were especially relevant to their position in the tribe. . . . I spent a great deal of time acquiring, with apparent casualness, the personal histories of people whom I had not yet met—so that when I met them, I could divert the conversation along revealing lines. In this way, chance contacts at dances, in a store, at someone else's house, could be utilized. [1965: xxi]

Mead distinguished her fieldnotes on contemporary Omaha life from the "collection of traditions, once integrated, now merely coexistent," which Fortune transcribed in Boasian fashion. (Benedict, indeed, had selected the problem and secured funding for Fortune.) "One must differentiate clearly between accounts of events in the lives of known persons, where the actors and narrators are alive and known, and accounts of events recorded from the memories of the old, where the actors remain unknown" (1965: xiii).

The Mountain Arapesh

A little more than a year after leaving the Omaha, and with three Manus and two Omaha books completed, Mead and Fortune began a three-culture study on the island of New Guinea in December 1931. An American Museum of Natural History Voss Fund grant gave Mead considerable freedom to study "the way sex roles were stylized in different cultures" (Howard 1984: 127–28). The first eight months were spent in the 212-person Mountain Arapesh village of Alitoa. Fortune focused on Arapesh language and external relations, Mead on everything else. From this work, in a culture Mead found with "few ceremonies and little elaboration, very thin" (1972: 197), she would publish 700 double-column pages, a massive five-part ethnography that tells us much about how she produced and processed her fieldnotes (Mead 1938, 1940, 1947, 1949).[4] She wrote only a little, and

---

[4]Only Part I (Mead 1938) is not printed in double columns.

Fortune nothing at all, on the other two cultures they would "do," the Mundugumor and Tchambuli.[5]

In Alitoa Mead kept four categories of fieldnotes, each retyped from the handwritten notes she recorded on her notepad as she moved through the village or interviewed informants. First was a chronological account of village life.

> I spent a good part of the morning in the village, sitting with the people, playing with the children, watching some craft, or casually questioning about some event. . . . During the day I recorded everything which seemed significant. In the late afternoon I walked through the village . . . and checked up on every house and its inhabitants to find where they were and where they had been that day.

A list of nineteen types of data answers the anticipated question of what she considered "significant" events; it includes the presence or absence in Alitoa of each resident, speeches, quarrels, visitors, announced plans, and "government demands which upset the ordinary routine" (1947:241).[6]

This account forms the basis of "The Record of Events," some 112 double-column pages covering January 28 to August 16, 1932 (1947: 276–388). To it, Mead added material from her second category of fieldnotes, slips describing informal behavior and "discrete items which come up in the course of group conversations, but are essentially accidental to the trend of that conversation" (1940: 326–27, 329); and from her third category, descriptions of longer events such as seances (1947: 242). The "Record" is thus a slightly amended reproduction of her chronological fieldnotes. Mead admits that "for the reader, a detailed presentation such as this is bound to be tedious and unmanageable" (1947: 242). Accordingly, she provides a village plan, prose portraits of Alitoa residents, a checklist of inhabitants of each household, and a table of marriages.

Mead viewed her Arapesh ethnography with its division into generalizing sections and supporting materials—descriptive data, texts, lists, and the "Record"—as "an experiment in method of presentation" (Mead 1938: 150–51; 1947: 173; cf. McDowell 1980). It can also

---

[5]On the fieldnotes from this research, see Howard (1984: 139, 142) and McDowell (1980: 295 and n. 23).

[6]In May, Mead discontinued noting the presence or absence of villagers (1947: 359). She appends to "The Record of Events" (see next paragraph) a record of her observations of fifty minutes of village life (1947: 414–15).

be read as a critique of Malinowski's multivolume presentation of his fieldwork data. Mead recognized, of course, that events have multiple, functionally related aspects—"As complicated an event as a quarrel between kindred in which sorcery is invoked after a feast is in progress has many facets"—and intended the "Record" to illustrate this fact. Rather than describe more than once any feast-quarrel-sorcery event, however, Mead refers repeatedly to the "Record" in the first three topical parts of *The Mountain Arapesh*. "Use of an event to illustrate first one type of discussion, then another, necessarily makes for much repetition. The *Diary* presentation is designed to obviate all these difficulties" (1947: 173).

Mead's fourth category of fieldnotes comprised transcriptions of her six "sessions" with Unabelin, a twenty-year-old from a neighboring Arapesh village who was fluent in the pidgin he had acquired during two years in the gold fields (Mead 1949). Produced "when he was seated with me at the table at the back of the verandah," these were neither Boasian texts nor a life history but rather "accumulated notes" of myths, interview responses, comments on events and customs, and personal narrative. Retyped in pidgin from scratch notes while Mead was in Alitoa, they are presented in English translation.[7] At 63 pages, more than half as long as "The Record of Events," the "Sessions with Unabelin" are a fieldnote appendix, much less integrated than "The Record" with the preceding parts of the ethnography.

Like Malinowski, Mead is explicit that she worked constantly with her fieldnotes while in the field, and she includes examples of the feedback between data collection and evolving generalization (1940: 326–35). "I spent hours analyzing data or preparing lists so that I could get the largest amount of material in a few minutes" (1940: 338). She also mentions her reading of Geza Roheim while in Alitoa, and the stimulus this provided to data analysis (1940: 331). On a negative note, she states that she did not have access to Fortune's fieldnotes, as he did to "seventy-five per cent of mine" (the chronological fieldnotes and longer event records), when she drafted Parts I–IV of *The Mountain Arapesh* in 1935–36 (Mead 1940: 326n). By that time Gregory Bateson had entered their lives, and Mead and Fortune had separated and divorced.[8]

[7]The sixth session includes a passage typed from scratch notes only in 1946 (Mead 1949: 366); this is the longest admitted interval I have come across between recording scratch notes and typing them.

[8]Bateson and Mead conducted fieldwork together in Bali and among the New Guinea Iatmul during 1936–39. This involved extensive use of photography, and the

Mead's Reflections on Fieldnotes

In 1953 Mead returned to Manus. Her fieldnote practice (1956: 481–501) was much like that of her earlier research, although she noted how much more detailed her descriptive notes were than those of 1928–29. She also did more direct typing of informant statements, as she had in Iatmul in 1938 (1977: 297). For this field trip Mead kept a journal, briefly listing the major events of the day, and she had adopted the term "scenarios" to refer to titled observation episodes included in her "Running Account."

It is ironic that Mead, who so valued and indeed pioneered problem-oriented ethnography early in her career (1933: 9, 14–15; 1962: 125–26), turned against it in later years. She found the quantitative, experimental-model approaches of Clyde Kluckhohn, John Whiting, and others misdirected (1962: 134–35) and denigrated the kind of testing and systematic data-gathering that, in essence, defined her own first fieldwork in Samoa (as directed by Boas) and in Manus, if not in Alitoa or Bali (1972: 144). In a 1965 letter written in Manus she expressed preference for empathy over controlled fieldnote recording. "If you surrender fully enough to the culture, this will itself inform your further choices and provide new problems, home-grown for the fieldworker's perception" (1977: 282).

Mead's final statement on the subject, "The Art and Technology of Fieldwork," affirmed wide-ranging fieldnote attention to "grasping as much of the whole as possible" over problem-oriented fieldnote records (1970: 250, 254, 256–57). Instead of the direction in which her own work had pointed, and which the profession in large part followed, she argued at last for the more protean Malinowskian approach.

> The field worker is engaged in building a systematic understanding of the culture he is studying, weighing each new item of information, reacting to each discrepancy, constructing hypotheses about what he may encounter next. This systematic understanding—his total apperceptive mass of knowledge—provides him with a living, changing, analytical system which simultaneously correctly or incorrectly files information received . . . and so defines the search for new information. As he is attempting to build an understanding of the whole, before specializing in any aspect, it follows that the greater the degree of

resulting ethnography featured interpretations of their visual data (Mead 1970: 258–59, Plates I–XVI; 1977: 212–14); the role of fieldnotes in this research is considered briefly in the essay "Fieldnotes and Others," in Part IV of this volume.

simultaneity of observations on many aspects of the culture, the higher
the chance of using the cross-referencing provided by parallels . . . or by
contrast. [1970: 247]

A good description of headnotes, perhaps, but a much weaker direc-
tive for writing and typing than any of Mead's pronouncements on
fieldnotes between 1928 and 1956.

From the 1920s to the 1960s

The years 1925–60 have been characterized as the "classical period" of American and British "socio-cultural anthropology" (Stocking 1983b: 8). During these decades fieldnote practice assimilated the
advances of Malinowski and Mead (even if she received less professional acknowledgment), though the approaches of Boas and Rivers
maintained currency as well.[9] Voget (1960) identifies a shift from the
1925–40 "culturalism-functionalism-holism"—in which British functionalism was complemented by American concerns for pattern and
cultural consistency—to growing interests during 1940–60 in interaction, individual behavior, and complexity. Nonetheless, concern
with "all aspects of the life of the people," with "the whole culture"
(Bennett 1948: 672; cf. Evans-Pritchard 1951: 77), persisted through
these decades, and wide-ranging fieldnotes appear to have been the
goal of most ethnographers.

American and British holism had their differences, however, whose
origins may be discerned in the institutional analyses of Malinowski
and the problem-focused studies of Mead. John Bennett, in a 1948
review of fieldwork methods, noted the tendency of American anthropologists to begin their fieldwork with a particular problem, and
widen from there; he cited Robert Redfield's study of the folk–urban
continuum in Yucatan as an example. British anthropologists, with
Bateson's *Naven* the example, preferred to narrow their research during the course of fieldwork, allowing problems to emerge in the field.
"These two approaches both produce meaningful studies" (Bennett
1948: 681–82).

Evans-Pritchard, a Malinowski student, was emphatic that the institutional focus "on a people's law, on their religion, or on their

[9]The myth of Cushing's "going native" remained a cautionary warning about the
limits of participant-observation.

economics, describing one aspect of their life and neglecting the rest," was a post-fieldwork decision about writing ethnography; holistic fieldnotes should cover "their entire social life and . . . the whole social structure" (1951: 80. See Marcus and Fischer 1986: 56; Kuper 1947: 5–7). Postwar social anthropologists would amend this position: the ethnographer might structure fieldwork around problems as long as those problems arose "from the people themselves," from "the grain of the field" (Beattie 1965: 2–3; Beteille 1975: 102; Middleton 1970: 1, 6; Srinivas et al. 1979: 8. See also Evans-Pritchard 1951: 75). Whatever its roots, by the 1960s the "methodical ethnography" (Beals 1978) or "problem-oriented" study had all but chased out the "holistic monograph" (Tax 1976: ix–x. Cf. Johnson 1987; Lewis 1953: 15; Powdermaker 1966: 237).

As British anthropologists adopted more pointed fieldwork problems and more Americans ventured beyond summer fieldwork seasons in familiar North American terrains, "there was a gradual convergence . . . in the strategies adopted for fieldwork and similarities in the techniques employed" (Urry 1984a: 60). What is remarkable is that this occurred with so little training of students in fieldwork practice. "For the most part . . . fieldwork training was a matter of learning by doing, . . . of 'sink-or-swim.' . . . Fieldwork was enacted more than it was analyzed" (Stocking 1983b: 8; cf. Mead 1972: 142–43). The inattention to fieldwork training under Boas at Columbia continued to mark the department (Freilich 1970b: 186; Landes 1970: 121, 122; Wagley 1983: 1), and there are at least four different stories told of Kroeber's lack of interest in discussing fieldwork methods with students (Agar 1980: 2; Jackson, this volume; Nader 1970: 98; Wagley 1983: 1). Beattie remarks of the early postwar years that "it was unusual in English anthropology courses at that time (it still is) to give very detailed formal instructions on methods of field research" (1965: 5; cf. Middleton 1970: 3).

In both the United States and England, despite the flurry of personal fieldwork accounts from the 1960s on, training remained "informal" at best (Stocking 1983b: 8). In the Manchester "Field Seminar" in the late 1960s, Shokeid recalls "almost no reference to the process of data gathering" (1988: 32). Perhaps the most important teaching channel during all these years was contact between students just returned from the field and those about to leave. Wagley's mention of this, and of advice from experienced ethnographers in New York and upon arrival in Guatemala in 1937, is especially revealing (1983); so is Beattie's

account of similar experiences at Oxford and in East Africa in the early
1950s (1965: 5, 6, 37, 39).

Developing Fieldnote Practice: The United States

The decades from the 1920s through the 1960s encompass massive
change in the fieldwork practice of American anthropologists. These
years saw a number of shifts: from salvaging the past to studying the
present; from studying the total culture to a focus on problems; from
interest in customs to concern for social processes; from reliance on the
seated informant to participant-observation; from paying for informant time to a concern with rapport; from transcription to inscription
and description; from texts to fieldnotes and records; "from ethnology
to cultural anthropology" (Stocking 1976: 13).

Ethnography based upon texts from one or a few seated informants
by no means ended with Boas, although others, like Lowie (1960)
would produce less raw, more readable results. It was Cornelius Osgood, however, a 1930 University of Chicago Ph.D., who out-Boased
Boas with his three volumes on Canadian Ingalik Indian culture. This
remarkable salvage effort during 1937 was based upon more than 500
hours of transcription with one informant, who was paid by the
hour. Osgood's questions opened the process, but Billy Williams easily caught on, having learned the culture in similar sessions with
his grandfather, and Osgood read back his fieldnotes to Williams
for correction and expansion (Osgood 1940). Casagrande's single-
informant work in 1941 also harked back to Boas, as Ojibwa Indian
John Mink was urged, successfully, "to understand our interest in the
general culture pattern rather than the particular instance" (1960a: 472).

Working with paid informants was still acceptable fieldwork practice into the 1950s (Friedrich 1986: xvi). Perhaps the most Boasian use
of informant-text transcription was the work of anthropologists in
Chiapas, Mexico, in the 1950s and 1960s. Reviewing a study of Tzotzil
medicine, Vogt reveals:

> Following a research strategy that all of us from Chicago, Harvard, and
> Stanford have found to be productive, Holland located a bilingual
> informant and trained him to operate a tape recorder and to transcribe
> tapes of curing ceremonies into written Tzotzil and to type the materials
> with an interlinear translation. [1965: 525][10]

[10] Vogt's later account (1979) of the Harvard Chiapas Project details more wide-
ranging fieldwork methods.

Transcription of texts as an occasional method, subordinate to partici-pant-observation, of course continued to be used by most anthropolo-gists, as in Watson's sessions on Agarabi initiation (discussed in "A Vocabulary for Fieldnotes," Part II, this volume) or Mitchell's two-hour transcription of an account of a New Guinea Wape feud (1978: 91).

The more usual approach has been problem-focused participant-observation, with wide-ranging fieldnotes and separate records of particular types of data. Kluckhohn, spending summers in fieldwork among the Navajo from the 1920s on, began in 1932 to focus upon witchcraft, within a broad array of ethnographic interests. His book *Navajo Witchcraft* scrupulously details its fieldnote sources: (1) field-notes written during 132 interviews with ninety-three informants, most conducted with an interpreter, ranging from 2 to 91 pages in length (twenty-five of these, focused exclusively on witchcraft, were conducted during the early 1940s); (2) fieldnotes from conversations, mainly in Navajo, written soon afterward, ranging from a few lines to 10 pages; (3) notes on witchcraft from whites; (4) notes on overheard Navajo gossip about witchcraft; (5) 87 pages of fieldnotes from eleven other ethnographers, including the "running notes" of Alexander and Dorothea Leighton (Kluckhohn 1944: 15–17, 244–52).

Like Mead's *Mountain Arapesh* with its use of supporting materials, Kluckhohn's monograph is divided into topical and interpretive sec-tions, plus appendixes that reproduce "almost all statements of any length which have been made to me about Navaho witchcraft" (1944: 21). He admits that these fieldnotes, set in double columns and small type, are "enormously detailed . . . and not easy to read." Few eth-nographers would ever again be as candid about their fieldnote evi-dence.

Tax's research in a Guatemalan municipio took place during field seasons from 1935 to 1941 while he was on the Carnegie Institution staff. His earlier participant-observation prepared the way for his collection in 1940–41 of extensive economic records of land owner-ship and use, agricultural labor, yields, prices, and measures of wealth; these are the heart of his ethnography (Tax 1953: x, 188–91). His fieldnotes were microfilmed and made available to libraries in 1950 (1953: x, 224); this alternative to Mead's and Kluckhohn's documenta-tion has also been a rare occurrence.

The Spicers' 1935–36 fieldwork in a Yaqui Indian neighborhood in Tucson, Arizona, demonstrated the infusion of British social anthro-pology that Radcliffe-Brown's 1931–36 stay brought to the University of Chicago (Spicer 1940: xxiv–xxvi). Like their fellow Chicago students the Embrees, in the field in Suye Mura at the same time, the Spicers' wide-ranging fieldwork produced chronological fieldnotes of the events, rituals, and conversations they observed and heard over one year. These were supplemented by records filed under each person's name, seated interviews following events observed, and life histories (Spicer 1988). Interviews were wide-ranging at first and narrowed later; notes were written following the interviews.

Charles Wagley's 1937 and 1939–40 fieldwork illustrates how the changes in fieldwork practice were occurring even without direct British influence. Wagley (see 1983) was a student of Benedict's and part of a group that she and Boas sent to work among Brazilian Indians (Landes 1970: 121). Mead's work had no direct influence on Wagley; she gave one lecture on field methods at Columbia during his student days, but he did not attend. He did "of course" read Malinowski's *Argonauts*. His first six-month field trip to a Maya-speaking Guatemalan community utilized paid informants, an interpreter who later became an assistant and wrote fieldnotes for Wagley, text transcriptions, and also participant-observation in homes, the town hall, fields, and rituals. In his Tapirape research he had to learn the language, and he could not pin down informants for interviews or transcription even by paying them. The Boasian touches disappeared as participant-observation and wide-ranging descriptive fieldnotes took over, supplemented by records of the daily activities of ten Tapirape men (Wagley 1977: 19–20, 53).

While Wagley was in Guatemala and Brazil, William Foote Whyte spent 1937–40 in a Boston Italian neighborhood doing research for *Street Corner Society* (1943), "in many ways the sociological equivalent of *Argonauts of the Western Pacific*" (Van Maanen 1988: 39). Whyte read Malinowski, but the personal links from Radcliffe-Brown to Warner to Chapple and Arensberg were probably more influential; only later did he take his Ph.D. in sociology rather than anthropology (Whyte 1955: 286–87; 1984: 14–15. Cf. Kelly 1985). With ample support and freedom to follow his instincts, Whyte made the most of speech-in-action, learning to watch and listen at street corners, gambling locations, bowling alleys, and political meetings (1955: 298, 303). Reports of this activity, rather than formal interviews, formed the bulk of his chronological fieldnotes, which he typed immediately following participant-observation episodes (1955: 297, 302, 307). As secretary of a club and a political campaign, he occasionally took notes during events, and he transcribed texts of political speeches as he heard them

(1955: 305, 312). He used records only for some 106 positional mappings and for initiation interaction sequences at club meetings, based on scratch notes and memory; these data, collected over six months, were used to generate group structure and revealed the emergence of two factions (1955: 333–35). Like Malinowski, Whyte constantly analyzed his data while in the field (1955: 280), also developing an index that I return to in the essay "On Ethnographic Validity" (Part V, this volume).

The growing significance of records in American fieldwork is particularly evident in Oscar Lewis's research in Tepotzlan, Mexico, in 1943–44, 1947, and 1948 (Lewis 1951: ix–xxi). What had been intended as a problem-focused "personality study," utilizing Redfield's 1926 ethnography of the village as a base, was transformed into a holistic "historical, functional, . . . and configurational" project as the impact of change and doubts about Redfield's characterization of interpersonal life registered with Lewis. In 1943–44 his team of fifteen professionals and students, plus local assistants, assembled an ethnographic census, psychological tests, and quantitative records on land, labor, and wealth. The primary focus for wide-ranging fieldnotes was a series of seven family studies conducted by Lewis, a colleague, and five Mexican students. These averaged 250 typed pages (Lewis 1950), and one became the beginning point of continuing research by Lewis through 1963 (Lewis 1959: 21–57; 1964).

By the 1950s, problem-focused research was the norm, and fieldnotes in the Mead pattern—problem first, general culture second—were the practice. Clifford and Hildred Geertz were part of a six-member team studying the Javanese town of Modjokuto in 1953–54. Each member had a separate project: the Geertzes covered religion and the family (C. Geertz 1960; H. Geertz 1961); the others investigated marketing, rural villages, town organization, and the Chinese minority. Clifford Geertz's chronological fieldnotes of events, conversations, and seated interviews were typed from scratch notes and written progressively more and more in Javanese (1960: 383–385). Hildred Geertz's fieldnotes focused on participant-observation and interviews with forty-five families. Roland Force's problem-focused 1954–56 research on leadership in Palau, in Micronesia, similarly resulted in typed fieldnotes originating in scratch notes, but his were organized according to topics. His most significant records were notes on Palauan concepts mentioned in earlier ethnographies and copied by him onto cards to use in interviews (1960: 177–80).

By the 1960s the practice of return visits and continuing long-term research—like that of Kluckhohn and Lewis—had become more common. Masses of fieldnotes accumulated, but accounts are few of how they are organized and used in writing. George Foster (1979a) has written a comprehensive overview concerning his research in Tzintzuntzan, Mexico, which began in 1945–46 and continued annually from 1958. By the 1970s his files consisted of ten boxes of five- by eight-inch sheets. Four were fieldnotes proper: three of "basic data of many types" organized according to the Human Relations Area Files (HRAF) categories he had begun using in 1945, and another of notes on health and medical topics. The six boxes of records comprised one of 400 dreams, one of Thematic Apperception Tests (TAT), two of vital statistics for two hundred years of the village's history, and two of individual data on 3,000 persons (1979a: 169–70).

Developing Fieldnote Practice:
British Social Anthropology

The cohesiveness of Boasian anthropology in the United States was dissolving by the 1930s; tours and stays by Malinowski in 1926, 1933, and 1938–42 and by Radcliffe-Brown in 1926 and 1931–36 constituted one competing source of influence (Ebihara 1985; Jackson 1986: 110; Kelly 1985; Stocking 1976; Urry 1984a: 59). In Britain the cohesiveness of Malinowskian anthropology, later consolidated (or narrowed) by Radcliffe-Brown (Fortes 1957; Hackenberg 1973: 303–7; Kuper 1973; Stocking 1984b: 179), emerged with full force in the 1930s and continued into the 1960s.

The medium of transmission for Malinowski's fieldwork practice was his LSE seminar, which began in 1924. Here the reading aloud of Malinowski's writing projects, as well as his pontifications on methods and fieldnote analysis, set standards his students would attempt to meet, and surpass. Among the earliest students were E. E. Evans-Pritchard, Raymond Firth, Hortense Powdermaker, Isaac Schapera, and Audrey Richards. Others would include Gregory Bateson, Camilla Wedgwood, C. W. M. Hart, Lucy Mair, Edmund Leach, Max Gluckman, and—among the Rockefeller-funded International African Institute cadre of 1933–34—Meyer Fortes, Hilda Kuper, and S. F. Nadel (Firth 1957; Hart 1970; Kuper 1973; Kuper 1984: 198–99; Lutkehaus 1986; Richards 1939: 291; Salat 1983: 63; Stocking 1983a: 111–12; Wayne 1985: 536–37).

The early fieldwork of this group still showed traces of the British anthropology in which Malinowski had been trained. Evans-Pritchard, in his 1926–30 fieldwork among the Azande, relied heavily upon informants and transcribed texts, including those recorded by his Zande clerk (Evans-Pritchard 1932: 294–98, 336; 1937: 2, 7; 1940: 9, 15). Unable to live in a Zande community, Evans-Pritchard found time on his hands, he later told Hart (1970: 155), "and had only been able to combat it by a rigid determination to take notes, about something, no matter how boring or trivial, every single day he was in the field." Schapera, from 1929 on, combined fieldnotes based on participant-observation with heavy reliance on text transcription from key informants, including literate Tswana assistants who wrote their own (Comaroff and Comaroff 1988: 558–60; Schapera 1935. Cf. Kuper 1947: 3). Generally, however, texts of oral performances such as folktales disappeared from social anthropologists' fieldnotes; not until the late 1960s did interest in rhetoric, delivery, and audience response lead to a revival of textual attention (Finnegan 1969). Genealogical method also continued to be important to the Malinowski students (Evans-Pritchard 1940; Hart 1970: 160–61; Kuper 1947: 3; Powdermaker 1966: 78), and, with greater attention to recitational pragmatics, it would remain so into the 1950s (Lewis 1977; Madan 1975: 137–38, 142–46; Middleton 1970: 32–35).

Firth's 1928–29 fieldwork, for which his teacher was "saving" Tikopia from other researchers (Larcom 1983: 176n), was a comprehensive demonstration of Malinowskian speech-in-action participant-observation; notes were taken in view of the Tikopia (Firth 1936: 5, 6, 10). So was Evans-Pritchard's Nuer fieldwork in visits between 1930 and 1936, even if the Nuer themselves—rather than Malinowski, with whom he had broken—pushed him in that direction (1940: 11, 13, 15). The students were also beginning to define problems earlier, even before fieldwork, and to acquire masses of quantitative records. Focusing on diet and crop production among the Bemba, Richards (1935) advocated quantitative analysis of marriage, divorce, and labor migration rates, using systematic village censuses and "not merely a set of the most voluble informants who are only too ready to haunt the tent door." Firth, in his 1939–40 study of Malay fishermen, collected extensive economic "records," as well as fieldnotes from wide-ranging participant-observation (1966: 357–61).

Postwar social anthropology consolidated these gains of the 1930s, as Beattie's and Middleton's valuable accounts of their early 1950s fieldwork in Uganda illustrate. Doing holistic research, with problems emerging from "the grain of the field," both anthropologists also collected extensive quantitative records on household composition, marriage, and career histories of chiefs (Beattie 1965: 34, 36–37, 39–41, 54; Middleton 1970: 3, 65–66). In the Malinowskian pattern, the periods between "tours" were used for preliminary analysis and reports, but fieldnotes were also analyzed in the field (Beattie 1965: 8, 24; Middleton 1970: 1, 59–60; cf. Evans-Pritchard 1951: 76). Middleton rewrote his scratch notes soon after taking them (1970: 33, 64), but Srinivas, bringing Radcliffe-Brownian social anthropology to India in 1948, found this impossible; he was not able to return to them for analysis until 1950 (1987: 139–40). Suffering a similar lack of privacy in which to read and write, Maybury-Lewis, in his Shavante fieldwork in 1958, could not analyze his fieldnotes based on speech-in-action until after he left Brazil (1967: intro. [n.p.]). After working over their fieldnotes, both Srinivas and Maybury-Lewis returned for further fieldwork.

In 1951 and 1967, and again in 1984, groups of British anthropologists registered their collective prescriptions for fieldwork practice. Published in 1951, the sixth edition of *Notes and Queries on Anthropology* (Seligman 1951) had been under a committee's revision since 1936, interrupted by World War II.[11] Radcliffe-Brown played a key role, as did the Malinowski students Firth, Evans-Pritchard, and Fortes. Unlike the original of 1874, this edition was aimed at professional anthropologists. The section on fieldwork methods began on a Malinowskian note: "Direct observation supplemented by immediate interrogation is the ideal course." Only two pages were devoted to fieldnotes: it was recommended that notes be written as soon as possible, in public if the informants did not object, and should cover "events observed and information given"; records of "prolonged activities or ceremonies" and a journal (in the strict sense) should be kept as well. Scratch notes

---

[11] The volume clearly looked backward rather than forward. Among its recommendations: "A sporting rifle and a shotgun are, however, of great assistance in many districts where the natives may welcome extra meat in the shape of game killed by their visitor. . . . As a rule beads, cotton cloth and coloured handkerchiefs are valued inasmuch as they are already local articles of trade; preferences can be discovered from the traders in the nearest market town. . . . If it is impossible to have local natives as attendants, it is better to have 'boys' who regard the natives as dangerous, or even as cannibals, rather than those who despise them as slaves or inferiors. If the servants are not natives of the district, it may be advisable to camp well away from the village and to allow them to go into the village only if they are on a definitely friendly footing with the natives" (Seligman 1951: 29, 33, 41). Me Tarzan, you Jane? See Crick 1982: 18.

recorded during events were advised, to assist later questioning of "observers or participants . . . and to obtain fuller details and explanations (for this, see Köbben 1967: 42). Just one paragraph addressed texts. Six pages, in contrast, were devoted to the genealogical method, with some passages paraphrasing Rivers. Three pages featured an excellent discussion of sampling, covering its powers and limitations (Seligman 1951: 27, 36, 45–46, 49–50, 50–55, 56–58).

The Craft of Social Anthropology (Epstein 1967) was the product of Max Gluckman's Manchester students and colleagues. It included papers on quantitative approaches to census and household records, sampling and surveys, divorce and genealogies, and economic data. Other chapters covered "case" records in studies of law and witchcraft. Gluckman's introduction and the paper by van Velsen were concerned with how "extended cases" recorded in chronological fieldnotes could be analyzed in ethnographic writing; I return to these ideas in Part V, in the essay "On Ethnographic Validity." Certainly a consolidation of approach, based on considerable ethnographic work by its authors in South Africa, Zambia, Malawi, and India, and with full control of the British literature, it was a volume firmly in the Malinowski tradition.

The first in a series on research methods, *Ethnographic Research: A Guide to General Conduct* (Ellen 1984), draws heavily on the American fieldwork and personal account literature, and reveals few after-effects of the transactionalism, structuralism, structural Marxism, and symbolic anthropology (Turner variant) that captivated British anthropologists in the 1960s and 1970s (Ortner 1984). Ellen's view of the varieties of fieldnote data is consistent with this volume's essays; it is cited accordingly in my essay "A Vocabulary for Fieldnotes" (this volume, Part II). The volume's quantitative profile is smooth, assumed, characteristically BSA. Holy's (1984) chapter on theory is a well-argued, low-key presentation in the interpretive vein more assertively represented in American anthropology by the 1980s (see also Tonkin's contribution in Ellen 1984, and Crick 1982). Malinowski would rest easy with this book.

From the 1960s to the 1980s

Fieldnote practice to the 1960s, as we have seen, can be traced in prefaces and appendixes. For the 1960s, 1970s, and 1980s the picture is murkier, despite the many personal accounts. The history of these postclassical years is so far one of theory rather than of fieldwork practice. Tellingly, Ortner is able to review the theoretical "movements" of these years with reference to few ethnographies. Structuralism and Schneider-style symbolic anthropology had little or no need for wide-ranging fieldnotes (Ortner 1984: 136, 130. Cf. Marcus and Cushman 1982: 37; Van Maanen 1988: 130). Neither did cultural ecology; to the extent that it sponsored fieldwork, it led more to records than to fieldnotes proper (Ortner 1984: 134. Cf. Johnson 1987: 28–29; Marcus and Cushman 1982: 61–62).[12] Cognitive anthropology, not reviewed by Ortner, has been similarly oriented to formal records (Agar 1980; Conklin 1968: 174–75; Van Maanen 1988: 130–31). Structural Marxism and political economy both produced their exemplary work by using historical documents or reanalyzing ethnographic cases (Ortner 1984: 139, 142); this is also true of Sahlins's "practice" model (Ortner 1984: 155–57).

Fieldnotes played a more significant role in the ethnographic interests in public behavior and rituals found in the symbolic anthropologies of Geertz and Turner and their followers. Yet Ortner notes a weak and declining "systematic sociology" in this work (1984: 131–32, 134; cf. Johnson 1987: 29), as she also does of cultural ecology and political economy (1984: 134, 143). The remedy is in an emerging focus on "practice": on "praxis, action, interaction, activity, experience, performance"; on "the doer . . . agent, actor, person, self, individual, subject"; and on "transactions, projects, careers, development cycles, and the like" (1984: 144, 158).[13] All this certainly points in the direction of renewed need for wide-ranging fieldnotes. Two bodies of work perhaps also pointing in this direction are those of 1960s transactionalism, only briefly mentioned by Ortner (1984: 144–45 n.14), and feminist ethnography, oddly left out of her canvass (see Caplan 1988).

Two others, which Ortner clearly favors, are an ethnography-based historical approach and a renascent psychological anthropology (1984: 158–59, 151). These bodies of work, some richly ethnographic, are reviewed at length by Marcus and Fischer (1986) under the banner of

---

[12]The exception, as Ortner mentions, was Rappaport's *Pigs for the Ancestors* (1968). See also Lee (1979) on wide-ranging ecologically oriented work by the Kalahari Research Project.

[13]This contrasts with the ethnographically dead hand of the new historical anthropology and its focus on "time, process, duration, reproduction, change, development, evolution, transformation" (Ortner 1984: 158).

"experimental ethnography." Assaying its development between 1973 and 1982, they argue for a theoretical rapprochement between interpretive ethnography and political economy. To the extent that they discuss how fieldnote materials are used in textual construction, they limit themselves to interview-driven work, particularly that of "the Morocco Trio"—Rabinow, Crapanzano, and Dwyer (see also Clifford 1983: 133–35; Geertz 1988: 91–101). An assessment of how fieldnotes are used in the more ethnographically wide-ranging work that Marcus and Fischer review (work by Robert Levy, Waud Kracke, Gananath Obeyesekere, Edward Schieffelin, Steven Feld, Bradd Shore, and June Nash) is sorely needed.[14]

So is a new body of retrospective accounts of fieldwork practice like those that help make possible a history of fieldnotes for the "classical period," or for the ethnography of the 1970s and 1980s represented in this volume (see Friedrich 1986 for a model). Unfortunately, most of the "confessional" personal accounts from the 1970s and 1980s tell us little or nothing about writing fieldnotes (Alland 1975; Barley 1983, 1986; Cesara 1982; Gearing 1970; Mitchell 1978; Romanucci-Ross 1985; Turner 1987; Werner 1984).

Fieldnotes and Science

Tension between scientific and humanistic definers of anthropology has long wracked American anthropology (Berreman 1968: 368–69; Ebihara 1985: 114; Johnson 1978: 42–43, 60–64, 205–6; Lewis 1953: 4–5; Marcus and Cushman 1982: 45; Stocking 1974a: 17–19). A "hard science" challenge in the 1950s (Johnson 1987) provoked the fierce debates (and ethnographic retreats) of the 1960s and 1970s that Ortner (1984) so well surveys. From the 1970s on an equally challenging "interpretive response" (Johnson 1987. See Holy 1984; Marcus and Fischer 1986) has fueled new and old fires. Battle lines, name-calling, and mockery abound. A participant in an American Anthropological Association meeting told Agar, "If one more person calls me a logical positivist I'm going to punch them in the nose" (1980: 176). A 1989 AAA panel was devoted to "Anti-Anti-Science."

The implication of the scientific-quantitative approach is to devalue

[14]What is "experimental" (see the Marcus and Fischer 1986 subtitle) is, of course, in the eye of the beholder. Let us resist premature canonization. Other noteworthy ethnographies important to assessing the 1973–82 period that Marcus and Fischer survey include those listed in Part A of the Appendix to this essay.

wide-ranging fieldnotes and to focus fieldwork practice upon record collection. A nod is given to the results of participant-observation but only for the exploratory or background qualities it provides for the "hard data" of records, the object of nearly all "methodological" attention (Agar 1980: 70, 112–13, 119, 135, 177; Brim and Spain 1974: 96–97; Cohen and Naroll 1970: 9–10; Edgerton and Langness 1974: 32–33; Johnson 1978: 9–11, 204–5; LeVine 1970: 183, 185; Lewis 1953: 6; Pelto and Pelto 1973: 269, 274; Pelto and Pelto 1978: 69; Spindler and Goldschmidt 1952: 210; Whiting and Whiting 1978: 58. Cf. Honigmann 1976: 243; Hughes 1960: 501). Humanist-interpretive defenders of participant-observation have painted only a hazy, poorly focused picture of how wide-ranging fieldnotes are utilized in the writing of ethnography (Geertz 1973: 3–30; Geertz 1983: 55–70; Honigmann 1970b; Nash and Wintrob 1972; Van Maanen 1988; Wolff 1964; Cf. Shankman 1984). If we are to come back from the field with anything more than empathy, a rapport high, and headnotes, then the relationship of our fieldwork documentation to ethnographic writing must be clear and sharp. Too many of the attempts to reconcile the debated positions—"both sides are right"—amount to veiled statements that "my side is more right." From the point of view of the user of wide-ranging fieldnotes, both sides are wrong.

British anthropology has been relatively immune to the invective and trumpets of the American science-humanism debates. Malinowski and many of his students were trained first in scientific disciplines; counting and quantification, as we have seen, came almost naturally, part of business as usual. Bateson, trained first in biology, well expressed the need both for "loose thinking" in fieldwork and for "strict thinking" in formalizing and operationalizing ethnographic analysis as one moves to writing. Both were part of science, as he saw it; and anthropology, though concerned with the "feel" and "ethos" of a culture, was a science. "There is, I think, a delay in science when we start to specialize for too long either in strict or loose thinking." In terms perhaps anticipating Thomas Kuhn, Bateson concluded: "When the concepts, postulates, and premises have been straightened out, analysts will be able to embark upon a new and still more fruitful orgy of loose thinking, until they reach a stage at which again the results of their thinking must be strictly conceptualized" (1941: 67–68).

The melding, or acceptance, of scientific and humanist perspectives was also evident in Evans-Pritchard's authoritative pronouncements. Within a single essay he could state first, "Without theories and hypotheses anthropological research could not be carried out, for one only finds things, or does not find them, if one is looking for them"; and then, "The imaginative insight of the artist . . . is required in interpretation of what is observed." The anthropologist, he asserted, must have "a feeling for form and pattern, and a touch of genius" (1951: 64, 82).

Evans-Pritchard was an ethnographer, not an ideologue. To him the value of both hypothesis and art in doing fieldwork and writing ethnography was self-evident. It is significant that an important push toward science in American anthropology came in the 1930s from George Peter Murdock (Ebihara 1985: 108, 110; Stocking 1976: 17–18), whose ethnographic experience was minor. John and Beatrice Whiting, his students during those years, recall learning "how to formulate and test hypotheses, the meaning of probability statistics, and the value of the experimental method" (1978: 41–43). From Murdock's interests in testing cross-cultural hypotheses arose the 1938 clarion call for standardization, *Outline of Cultural Materials* (Conklin 1968: 174).

Fed also through growing contact in the 1930s and 1940s with sociologists and psychologists (Stocking 1976: 9–13), the increasing pressures toward making anthropology more of a behavioral science were ready to burst by the early 1950s. In a 1953 review, "Controls and Experiments in Field Work," Lewis noted that only seven articles on field methods had been published in the *American Anthropologist* between 1930 and 1953, and four of them had been about language. Recent trends stressing quantification could be pointed to, however, and the gauntlet had been thrown down in 1952 with the first published American fieldwork report based on an explicit experimental design (1953: 14, 6–9, 20).

That paper, a study of Menomini Indian acculturation (Spindler and Goldschmidt 1952), utilized the rhetoric of behavioral science: laboratory setting, control group, sociological and psychological variables, chi-square. But in fact, its sample was not random, making the statistical test dubious; and ethnographic knowledge was used to supply the background, select the variables, and interpret the results, thus providing the validity that an abstract research design never has by itself. As an exercise in counting (see Johnson and Johnson, this volume) it was fine ethnography, but the role of headnotes and fieldnotes in structuring the study was devalued, despite lip service to "the time-honored tools of the trade." Many more hypothesis-testing studies over the next three and a half decades would be less charitable to ethnography.

The radical impact of this behavioral science approach can be appreciated in David Aberle's narrative of the course of research for his classic ethnography *The Peyote Religion among the Navaho* (1966: 227–43). The Bureau of Indian Affairs (BIA) recruited Aberle to study the peyote "cult" in 1949 and supported his fieldwork during two summer seasons. From the beginning Aberle defined his objective as an account of the differential appeal of the peyote religion. This led to interviews and participant-observation at peyote rituals all over the Navajo reservation. While he acknowledged that intensive study of one or two communities would have yielded finer-grained data on the interpersonal influences leading to peyote use, his wide-ranging survey made possible the detailed history of the movement and appreciation of community variation on the reservation.

For the third season, lacking further BIA funds, he applied to the National Institute of Mental Health (NIMH). On advice from quantitative experts, he prepared a detailed questionnaire and a structured interview; an assistant spent the summer of 1951 collecting interviews and completed questionnaires, and Aberle continued wide-ranging fieldwork.

The more detailed proposal needed for NIMH renewal in the summer of 1952 was couched in appropriate language: hypothesis, variables, operationalization. Nonetheless, Aberle decided than an open-ended topical interview was what he wanted; fieldnotes from four of these interviews are included in an appendix to his book (1966: 380–98). With a Ford Foundation Behavioral Studies grant to analyze his data, Aberle consulted the Survey Research Center of the University of Michigan. The Center looked askance at Aberle's interviews, which did not fall easily into codable "items." This fact, plus his contacts with sociologists and social psychologists, led him to use a standardized interview schedule and a random sample in his 1953 summer work. Statistical analysis of these data confirmed at ".05 or better" that the only significant variable associated with peyote acceptance was the government-enforced livestock reduction scheme.

The host of social and cultural factors that Aberle had also investigated "had gone by the board," he said. But these topics are well covered in his richly contextualized monograph, which is the fruit of six summers of fieldwork and much more than a report on the results of his 1953 research design. Though even that had not satisfied the statisticians, Aberle's "Postscript, 1965" pointed in the direction of greater utilization of fieldnotes, not more perfect records:

> I think this book might have been more evocative than it is. I am not sure that I have conveyed the dignified and serious atmosphere of a peyote meeting, the passionate and zealous religious conviction that inspires so many peyotists, or their certainty that through peyote they have indeed found a cure of souls and bodies [1966: 419]

If by the mid-1960s some, like Aberle, were viewing quantitative hypothesis-testing as just another technique, and not the New Order, others were preparing for the high tide of science of the 1970s.

As the decade opened, in the preface to *A Handbook of Method in Cultural Anthropology* Ronald Cohen announced: "Our own desire is to see anthropology become a progressively more rigorous and scientific branch of the social sciences. . . . We eschew culture-specific studies with the explanation of the culture as a major goal, and focus instead on the nomothetic goals." Enunciating a view more extreme than that of other quantitative proponents, Cohen made his choices clear: "To study the Trobrianders is one thing; to study their divorce rate and the theoretically predicted correlates of it is quite another" (Cohen 1970: vi, viii, ix).

Opposed to those who used quantitative records along with wide-ranging fieldnotes was a new "quantitative extreme" whose studies "consist mainly of statistical testing of theoretical constructs. Some anthropologists, we suppose, would not consider these works to be 'ethnographic' in any sense" (Pelto and Pelto 1973: 274; cf. Agar 1980: 10). Brim and Spain's *Research Design in Anthropology* (1974) set the standard for this camp, one perhaps even stronger in the 1980s than in the 1970s (Agar 1980: 76). Significantly, there is no mention at all of fieldnotes in their book.

Neither was there in Edgerton and Langness's *Methods and Styles in the Study of Culture* (1974); as in the Peltos' *Anthropological Research: The Structure of Inquiry* (1978; first edition 1970, P. Pelto alone), and Johnson's *Quantification in Cultural Anthropology* (1978), the primary concern was with techniques to produce particular forms of fieldwork records and their analysis.[15] The Peltos, however, had a short section on fieldnotes, aimed at making description more concrete; they also

---

[15]I was an enthusiastic participant of this 1970s movement. See Johnson 1978: x, 110–13, 173–77; Pelto and Pelto 1978: xii, 84–85, 87, 213; Sanjek 1971, 1977, 1978.

had a valuable passage on "event analysis," at the heart of what goes into wide-ranging fieldnotes (1978: 69–71, 200–207). Johnson did not discuss fieldnotes, but he did present his random-visiting approach (1978: 87–91, 106–10), which can be used to organize participant-observation and provide a measure of comprehensiveness to anthropological fieldnotes (Johnson and Johnson, this volume).

Even before the interpretive challenge gathered full steam in the late 1970s, a humanist reaction to the scientific and quantitative arguments (not quite the same thing; cf. Friedrich 1986: 211–13; Johnson 1978: 184; Johnson and Johnson, this volume) was registered. Wolff presented what might be termed the "qualitative extreme," arguing for a deliberate, gnostic "surrender-to" the culture one studies, with "total involvement, suspension of received notions, pertinence of everything, identification. . . . When some sort of order reappears, he knows he is emerging from surrender, and as he emerges he tries to recognize the differentiations in the new structure" (1964: 237, 242–43, 251). Wide-ranging fieldnotes accompanied this process (Wolff 1960), but questions about reliability and validity were beside Wolff's point. Nash and Wintrob (1972) advocated personal accounts of fieldwork as an alternative to the ethnographic genre that most of the quantitative advocates (certainly Edgerton and Langness, the Peltos, and Johnson) were attempting to expand. Honigmann (1976: 244), a most seasoned fieldworker (cf. Honigmann 1970a), reacted to the neglect of participant observation in Naroll and Cohen (1970)—despite his own contribution to it—and in Edgerton and Langness (1974) and in Pelto (1970). He stressed the role of "an observer's sensitivity, depth of thought, speculative ability, speculative freedom, imagination, intuition, intellectual flexibility." It is as difficult to deny the need for such qualities as it is to gauge their presence and force.

But even before the 1970s had begun, Gerald Berreman had predicted the future.

> Unless methodology is made explicit in ethnography, its practitioners are likely to diverge, on the one hand, into those (probably a large majority) who take refuge in scientism, who seek rigor at the expense of . . . content, insight, and understanding, and who get farther and farther away from the realities of human social life—from culture as it is lived. . . . On the other hand will be those (probably a minority) who have no pretense to being scientific, whose statements, while they may

be insightful, bear no demonstrable validity, who are essentially creative writers on anthropological topics. [1968: 369][16]

One wonders what the current headcount might be, and how many would choose not to be counted in either camp. Identifying the "explicit" place of wide-ranging fieldnotes in ethnographic writing— something other than hypothesis-testing or empathic interpretation— is something we shall return to in the final section of this book.

Speech-in-Action and Interview Fieldnotes

Informant verbal materials are grist for both the anthropological scientist's and humanist's mills. They are entered in fieldnotes to provide "a description of the situation as the native sees it, looking from the inside out." They complement observation, the description of the situation as the ethnographer sees it, "looking from the outside in" (Paul 1953: 422).

But speech does not float free. What a fieldworker hears an informant say occurs within a "speech event," a happening composed of participants, setting, intentions, and other social and linguistic elements (Agar 1980: 91–92; Briggs 1986). From the earlier ethnographic days of inquisition, of merely noting responses to the fieldworker's queries, the range of speech events in which ethnographers listen has expanded. Malinowski and Mead added speech-in-action events to the scheduled questions and text transcriptions with seated informants which their predecessors had introduced. These advances now form the ethnographic commons (see Geertz 1973: 17, 20–21, 30, 45).

The speech events of fieldwork range along two continuums. The first is situational: *from* speech events in which the ethnographer comes to the informant (in settings where the informant would be present anyway) *to* speech events in which the informant comes to the ethnographer and assumes the seated informant role. The second continuum is one of control: *from* events where the informant speaks freely *to* events where the ethnographer actively directs the informant's speech.

---

[16]Today ethnographic creative writing is welcomed by the Smithsonian Institution Press Series in Ethnographic Inquiry. Van Maanen (1988) sees "Impressionistic Tales"

The situation continuum is split between the informant's turf—
"finding them where they are" (Hughes 1960: 496)—and the ethnographer's turf. Sometimes, however, the ethnographer takes over
the informant's turf temporarily and talks with the informant in her or
his home, or in a church after the service. The turf then becomes the
ethnographer's; the informant is not in exactly the place she or he
would otherwise be, doing what she or he would otherwise be doing.
Speech events that transpire on the informant's turf are those appropriately called speech-in-action. Those on the ethnographer's own *or*
appropriated turf are interviews (interventions).

The control continuum is divided into sectors where the informant
controls what she or he says; sectors where control is shared by
informant and ethnographer; and sectors where the ethnographer controls the informant's speech, or attempts to. "Sharing" is always negotiation. Analysts of participant-observation have noted both the value
of "volunteered," spontaneous informant statements (Becker and Geer
1960: 287; Paul 1953: 449) and the importance of directed interviews
(Beattie 1965: 25, 30; Paul 1953: 442). A look through this situa-
tion/control frame may help us to see how verbal materials enter
ethnographers' fieldnotes and records.

Informant's turf; informant in control.   Situated listening is an under-
appreciated weapon of ethnography (Powdermaker 1966: 108). In a
paper on interviewing, Malinowski's student Nadel (1939: 321) called
attention to the fieldworker's overheard "information obtained *ad hoc*
from people whom he watches at work or in the act of carrying out
some particular activity." Kluckhohn's fieldnotes on Navajo-Navajo
gossip about witchcraft (1944) are a good example. Nadel called these
occasions "chance interviews," but they are neither interviews nor
only the result of chance. Transcribing texts as they are performed is a
deliberate research strategy (Whyte 1955: 305, 312). And more regularly, like Mead among the Omaha, or Agar "hanging out" with New
York City junkies (1980: 109), or Middleton among the Lugbara
(1970: 63), ethnographers purposefully put themselves in events where
they will hear, and later write what they hear in their fieldnotes.
Whyte's prime informant, Doc, understood well the value of listening.

---

as one species of ethnography; ethnography in its historic form has become "Realist
Tales."

Go easy on that "who," "what," "why," "when," "where" stuff, Bill. You ask those questions, and people will clam up on you. If people accept you, you can just hang around, and you'll learn the answers in the long run without even having to ask the questions. [Qtd. in Whyte 1955: 303]

Informant's turf; control shared.   Too often "the long run" is more time than an ethnographer can afford. Conversations with informants in their habitual locations serve to teach the ethnographer what to look and listen for, to confirm and disconfirm hypotheses and patterns, and to help plan future situated observation and listening (cf. Beteille 1975: 108; Powdermaker 1966: 76). "Accompanying an informant on a walk through the village . . . will stimulate conversation and provide an abundance of leads for later interviews" (Paul 1953: 446). This is the stuff of participant-observation, a basic source of fieldnote entries. As ethnographers learn the conventions of local speech events, they enter them appropriately (Briggs 1986; Holy 1984; Rosaldo 1980), as Whyte learned to do from Doc. Listening and conversation then go hand in hand.

You might ask informal questions while working with an informant on a harvest; you might ask during a group conversation over coffee; or you might ask while watching a ceremony. . . . while doing minimal harm to the natural flow of events into which your questions intrude. [Agar 1980: 90]

Informant's turf; ethnographer in control.   Directed questioning becomes more important as problems are followed, events connected, and holes in records identified. Ordinarily, ethnographers satisfy such needs in interviews, but recourse to informants in their everyday settings may be used to obtain specific information as well. Middleton learned a great deal in this manner but "would always try not to guide the conversation too much" (1970: 64). In Alitoa, Mead writes, "the village was very compact and I went the length of it to ask a single question" (1940: 338). Ethnographers frequently gather census data over time rather than in directed interviews (Spicer 1940: xxiv–xxv); requests for missing pieces of information to complete record files are introduced into "natural" conversations with informants (Mead 1965: xxi).

Ethnographer's turf; informant in control.   Nondirected sessions between seated informants and ethnographers are a usual ingredient of fieldwork (Middleton 1970: 64–65). "Extended interviews were . . . conducted . . . in the homes of the villagers or of the investigators. Chiefly the objective was to get the person interviewed to talk about anything in which he was interested. . . . The interviews took the form of casual conversations" (Spicer 1940: xxvi). A little further along the continuum, when "the ethnographer may do nothing more than suggest a broad area and sit back while the informant talks for half an hour" (Agar 1980: 105), we may speak of an "informal interview." Even more directed "open-ended interviews" are used

> when part of the interviewing task is to determine the areas and dimensions along which interviewing is to proceed. The characteristic approach is neither directive nor nondirective, but a compromise and shuttle between the two extremes; a question is asked or a topic suggested, and the respondent is allowed to answer as he sees fit. [Paul 1953: 445]

Perhaps the best label for all points along this segment of the interview continuum is "discovery interviews" (Plath 1980: 29).

Ethnographer's turf; control shared.   As the research "funnel" narrows (Agar 1980: 13. Cf. Bennett 1948: 687; Bohannan 1981; Middleton 1970), interview topicality becomes focused and nuanced from the ethnographer's perspective, but the informant is still encouraged to expand and elaborate as he or she sees fit. "The interview structure is not fixed by predetermined questions, as it is in the questionnaire, but is designed to provide the informant with freedom to introduce materials that were not anticipated by the interviewer" (Whyte 1960: 352). The order of questions may vary; the informant may introduce additional topics, to be brought back only gently to the ethnographer's problem; the interview may be taped, or notes may be written as it transpires, or afterward (Nadel 1939; Whyte 1960). This is the ethnographic interview par excellence—not quite formal, not really informal. Aberle's four Navajo interview transcripts are a good published example of its results (1966: 380–98). It is used particularly to learn more about observed events and informant interpretations (Beattie 1965: 25, 30), and to recover similar information about events that occurred before the ethnographer's arrival or are removed in space from the researcher's immediate purview (Paul 1953: 442; Mead 1940: 336).

Ethnographer's turf; ethnographer in control.   Formal interviews with seated informants are coercive speech events, structured by the class and culture of the ethnographer, not the informant (Briggs 1986). But even here there is a range—formal questionnaires permitting only short or even pre-set answers are at one extreme (Agar 1980: 90). With formal interviews we are in the domain of records, as we may be also with notes on long ethnographic interviews (see Lederman, this volume). Anthropologists generally conduct formal interviews only in conjunction with more wide-ranging participant-observation and fieldnotes (Middleton 1970: 65–66), though the "quantitative extreme" may be an exception. Psychological tests, text transcriptions, and economic, demographic, and genealogical records fall within the formal interview sector. Less control and more conversational negotiation—usually involving the ethnographer's attuning the informant to interview goals—mark life history interviews (Adair 1960) and those on daily behavior sequences (Bohannan 1981: 42; Sanjek 1978).[17]

I suspect that much contemporary ethnography, particularly in urban settings, is composed largely on the fieldnotes/record borderland of ethnographic interviews, often with topics established before fieldwork begins. To the extent that we avoid the discoveries of speech-in-action and move off the informant's turf, ethnography is impoverished. With interview-based research, "the field" is approached indirectly or even shut out (Powdermaker 1966: 222). Ethnographers need to see as much of their informants' turf as they can, even in urban settings where doing so is difficult (see Bohannan 1981; Keiser 1970; Wolcott 1975). We must not narrow the funnel too early.

Mead was dissatisfied with interviews, favoring "the fine detail of behavior of identified persons" (1977: 275). We may note that much of the presentation and recent discussion of "the Morocco Trio" is focused on their "dialogic" and "interlocutory" interview work, not on speech-in-action or observations made on the informants' turf (Clifford 1983: 133–35, 1986: 14–15; Geertz 1988: 91–101; Marcus and Fischer 1986: 34, 36, 56–58, 69–73, 183; Rabinow 1986: 245–46, 251; Van Maanen 1988: 137). Rabinow's fieldwork consisted mainly of interviews (1977: 38–39, 104–5, 119); his use of one paid "chief informant" puts his fieldwork, with his reflections on it, next to that of Boas and Osgood, not Malinowski, Mead, and their legatees.

[17] Agar (1980: 106) characterizes my network interviews (Sanjek 1978) as "informal." They were not. Generally, he applies "informal interview" to a much wider range than I do—from situated listening to ethnographic interviews.

Funding Fieldnotes

A mercenary theory of fieldnotes may seem outlandish at first, but we are looking at practice, so let's get practical. Most anthropologists are paid to do their fieldwork ("supported"), with more or fewer strings attached. Nowadays, most spin their own strings in individual research proposals submitted (in the United States) to the National Science Foundation or other government and private agencies. We do not yet have a detailed historical "political economy" of funding processes for anthropological research (Stocking 1985: 138), but from the 1920s to the early 1950s it was usual for major funding sources to grant or establish large amounts in the departments and research organizations that recruited and regranted fieldworkers. We underappreciate the extent to which so much anthropological fieldwork, including most of the lasting contributions before the 1960s, was *not* initiated by individual researchers in individual proposals. Larger designs and projects were a cushion between fieldworker and funder.

In 1920 there was a total of forty American Ph.D.s in anthropology. Their research was funded largely through museums, private benefactors (including Elsie Clews Parsons, a Boas stalwart), and the Bureau of American Ethnology, still the main sponsor of fieldwork (Stocking 1976: 9; 1985: 113–14, 140). Boas controlled or influenced much of this research support, and his research agenda structured the profession. During the 1920s forty more Ph.D.s (in four fields) were awarded, and 154 during the 1930s (Frantz 1985: 85). Margaret Mead's fellowship proposals—to the Rockefeller-funded National Research Council and Social Science Research Council for her Samoa and Manus fieldwork—were the exception; as with their problem focus, they were precursors of anthropology in the 1950s and later. Even in the 1930s, these individual fellowships were "few in number and highly competitive" (Wagley 1983: 3).

Not only Mead's early fieldwork but the majority of fieldwork projects of American and British anthropologists trained in the interwar years were funded by the Rockefeller Foundation and the Laura Spelman Rockefeller Memorial (Stocking 1985: 139). In the United States the support was channeled through organized programs: a Yale–American Museum of Natural History–Bishop Museum cooperative effort for Polynesian ethnography from 1919; the Laboratory of Anthropology at Santa Fe, New Mexico, for summer fieldwork from 1928; continuing research block-grants to the University of Chicago's department of anthropology and the Yale Institute of Human Relations from 1929; and the Tulane Middle American Research Bureau from 1931 (Ebihara 1985: 103; Stocking 1976: 11; Stocking 1985: 119–20, 122, 125, 129; Wagley 1983: 3). Rockefeller funds for industrial research at Harvard were also available for anthropological fieldwork under W. Lloyd Warner in Yankee City, in Natchez, Mississippi, and in Ireland (Kelly 1985: 125; Stocking 1985: 129, 139).[18]

At the Australian National Research Council some $250,000 in Rockefeller funds for Australian and Melanesian fieldwork—including that of Firth, Powdermaker, Fortune, and Warner—was controlled by Radcliffe-Brown during his 1926–31 tenure at Sydney and by his successors (Firth 1936: xvii; Kelly 1985: 124; Powdermaker 1966: 42, 54; Stocking 1985: 121). Under Malinowski's direction, Rockefeller money funded the cohort of International African Institute fellows between 1931 and 1936 (Stocking 1985: 123–27). By the late 1930s, when Rockefeller largesse had ended, more than two million dollars worldwide had gone to fund anthropological research in less than two decades (Stocking 1984b: 177; 1985: 138).

Other sources of funding also existed. Government funds were available in South Africa, the Sudan, and (from 1938, with the foundation of the Rhodes-Livingstone Institute) in British central Africa (Comaroff and Comaroff 1988: 558; Evans-Pritchard 1937: vii; Evans-Pritchard 1940: vii; Stocking 1984: 177). The Carnegie Institution supported Meso-American research, including that of Tax (Stocking 1985: 139–40). Mead had American Museum of Natural History support in New Guinea and Bali (1972: 196–97). The Columbia department was less blessed than Yale's, Harvard's, or Chicago's, with only modest access to Rockefeller money (Stocking 1985: 118–19), but Boas and Benedict were able to subsidize students with small amounts from private donors (Mead 1959b: 66, 341–42, 353; Stocking 1976: 12; Wagley 1983: 3). William Foote Whyte (1955) enjoyed a four-year Harvard Junior Fellowship. Fieldworkers during those years were a scarcer commodity than today, and they controlled both ends of most of their strings, being relatively free to conduct wide-ranging studies

[18]The same Rockefeller foundation initiatives also funded the sociology program at the University of Chicago (Bulmer 1984). With a strong fieldwork orientation from Robert Park, father-in-law of Robert Redfield, a research tradition that shares the ethnographic method with anthropology flourished. In this volume, I draw upon writings of Becker and Geer, Hughes, Siu, and Whyte (who came close to independent invention) from within this tradition.

and to record wide-ranging, detailed fieldnotes. Their circumstances were more like those of Malinowski's Trobriand work than of the tightly controlled research designs required by funding agencies in the 1950s and later.

American government funding of anthropological fieldwork picked up some of the slack in the late 1930s and early 1940s, and more extensively in the later 1940s, as the "good neighbor policy" led to Smithsonian Institution and State Department support for Latin American research, often in collaboration with local anthropologists. But tensions between ethnographic interests in wide-ranging research and shaping by the funder were now becoming more evident (Foster 1979a, 1979b; Goldschmidt 1979; Kelly 1985: 134; Lewis 1951: ix; Stocking 1976: 33–37). Staff research positions all but disappeared by the early 1950s, and increasing student enrollments drew anthropologists out of government and into academia (Goldschmidt 1985).

University-based research projects in the late 1940s and the 1950s afforded many of the same holistic fieldwork opportunities that the interwar ethnographers had enjoyed, though recruitment was by project organizers who wrote the project proposals. Notable fieldwork projects included Stewart's Puerto Rico team in the late 1940s, funded by the Rockefeller Foundation (Steward 1956: v); the 1953–54 Harvard team in Modjokuto, Java, organized by Douglas Oliver and funded by the Ford Foundation (Geertz 1960: ix); the Yale–Hawaii–Bishop Museum project in Micronesia, funded by the Carnegie Foundation in the 1950s (Force 1960: 7); and the Six Cultures project, with 1954–56 fieldwork supervised by the Whitings and funded by the Ford Foundation (Whiting and Whiting 1978: 49).

Despite the continuing importance of similar research projects into the 1980s, the dominant form of research support became the individual grant, from the National Institute for Mental Health or the National Science Foundation or, particularly for "area studies," the foundation-supported Social Science Research Council. With increasing competition for research funds from the 1950s on, individual submissions became more precise, more detailed, more problem-focused, and no doubt longer. More strings tied the fieldworker. Consequently, records became more important in field research, and the 1970s methods literature grew in response; fieldnotes proper receded in professional importance to near-neglect.

A similar transition took place in Britain. In 1946 the newly created Colonial Social Science Research Council (CSSRC) began to award grants for anthropological fieldwork. Firth, Schapera, Leach, and Stanner were dispatched to Southeast Asia and to East and West Africa to survey research priorities. In 1947 a grant was made to the Rhodes-Livingstone Institute for regrants to individual fieldworkers; these became the core of the Gluckman-Manchester school (Richards 1977: 175–76; cf. Epstein 1967). That same year Firth at the LSE found a shortage of fieldworkers as he recruited four anthropologists to carry out studies Leach had identified in Sarawak (Morris 1977: 203, 205–6). In 1949 Middleton found CSSRC and other support for his Lugbara fieldwork "relatively easy to obtain" (1970: 2). But by 1955 only one or two "very competitive" CSSRC grants were awarded, and in 1966 the program ended, though other government research funds replaced it (Chilver 1977; Lewis 1977). The Manchester extended team project also ended as Zambia moved to independence in 1965.

Government funding of individual grants steered anthropologists in the direction of hypothesis-testing and experimental design (Goldschmidt 1985: 168; LeVine 1970: 184; Middleton 1970: 3). The flexibility that anthropologists had enjoyed began to diminish in the early 1950s (Paul 1953: 432). Aberle's experience as he moved from old-time fieldwork under waning Bureau of American Ethnology support to NIMH-funded random sampling is a microcosmic portrait of a shift affecting the entire profession. Agar has sketched the realities of what government research applications and panels demand (1980: 37, 58, 68, 123, 176; see Johnson and Johnson, this volume): "They will want to see some hypotheses, some operationally defined variables, a sampling design, and a specification of questionnaires and/or experimental procedures. It would be foolish of an ethnographer not to expect such questions" (1980: 175).

Many anthropologists have embraced these changes in fieldwork strategies. Cognitive and social factors have been involved as well as economic ones. The logic of ethnographic research drove Richards to raise the question of why the ethnographer (Malinowski, or others) chose particular events to record. Mead began her Samoa and Manus fieldwork with intellectual problems, and she constructed her proposals and fieldwork around them. Socially, as Stocking points out (1976: 9–13), anthropologists in the interwar years, particularly in both smaller and in larger midwestern departments, interacted more frequently with sociologists and psychologists. "Social science" called for more structured, even quantitative evidence: for hypothesis-testing, for fieldwork data-sets, for records rather than fieldnotes.

The point, of course, is not fieldnotes versus records but the neglect of the value of wide-ranging fieldnotes. Ethnography cannot live by records alone. The desirability of systematic, quantitative fieldwork methods is accepted by nearly all anthropologists; what is at issue is whether they are best employed in later or earlier stages of fieldwork (Agar 1980; Bennett 1948; Firth 1966: 355; Middleton 1970: 6; Tax 1953: x; Whiting and Whiting 1970: 288). I return to the importance of wide-ranging fieldnotes for constructing ethnography in the essay "On Ethnographic Validity."

A Return to Ethnography

All roads lead to a return to ethnography in the 1990s. Interest in ethnography among the textualists (Clifford 1983, 1988; Clifford and Marcus 1986; Geertz 1988; Marcus and Cushman 1982; Marcus and Fischer 1986; Schweder 1986, 1988; Van Maanen 1988) is obvious and is commented upon throughout this volume. By a "return," of course, I do not mean that anthropologists have ever abandoned ethnography; a rich and distinctive ethnographic literature has been building even in the years since those surveyed (incompletely) by Marcus and Fischer (1986).[19]

We see in this work, as in that of the 1970s and early 1980s (see note 14) a variety of approaches and often a blending in the same study of interests in history, political and economic organizational constraints, identity and personhood, intention, and the interactional construction of social forms. This body of ethnography shows concern for both "moves and projects" and "systematic sociology" (Ortner 1984) which a wide-ranging but theory-directed ethnographic scrutiny should entail. If the theoretical movements of the 1960s and 1970s undervalued ethnography, the ethnography of the 1970s and 1980s absorbs but often underplays those theoretical movements. Theory informs; it need not be worn on one's sleeve.

There is clearly an opinion in this collective work that theory is a tool for ethnographic understanding and that such understanding is a valuable goal in its own right. The 1970 reveille calling for anthropology to "eschew culture-specific studies with the explanation of the culture as a major goal, and focus instead on the nomothetic goals"

[19] See Appendix to this essay, Part B.

(Cohen 1970: viii) may now be playing in reverse. No voice in the ethnographic chorus champions a study of the "theoretically predicted correlates of Trobriand divorce rates" as more valuable than what Malinowski taught us.

There is also in this ethnographic work the hint that separate political, symbolic, economic, legal, urban, medical, and psychological anthropologies may be folding back into a broader anthropology. In a new volume on legal anthropology the editors join those who question whether an "anthropology of law" is not a narrowing course.

> Studies of kinship, anthropological economics, "tribal" politics, and the anthropology of religion have also been criticized for being too isolated from major integrative theory in social anthropology. Once "narrowness" was useful for theory-building at a particular stage in social anthropology's development. But many . . . have returned to studying the interrelatedness of institutions and social action as they bring history and political economy into their ethnographies. [Starr and Collier 1989: 2–3; cf. Goldschmidt 1985: 172]

Here "ethnographies" are where theory winds up and demonstrates its worth, not the other way round (Geertz 1973: 25–28; Marcus and Cushman 1982: 59; Marcus and Fischer 1986: 185). Several important theoretical works of the 1980s share this concern for ethnography, not nomothetics; for ethnographic understanding, not the explanation in one master theory of everything that has ever happened to human beings in the past 100,000 years.[20]

There are indications too among the for-ethnography forces that the radical challenges of both 1950s science and 1970s interpretationism can be domesticated in an emerging ethnographic practice. Assessing them both, Allen Johnson writes:

> Today's ethnographies are superior in their own special ways: those compiled by believers in the experimental method achieve greater precision in measurement and analysis than the Boasians ever thought possible, and those written by interpretationists often take us closer to the lives of other peoples than mere numbers ever could. But practitioners of both approaches have focused, almost without exception, on specific cultural practices, leaving no one to amass the comprehensive cultural descriptions that give meaning to those practices. . . . There are still a few scholars—positivists and interpretationists alike—who strive

[20]See Appendix, Part C.

for comprehensiveness in their descriptions of other cultures, even while admitting this is an unattainable ideal, and who are equally at home examining functional connections or interpreting spoken and written texts. [1987: 30]

From a British perspective, and commenting on a variety of interpretive insights, Pat Caplan concludes:

> This current reflexive movement should not be over-estimated; the number of practitioners is relatively small, and the same names recur with almost monotonous regularity. Furthermore, the number of those actually writing "experimental ethnography" (as opposed to an anthropology of ethnography) is even smaller. . . . Nor should we overestimate its innovativeness; we can find long-standing debates in anthropology which presage these developments. Questions such as . . . whether or not it is possible to do truly objective ethnography have been around for a long time. [1988: 9]

It is fascinating to see how this domestication works itself out in Dennis Werner's *Amazon Journey: An Anthropologist's Year among Brazil's Mekranoti Indians*. Among the most recent and most ethnographically rich of the personal accounts, it is written by one who admits, "While I was still in graduate school, a fellow student once complained that every time I opened my mouth numbers came out" (1984: 10). Werner used several quantitative approaches in his fieldwork and, unlike the authors of other narratives in this genre, described these "scientific" studies and integrated their results in the text. His account of using Johnson's random visiting method is particularly interesting (1984: 75–76). Yet the "feel" of the field and of Mekranoti culture also comes alive in the book. Werner is successful in

> showing what it was like to be confronted with hundreds of new people speaking a strange language and doing strange things. I tried to convey the bungling awkwardness of plopping oneself down uninvited and ignorant, among a foreign people, and the sense of satisfaction in gradually growing to understand them. [1984: 9–10]

A final theme in much of the recent ethnography, and one I hope will become even stronger in the 1990s, involves its "critical flavor" and "political angle" (Ortner 1984: 147, 149). In typologizing ethnography Van Maanen has made a mistake in contrasting "realist tales," which are what anthropological ethnography is, with "critical tales" that "shed light on larger social, political, symbolic, or economic issues" (1988: 127). These are not opposing forms. Rather, a critical element may be either weaker or stronger in any ethnography, but it is this element that gives the work meaning and purpose. Both our theoretical and ethnographic productions are, at last, subordinate to the social, political, symbolic, and economic issues that move and motivate us. These never permit escape. There are Science, and scientists; Interpretation, and interpretationists; (realist) Ethnography, and (critical) ethnographers.

The "special quality of anthropology," Goldschmidt writes, "is: holism, contextualization, the preserved sense of the human scene as exquisitely complex and intricately articulated" (1985: 172). This ethnographic challenge will continue in the 1990s and beyond. We can only agree with Ortner (1984: 160) that "a lot of work remains to be done."

Bring out the notebooks. We will continue to need fieldnotes to do it.

APPENDIX: ETHNOGRAPHY 1973–1988

Part A: 1973–82

Barth, Fredrik. 1975. *Ritual and Knowledge among the Baktaman of New Guinea.* New Haven, Conn.: Yale University Press.

Beidelman, T. O. 1982. *Colonial Evangelism: A Socio-Historical Study of an East African Mission at the Grassroots.* Bloomington: Indiana University Press.

Blackman, Margaret. 1981. *During My Time: Florence Edenshaw Davidson, a Haida Woman.* Seattle: University of Washington Press.

Blok, Anton. 1974. *The Mafia of a Sicilian Village, 1860–1960: A Study of Violent Peasant Entrepreneurs.* New York: Harper Torchbooks.

Bluebond-Langner, Myra. 1977. *The Private Worlds of Dying Children.* Princeton, N.J.: Princeton University Press.

Bond, George C. 1976. *The Politics of Change in a Zambian Community.* Chicago: University of Chicago Press.

Cohen, Abner. 1981. *The Politics of Elite Culture: Explorations in the Dramaturgy of Power in a Modern African Society.* Berkeley: University of California Press.

Fernandez, James W. 1982. *Bwiti: An Ethnography of the Religious Imagination in Africa.* Princeton, N.J.: Princeton University Press.

Freeman, James M. 1979. *Untouchable: An Indian Life History.* Stanford, Calif.: Stanford University Press.

Goldschmidt, Walter. 1976. *The Culture and Behavior of the Sebei.* Los Angeles: University of California Press.

Gough, Kathleen. 1981. *Rural Society in Southern India.* Cambridge: Cambridge University Press.

Harris, Grace. 1978. *Casting Out Anger: Religion among the Taita of Kenya.* Cambridge: Cambridge University Press.

Herdt, Gilbert. 1981. *Guardians of the Flutes: Idioms of Masculinity.* New York: McGraw-Hill.

James, Wendy. 1980. *Kwamin Pa: The Making of the Uduk People.* Oxford: Oxford University Press.

Janzen, John M. 1978. *The Quest for Therapy: Medical Pluralism in Lower Zaire.* Berkeley: University of California Press.

Kleinman, Arthur. 1980. *Patients and Healers in the Context of Culture: An Exploration of the Borderland between Anthropology, Medicine, and Psychiatry.* Berkeley: University of California Press.

Lamphere, Louise. 1977. *To Run After Them: Cultural and Social Bases of Cooperation in a Navajo Community.* Tucson: University of Arizona Press.

Lee, Richard. 1979. *The !Kung San: Men, Women, and Work in a Foraging Society.* Cambridge: Cambridge University Press.

Lindenbaum, Shirley. 1979. *Kuru Sorcery: Disease and Danger in the New Guinea Highlands.* Palo Alto, Calif.: Mayfield.

Meggitt, Mervyn. 1977. *Blood Is Their Argument: Warfare among the Mae Enga Tribesmen of the New Guinea Highlands.* Palo Alto, Calif.: Mayfield.

Myerhoff, Barbara. 1978. *Number Our Days.* New York: Simon & Schuster.

Obbo, Christine. 1980. *African Women: Their Struggle for Economic Independence.* London: Zed.

Ortner, Sherry. 1978. *Sherpas through Their Rituals.* New York: Cambridge University Press.

Ottenberg, Simon. 1975. *Masked Rituals of the Afikpo: The Context of an African Art.* Seattle: University of Washington Press.

Parkin, David. 1978. *The Cultural Definition of Political Response: Lineal Destiny among the Luo.* London: Academic Press.

Plath, David. 1980. *Long Engagements: Maturity in Modern Japan.* Stanford, Calif.: Stanford University Press.

Robertson, A. F. 1978. *Community of Strangers: A Journal of Discovery in Uganda.* London: Scolar Press.

Roy, Manisha. 1975. *Bengali Women.* Berkeley: University of California Press.

Saberwal, Satish. 1976. *Mobile Men: Limits to Social Change in Urban Punjab.* New Delhi: Vikas.

Scheper-Hughes, Nancy. 1979. *Saints, Scholars, and Schizophrenics: Mental Illness in Rural Ireland.* Berkeley: University of California Press.

Scudder, Thayer, and Elizabeth Colson. 1980. *Secondary Education and the Formation of an Elite: The Impact of Education on Gwembe District, Zambia.* London: Academic Press.

Sexton, James, ed. 1982. *Son of Tecum Uman: A Maya Indian Tells His Life Story.* Tucson: University of Arizona Press.

Smith, Robert J., and Ella Lury Wiswell. 1982. *The Women of Suye Mura.* Chicago: University of Chicago Press.

Srinivas, M. N. 1976. *The Remembered Village*. Berkeley: University of California Press.

Weiner, Annette. 1976. *Women of Value, Men of Renown: New Perspectives on Trobriand Exchange*. Austin: University of Texas Press.

Wikan, Unni. 1982. *Behind the Veil: Women in Oman*. Baltimore, Md.: Johns Hopkins University Press.

Witherspoon, Gary. 1975. *Navajo Kinship and Marriage*. Chicago: University of Chicago Press.

Part B: 1983–88

Abu-Lughod, Lila. 1987. *Veiled Sentiments: Honor and Poetry in a Bedouin Society*. Berkeley: University of California Press.

Barth, Fredrik. 1983. *Sohar: Culture and Society in an Omani Town*. Baltimore, Md.: Johns Hopkins University Press.

———. 1987. *Cosmologies in the Making: A Generative Approach to Cultural Variation in Inner New Guinea*. Cambridge: Cambridge University Press.

Basso, Ellen. 1985. *A Musical View of the Universe: Kalapalo Myth and Ritual Performances*. Philadelphia: University of Pennsylvania Press.

Beneria, Lourdes, and Martha Roldan. 1987. *The Crossroads of Class and Gender: Industrial Homework, Subcontracting, and Household Dynamics in Mexico City*. Chicago: University of Chicago Press.

Caplan, Lionel. 1987. *Class and Culture in Urban India: Fundamentalism in a Christian Community*. Oxford: Oxford University Press.

Comaroff, Jean. 1985. *Body of Power, Spirit of Resistance: The Culture and History of a South African People*. Chicago: University of Chicago Press.

Daniel, E. Valentine. 1984. *Fluid Signs: Being a Person the Tamil Way*. Berkeley: University of California Press.

Forrest, John. 1988. *Lord I'm Coming Home: Everyday Aesthetics in Tidewater North Carolina*. Ithaca: Cornell University Press.

Friedrich, Paul. 1986. *The Princes of Naranja: An Essay in Anthrohistorical Method*. Austin: University of Texas Press.

Grillo, Ralph. 1985. *Ideologies and Institutions in Urban France: The Representations of Immigrants*. Cambridge: Cambridge University Press.

Humphrey, Caroline. 1983. *The Karl Marx Collective: Economy, Society and Religion in a Siberian Collective Farm*. Cambridge: Cambridge University Press.

Jackson, Jean. 1983. *The Fish People: Linguistic Exogamy and Tukanoan Identity in Northwest Amazonia*. New York: Cambridge University Press.

Kugelmass, Jack. 1986. *The Miracle of Intervale Avenue: The Story of a Jewish Congregation in the South Bronx*. New York: Schocken.

Lan, David. 1985. *Guns and Rain: Guerrillas and Spirit Mediums in Zimbabwe*. London: James Currey.

Lederman, Rena. 1986. *What Gifts Engender: Social Relations and Politics in Mendi, Highland Papua New Guinea*. New York: Cambridge University Press.

Lutz, Katherine. 1988. *Unnatural Emotions: Everyday Sentiments on a Micronesian*

Atoll and Their Challenge to Western Theory. Chicago: University of Chicago Press.

McDonough, Gary. 1986. *Good Families of Barcelona: A Social History of Power in the Industrial Age*. Princeton, N.J.: Princeton University Press.

MacGaffey, Janet. 1987. *Entrepreneurs and Parasites: The Struggle for Indigenous Capitalism in Zaire*. Cambridge: Cambridge University Press.

Moore, Sally Falk. 1986. *Social Facts and Fabrications: "Customary" Law on Kilimanjaro, 1880–1980*. Cambridge: Cambridge University Press.

Myers, Fred. 1986. *Pintupi Country, Pintupi Self: Sentiment, Place, and Politics among Western Desert Aborigines*. Washington, D.C.: Smithsonian Institution Press.

Obeyesekere, Gananath. 1984. *The Cult of the Goddess Pattini*. Chicago: University of Chicago Press.

Ohnuki-Tierney, Emiko. 1984. *Illness and Culture in Contemporary Japan: An Anthropological View*. Cambridge: Cambridge University Press.

Ong, Aiwha. 1987. *Spirits of Resistance and Capitalist Discipline: Factory Women in Malaysia*. Albany: State University of New York Press.

Rigby, Peter. 1985. *Persistent Pastoralists*. London: Zed.

Rosen, Lawrence. 1984. *Bargaining for Reality: The Construction of Social Relations in a Muslim Community*. Chicago: University of Chicago Press.

Shokeid, Moshe. 1988. *Children of Circumstances: Israeli Emigrants in New York*. Ithaca: Cornell University Press.

Siu, Paul C. P. 1987. *The Chinese Laundryman: A Study of Social Isolation*. New York: New York University Press.

Spicer, Edward H. 1988. *People of Pascua*. Tucson: University of Arizona Press.

Tambiah, Stanley Jeyaraja. 1984. *The Buddhist Saints of the Forest and the Cult of the Amulets*. New York: Cambridge University Press.

Weatherford, J. McIver. 1985. *Tribes on the Hill*. South Hadley, Mass.: Bergin & Garvey.

Whitehead, Harriet. 1987. *Renunciation and Reformulation: A Study of Conversion in an American Sect*. Ithaca: Cornell University Press.

Yanagisako, Sylvia. 1985. *Transforming the Past: Tradition and Kinship among Japanese Americans*. Stanford, Calif.: Stanford University Press.

Part C: Comparative and Theoretical Works, 1980s

Ardener, Shirley, ed. 1981. *Women and Space: Ground Rules and Social Maps*. London: Croom Helm.

Brenneis, Donald, and Fred Myers, eds. 1984. *Dangerous Words: Language and Politics in the Pacific*. New York: New York University Press.

Briggs, Charles. 1986. *Learning to Ask: A Sociolinguistic Appraisal of the Role of the Interview in Social Science Research*. New York: Cambridge University Press.

Callan, Hillary, and Shirley Ardener, eds. 1984. *The Incorporated Wife*. London: Croom Helm.

Collier, Jane F., and Sylvia Yanagisako, eds. 1987. *Gender and Kinship: Essays toward a Unified Analysis*. Stanford, Calif.: Stanford University Press.

Fernandez, James. 1986. *Persuasions and Performances: The Play of Tropes in Culture.* Bloomington: Indiana University Press.

Hannerz, Ulf. 1980. *Exploring the City: Inquiries toward an Urban Anthropology.* New York: Columbia University Press.

Holland, Dorothy, and Naomi Quinn, eds. 1987. *Cultural Models in Language and Thought.* New York: Cambridge University Press.

Holy, Ladislav, and Milan Stuchlik. 1983. *Actions, Norms, and Representations: Foundations of Anthropological Inquiry.* Cambridge: Cambridge University Press.

Marcus, George, ed. 1983. *Elites: Ethnographic Issues.* Albuquerque: University of New Mexico Press.

Ortner, Sherry, and Harriet Whitehead, eds. 1981. *Sexual Meanings: The Cultural Construction of Gender and Sexuality.* Cambridge: Cambridge University Press.

Parkin, David, ed. 1982. *Semantic Anthropology.* London: Academic Press.

Schneider, David M. 1984. *A Critique of the Study of Kinship.* Ann Arbor: University of Michigan Press.

Tambiah, Stanley Jeyaraja. 1985. *Culture, Thought, and Social Action: An Anthropological Perspective.* Cambridge, Mass.: Harvard University Press.

White, Geoffrey, and John Kirkpatrick, eds. 1985. *Person, Self, and Experience: Exploring Pacific Ethnopsychologies.* Berkeley: University of California Press.

REFERENCES

Aberle, David. 1966. *The Peyote Religion among the Navaho.* New York: Wenner-Gren Foundation.

Adair, John. 1960. A Pueblo G.I. In Casagrande 1960b, 489–503.

Adams, Richard N., and J. Preiss, eds. 1960. *Human Organization Research.* Homewood, Ill.: Dorsey.

Agar, Michael H. 1980. *The Professional Stranger: An Informal Introduction to Ethnography.* New York: Academic Press.

Alland, Alexander, Jr. 1975. *Where the Spider Danced.* New York: Anchor Press.

Barley, Nigel. 1983. *Adventures in a Mud Hut: An Innocent Anthropologist Abroad.* New York: Vanguard Press.

———. 1986. *Ceremony: An Anthropologist's Misadventures in the African Bush.* New York: Holt.

Bartlett, F. C., et al., eds. 1939. *The Study of Society.* London: Routledge & Kegan Paul.

Bateson, Gregory. 1941. Experiments in Thinking about Observed Ethnological Materials. *Philosophy of Science* 8:53–68.

Beals, Alan R. 1978. *The Remembered Village* as Ethnography. *Contributions to Indian Sociology* 12:109–15.

Beattie, John. 1965. *Understanding an African Kingdom: Bunyoro.* New York: Holt, Rinehart & Winston.

Becker, Howard, and Blanche Geer. 1960. Participant Observation: The Analysis of Qualitative Field Data. In Adams and Preiss 1960, 267–89.

Bennett, John. 1948. The Study of Cultures: A Survey of Technique and Methodology in Field Work. *American Sociological Review* 13:672–89.

Berreman, Gerald D. 1968. Ethnography: Method and Product. In *Introduction to Cultural Anthropology: Essays in the Scope and Methods of the Science of Man,* ed. James A. Clifton, 336–73. Boston: Houghton Mifflin.

Beteille, André. 1975. The Tribulations of Fieldwork. In Beteille and Madan 1975, 99–113.

Beteille, André, and T. N. Madan, eds. 1975. *Encounter and Experience: Personal Accounts of Fieldwork.* Honolulu: University of Hawaii Press.

Boas, Franz. 1888 [1964]. *The Central Eskimo.* Lincoln: University of Nebraska Press.

———. 1938 [1944]. Methods of Research. In *General Anthropology,* ed. Franz Boas, 666–86. Madison, Wis.: United States Armed Forces Institute.

———. 1966. *Kwakiutl Ethnography.* Ed. Helen Codere. Chicago: University of Chicago Press.

Bohannan, Paul. 1981. Unseen Community: The Natural History of a Research Project. In Messerschmidt 1981, 29–45.

Boissevain, Jeremy. 1970. Fieldwork in Malta. In Spindler 1970, 58–84.

Briggs, Charles. 1986. *Learning to Ask: A Sociolinguistic Appraisal of the Role of the Interview in Social Science Research.* New York: Cambridge University Press.

Brim, John A., and David H. Spain. 1974. *Research Design in Anthropology: Paradigms and Pragmatics in the Testing of Hypotheses.* New York: Holt, Rinehart & Winston.

Bulmer, Martin. 1984. *The Chicago School of Sociology: Institutionalization, Diversity, and the Rise of Sociological Research.* Chicago: University of Chicago Press.

Caplan, Pat. 1988. Engendering Knowledge: The Politics of Ethnography. *Anthropology Today* 4 (5): 8–12; 4 (6): 14–17.

Casagrande, Joseph B. 1960a. John Mink, Ojibwa Informant. In Casagrande 1960b, 467–88.

———, ed. 1960b. *In the Company of Man: Twenty Portraits of Anthropological Informants.* New York: Harper Torchbooks.

Cesara, Manda. 1982. *Reflections of a Woman Anthropologist: No Hiding Place.* New York: Academic Press.

Chilver, Sally. 1977. The Secretaryship of the Colonial Social Science Research Council: A Reminiscence. *Anthropological Forum* 4:239–48.

Clifford, James. 1983. On Ethnographic Authority. *Representations* 1 (2): 118–46.

———. 1986. Introduction: Partial Truths. In Clifford and Marcus 1986, 1–26.

———. 1988. *The Predicament of Culture: Twentieth-Century Ethnography, Literature, and Art.* Cambridge, Mass.: Harvard University Press.

Clifford, James, and George E. Marcus, eds. 1986. *Writing Culture: The Poetics and Politics of Ethnography.* Berkeley: University of California Press.

Codere, Helen. 1959. The Understanding of the Kwakiutl. In Goldschmidt 1959, 61–75.

———. 1966. Introduction. In Boas 1966, xi–xxxii.

Cohen, Ronald. 1970. Preface. In Naroll and Cohen 1970, v–x.

Cohen, Ronald, and Raoul Naroll. 1970. Method in Cultural Anthropology. In Naroll and Cohen 1970, 3–24.

Cole, Douglas. 1983. "The Value of a Person Lies in His Herzensbildung": Franz Boas' Baffin Island Letter-Diary, 1883–1884. In Stocking 1983c, 13–52.

Comaroff, Jean, and John L. Comaroff. 1988. On the Founding Fathers, Fieldwork, and Functionalism: A Conversation with Isaac Schapera. *American Ethnologist* 15:554–65.

Conklin, Harold. 1968. Ethnography. In *International Encyclopedia of the Social Sciences,* ed. David Sills, 5:172–78. New York: Free Press.

Crick, Malcolm. 1982. Anthropological Field Research, Meaning Creation, and Knowledge Construction. In *Semantic Anthropology,* ed. David Parkin, 15–37. London: Academic Press.

Cushing, Frank Hamilton. 1882–83. My Adventures in Zuni. *Century Illustrated Monthly Magazine* 25:191–207, 500–511; 26:28–47.

De Laguna, Frederica. 1977. *Voyage to Greenland: A Personal Initiation into Anthropology.* New York: Norton.

DeMallie, Raymond. 1982. Preface. In Robert H. Lowie, *Indians of the Plains* (1954), v–xviii. Lincoln: University of Nebraska Press.

Ebihara, May. 1985. American Anthropology in the 1930s: Contexts and Currents. In Helm 1985, 101–21.

Edgerton, Robert, and L. L. Langness. 1974. *Methods and Styles in the Study of Culture.* Novato, Calif.: Chandler & Sharp.

Ellen, R. F., ed., 1984. *Ethnographic Research: A Guide to General Conduct.* San Diego: Academic Press.

Epstein, A. L., ed. 1967. *The Craft of Social Anthropology.* London: Social Science Paperbacks.

Evans-Pritchard, E. E. 1932. The Zande Corporation of Witchdoctors. *Journal of the Royal Anthropological Institute* 62:291–336.

———. 1937. *Witchcraft, Oracles, and Magic among the Azande.* Oxford: Oxford University Press.

———. 1940. *The Nuer.* Oxford: Oxford University Press.

———. 1951. *Social Anthropology.* New York: Free Press.

Finnegan, Ruth. 1969. Attitudes to the Study of Oral Literature in British Social Anthropology. *Man* 4:59–69.

Firth, Raymond. 1936 [1963]. *We, the Tikopia: A Sociological Study of Kinship in Primitive Polynesia.* Boston: Beacon Press.

———, ed. 1957. *Man and Culture: An Evaluation of the Work of Bronislaw Malinowski.* New York: Harper Torchbooks.

———. 1966. *Malay Fishermen: Their Peasant Economy.* Hamden, Conn.: Archon Books.

———. 1967. Introduction. In Malinowski 1967, xi–xix.

———. 1981. Bronislaw Malinowski. In *Totems and Teachers: Perspectives on the History of Anthropology,* ed. Sydel Silverman, 101–39. New York: Columbia University Press.

Force, Roland. 1960. *Leadership and Cultural Change in Palau.* Chicago: Chicago Natural History Museum.

Fortes, Meyer. 1957. Malinowski and the Study of Kinship. In Firth 1957, 157–88.

Foster, George M. 1979a. Fieldwork in Tzintzuntzan: The First Thirty Years. In Foster et al. 1979, 165–84.

———. 1979b. The Institute of Social Anthropology. In Goldschmidt 1979, 205–16.

Foster, George M., Thayer Scudder, Elizabeth Colson, and Robert V. Kemper, eds. 1979. *Long-Term Field Research in Social Anthropology.* New York: Academic Press.

Frantz, Charles. 1985. Relevance: American Ethnology and the Wider Society, 1900–1940. In Helm 1985, 83–100.

Freilich, Morris, ed. 1970a. *Marginal Natives: Anthropologists at Work.* New York: Harper & Row.

———. 1970b. Mohawk Heroes and Trinidadian Peasants. In Freilich 1970a, 185–250.

Friedrich, Paul. 1986. *The Princes of Naranja: An Essay in Anthrohistorical Method.* Austin: University of Texas Press.

Gearing, Frederick. 1970. *The Face of the Fox.* Chicago: Aldine.

Geertz, Clifford. 1960. *The Religion of Java.* New York: Free Press.

———. 1973. *The Interpretation of Cultures.* New York: Basic Books.

———. 1983. *Local Knowledge: Further Essays in Interpretive Anthropology.* New York: Basic Books.

———. 1988. *Works and Lives: The Anthropologist as Author.* Stanford, Calif.: Stanford University Press.

Geertz, Hildred. 1961. *The Javanese Family: A Study in Kinship and Socialization.* Glencoe, Ill.: Free Press.

Gladstone, Jo. 1986. Significant Sister: Autonomy and Obligation in Audrey Richards' Early Fieldwork. *American Ethnologist* 13:338–62.

Golde, Peggy, ed. 1970. *Women in the Field: Anthropological Experiences.* Chicago: Aldine.

Goldschmidt, Walter, ed. 1959. *The Anthropology of Franz Boas.* San Francisco: Chandler.

———, ed. 1979. *The Uses of Anthropology.* Washington, D.C.: American Anthropological Association.

———. 1985. The Cultural Paradigm in the Post-War World. In Helm 1985, 164–76.

Green, Jesse, ed. 1979. *Zuni: Selected Writings of Frank Hamilton Cushing.* Lincoln: University of Nebraska Press.

Gronewold, Sylvia. 1972. Did Frank Hamilton Cushing Go Native? In *Crossing Cultural Boundaries:* The Anthropological Experience, ed. Solon Kimball and James B. Watson, 33–49. San Francisco: Chandler.

Gruber, Jacob. 1970. Ethnographic Salvage and the Shaping of Anthropology. *American Anthropologist* 72:1289–99.

Hackenberg, Robert. 1973. Genealogical Method in Social Anthropology: The Foundations of Structural Demography. In Honigmann 1973, 289–325.

Hart, C. W. M. 1970. Fieldwork among the Tiwi, 1928–1929. In Spindler 1970, 142–63.

Helm, June, ed. 1985. *Social Contexts of American Ethnology, 1840–1984*. Washington, D.C.: American Ethnological Society.

Hinsley, Curtis M., Jr. 1981. *Savages and Scientists: The Smithsonian Institution and the Development of American Anthropology, 1846–1910*. Washington, D.C.: Smithsonian Institution Press.

——. 1983. Ethnographic Charisma and Scientific Routine: Cushing and Fewkes in the American Southwest, 1879–1893. In Stocking 1983c, 53–69.

Holy, Ladislav. 1984. Theory, Methodology, and the Research Process. In Ellen 1984, 13–34.

Honigmann, John J. 1970a. Field Work in Two Northern Canadian Communities. In Freilich 1970a, 39–72.

——. 1970b. Sampling in Ethnographic Fieldwork. In Naroll and Cohen 1970, 266–81.

——, ed. 1973. *Handbook of Social and Cultural Anthropology*. Chicago: Rand McNally.

——. 1976. The Personal Approach in Cultural Anthropological Research. *Current Anthropology* 17:243–61.

Howard, Jane. 1984. *Margaret Mead: A Life*. New York: Fawcett Crest.

Hughes, Everett C. 1960. The Place of Field Work in Social Science. In *The Sociological Eye: Selected Papers*, 496–506. Chicago: Aldine, 1971.

Jackson, Walter. 1986. Melville Herskovits and the Search for Afro-American Culture. In *Malinowski, Rivers, Benedict, and Others: Essays on Culture and Personality*, ed. George W. Stocking, Jr., 95–126. Madison: University of Wisconsin Press.

Jacobs, Melville. 1959. Folklore. In Goldschmidt 1959, 119–38.

Johnson, Allen. 1978. *Quantification in Cultural Anthropology*. Stanford, Calif.: Stanford University Press.

——. 1987. The Death of Ethnography: Has Anthropology Betrayed Its Mission? *The Sciences* 27 (2): 24–31.

Kaberry, Phyllis. 1957. Malinowski's Contribution to Fieldwork Methods and the Writing of Ethnography. In Firth 1957, 71–91.

Keiser, R. Lincoln. 1970. Fieldwork among the Vice Lords of Chicago. In Spindler 1970, 220–37.

Kelly, Lawrence. 1985. Why Applied Anthropology Developed When It Did: A Commentary on People, Money, and Changing Times, 1930–1945. In Helm 1985, 122–38.

Kluckhohn, Clyde. 1944 [1967]. *Navaho Witchcraft*. Boston: Beacon Press.

Knight, Rolf. 1978. *Indians at Work: An Informal History of Native Indian Labour in British Columbia, 1858–1930*. Vancouver: New Star Books.

Köbben, A. J. F. 1967. Participation and Quantification; Field Work Among the Djuka (Bush Negroes of Surinam). In *Anthropologists in the Field*, ed. D. G. Jongmans and P. C. W. Gutkind, 35–55. New York: Humanities Press.

Kuper, Adam. 1973. *Anthropologists and Anthropology: The British School, 1922–1972*. New York: Pica Press.

Kuper, Hilda. 1947. *An African Aristocracy: Rank among the Swazi*. London: Oxford University Press.

——. 1984. Function, History, Biography: Reflections on Fifty Years in the British Anthropological Tradition. In Stocking 1984a, 192–213.

Landes, Ruth. 1970. A Woman Anthropologist in Brazil. In Golde 1970, 117–39.

Langham, Ian. 1981. *The Building of British Social Anthropology: W. H. R. Rivers and His Cambridge Disciples in the Development of Kinship Studies, 1898–1931.* Boston: Reidel.

Larcom, Joan. 1983. Following Deacon: The Problem of Ethnographic Reanalysis, 1926–1981. In Stocking 1983c, 175–95.

Leach, Edmund. 1957. The Epistemological Background to Malinowski's Empiricism. In Firth 1957, 119–37.

Lee, Richard. 1979. Hunter-Gatherers in Process: The Kalahari Research Project, 1963–1976. In Foster et al. 1979, 303–21.

LeVine, Robert. 1970. Research Design in Anthropological Field Work. In Naroll and Cohen 1970, 183–95.

Lewis, I. M. 1977. Confessions of a 'Government' Anthropologist. *Anthropological Forum* 4:226–38.

Lewis, Oscar. 1950. An Anthropological Approach to Family Studies. *American Journal of Sociology* 55:468–75. Cited from rpt. in Lewis 1970, 81–19.

——. 1951. *Life in a Mexican Village: Tepoztlan Restudied.* Urbana: University of Illinois Press.

——. 1953. Controls and Experiments in Fieldwork. In *Anthropology Today,* ed. A. L. Kroeber, 452–75. Chicago: University of Chicago Press. Cited from rpt. in Lewis 1970, 3–34.

——. 1959. *Five Families: Mexican Case Studies in the Culture of Poverty.* New York: Wiley.

——. 1964. *Pedro Martinez: A Mexican Peasant and His Family.* New York: Random House.

——. 1970. *Anthropological Essays.* New York: Random House.

Lowie, Robert H. 1960. My Crow Interpreter. In Casagrande 1960b, 427–37.

Lutkehaus, Nancy. 1986. "She Was *Very* Cambridge": Camilla Wedgwood and the History of Women in British Social Anthropology. *American Ethnologist* 13:776–98.

McDowell, Nancy. 1980. The Oceanic Ethnography of Margaret Mead. *American Anthropologist* 82:278–303.

Madan, T. N. 1975. On Living Intimately with Strangers. In Beteille and Madan 1975, 131–56.

Malinowski, Bronislaw. 1916. Baloma; The Spirits of the Dead in the Trobriand Islands. *Journal of the Royal Anthropological Institute* 46:353–431. Cited from rpt. in Malinowski 1948, 149–274.

——. 1922 [1961]. *Argonauts of the Western Pacific.* New York: Dutton.

——. 1926. *Myth in Primitive Psychology.* New York: Norton. Cited from rpt. in Malinowski 1948, 93–148.

——. 1935 [1978]. *Coral Gardens and Their Magic.* New York: Dover.

——. 1948. *Magic, Science, and Religion and Other Essays.* New York: Anchor Books.

———. 1967. *A Diary in the Strict Sense of the Term*. New York: Harcourt, Brace & World.

Malinowski, Bronislaw, and Julio de la Fuente. 1982. *Malinowski in Mexico: The Economics of a Mexican Market System*. London: Routledge & Kegan Paul.

Marcus, George E., and Dick Cushman. 1982. Ethnographics as Texts. *Annual Review of Anthropology* 11:25–69.

Marcus, George E., and Michael M. J. Fischer. 1986. *Anthropology as Cultural Critique: An Experimental Moment in the Human Sciences*. Chicago: University of Chicago Press.

Maud, Ralph. 1989. The Henry Tate-Franz Boas Collaboration on Tsimshian Mythology. *American Ethnologist* 16:158–62.

Maybury-Lewis, David. 1967. *Akwe-Shavante Society*. Oxford: Oxford University Press.

Mead, Margaret. 1928. *Coming of Age in Samoa: A Psychological Study of Primitive Youth for Western Civilization*. New York: Morrow.

———. 1930a [1969]. *Social Organization of Manu'a*. Honolulu: Bernice P. Bishop Museum.

———. 1930b. *Growing Up in New Guinea: A Comparative Study of Primitive Education*. New York: Morrow.

———. 1932a. An Investigation of the Thought of Primitive Children, with Special Reference to Animism. *Journal of the Royal Anthropological Institute* 62:173–90. Cited from rpt. in Mead 1978, 102–18.

———. 1932b [1966]. *The Changing Culture of an Indian Tribe*. New York: Capricorn.

———. 1933. More Comprehensive Field Methods. *American Anthropologist* 35:1–15.

———. 1934. *Kinship in the Admiralty Islands*. Anthropological Papers 34: 183–358. New York: American Museum of Natural History.

———. 1938. *The Mountain Arapesh, I. An Importing Culture*. Anthropological Papers 36:139–349. New York: American Museum of Natural History.

———. 1939. Native Languages as Field Work Tools. *American Anthropologist* 41:189–205.

———. 1940. *The Mountain Arapesh, II. Supernaturalism*. Anthropological Papers 37:317–451. New York: American Museum of Natural History.

———. 1947. *The Mountain Arapesh, III. Socioeconomic Life. IV. Diary of Events in Alitoa*. Anthropological Papers 40: 163–419. New York: American Museum of Natural History.

———. 1949. *The Mountain Arapesh, V. The Record of Unabelin with Rorschach Analysis*. Anthropological Papers 41: 285–340. New York: American Museum of Natural History.

———. 1956. *New Lives for Old: Cultural Transformation—Manus, 1928–1953*. New York: Morrow.

———. 1959a. Apprenticeship under Boas. In Goldschmidt 1959, 29–45.

———. 1959b. *An Anthropologist at Work: Writings of Ruth Benedict*. Boston: Houghton Mifflin.

———. 1962. Retrospects and Prospects. In *Anthropology and Human Behavior,* ed. Thomas Gladwin and William Sturtevant, 115–49. Washington, D.C.: Anthropological Society of Washington.

———. 1965. Consequences of Racial Guilt, Introduction: 1965. In Mead 1932b.

———. 1969. Introduction to the 1969 Edition. In Mead 1930a.

———. 1970. The Art and Technology of Fieldwork. In Naroll and Cohen 1970, 246–65.

———. 1972. *Blackberry Winter: My Earlier Years.* New York: Morrow.

———. 1974. *Ruth Benedict.* New York: Columbia University Press.

———. 1977. *Letters from the Field, 1925–1975.* New York: Harper & Row.

———. 1978. The Evocation of Psychologically Relevant Responses in Ethnological Fieldwork. In Spindler 1978, 89–139.

Messerschmidt, Donald A., ed. 1981. *Anthropologists at Home in North America: Methods and Issues in the Study of One's Own Society.* New York: Cambridge University Press.

Middleton, John. 1970. *The Study of the Lugbara: Expectation and Paradox in Anthropological Research.* New York: Holt, Rinehart & Winston.

Mitchell, William. 1978. *The Bamboo Fire: An Anthropologist in New Guinea.* New York: Norton.

Morris, H. S. 1977. Constraints on Research in Colonial and Post-colonial Sarawak. *Anthropological Forum* 4:198–214.

Nadel, S. F. 1939. The Interview Technique in Social Anthropology. In Bartlett et al. 1939, 317–27.

Nader, Laura. 1970. From Anguish to Exultation. In Golde 1970, 95–116.

Naroll, Raoul, and Ronald Cohen, eds. 1970. *A Handbook of Method in Cultural Anthropology.* New York: Columbia University Press.

Nash, Dennison, and Ronald Wintrob. 1972. The Emergence of Self-Consciousness in Ethnography. *Current Anthropology* 13:527–42.

Ortner, Sherry. 1984. Theory in Anthropology since the Sixties. *Comparative Studies in Society and History* 26:126–66.

Osgood, Cornelius. 1940. Informants. In *Ingalik Material Culture,* 50–55. New Haven: Yale University Publications in Anthropology.

Pandey, Triloki Nath. 1972. Anthropologists at Zuni. *Proceedings of the American Philosophical Society* 116:321–37.

Parezo, Nancy. 1985. Cushing as Part of the Team: The Collecting Activities of the Smithsonian Institution. *American Ethnologist* 12:763–74.

Paul, Benjamin. 1953. Interview Techniques and Field Relationships. In *Anthropology Today,* ed. A. L. Kroeber, 430–51. Chicago: University of Chicago Press.

Pelto, Pertti J. 1970. *Anthropological Research: The Structure of Inquiry.* New York: Harper & Row.

Pelto, Pertti J., and Gretel H. Pelto. 1973. Ethnography: The Fieldwork Enterprise. In Honigmann 1973, 241–88.

———. 1978. *Anthropological Research: The Structure of Inquiry.* 2d ed. New York: Cambridge University Press.

Piddington, Ralph. 1957. Malinowski's Theory of Needs. In Firth 1957, 33–51.

Plath, David. 1980. *Long Engagements: Maturity in Modern Japan*. Stanford, Calif.: Stanford University Press.

Powdermaker, Hortense. 1966. *Stranger and Friend: The Way of an Anthropologist*. New York: Norton.

Rabinow, Paul. 1977. *Reflections on Fieldwork in Morocco*. Berkeley: University of California Press.

———. 1986. Representations Are Social Facts: Modernity and Post-Modernity in Anthropology. In Clifford and Marcus 1986, 234–61.

Rappaport, Roy. 1968. *Pigs for the Ancestors: Ritual in the Ecology of a New Guinea People*. New Haven, Conn.: Yale University Press.

Richards, Audrey I. 1935. The Village Census in the Study of Culture Contact. *Africa* 8:20–33.

———. 1939. The Development of Field Work Methods in Social Anthropology. In Bartlett et al. 1939, 272–316.

———. 1957. The Concept of Culture in Malinowski's Work. In Firth 1957, 15–31.

———. 1977. The Colonial Office and the Organization of Social Research. *Anthropological Forum* 4: 168–89.

Rivers, W. H. R. 1906. *The Toda*. London: Macmillan.

———. 1910. The Genealogical Method of Anthropological Inquiry. *Sociological Review* 3:1–12. Cited from rpt. in Rivers 1914, 97–109.

———. 1914 [1968]. *Kinship and Social Organization*. London: Athlone Press.

Rohner, Ronald, comp. and ed. 1969. *The Ethnography of Franz Boas: Letters and Diaries of Franz Boas Written on the Northwest Coast from 1886 to 1931*. Chicago: University of Chicago Press.

Rohner, Ronald, and Evelyn Rohner. 1969. Franz Boas and the Development of North American Ethnology and Ethnography. In Rohner 1969, xiii–xxx.

Romanucci-Ross, Lola. 1985. *Mead's Other Manus: Phenomenology of the Encounter*. South Hadley, Mass.: Bergin & Garvey.

Rosaldo, Renato. 1980. *Ilongot Headhunting, 1883–1974: A Study in Society and History*. Stanford, Calif.: Stanford University Press.

Salat, Jana. 1983. *Reasoning as Enterprise: The Anthropology of S. F. Nadel*. Göttingen: Herodot.

Sanjek, Roger. 1971. Brazilian Racial Terms: Some Aspects of Meaning and Learning. *American Anthropologist* 73:1126–43.

———. 1977. Cognitive Maps of the Ethnic Domain in Urban Ghana: Reflections on Variability and Change. *American Ethnologist* 4:603–22.

———. 1978. A Network Method and Its Uses in Urban Anthropology. *Human Organization* 37:257–68.

Schapera, I. 1935. Field Methods in the Study of Modern Culture Contacts. *Africa* 8:315–28.

Schneider, David M. 1968. Rivers and Kroeber in the Study of Kinship. In Rivers 1914, 7–16.

Schweder, Richard. 1986. Storytelling among the Anthropologists. *New York Times Book Review*, September 20, pp. 1, 38–39.

———. 1988. The How of the Word. *New York Times Book Review,* February 28, p. 13.

Seligman, Brenda Z., ed. 1951. *Notes and Queries on Anthropology,* 6th ed. London: Routledge & Kegan Paul.

Seligman, C. G. 1910. *The Melanesians of British New Guinea.* Cambridge: Cambridge University Press.

Shankman, Paul. 1984. The Thick and the Thin: On the Interpretive Theoretical Program of Clifford Geertz. *Current Anthropology* 25:261–79.

Shokeid, Moshe. 1988. Anthropologists and Their Informants: Marginality Reconsidered. *Archives Européennes de Sociologie* 29:31–47.

Siu, Paul C. P. 1987. *The Chinese Laundryman: A Study of Social Isolation.* New York: New York University Press.

Slobodin, Richard. 1978. *W. H. R. Rivers.* New York: Columbia University Press.

Smith, Marian. 1959. Boas' "Natural History" Approach to Field Method. In Goldschmidt 1959, 46–60.

Spicer, Edward H. 1940. *Pascua: A Yaqui Village in Arizona.* Chicago: University of Chicago Press.

———. 1988. *People of Pascua.* Tucson: University of Arizona Press.

Spindler, George D., ed. 1970. *Being an Anthropologist: Fieldwork in Eleven Cultures.* New York: Holt, Rinehart & Winston.

———, ed. 1978. *The Making of Psychological Anthropology.* Berkeley: University of California Press.

Spindler, George D., and Walter Goldschmidt. 1952. An Example of Research Design: Experimental Design in the Study of Culture Change. *Southwestern Journal of Anthropology* 8:68–82.

Srinivas, M. N. 1987. *The Dominant Caste and Other Essays.* Bombay: Oxford University Press.

Srinivas, M. N., A. M. Shah, and E. A. Ramaswamy, eds. 1979. *The Fieldworker and the Field: Problems and Challenges in Sociological Investigation.* Delhi: Oxford University Press.

Starr, June, and Jane F. Collier. 1989. Introduction: Dialogues in Legal Anthropology. In *History and Power in the Study of Law: New Directions in Legal Anthropology,* ed. June Starr and Jane F. Collier, 1–28. Ithaca: Cornell University Press.

Steward, Julian. 1956. *The People of Puerto Rico.* Urbana: University of Illinois Press.

Stocking, George W., Jr., ed. 1974a. *The Shaping of American Anthropology, 1883–1911: A Franz Boas Reader.* New York: Basic Books.

———. 1974b. Empathy and Antipathy in the Heart of Darkness. In *Readings in the History of Anthropology,* ed. Regna Darnell, 281–87. New York: Harper & Row.

———. 1976. Ideas and Institutions in American Anthropology: Toward a History of the Interwar Period. In *Selected Papers from the American Anthropologist, 1921–1945,* ed. George W. Stocking, Jr., 1–53. Washington, D.C.: American Anthropological Association.

———. 1983a. The Ethnographer's Magic: Fieldwork in British Anthropology from Tylor to Malinowski. In Stocking 1983c, 70–120.

——. 1983b. History of Anthropology: Whence/Whither. In Stocking 1983c, 3–12.

——, ed. 1983c. *Observers Observed: Essays on Ethnographic Fieldwork*. Madison: University of Wisconsin Press.

——, ed. 1984a. *Functionalism Historicized: Essays on British Social Anthropology*. Madison: University of Wisconsin Press.

——. 1984b. Radcliffe-Brown and British Social Anthropology. In Stocking 1984a, 133–91.

——. 1985. Philanthropoids and Vanishing Cultures: Rockefeller Funding and the End of the Museum Era in Anglo-American Anthropology. In *Objects and Others: Essays on Museums and Material Culture,* ed. George W. Stocking, Jr., 112–45. Madison: University of Wisconsin Press.

Tax, Sol. 1953. *Penny Capitalism: A Guatemalan Indian Economy*. Smithsonian Institution Institute of Social Anthropology Publication 16. Washington, D.C.: U.S. Government Printing Office.

——. 1976. Foreword. In M. N. Srinivas, *The Remembered Village,* ix–xi. Berkeley: University of California Press.

Tonkin, Elizabeth. 1984. Participant Observation. In Ellen 1984, 216–23.

Turner, Edith. 1987. *The Spirit and the Drum: A Memoir of Africa*. Tucson: University of Arizona Press.

Urry, James. 1973. *Notes and Queries on Anthropology* and the Development of Field Methods in British Anthropology, 1870–1920. *Proceedings of the Royal Anthropological Institute of Great Britain and Ireland for 1972,* pp. 45–57.

——. 1984a. A History of Field Methods. In Ellen 1984, 35–61.

——. 1984b. Englishmen, Celts, and Iberians: The Ethnographic Survey of the United Kingdom, 1892–1899. In Stocking 1984a, 83–105.

Van Maanen, John. 1988. *Tales of the Field: On Writing Ethnography*. Chicago: University of Chicago Press.

Voget, Fred. 1960. Man and Culture: An Essay in Changing Anthropological Interpretation. *American Anthropologist* 62: 943–65.

Vogt, Evon Z. 1965. Review of William Holland, *Medicina Maya en los altos de Chiapas: Un estudio del cambio socio-cultural. American Anthropologist* 67:524–26.

——. 1979. The Harvard Chiapas Project: 1957–1975. In Foster et al. 1979, 279–301.

Wagley, Charles. 1977. *Welcome of Tears: The Tapirape Indians of Central Brazil*. New York: Oxford University Press.

——. 1983. Learning Fieldwork: Guatemala. In *Fieldwork: The Human Experience,* ed. Robert Lawless, Vinson H. Sutlive, Jr., and Mario D. Zamora, 1–17. New York: Gordon & Breach.

Walker, Anthony. 1986. *The Toda of South India: A New Look*. Delhi: Hindustan.

Wayne (Malinowska), Helena. 1985. Bronislaw Malinowski: The Influence of Various Women on His Life and Works. *American Ethnologist* 12:529–40.

Weiner, Annette. 1983. Ethnographic Determinism: Samoa and the Margaret Mead Controversy. *American Anthropologist* 85:909–19.

Werner, Dennis. 1984. *Amazon Journey: An Anthropologist's Year among Brazil's Mekranoti Indians*. New York: Simon & Schuster.

White, Leslie A. 1963. *The Ethnography and Ethnology of Franz Boas*. Austin: Texas Memorial Museum.

Whiting, Beatrice, and John Whiting. 1970. Methods for Observing and Recording Behavior. In Naroll and Cohen 1970, 282–315.

——. 1978. A Strategy for Psychocultural Research. In Spindler 1978, 39–61.

Whyte, William Foote. 1943. *Street Corner Society*. Chicago: University of Chicago Press.

——. 1955. Appendix: On the Evolution of "Street Corner Society." In *Street Corner Society*, enl. ed., 279–358. Chicago: University of Chicago Press.

——. 1960. Interviewing in Field Research. In Adams and Preiss 1960, 352–73.

——. 1984. *Learning from the Field: A Guide from Experience*. Beverly Hills, Calif.: Sage.

Wolcott, Harry F. 1975. Feedback Influences on Fieldwork; or, A Funny Thing Happened on the Way to the Beer Garden. In *Urban Man in Southern Africa,* ed. Clive Kileff and Wade Pendleton, 99–125. Gwelo, Rhodesia [Zimbabwe]: Mambo Press.

Wolff, Kurt. 1960. The Collection and Organization of Field Materials: A Research Report. In Adams and Preiss 1960, 240–54.

——. 1964. Surrender and Community Study: The Study of Loma. In *Reflections on Community Studies,* ed. Arthur J. Vidich, Joseph Bensman, and Maurice R. Stein, 233–63. New York: Wiley.

PART IV

Fieldnotes in Circulation

After a few months in India, I was sitting in my hut reading a book by lantern, relaxing to the background noises of evening in the *tanda*. Suddenly the door opened, and taking great liberties with translation, I heard, "Where's your notebook? We're having an important ceremony out here. What's the matter, you're not working tonight?"

—MICHAEL AGAR

GEORGE C. BOND

Fieldnotes: Research in Past Occurrences

This essay constitutes a preliminary foray into a heavily guarded, well-secured, and rarely exposed terrain. The terrain is one marked by secrecy and taboos, and what I have to say about it must be considered as tentative, subjective, personal, and strictly confidential. I had thought of writing in Tumbuka or, even better, a language without a script. Fieldnotes are an anthropologist's most sacred possession. They are personal property, part of a world of private memories and experiences, failures and successes, insecurities and indecisions. They are usually carefully tucked away in a safe place. To allow a colleague to examine them would be to open a Pandora's box. They are, however, an important key to understanding the nature of what anthropologists do; they are the records of our findings, if not of our own self-discovery as artists, scientists, and—more accurately—*bricoleurs*, assembling cultures from the bits and pieces of past occurrences. They imply a degree of deception and a hint of imagination and fabrication.

What are fieldnotes? Fieldnotes have at least two sets of qualities;

I am grateful to Lambros Comitas, Robert Jay, David Lewis, Terence Ranger, Roger Sanjek, and William Shack for their valuable comments.

Robert Jay and the late Lucy Mair and Philip Staniford served as my trusted colleagues, friends, guides, critics, and arbiters. Many of the ideas that appear here were discussed with them in the 1960s.

they possess attributes of both written texts and discourses. They
appear to have the security and concreteness that writing lends to
observations, and as written texts they would seem to be permanent,
immutable records of some past occurrence, possessing the stamp of
authority of an expected professional procedure. But there is that
personal, parochial, subjective, indefinable quality about them. They
are shorthand statements, *aides-mémoire* that stimulate the re-creation,
the renewal, of things past. For the fieldworker, fieldnotes stimulate
and are part of human experiences. The notes are thus living, mutable
texts; they are a form of discourse whose content is subject to constant
re-creation, renewal, and interpretation. The immutable documents
and the mutable experiences stand in a dialectical relationship, denying
the possibility of a single reality or interpretation.

   Further, the document both as written text and as living occurrence
is placed in jeopardy with each additional period of field research. The
immutable and the mutable are refractions of historical situations;
through published ethnographic constructions they may become part
of local historical configurations. It is fieldnotes as part of local historical situations that I want to explore here, after putting fieldnotes into
some sort of context as neither quite discourse nor fully text.

Fieldnotes: Neither Discourse nor Text

   In his important article "The Model of the Text: Meaningful Action
Considered as a Text," Paul Ricoeur argues for applying the methodology of text interpretation as a paradigm for interpreting meaningfully
oriented behavior (1981a: 203). The exposition is subtle, complex, and,
in Fernandez's view (1985: 16), problematic for the colloquial orientation of the anthropological endeavor. Ricoeur attempts to suggest the
manner in which the temporally immediate, situationally and culturally specific subject may be removed to the nontemporal, subject-
dissociated, universal range of its self-created audience. The contrast is
one between discourse and text. Discourse is an instance of speech or,
for the human sciences, of meaningful action. It has the following four
traits: it is realized temporally and in the present; it is self-referential; it
is always about something, "a world that it claims to describe, to
express, or to represent"; and it is the medium of exchange for all
messages (1981a: 198). It is of the same order as *parole*. Text is something more in that it decontextualizes discourse, removes it from the

particularities of speakers and location (Fernandez's colloquial situation), and reconstitutes it as an element in a linguistic or social system, situated outside of time. For Ricoeur, "the text is a discourse fixed by writing" (1981b: 146). With writing, the discourse is transformed into something with its own four qualities: it is fixed, autonomous, important, and open. So too with human action.

Ricoeur takes his four criteria for a text and applies them to meaningful action (1981a: 203–7). Fixation entails detaching the meaning of action from the particular event of action. The transcendent features of discourse and of action become fixed, capturing the transient tracer elements like flies in amber. Through textualization action becomes autonomous, detached from its agent, with intended and unintended consequences. An event's meaning gains importance when it is emancipated from its situational context, the social conditions of its production. And finally, human action is to be taken as open work whose meaning is in suspense, allowing for interpretations.

For me, fieldnotes lie between discourse and text. True, they are written materials and thus have the properties of texts. They may be read, though not always easily. According to Ricoeur, writing calls for reading, and for him the writing-reading relation is not of the same order as "a dialogue with the author through his work" (1981b: 146). He goes on to say in his article "What Is a Text?" that "the book divides the act of writing and the act of reading into two sides, between which there is no communication. The reader is absent from the act of writing; the writer is absent from the act of reading" (1981b: 146–47). That this situation does not apply to fieldnotes points to their possible limitation and weakness as texts and yet their generality and strengths as selective observations of a fragmented reality. Fieldnotes are written by the reader who reads them, and in each reading there is a dialogue, a questioning of their relation to reality, to a body of remembered experiences set within the larger corpus of field data. Fieldnotes fix a selected reality and lack autonomy in that they are tied intimately to situation and context. They are a constant source of answers and also of questions. Both answers and questions are related to the sociological imagination of the author—or an academic tutor or trusted colleague.

But trust is not always sufficient encouragement to expose one's unedited corpus of field materials, notebooks, journals, and diaries. The fieldworker is both an artist and a researcher, engaging in creative thoughts and constructions as well as making scientific observations and discoveries. Even tutors and colleagues are rarely allowed into this inner domain in which personal experiences provide the basis of recorded observations. The questions of others do help to stabilize and structure a portion of the corpus, to link fieldnotes to anthropological issues and problems. Colleagues and tutors serve as guides, critics, and arbiters drawing acts of personal creation into the domain of public texts, as monitors helping the fieldworker to delineate the appropriate limits of generalizations related to his or her fieldnotes and experiences.

Fieldnotes are part of those experiences and establish a dialogue with past occurrences. As texts, they only partially fix discourse. They are part of a complex personal and collective negotiation of some past reality that contributes to the recounting and making of history, not just to its description and analysis. As an anthropologist who has engaged in the continuous study of a population, the Yombe of northern Zambia, and a community, the Chiefdom of Uyombe, I view fieldnotes as experiments in interpretation. They are partial constructions of complex social and historical configurations. They are part of the process of a negotiated and refracted reality, constructed in the interplay with our local tutors and informants, our observations, and our theories. They contain principles that gain in interpretive force through observation, experimentation, and progressive contextualization leading toward general statements.

Fieldnotes, like texts, have the appearance of immutability. But like discourse, they appear to require contexts. Barth makes the point in his preface to *The Social Organization of the Marri Baluch*. In 1955 the Pehrsons had been doing fieldwork among the Marri Baluch for about eight months when Robert Pehrson died. On the basis of their extensive fieldnotes, Barth set about to write an ethnography of the Marri. Of his initial effort to do so, he observed:

> My repeated attempts at writing up this material were most frustrating. Lacking any kind of connected analysis from Robert Pehrson's hand, I found it impossible to work systematically with the notes; . . . I finally decided that the failure might be caused by the lack of adequate political and ecological data and that in any case the only hope of success lay in being able myself to visit the area. [1966: ix]

Only after spending five weeks in the field, retracing Pehrson's steps, was Barth able to write. Even then, he found it difficult to identify the critical supplementary data he needed to make Pehrson's fieldnotes into a monograph. He recognized that information vital to the task of anthropological analysis is "fairly consistently excluded from our field notes" and that what is missing is not easily apprehended. The supplementary data, he concluded, were "mainly connected with the concrete 'stage' or setting in which social life takes place" (1966: x–xi).

One may suggest that his frustration and his dilemma stemmed from his theoretical orientation and perspective, which emphasized the physical and social parameters related to decisions and choices. As Barth observed, "The interpretation of actions, both in a strategic means-ends perspective and as messages or communications, depends on this knowledge and case material remains highly ambiguous when it is lacking" (1966: xi). One may suggest that there is no cumulative effect of the "progressive contextualization" (Vayda 1983) of recorded occurrences without some knowledge or understanding of basic local principles of sociocultural life. These are principles that the anthropologist learns or acquires from observation and experience. A fieldworker learns the basic rules or suffers the consequences, as did Evans-Pritchard in his sojourn with the Nuer. These rules, the parameters for choices, decisions, and other forms of meaningful action, do not always enter the pages of notebooks but remain part of the unrecorded corpus of things past. When we review our notes, we fill in the gaps; we give order to the immutable text. Our knowledge interpenetrates the fieldnotes, transforming them into something other than what they at first seem. And in this very process the reality of text is transformed into discourse and reinstates the primacy of interlocution and interlocation. And yet the text takes on new and renewed meaning, transcending both time and place, both agent and message. It is, as it were, freed from its parochial cultural moorings; it enters the domain of historical endeavors.

In his book *The Idea of History,* Collingwood circumscribes the notion of a historian and provides a rudimentary basis for distinguishing historians from field anthropologists. He observes simply that "the historian is not an eyewitness of the facts he desires to know" (1961: 282), a view that I do not fully share. Collingwood is concerned with the idea of history and the locus of historical enactment—fieldnotes are, after all, documents of past occurrences. For Collingwood, "the historian must re-enact the past in his own mind," and though one must treat this perspective with caution, it points toward the interplay of the past and the present and the presence of memory. He makes the point that "historical knowledge is that special case of memory where the object of present thought is past thought, the gap between present and past being bridged not only by the power of present thought to think of the past, but also by the power of past thought to reawaken itself in the present" (1961: 294). Recognizing the limitations of memory, he requires evidence such as texts. But so too does the field anthropologist require evidence to support the validity of his memories, and this evidence is provided in fieldnotes. In this manner the quality of sociological memory and of human experience is enhanced by materials written at the time of past occurrences. The one anchors the other, though sometimes in different configurations. That is, fieldnotes as selective records of refracted past occurrences may not always accord with memory. The strength or viability of one or the other may be explored by returning to the field.

By now it should be apparent that I take fieldnotes to be experimental forms that connect the ethnographer both to the particularities of the field and to the general contours of sociological theory. They are not only descriptions but also part of a process of translation (Clifford 1983: 127) and interpretation. They are often the product of a negotiated construction of reality. They are for me a refraction of historical situations and may themselves become part of historical processes. It is to this last assertion that I now turn.

The Historical Context of Field Research

My initial tours of fieldwork were undertaken in the 1960s, a period marked by social and political protest but not, as some might claim, fundamental economic transformations. The historical events of this period overwhelmed functionalism, exposing its limitations as theory, method, and ideology. They brought into question the possibility of an objective social science based upon Durkheim's first rule that social facts must be considered as things, and its corollary that "all preconceptions must be eradicated" (1958: 14, 31).

The sixth edition of *Notes and Queries* enshrined these presuppositions and gave them an illusion of impenetrable concreteness. It made the claim that unless the investigator has received scientific training, "his observations will certainly be hampered by preconceived attitudes of mind" (Seligman 1951: 27): it was indispensable for fieldworkers to distinguish clearly between observation and interpretation, theory and fact; descriptive notes and records of investigation are an essential part of the facts. How it is possible to make such distinctions and separations is not made clear in *Notes and Queries*. Fieldnotes are by their very nature selective, negotiated acts of interpretation. We are not what we observe, and only fragments of our observations find their way into our notes. Of course, from a perspective outside anthropology, fieldnotes are mere symbols, but in the internal scheme of our endeavor they have become things in themselves, texts removed from the situation of their production.

Never was this order of confusion between fieldnotes and their production given more concreteness and elevated to higher authority than in the works of the lads of Manchester. There fieldnotes were treated as facts, as concrete things, as sources of authority, as weapons in the struggle to gain the high ground of functionalist debate. Central Africa became the proving ground, an almost exclusive preserve of Manchester. Meticulous and detailed ethnographic coverage of human activities was a standard to which one was expected to conform.

Two properties of the Mancunian ethnographic and field method—the extended case approach, and situational analysis—may be used to establish context for the discussion that follows. The first property is the interpretive, legal perspective employed in the careful analysis of case and extended case materials. It is intended to establish social precedent and regularities. The second aspect is the analysis of social situations to "show how variation can be contained within the structure" (Mitchell 1964: xiii). Van Velsen makes the point that "situational analysis is a method of integrating variations, exceptions and accidents into descriptions of regularities." He claims that it is "particularly suitable for the study of unstable and non-homogeneous societies and communities" (1964: xxviii). The key lies in the fine-grained presentation of actors in a variety of situations, and the means of this presentation lies in the copious inclusion of fieldnotes in the ethnographic texts both as a record and as a check on the "author's interpretations and conclusions" (1964: xxvii). Though one may question those interpretations and conclusions, the fieldnotes retain an essentially fundamental, unquestioned integrity as facts. Fieldnotes enshrined in texts become immutable. The reader, as in a work of history, has the documents before him. Fieldnotes establish the authority of the ethnographer and his texts.

Situational analysis includes the voices of the people studied and describes the situation of actors in immediate structures. It does not, however, include the actors as sociological critics or relate their circumstances and human condition to historical processes. Sandombu (Turner 1957), Chanda (Epstein 1961), and Meya (van Velsen 1964) are treated as symbols for a type of sociological analysis. There is here the inherent problem of appropriation and unwitting exclusion. Let me put this less cryptically. Fieldnotes cannot be the sole check, since they are themselves a fabrication, a construction based on a selected and negotiated reality. It is we who fix them and make them concrete. In doing so, we treat them as if they were things in themselves, removed from historical and social circumstances. Fieldnotes embodied in text are explored for their sociological principles but not for what they may tell us about history. Thus, Sandombu, Chanda, and Meya are re-moved from time and rendered speechless, passive actors of the anthropological enterprise.

My criticism of this Mancunian approach is intended as a salute to the excellence of its practitioners' fieldwork and fieldnotes and their subtle legal interpretive analysis of case materials. Their work formed part of the context for those of us who did research in central Africa in the early 1960s.

Fieldwork of the Long Duration

In their introduction to *Long-Term Field Research in Social Anthropology*, Foster et al. (1979: 9–10) distinguish three types of field studies: the single field study, the restudy, and the repeated or continuous study. The single field study is exactly that: one does fieldwork among a population and does not undertake further study. I engaged in such a one-shot effort for ten months among the Mende of Sierra Leone. The restudy involves an initial major study with a follow-up study some years later, chiefly to observe changes. The repeated or continuous study entails periodic return trips to explore change and to acquire "a deeper understanding of the culture itself." My own research among the Yombe of northern Zambia falls into this last category; it spans a period of eighteen years. The major fieldwork took place from 1963 to 1965; I returned for much shorter periods in 1973, 1976, and 1981. The first trip, though oriented toward a specific cluster of problems, pro-vided the opportunity to collect basic data on a range of topics. Subsequent trips were more focused and intended to explore change and continuity as well as to deepen my understanding of Yombe society and culture. It is from the perspective of such long-term study of a population and a community that my assertions about the nature of fieldnotes must be understood (Bond 1971, 1972, 1975, 1976, 1979a and b, 1982, 1987a and b).

Foster et al. point to three personal consequences of long-term study: changes occur in fieldworkers' research interests, skills, and standing as investigators (1979: 330–31). The researchers become known quantities in the field and are treated as social persons. They have a place in the past, and their work is understood. They may negotiate their own past; they are of the community and yet beyond it. Their standing within society has changed and so also has their vantage point. There is much assumed common ground, shared knowledge and experience, a situation that does not obtain for beginners in the field. Fieldworkers must learn how to read human behavior and social situations. They learn from experiences and observations.

The point is made more readily by a mistaken interpretation of an ethnographic situation than by a correct one. The following example will also help to illustrate the properties of fieldnotes as an intermediate form between discourse and textualization, with attributes of both forms. In my notes of 1965 I recorded this brief vignette (which I present in a truncated form):

> It is late evening and Kafa, a man in his late 40s, stands in front of his store. His son Musu is playing with his friends. Kafa walks forward, stops and calls Musu to come. He says "Zane Kuno Imwe" (Come here you). He stands with his head slightly tilted, his eyes looking away and his hands clasped before him. His knee is bent slightly forward.
>
> Kafa says to his son "Where is the sun?"
> Musu replies "The sun is so."
>
> Kafa   "Where are the chickens?"
> Musu   "They have gone home to roost."
>
> Kafa   "Where should you be?"
> Musu   "At home."
>
> Kafa   "I will be home shortly to help you with your schoolwork."
>
> Musu went home.

After recording this exchange, I approached Kafa and asked him whether he was always so attentive to his son. I had assumed that his behavior was a display of fond fatherly concern. Kafa told me that he would beat his son when he got home; that fathers and sons were adversaries, and grandfathers and grandsons friends, since they were brothers. The vignette and Kafa's explanation became a lesson in local custom, kinship, authority, and the symbolic significance of language use, posture, and gesture. A complex world of subtle local cultural nuances had opened to me.

The intellectually seductive qualities necessary for thick description (Geertz 1973: 3–33) through progressive contextualization and interpretation are present here. So let me be careful and limit my exposition to a few brief comments. After initially recording the occurrence, the next task was to assemble its elements, guided by my observations, by Kafa's interpretation, and by a given body of sociological description and theory—a body of theory that in my opinion must be treated with caution.

Kafa's use of language, posture, and gesture reversed one order of authority and yet at the same time acknowledged another one in the making, the one contained in the progressive development of the other: men grow old and gradually relinquish their social position and authority to their heirs apparent.

I have moved rapidly and precipitously from a man disciplining his young son to a social and human condition. Let me explain. The elements of this unit of discourse included language, posture, gesture, and other forms of meaningful social action. In Tumbuka the use of the second person plural—"Zani Kuno, Imwe"—is the polite, respectful form, indicating social distance. The singular form "Za Kuno, Iwe" is usually used by a man to his young children, other minors, peers, and friends; it expresses social intimacy or subordination. A man expects his son to tilt his head, shift his gaze, clasp his hands, and bend his knees, leaning slightly forward—but not the reverse. During the conversation I recorded, the immediate (or present) ordering of authority and seniority had been reversed: the father assumed the cultural manners expected of a son, with all the animus that that implies. Substance belied cultural form, however; there was a tension between the form and substance of authority, but within the form there was anticipation, a recognition of future relationships. With growing age a man gradually relinquishes his social position and authority to his heir apparent. The prospective heir becomes a quasi-father to his siblings and the father a quasi-grandfather. At the level of discourse, however, the vignette was one of a father reprimanding his son.

The message was simple and yet complex. It was situational, yet it formed the basis for generalizable statements about Yombe kinship structure and culture. The vignette was one occurrence, an experiment in individual and collective interpretation. It was a shared experience, a negotiated construction of a speck of cultural reality.

I subsequently discussed the incident with Kafa, and his interpretation in bits and pieces entered my fieldnotes. Thus, my notes contain my observation and initial interpretation, Kafa's interpretation, and a further accumulation of recorded materials. I have now added one more interpretation, and I am sure there could be others.

In 1981 (sixteen years later) I again met Musu, who did not remember this specific incident. My fieldnotes had retained the vignette and jogged my memory; the memory and the vignette were now mine and not his; both he and Kafa accepted the authority of my fieldnotes and memories. I had entered their personal (or individual) histories and, in a minor way, framed the events of their past. My fieldnotes had become a minor force to be reckoned with. My interpretation of Musu's progression was given some credence; by 1981 he had assumed many of his father's responsibilities and was treated as a quasi-father by his younger siblings.

Over the period of a long-term association with a population and a community, the fieldworker enters into a special relationship with local history. He or she becomes a chronicler of events and assumes a degree of authority over the past, especially in a situation of rapid social change. Scudder and Colson make the interesting point that in long-term studies "the people who are the focus of the study become more the product of their own history and less the exemplars of cultural patterns" (1979: 251). When applied to the Yombe of northern Zambia, this observation makes a great deal of sense. The anthropologist is also a part of that production, however.

This brings me to the second situation I wish to consider, one in which ethnographic materials enter into and become part of the formulations of local political history. During my fieldwork in 1963–65, one of the topics I investigated was the nature of Yombe politics (Bond 1976). The political situation in Zambia and Uyombe was complicated and multifaceted. One important facet of politics centered on the chief and the royal clan. The royal clan consisted of six agnatic branches. Each branch had its own territorial base and rights and privileges related to chieftainship and the royal clan council. These rights and privileges had become fixed only during colonial rule, however, and their legality and legitimacy remained a constant issue. There was much intrigue and maneuvering as each branch sought to strengthen

its political position and its authority and power. The political struggles of these branches involved not only Uyombe but also the colonial
and, after independence, the Zambian state.

The history and genealogy of any branch were essential items in its
claims to royal status, rights, and privileges. They were treated as a
form of valued property held in trust by senior men as the heads of
royal branches and by prominent, loyal "sister's sons." These men
were local historians whom the Yombe treated as authorities on local
custom and practice. Many became my tutors, instructing me in
various fields of Yombe social life. In 1964–65 I traveled through
Uyombe, recording branch histories and genealogies as told by these
senior men. The fact that, unfortunately, most of these men are now
dead has lent an unintentional degree of authority to my written
versions of their oral accounts.

In their oral form these historical accounts had the properties of a
kaleidoscope with elements being rearranged into different configurations from one royal segment and branch to another and from one
period to the next. They were mutable, plastic forms whose shapes
were nevertheless governed by literary and structural principles. They
were thick descriptions of Yombe history and politics. The elements
were neither fixed nor autonomous but often manipulated to accord
with political interests, shifting political alliances and opportunities,
and power relationships. Textualization fixed these historical accounts
and removed them from the hurly-burly and historical progression of
Yombe politics. The written texts had captured and preserved a mo-
mentary reality, removing human action from historical time. The
message of the word, of speech, had been released from its human
authors and their social condition, rendering it without force, power-
less in political contention. Or so I thought. I had myself removed
these historical accounts from the realm of discourse, inscribed them
in my fieldnotes, and then published them as part of an ethnographic
study. Interpretations might change but not the written texts.

But the Yombe have their own views about history and the permanence of texts. They restored the mutable attributes to these recorded
materials and returned them to the level of discourse and fieldnotes, a
condition intrinsic to my monograph. I had entered into their collective history and returned their text to them, and unwittingly my
monograph had become a part of their history.

In 1979 Chief Punyira died. He had ruled for more than fifty years,
and during his long reign most of the senior local historians had died.
From his death through 1981 there ensued a bitter battle over succes-

sion to the chieftainship. The struggle was waged in the National Assembly, the courts, and the president of Zambia's office, to say nothing of Uyombe itself. My monograph became an important source of historical materials and was brought into the fray of local politics. It could be used by either major faction without jeopardizing their claims. What was in jeopardy was the historical materials it contained and my rendering and interpretation of them. By 1981 one faction had gained the upper hand, and their man was tentatively recognized as the chief by the central government.

The new chief, Edwall, arranged for his inauguration, inviting important regional Zambian dignitaries. His supporters and sisters' sons returned home from the copper belt to assist in the preparations. I was assigned the task of typing up the history of the royal clan and Edwall's royal branch. The writing was to be undertaken by two of his branch's sisters' sons, one of whom would be master of ceremonies and read the prepared historical account. The evening prior to the inauguration, I was handed a copy of my book with slight but significant lettered changes in events and characters: the opposing faction had been transformed into usurpers and made into commoners, though the basic principles of my analysis had been retained and accepted as the framework of Yombe history. I was told to put the changes into my fieldnotes and include them in the next edition of my monograph.

The next day the history was read at the inauguration; copies were distributed to government and party officers and sent to the appropriate government ministries in Lusaka. Their, my, and now our text had become part of Yombe historical reality and had acquired a temporary authority—but not as a document removed from its authors and their political situation. In its enactment at the inauguration the historical account had been reinstated as discourse, fieldnotes, and text. It was now a Yombe history, a document produced by Yombe, and had itself contributed to their history. It had been restored to its cultural setting, representing the multiple voices of its authors and their relation to power.

Appropriation and Exclusion

I have attempted to explore the nature of fieldnotes as discourse and as text. I have done so by searching for the meaning of fieldnotes as a form that bridges the gap between an idea of history and the practice of anthropology. Fieldnotes are a product of past interactions and contain a refraction of past occurrences. They are neither fully discourse nor fully texts but possess attributes of both. They unite the culturally and historically specific with the analytically general. They are tied into a local world of knowledge and yet transcend it, providing the preliminary base for synthetic cultural constructions. They are fixed, autonomized, and open, yet they are mutable, dependent, and closed. They are the products of multivocality, the creation of a number of voices. They are the arena of experimentation, translation, and interpretation. They are acts of collaboration, negotiated constructions of specks of reality whose reality is not always discernible. They bare the weaknesses and strengths of an honored methodology, participant-observation. The investigator, the filter through which observations are made and notes inscribed, is at last the principle agent of his or her own recorded reality.

The view of fieldnotes I have expounded reveals the ideological nature of a central anthropological claim that anthropology is holistic.[1] Fieldnotes take the measure of this assertion. The notion of being holistic is based on the most imprecise of instruments, the "scientifically trained investigator," and the most fragmentary of evidence, fieldnotes. An irony lies in the fact that as we have increasingly refined the research techniques that might enable us to encompass the whole, we have progressively moved away from our holistic assertions. Perhaps it is our sociological imaginations and our constant sojourns with history that enable us to be master builders. It is certainly not our fieldnotes that allow us such liberties of social and cultural construction.

Fieldnotes are written texts but texts of a particular type. As notes, they may serve as *aides-mémoire,* stimulating memory of past occurrences and awakening sociological imagination. They may interact with the knowledge of social and cultural principles that the investigator has learned as an observer of and a participant in a way of life. They may also interact with the memories and ongoing occurrences of local tutors and informants. But memory, for all of us, is often an untrustworthy companion and requires the written texts as evidence of some past occurrence.

It is within fieldnotes that we find our own voices and the voices of our tutors and the other people with whom we have lived and studied.

---

[1] I am indebted to Professor Comitas for pointing out the relation of fieldnotes to the notion of a holistic anthropology. See also Johnson and Johnson in this volume.

These voices are sometimes harsh and dissonant. The production of fieldnotes, a form of text, need not be predicated on common understandings and a shared tradition, as Rabinow suggests; the understanding may be one-sided and the tradition theirs, not ours. But Rabinow is recognizing a larger point: namely, the risks of distortions in "making textual production the guiding metaphor of the anthropological encounter" (1985: 6). Fieldnotes recorded by the fieldworker are refractions of social life but not themselves that social life. They are recorded fragments of past occurrences.

Fieldnotes run the risk of being a form of appropriation. My fieldnotes contain fragments of the histories of individuals and collectivities. These fragments may be minor vignettes, forgotten by the individuals involved. They gain persistence by having been recorded in fieldnotes and may have their meaning enhanced through progressive ethnographic and theoretical contextualization and interpretation. They may even find their way into published materials as "apt illustrations" of sociological principles. But these examples and the principles they illustrate may be placed in jeopardy when they are reintroduced into their original cultural milieu. In their turn the local population may use the text and reinstate it as discourse, making new interpretations possible. But the text treated as discourse has ceased to be solely theirs; our sociology enters into and becomes a feature of their history.

The reverse occurs very infrequently; rarely does their sociology shape our history. Authority, appropriation, and exclusion thus become central issues in the anthropological endeavor. Clifford has written persuasively on ethnographic authority, so I need not pursue it here. But exclusion and appropriation remain dark areas within the academy and deserve some brief mention. To get at these issues, Rabinow sees the need for an anthropology of anthropology: that is, an exploration of the complex constraints within which knowledge is produced and received. He makes the interesting observation that the taboo against specifying the power relations in the production of texts "is much greater than the strictures against denouncing colonialism" (1986: 253). Rabinow fails to grasp the significant point that the politics of the academy is the politics of society (or of societies) expressed in various fundamental forms of appropriation and exclusion. As Ellen Lageman makes clear in her history of the Carnegie Corporation (1987, 1988) and Joan Vincent in her broad, sweeping analytic social history of the development of political anthropology (1990), the politics of knowledge is a central feature of power relations.

Appropriation and exclusion are too complex to probe deeply in a

discussion primarily concerned with the personal documents that anthropologists generate and then use to construct the societies and
cultures of "others." In a most rudimentary and yet complex way,
fieldnotes are a means of thinking and speaking about local populations. The ethnographic text based upon these thoughts and words,
however, becomes a way of acting toward and upon them. Since it is
very rarely placed in contention, reduced to discourse, it becomes a
thing in itself. The critical voices of indigenous scholars are usually
absent from the field of academic discourse. The integrity and accuracy of fieldnotes are rarely subjected to indigenous scrutiny. Under
these and other conditions it becomes comparatively easy to appropriate the history of others as, at the same time, our history and sociology
becomes increasingly theirs. The academy remains one of the central
bastions for defining the other, and anthropology one of the champions.

REFERENCES

Barth, Fredrik. 1966. Preface. In Robert H. Pehrson, *The Social Organization of the Marri Baluch,* comp. and ed. Fredrik Barth, vii–xii. Chicago: Aldine.
Bond, George C. 1971. A Caution to Black Africanists. *Phylon* 32: 94–98.
———. 1972. Kinship and Conflict in a Yombe Village. *Africa* 42: 275–88.
———. 1975. Minor Prophets and Yombe Cultural Dynamics. In *Colonialism and Change,* ed. Maxwell Owusu, 145–62. The Hague: Mouton.
———. 1976. *The Politics of Change in a Zambian Community.* Chicago: University of Chicago Press.
———. 1979a. Religious Co-existence in Northern Zambia: Intellectualism and Materialism in Yombe Belief. *Annals of the New York Academy of Sciences* 318:23–36.
———. 1979b. A Prophecy That Failed: The Lumpa Church of Uyombe, Zambia. In *African Christianity: Patterns of Religious Continuity in Africa,* ed. George Bond, Walton Johnson, and Sheila Walker, 137–60. New York: Academic Press.
———. 1982. Education and Social Stratification in Northern Zambia: The Case of Uyombe. In *Social Stratification and Education in Africa,* ed. George Bond. Special issue, *Anthropology and Education Quarterly* 13:251–67.
———. 1987a. Religion, Ideology, and Property in Northern Zambia. In *Studies in Power and Class in Africa,* ed. I. L. Markovitz, 170–88. New York: Oxford University Press.
———. 1987b. Ancestors and Protestants. *American Ethnologist* 14:52–77.
Clifford, James. 1983. On Ethnographic Authority. *Representations* 1:118–46.
Collingwood, R. G. 1961. *The Idea of History.* London: Oxford University Press.
Durkheim, Emile. 1958. *The Rules of Sociological Method.* Glencoe, Ill.: Free Press.

Epstein, A. L. 1961. The Network and Urban Social Organization. *Rhodes-Livingstone Institute Journal* 29:28–62.

Fernandez, James W. 1985. Exploded Worlds—Text as a Metaphor for Ethnography (and Vice Versa). *Dialectical Anthropology* 10:15–27.

Foster, George M., Thayer Scudder, Elizabeth Colson, and Robert V. Kemper, eds. 1979. *Long-Term Field Research in Social Anthropology.* New York: Academic Press.

Geertz, Clifford. 1973. *The Interpretation of Cultures.* New York: Basic Books.

Lagemann, E. C. 1987. The Politics of Knowledge: The Carnegie Corporation and the Formulation of Public Policy. *History of Education Quarterly* 27 (summer): 206–20.

———. 1988. *The Politics of Knowledge: A History of the Carnegie Corporation of New York.* Middletown: Wesleyan University Press.

Mitchell, J. C. 1964. Foreword. In Jaap van Velsen, *The Politics of Kinship,* v–xiv. Manchester: Manchester University Press.

Rabinow, Paul. 1985. Discourse and Power: On the Limits of Ethnographic Texts. *Dialectical Anthropology* 10:1–15.

———. 1986. Representations Are Social Facts: Modernity and Post-Modernity in Anthropology. In *Writing Culture: The Poetics and Politics of Ethnography,* ed. James Clifford and George E. Marcus, 234–62. Berkeley: University of California Press.

Ricoeur, Paul. 1981a. The Model of the Text: Meaningful Action Considered as a Text. In Thompson 1981, 197–222.

———. 1981b. "What Is a Text? Explanation and Understanding." In Thompson 1981, 145–65.

Scudder, Thayer, and Elizabeth Colson. 1979. Long-Term Research in Gwembe Valley, Zambia. In Foster et al. 1979, 227–54.

Seligman, Brenda Z. ed. 1951. *Notes and Queries on Anthropology.* 6th ed. London: Routledge & Kegan Paul.

Thompson, J. S., ed. 1981. *Paul Ricoeur, Hermeneutics, and the Human Sciences.* Cambridge: Cambridge University Press.

Turner, Victor W. 1957. *Schism and Continuity in an African Society.* Manchester: Manchester University Press.

Van Velsen, Jaap. 1964. *The Politics of Kinship.* Manchester: Manchester University Press.

Vayda, Andrew P. 1983. Progressive Contextualization: Methods for Research in Human Ecology. *Human Ecology* 11:265–81.

Vincent, Joan. 1990. *Anthropology and Politics: Visions, Traditions, and Trends.* Tucson: University of Arizona Press.

CHRISTINE OBBO

Adventures with Fieldnotes

This essay presents my experiences as a fieldnote-taker, both in Africa and in the West, and considers the interest of others in my notes—city officials and foreign colleagues in Uganda, and community information brokers and academics in the United States. As an anthropologist I have faced the same issues that confront many others: issues of protecting my data from misuse and of protecting my informants in a highly charged political situation. But as a Third World anthropologist, I have found my experiences with Western academics also mirroring the historical relationship between the West and the so-called "people without history" (Wolf 1982. See also Asad 1973; Chilungu 1976; Gough 1968). My fieldnotes were a record of my findings and feelings, yet on occasion they seemed to take on a life of their own in the social situations that surround fieldwork. Sometimes they were perceived by others as tokens of power. My adventures with fieldnotes opened for me a window on the politics of anthropological knowledge.

To Share or Not to Share

The concern over who should have access to fieldnotes is an ethical problem for all anthropologists. Once others read them, the uses made of fieldnotes are no longer controllable by the ethnographer. The problem is threefold. First, in the cutthroat, publish-or-perish climate of academia, some scholars may be ruthless in using someone else's fieldnotes to advance their own careers; others, fearing the worst, may worry unduly about protecting their work. However, considerations of self-protection in relation to fieldnotes are important, especially in the early stages of one's academic career. After all, fieldnotes are not copyrighted. Second, anthropologists increasingly work in settings where the people studied can read what is written about them. Even when pseudonyms are used in publications, communities and informants are often identifiable in fieldnotes. An indiscreet reader of others' fieldnotes may put fieldworkers or their sources in trouble by revealing the names of informants, especially in connection with unsavory activities or the confidential revelation of community "secrets." Third, where economic reprisal or political danger is an issue, anthropologists have a duty to protect their informants, particularly when working in countries with fascist or other sorts of authoritarian regimes. I often had access to information about embarrassing or illegal activities of poor urbanites which I did not want to publish for consumption by the political regime or non-Africans.

As a non-Western anthropologist, I have faced two problem areas in addition to these three. First, Western colleagues conducting parallel research have on occasion attempted to get an assistant "on the cheap" by reading my fieldnotes with the intent of using them. Second, Westerners, both academics and others, have responded to my fieldwork in their home countries in ways that reveal their discomfort when the accustomed power relationships between anthropologist and "native" are reversed. The fieldnotes of a non-Westerner studying Americans upsets and makes them anxious because they feel that their culture is on the line.

The Employed and the Unemployed

Like most cities, Kampala, the capital of Uganda, has its employed and unemployed urbanites (see Obbo 1975, 1976, 1980). The employed stereotype the unemployed as the poor, thieves, or prostitutes, regardless of the empirical evidence in their own everyday lives. It was not surprising, therefore, when I decided to study Wabigalo-Namuwongo, one of the low-income suburbs, that some of the officials at the National Research Council were patronizing and dismissive. They wondered what there was to study among the people they viewed from their office windows as "barefoot, most often drunk." The City Council officials assumed the same attitude: "What is the use of studying what is known? The poor are a nuisance who blight the city streets as they hawk food and other merchandise."

A few weeks after I started my study, I began to seize every opportunity I could to convince city officials that the low-income urbanites among whom I worked were law-abiding persons engaged in legitimate economic activities. When I accompanied trade license applicants from my fieldwork neighborhood to the City Council offices, I would press the point that Wabigalo-Namuwongo people desired, above all, to operate legally. I had discovered that most low-income dwellers who operated without licenses did so because of the whims of bureaucrats, not because of their desire to avoid licensing.

City officials were content with this state of affairs. It enabled them to perpetuate the public myths about the unemployed while privately supplementing their incomes by extracting payments from license applicants—both successful and unsuccessful: poor city dwellers had to pay bribes to license-granting officials as well as legal license fees. Further, it was no secret that those without licenses could avoid police raids only by paying protection money to city agents. Whether one was taken to court and fined or paid someone to avert a raid, the result was loss of money. Consequently, when City Council employees demanded bribes for licenses or protection, the poor willingly paid up.

People borrowed money and often went heavily into debt to speed up the processing and granting of licenses for house construction, beer brewing, alcohol distilling, and food vending. Unlicensed, these were the activities subject to fines or protection payoffs to chiefs, policemen, or licensing officers. While a few informal-sector operatives went unlicensed because they objected to paying bribes for licenses, the majority of those operating illicitly could not afford bribes and thus had no choice. Yet sometimes an unlicensed self-employed operator would lose up to three months' earnings in a day. If the poor were not "unemployed," city officials were nonetheless busy in keeping the "unemployed" poor. As one person put it, "The rich want to keep us poor all the time. We work hard to improve our lives, but they do not want to see us with money."

I was caught in a double bind. On the one hand, I wanted to correct the official stereotyping of low-income urbanites as unemployed law-breakers. On the other hand, I knew that calling attention to their economic success made them even more vulnerable to extortion and raids. The poor who were trying hard to survive in the city found their economic contributions dismissed, and their incomes arbitrarily and coercively appropriated. Having licenses did not mean an end to exploitation for restaurant owners, distillers, bar owners, furniture makers, shoe repairers, and market vendors, who had to renew their licenses periodically. In addition, goods or services extracted from them without payment by city agents represented losses. Some business operators told me that in order to make up for exploitation by city officials, they overcharged all other elite and nonneighborhood customers.

In 1973 there was a shortage of rice, sugar, and cooking oil in Kampala. The traders in the low-income areas seemed to have limitless supplies that they continued to sell cheaply. The prices did go up, however, when elite customers began flocking to the areas for purchases. By 1974 the economic situation all over Uganda had deteriorated. Downtown merchants accused low-income hawkers of hoarding essential goods and depriving the merchants of business. Several police and military raids on low-income neighborhoods followed. These incursions did not discriminate between established operators and those hawkers whose downtown dealings were the target of the merchant complaints. Local dressmakers lost sewing machines, and distillers had equipment damaged. Many local operators then stopped dealing with outsiders or with people who had known or suspected connections to city agents.

Most informal-sector operators went underground. They restricted their dealings to networks of friends and friends of friends, and even these customers could make purchases only by prior arrangement. Food sellers, however, could not really go underground, and their patronage expanded. Consequently, owners of downtown restaurants complained that "their" clients were being "stolen" by "illegal" food sellers in "the slums." These vociferous restaurateurs were African businessmen who had benefited from the expulsion of Asians and who had hoped to make fortunes. The elusive customers were mainly salaried workers in the city, who went to the low-income area food sellers to eat or to make group arrangements for lunch deliveries to their workplaces. One told me, "The food was appetizing, the food was fairly priced—really underpriced—and it was tailored to the clients' tastes." By contrast, food in the downtown restaurants was "greasy, expensive, small portions of meat or chicken, and not varied." Since many of the restaurateurs were soldiers or their relatives, army raids and destruction of food sellers' shacks in the low-income areas became common.

As the economy of Uganda deteriorated to the collapsing point (see Southall 1980), the informal sector of petty production, reproduction, and distribution in the low-income areas replaced the downtown business area as the hub of the economy. People invented new words to describe business activities. Owners of downtown shops, for example, were labeled *mafuta mingi* ("a lot of oil"), comparing them to oil prospectors bent on pumping out as much wealth as possible before their wells—the former Asian-owned stores—dried up. *Magendo* were smugglers who sold manufactured goods at exorbitant prices. *Bayaaye* referred to unemployed youth who harrassed anyone with wealth and often joined the army of General Idi Amin, Uganda's ruler.

By 1979 downtown Kampala looked like an extension of the low-income areas. Salaried municipal and state government workers were driven by inflation to supplement income through informal-sector activities conducted during normal work hours. Many who had the financial capability smuggled in consumer goods, which they retailed at high prices. However, the production of many commodities (such as candles) and services (such as automobile repair), remained in the hands of operatives within the low-income neighborhoods.

As a stranger in Wabigalo-Namuwongo claiming to study people's activities, I was an object of suspicion. The military dictatorship depended upon spies. The people among whom I worked knew that and told me there were spies in the area. The two Wabigalo-Namuwongo chiefs, police officers, and other city agents frequently visited me to ask what I was writing about and what I had discovered. When I first arrived in the neighborhood, I had wanted to maintain independence and so had refused lodgings in the house of one chief and a rented room suggested by the other. I had also brought my own research assistant with me. The chiefs therefore had no influence over where I lived or whom I employed. This, I was told later, had established my neutrality in the eyes of local people. One woman told me toward the end of my fieldwork in 1973, "We were being harassed before you came." Still another considered it important to repeat in 1979, "Your initial actions earned our trust." The chiefs nonetheless attempted to use me as a source of information on illegal brewers, gin distillers, and dealers in stolen goods who worked at night and "sat" or slept by day.

I was fortunate that the chief who was most curious about my findings, and who often glanced over my fieldnotes, could not read. After discovering his weakness, I could afford not to hide my notes and hence not to provoke his curiosity. I learned to avoid providing direct answers, while appearing to be cooperative with these officials on whom I was dependent for security and, to some extent, good will. I knew that sharing my findings with the officials would only have helped them target their harassment of "illegal" brewers and traders, whose safety and good will were of major concern to me.

Research Assistant on the Cheap

I was privileged to attend Uganda's Makerere University, where field research was emphasized and encouraged. Since the 1950s the Makerere [formerly East African] Institute of Social Research has played an important role in fostering anthropological fieldwork in East Africa. Africans themselves, however, did not become primary investigators until the mid-1960s; until then they were employed only as research assistants. During the late 1960s and the 1970s, the period of my fieldwork, the research assistants were male, with no more than a junior high school education. While investigators trained their assistants in data collection, it was clear that distortions resulted from the double impact of a foreign researcher who did not speak local languages and assistants with limited skills in English.

Unlike other social scientists, anthropologists who could not learn the local languages were troubled by such barriers to their understanding of the actors' cultural points of view. Still more severe distortions of information resulted when research assistants consciously or unconsciously ignored, interpreted, or reformulated the responses of informants who (the assistants felt) had not provided a proper image of their society. Since information was only as good as its method of collection, shrewd investigators sought out local colleagues who would unwittingly play the role of unpaid research assistant. The midmorning and midafternoon tea hours at the Institute were social opportunities for conversation and brainpicking among fieldworkers. At times, a foreign researcher who had reached a point where it was difficult to get any more information, would make attempts to gain access to a colleague's fieldnotes.

As a first-time fieldworker, I now realize, I had the role of "assistant on the cheap" thrust on me by a foreign colleague who was working in

a low-income neighborhood similar to mine and who did not speak
the local language. I often talked with him during the tea breaks and
even took him on a tour of my fieldwork site. Some time later I
learned that he was verifying my findings with the Institute's research
assistants. Some of the assistants had friends and relatives in Wabigalo-
Namuwongo, a multi-ethnic neighborhood where my own ethnic
group was not represented. While it might seem innocent to ask,
"Christine says such and such; is it true?" this behavior threatened
confidences I had labored to establish and the rapport I had gained in a
neighborhood where many residents did not trust elites—African or
otherwise—and resented new investigators asking even more questions.

Furthermore, the research assistants my colleague was using to
verify my findings were all from an ethnic group different from mine.
My colleague was aware of the inter-ethnic antagonisms in Uganda
and knew that some of my findings might be misinterpreted by ethnic
chauvinists. It seemed to me that he was jeopardizing my relationships
both with the Institute research assistants and with my informants.
Luckily, my multilingualism and the trust I had already established
carried me through this episode. I took it as a vote of confidence in me
when one day I overheard a Wabigalo-Namuwongo woman advise
another, "Tell him [the foreigner] what he wants to hear." The assistant, who either shared the sentiment or did not care about the
content of the answers, did not translate this remark to my foreign
colleague.

I was upset with my colleague. While scholarly exchange and even
field site visits are valuable, he had jeopardized my work unneces-
sarily. It was clear to everyone that ethnicity was highly politicized,
that the antagonism of the masses toward elites was mounting, and
that Uganda's fascist regime was actively promoting distrust and ethnic hostilities among the populace. It was thoughtless to play dangerous games with other people's fieldwork.

This was not the end of the matter. At an international meeting the
colleague read a well-received paper. Some sections sounded like verbatim passages from my fieldnotes. I was flabbergasted as I listened.
After the session he came up to me and said, "You are probably upset
that I used your data. I wrote the paper at the last moment, and I did
not have time to show you." His stance was that it had been "fun" to
analyze my notes. My research assistant told me that a week before the
meeting this man had sat down in my office and read my fieldnotes.

My assistant had thought that he wanted to chat and did not question him. Behind my back I had been reduced to a research assistant, a pawn in that international division of labor in which natives provide data and Westerners analyze it.

Continuing interest in my fieldnotes presented me with more problems when I started writing my dissertation. A senior professor, who had heard from a colleague what I was working on, wrote to me, instructing me to send him all my data. My supervisor was astounded. Even a supervisor does not make such a demand.

Some time later I had as a house guest a foreign anthropologist working in the same geographical area and with interests similar to mine. One evening she did not accompany us out to dinner, becoming violently ill at the last moment. When we returned and told her what a good time we had had, she was upset, and in her anger made a "slip" of the tongue: "Where do you keep your fieldnotes? I could not find them anywhere." I did not answer, but I was privately amused. Because she had earlier demanded access to my fieldnotes, I had locked them in a trunk when I knew she was coming. Later, after reflection, I was angry. We had talked a lot—mostly, I had answered her questions— yet somehow she felt she had to see my notes. Worse still, this particular anthropologist had no need to do so because she was a competent fieldworker who "spoke the language like the natives." It was simply the old instinct that Western anthropologists were better at analyzing data than their counterparts from developing countries.

The foregoing incidents would appear trivial and funny but for the political implications of such acts. I suspect that many similar episodes mark the professional careers of other Third World anthropologists. Anthropology has been and still is a radical discipline. It is the only discipline that can competently study the "other" humanity not covered by the Western discourses. Although the consultant "bandwagon" to the Third World in the last two decades has produced many reports, most of them have been superficial "quick and dirty" research. At best, they have depended upon reworking and rephrasing anthropological writings. Foreign consultants often make a pretense of collaboration with local scholars for a week or a few months in the host country. When they return home and write their reports, the local experts who assisted them fail to be acknowledged, even in a footnote.

The omission reflects the persistent attitude that Westerners are best suited to interpret other peoples' actions and beliefs. This attitude becomes even more problematic when Western anthropologists disregard fellow anthropologists from these other countries. I believe that anthropological training gives Third World anthropologists a double consciousness that should make them ideal analysts—close to the experience, yet distant enough to analyze it. After all, the Western justification for studying others has often been that it would enable us to understand ourselves better. Should the rules change when the anthropologists who seek to understand themselves are not Westerners? Understanding ourselves through anthropological experiences may have been an ideal of the founders of anthropology, but in the intense competition to "be an expert," many anthropologists pay only lip service to this ideal.

In the West

Few anthropologists are comfortable with non-Western anthropologists studying Western cultures. They are encouraging about situations and topics that are likely to produce "symbolic" analyses rather than information that is to be taken seriously. Or they are interested in plans to study the poor, or minorities, or recent immigrants (see Galliher 1980; Nader 1969). When I once expressed a desire to understand the lifestyles of suburban Americans, a scholar who had gained prominence through his studies of African societies asked, "Will they not hate you?" I resisted a temptation to point out to him that this had never been an issue when he was studying Africans. The situation was basically simple to understand: the Africans are exotic, and they are far away and cannot question most interpretations of their societies and cultures; suburban culture is familiar and also close to most anthropologists. Abrahams (1986) highlights the feelings of intrusion, self-consciousness, and indifference he encountered in studying a Finnish village. Were not these issues also present in his earlier Tanzanian fieldwork?

My first experience with the problems of doing research in the West came when I joined a Regional and Urban Planning class project in a small midwestern town. My fieldwork led me to coffee, garden, and cookie clubs that provided people with an opportunity to socialize and vent their feelings about issues of concern to them. I was adopted by two informants who saw their role as information brokers who could tell me what was going on. I found that I could cope very well without their help. But in the interest of smooth relations I agreed to summarize my findings on town life, and let them respond. They each individually concluded that I was not depicting the community accurately. I continued my research but did not discover anything to contradict my findings.

In my research I had found problems that were also daily staples of the American mass media: wife battering, child abuse, and gay and mentally retarded children. These were what my self-appointed critics thought made for an inaccurate portrayal of suburban life; such problems were better ignored in this upper-middle-class neighborhood. Two years later one of my critics admitted that she had been amazed and shocked at how much I had been able to find out about the community. "Truth is brutal," she said. "Most people in the suburbs either repress or ignore the truth." I concluded that perhaps the real shock was that a foreigner, an African, could learn something about white Americans. At first I was patronized because I was from a developing country where everyone was assumed to be both starving and illiterate. I was not threatening until I systematically studied life in suburbia and discovered "truths" my critic did not expect me to find.

My second encounter with reactions to fieldwork in the West occurred when I lived in an academic community where anthropology was considered a "nice" subject, much like looking through *National Geographic* magazines. A good anthropologist was one who showed slides of his blond self standing next to dark natives, one whose office or home contained objects that nonspecialists could easily pronounce to represent "fecundity" or "ancestors." Anthropologists dealt with strange, exotic customs, not with humanity as a whole.

I began to teach a course in fieldwork methods for seniors majoring in anthropology. My purpose was not necessarily to make them anthropologists but to bring them an appreciation of the difficulties involved in studying people. I also wanted to impress upon them that anthropology can be done anywhere, not only in non-Western societies. "You are joking," had been the reaction of one student in an introductory class to whom I had assigned an anthropological study of an American school (Wolcott 1973).

The class engaged in participant–observation at the town bank, a 1940s-style diner, and a nursing home. They learned that more was involved in participant–observation than standing in one place for a period of time and noting what happened. I also introduced the students to the ethical dilemmas of anthropological research (Barnes 1967; Vidich et al. 1958; Whyte 1958) by assigning them an event or issue on the campus. The students felt they had learned much; occasional letters to me still describe the seminar as "an enriching experience."

When my academic colleagues learned about the seminar, they started teasing me about studying *them*. The teasing soon became more aggressive, with public accusations: "You're studying us, aren't you?" I told some that I was not "writing a novel" about them, so they had nothing to fear. Before long, once again, self-appointed information brokers appeared, attempting implicitly to interpret to me what was going on in the community and, in turn, translate what I was doing to the community at large. I distanced myself from these self-designated helpers, but they persisted in passing on to others what they thought I was about, even when I avoided conversations with them. Pressure mounted for me to socialize with certain people, presumably so that my experiences could be contained. Still others wanted to be friends because they had "participated in the civil rights movement," or considered themselves "different from mainstream people." The more I remained detached, the more efforts were exerted to have me talk about the research seminar, or to share my information about the community. When all this still produced no confession from me that I was indeed doing research, one of the self-appointed brokers blurted out in frustration, "Won't you step on the toes of those in power?" This was an admission that attempts to discover and contain what I was doing had failed.

As an African in this white community, I think I would have been an object of curiosity no matter what I had taught. My being an anthropologist and teaching students how to do fieldwork doubled the curiosity. This saga was in part the result of the dynamics of a small community where residents wanted to know all about others but to keep their own lives secret. Public knowledge freely circulating orally in such a community may be threatening when it appears, or threatens to appear, in print. Attempts to censure me through discussions failed in this instance because I had learned how to deal with the situation through my previous encounter in the midwestern suburb. Attempts to gain access to my "diaries" failed too. Though I was not doing fieldwork and thus was keeping no field diaries, the suspicion that I was "studying us" gave life and power to fieldnotes that did not exist.

From then on, I decided to start taking fieldnotes, not in English but in my own language.

Conclusion

From the first week of my fieldwork in Uganda in 1971, I realized that fieldnotes would be problematic because of the political climate at the time. What did not occur to me then was that adventures related to my fieldnotes were to be a part of my life as a professional anthropologist. During my fieldwork in Uganda, my fieldnotes on the illicit income-generating activities in Wabigalo-Namuwongo would have been a useful tool in the hands of many government agents and bureaucrats to justify their harassment of informal-sector operatives. At the Makerere Institute of Social Research, many foreign scholars used local research assistants. But some also shrewdly sought out local anthropologists and were not content with brain-picking during tea or coffee breaks but attempted access to fieldnotes as well. In the West I have found fieldwork among the literate problematic because they demand and seek access to research results, including fieldnotes, in an effort to ensure that only "truth" as they see it will be reported. I believe the reaction to my work would have been different if I had been dealing with the traditional subjects of research—the poor and minorities.

Fieldnotes are central to the enterprise of anthropology. I have deliberately written this essay on adventures with fieldnotes in the first person instead of using a distant and abstract style that allows for generalization. In trying to generalize, I discovered that the fieldnotes themselves became shadowy. I have reported in the first person because fieldwork is such a personal and subjective experience; how Western anthropologists and ordinary citizens react to a foreign anthropologist should be of interest to anthropologists at large.

The issues played out in my personal account—issues of assumed power, and professional recklessness—transcend the experience of a single anthropologist. As an African and a Ugandan, I come from an area that has been dominated by anthropological research and reportage. I therefore report in the first person to emphasize my position as representative of a subject population and to highlight how this influences the way others, perhaps unwittingly, perceive me.

REFERENCES

Abrahams, Ray. 1986. Anthropology among One's Affines. *Anthropology Today* 2 (2): 18–20.

Asad, Talal. 1973. Introduction. In *Anthropology and the Colonial Encounter,* ed. Talal Asad, 9–19. London: Ithaca Press.

Barnes, J. A. 1967. Some Ethical Problems in Modern Fieldwork. In *Anthropologists in the Field,* ed. D. G. Jongmans and P. C. W. Gutkind, 193–213. The Hague: Van Gorcum.

Chilungu, Simeon W. 1976. Issues in the Ethics of Research Method: An Interpretation of the Anglo-American Perspective. *Current Anthropology* 17:457–81.

Galliher, John F. 1980. Social Scientists' Ethical Responsibilities to Superordinates: Looking Up Meekly. *Social Problems* 27:298–308.

Gough, Kathleen. 1968. New Proposals for Anthropologists. *Current Anthropology* 9:403–7.

Nader, Laura. 1969. Up the Anthropologist—Perspectives Gained from Studying Up. In *Reinventing Anthropology,* ed. Dell Hymes, 284–311. New York: Random House.

Obbo, Christine. 1975. Women's Careers in Low Income Areas as Indicators of Country and Town Dynamics. In *Town and Country in Central and Eastern Africa,* ed. David Parkin, 288–93. London: Oxford University Press.

———. 1976. Dominant Male Ideology and Female Options: Three East African Case Studies. *Africa* 46:371–88.

———. 1980. *African Women: Their Struggle for Economic Independence.* London: Zed Press.

Southall, Aidan. 1980. Social Disorganization in Uganda: Before, during and after Amin. *Journal of Modern African Studies* 18:627–56.

Vidich, A., J. Bensman, R. Risley, R. Ries, and H. S. Becker. 1958. Comments on Freedom and Responsibility in Research. *Human Organization* 17:2–7.

Whyte, William F. 1958. Freedom and Responsibility in Research: The "Springdale" Case. *Human Organization* 17:1–2.

Wolcott, Harry F. 1973. *The Man in the Principal's Office: An Ethnography.* New York: Holt, Rinehart & Winston.

Wolf, Eric. 1982. *Europe and the People without History.* Berkeley: University of California Press.

NANCY LUTKEHAUS

Refractions of Reality: On the Use of Other Ethnographers' Fieldnotes

Both the late British anthropologist Camilla Wedgwood and I have carried out field research in the same village on Manam, a small island off the northeast coast of Papua New Guinea. I have had the benefit of her fieldnotes, in addition to the handful of her published papers, as a source of historical and ethnographic data to supplement my own. Because I had wanted to study the historical dynamics of political and

The archival research and fieldwork that gave me the opportunity to use Wedgwood's notes were funded by a Fulbright-Hayes (Australian-American Educational Foundation) fellowship, the National Institutes of Mental Health, and the Institute for Intercultural Studies. I thank the Archivist at the University of Sydney, Mr. Kenneth Smith, for permission to reproduce sections from Malinowski's letter to Camilla Wedgwood and portions from her notebooks; Marie Reay for her comments and advice regarding Wedgwood and her Manam material; and the late Peter Lawrence for arranging access to the Wedgwood papers at the Australian National University. The department of anthropology at the Research School of Pacific Studies, with which I was affiliated while in Australia, generously provided office space and support. I also thank Sir Raymond Firth, Gelya Frank, David Lipset, Rhoda Metraux, Roger Sanjek, Ann Stoler, and Michael Young for their incisive comments and helpful suggestions on an earlier version of this essay.

Portions of Malinowski's letters to Wedgwood are printed with the permission of his daughter, Helena Wayne.

economic change, I was interested in finding a field site in Melanesia where earlier anthropological research had been carried out. I was also concerned to find a research site where another female anthropologist interested in the lives of women had previously worked, as I particularly wanted to discover what changes, if any, there might have been in women's economic and political roles.

Nearly fifty years separated our research. Wedgwood went to Manam Island in 1933–34; I arrived there in 1978. Although she published several articles soon after she returned from the field (Wedgwood 1933, 1934a and b, 1935, 1937, 1938), when she died in 1955, at the relatively young age of fifty-four, she had not yet written a full ethnographic account of Manam society.[1] I was fortunate, therefore, to have had access to her fieldnotes, journals, and letters—housed at the University of Sydney—prior to going to Manam myself.[2]

This essay is an analysis of my personal experiences as an ethnographer using another ethnographer's fieldnotes, together with some background on Wedgwood's training in field methodology and preparation for field research, and observations about *her* experience working with still another ethnographer's fieldnotes.[3]

Wedgwood's Fieldwork and Notes

Malinowski's Advice to Wedgwood

Do not write with a pencil with anything like a soft lead—it rubs. Indelible pencils are *not* a sound proposition. If possible write legibly and write native words in script or block capitals—at least for the first time of using. When taking down genealogies and when referring to individuals for the first time indicate sex in brackets. Never destroy or

[1] An additional article, "Manam Kinship" (Wedgwood 1959), was published posthumously with the assistance of Marie Reay, her former student at the University of Sydney.

[2] Margaret Mead first suggested Manam Island to me as a possible field site where earlier research had been done by another female anthropologist. She had known Camilla Wedgwood and was aware that her field data were archived at Sydney, where Wedgwood had been affiliated with both the Women's College and the department of anthropology. It was with Mead's help that I got permission from the department of anthropology to use Wedgwood's field materials.

[3] For further information regarding Wedgwood's social and academic background, see Lutkehaus 1986.

erase anything in these books . . . [they] will contain a chaotic account in
which everything is written down as it is observed or told. To counter-
act this chaos, cross-reference the scheme or plan drawn up. This best
done in coloured chalks. Do not be parsimonious with paper.

These statements are excerpts from the notebook in which Wedgwood (1932–34: notebook, 5/18/32) recorded Malinowski's note-
taking advice to her as she prepared for her fieldwork in Manam. She
added that bound books, rather than tablets, should be used—with
numbered pages. As general advice she recorded the stricture not
to "refrain from noting things because you are sure you could not forget it," or because it is so familiar. "You will [this was underlined
three times] forget it." Ethnographic notebooks, Malinowski told her,
should include observations, informants' commentaries, texts (both
secular and sacred), day-to-day observations, and documents (maps,
plans, statistics, case histories). The ethnographer should

> write up temporary sketches of different activities, rites or ceremonies
> actually seen to preserve local colour, emotional feeling, etc. In particu-
> lar write up impressions received in [the] first few weeks. This may be
> done in letters home—duplicate copies kept.

Wedgwood then underlined the following admonition: "Note where-
in native interest lies—[to determine the] native sense of values."
    All of this will sound very familiar to anyone who has read Mali-
nowski's own statements about field methodology, especially those in
the first chapter of *Argonauts of the Western Pacific* (1922) and the conclusion to volume one of *Coral Gardens and Their Magic* (1935). All that is
lacking is Malinowski's exhortation to record the "imponderabilia of
actual life and typical behavior" (1922: 20).
    In his discussion of fieldwork in British anthropology, Stocking
(1983a) has analyzed Malinowski's methods and his mode of ethnographic presentation in *The Argonauts*. He points out that Malinowski
was not only intent on advancing himself in the role of "fieldworker as
hero" but also fundamentally concerned with convincing the novice
anthropologist that despite initial difficulties in fieldwork the task
could indeed be done. Malinowski's supportive and hortatory role is
well illustrated by some of his comments in a letter he wrote to
Camilla Wedgwood on May 5, 1933, five months after she had established herself in the field:

This I want very much to impress on you: fieldwork in its best form at first looks just like the thing which you are sending over. It must at first be chaotic, and put in the form of little odds and ends. One gets whole weeks of complete disillusionment and despondence [*sic*]. And then suddenly after months of toil and labour, one or two institutions suddenly fall into focus and one or two strokes allow us to build up the full picture. And this is the joy of fieldwork. But you must not expect it to happen immediately. So give full play to what you call your puritanic conscience and what I would define as B.M.'s honest to God Functional Method of fieldwork, and plod along. . . . I seem to recognize from your letters that information, as it ought to in Melanesia, is simply pouring into your open nets. Therefore, be patient, cheer up and stick to the Functional Method, which is only a different name for common sense. [Wedgwood 1932–34]

From Notes to Ethnography

Collecting information, however, is only the first stage in the process of field research. According to her notes on Malinowski's methodology, Wedgwood labeled the next stage the "Constructive Scheme." This involves first "the projection of every significant fact under all aspects of the culture" and, second, writing up the different cultural aspects as material accumulates. Thus, one develops "a sort of double entry: the analysis of x in terms of a through w; and the analysis of a, b, c, etc. in terms of x, x1, x2, etc." She cites land tenure as an example: an analysis of land tenure should include discussion of "the social, political, economic and religio-magical relations of man to the soil as sanctioned by native law and custom" (1932–34: notebook, 1932). Preliminary analysis of this sort should be done in the field, to identify gaps in one's data.

Wedgwood did not record such analyses in her field notebooks, but judging from Malinowski's letters to her, she was apparently including some preliminary analyses of her field data in her letters to him. At one point he suggested that he "cut out certain portions of your information and publish them in *Man* as it might be easier to do it out of informal letters than for you to have to stew over the writing up of an article."[4] Thus her letters, as partial dialogues between herself and interested others, provided the medium—and, apparently, the motivation—through which she conveyed some analysis.

[4]Malinowski's letter to Wedgwood: 8 May 1933. *Man* is a scholarly journal published by the Royal Anthropological Society.

1. Camilla Wedgwood playing cat's cradle with Oaruoaru outside her field house, Manam Guinea (1933). Courtesy National Library of Australia.

At the request of A. P. Elkin at the University of Sydney, however, she did write two articles for the journal *Oceania* while in the field. Her diary for May 19, 1933, notes that she started to work on the outline for a general article about Manam ethnography to send to Elkin (Wedgwood 1934a). Two months later she wrote a second article, about female puberty rites (Wedgwood 1933). She did not record drafts of these analyses of her data in her fieldnotes but must have written them separately. Her notes remain, in Malinowski's words, "the brute material of information."

In light of current interest within anthropology in the relationship between recorded observation and the writing of ethnography (cf. Clifford and Marcus 1986)—or, as Malinowski expressed it, the enormous distance between the "brute material of information . . . and the final authoritative presentation of results" (1922: 3–4)—it is interesting to note that Wedgwood went to the field with a distinct model of what an ethnography should include. Her notebooks contain an outline titled "Plan of Book," whose eleven sections cover all aspects of a society, from social morphology and the description of daily life to the preservation of law and order and the problems of culture contact (see the appendix to this essay). Although she never wrote up her field material in the form of a book-length ethnography, to some extent this outline must have served Wedgwood as a guide to her collection of data in the field, as it is reflected in her presentation of material in the articles she did publish.[5]

Wedgwood and Deacon's Fieldnotes

Wedgwood herself had worked with another person's fieldnotes before going to the field. A. C. Haddon, her mentor at Cambridge, had assigned her the task of editing an ethnography based on the fieldnotes, letters, and fragmentary bits of analysis about the Malekula of the New Hebrides left by the late Bernard Deacon, a brilliant young

[5] As Kaberry notes, the impact of Malinowski's influence on his students is especially evident in their publications during the early thirties (see, e.g., Wedgwood 1934a). In these they produced studies of particular institutions—such as kinship or land tenure—which utilized the functional approach for the organization of data (Kaberry 1957: 87). Organizing data under chapter headings makes these divisions appear as "inevitable" or "natural" categories rather than specific constructs of the Functional Method, because that method, as Malinowski put it, was "only a different name for common sense."

anthropologist whose career was cut short when he died of blackwater fever just before leaving the New Hebrides in 1927.[6]

I have also looked at Deacon's notes and can fully appreciate the difficulty Wedgwood had in making sense of them. They are very different from hers. She commented that the notes "vary in clarity from detailed accounts of one or two festivals of which Deacon was an eyewitness" to others so "confused and fragmentary as to require many weeks of labour before they could be understood, a pencilled scrawl on the back of an old envelope or a chance word in some other notebook often giving the necessary clue to their meaning" (Deacon 1934: xxxiii).[7]

There were three major problems with Deacon's notes: he seldom dated them; he did not indicate to which of several districts different notes pertained; and he wrote in various dialects plus a mixture of English and Malekulan languages. The notes contained little information about the lives of women or much about the people's daily affairs. As Wedgwood commented in her preface to *Malekula: A Vanishing People in the New Hebrides,* "This is not the book that Deacon would have written, it is only a compilation of what he left behind. . . . I am convinced that [the notes] do not contain all that he knew of the people and their ways" (Deacon 1934: xxxii–xxxiii).[8]

I mention Deacon's notes for two reasons. First, their lacunae and weaknesses illustrate the general problems of using another ethnographer's notes. Second, the fact that Wedgwood had the frustrating experience of working with them undoubtedly influenced the way she recorded her own field data. Her journal entry for July 3, 1933, for

[6]Deacon's contributions to anthropology are discussed in detail by Langham (1981) in his historical study of what he identifies as the "Cambridge School," as well as by Larcom (1983) (see no. 8 below). Margaret Gardiner has published some of Deacon's letters to her in her recent memoir (1984).

[7]In May 1928, Wedgwood wrote rather despairingly to her former professor at Cambridge W. E. Armstrong: "I am gradually breaking the back of the job of getting Deacon's notes into order, & discovering how much material there is. . . . My room is at present littered with genealogies & tables of comparative terms. . . . I suppose I shall eventually reduce it to an intelligible form, but at present I feel rather like Alice in Wonderland" (qtd. in Gardiner 1984: xvii).

[8]Joan Larcom (1983), an anthropologist who some fifty years later returned to the New Hebrides (now called Vanuautu) and worked among the Mewun, one of the groups Deacon had studied, has written about "following Deacon" and the use she has made of his work. Her essay discusses in particular the implications of some of the differences she found between his fieldnotes and Wedgwood's edited version of them.

example, recorded that she had started a catalogue of her photos to be sent back to the University of Sydney with the negatives: "If I should die, my editors will at least not suffer in that respect as I did from Bernard's very few and uncatalogued photos!" (Wedgwood 1932–34, Journal No. 3: 79). Both Wedgwood and Haddon bemoaned the fact that Deacon had not recorded the detail about everyday life which, Wedgwood implies, he would certainly have conveyed had he himself written up his field materials. This point raises a more general question about what ethnographers include in their notes. Is it likely, as Keesing states (1981: 7), that "much of what the ethnographer learns never goes into the notebooks" because it remains in the realm "that for lack of a better term, we can call the 'unconscious'—a knowledge of scenes and smells and people and sounds that cannot be captured in the written word"? I agree that much of our sensory response to persons and scenes does not go into our notes, but not because this information cannot be captured in the written word. That is a matter of skill: some people are better than others in conveying "a sense of place." Rather, I think the heart of the problem is that we all make certain unconscious assumptions about what is important or relevant to record.[9]

Wedgwood correctly believed that Deacon knew more than he conveyed in his notes. In fact, it was through reading letters he wrote to his girlfriend Margaret Gardiner and to other friends and colleagues that Wedgwood was able to garner information about Malekula that was lacking in his notes. Because their aim and audience differ, letters may attempt to evoke a less "objective" sense of persons and place than fieldnotes and thus often provide the very information that is not recorded in raw notes.[10]

Wedgwood commented that the clearest and most vivid notes were those describing events Deacon had actually witnessed. Her comment is testimony to Malinowski's point that fieldwork should focus on the recording of information about events that the ethnographer has participated in and can question individuals about directly (the methodol-

[9]See Barth's preface to his edition of Pehrson's notes on the Marri Baluch: "There may be kinds of information that are in fact vital to the task of anthropological analysis but are fairly consistently excluded from our field notes—in other words . . . we have conventional criteria for identifying observations as data that are inappropriate for the kinds of hypotheses and theories we wish to develop in our analysis" (Barth 1966: x).

[10]Deacon's letters from Malekula to his girlfriend in Cambridge show that information about fieldwork conveyed to a loved one may be quite different from what one writes to a colleague or mentor, more introspective than ethnographic (Gardiner 1984). I appreciate Michael Young's thoughtful comments on this point.

ogy that Clifford, in this volume, identifies as "description"). This contrasts with a primary dependence on questioning informants about specific categories of information, such as the "Notes and Queries" sort of interrogation that Rivers and Seligman advised (Clifford's "transcription").

Wedgwood's Field Materials

In contrast to Deacon, Wedgwood wrote her notes in a series of thirty-four neatly bound notebooks. They were so carefully dated—sometimes even indicating the time of day—that it was easy to follow the chronology of her fieldwork. She left the left-hand pages blank so that if she had new information to add later or a correction to make, she could insert it alongside the original version. She would write the new material in pencil or contrasting ink as a way of distinguishing the two versions.

Following Malinowski's prescriptions, her notes consist of recorded observations of daily activities, genealogical data, fragments of texts with interlineal translations, narrative descriptions of events and processes, and drawings diagraming such things as house construction and the parts of an outrigger canoe. (Haddon was particularly interested in comparative data on Oceanic canoes.)

Even with the clarity of her notes and their narrative format, however, I found that Wedgwood's letters, journals, and published articles were essential as corollary sources of information. In her journals she kept a daily record, providing detailed narrative descriptions of both special events and mundane daily occurrences. Her field materials also included sketch maps of settlement patterns, collections of plant specimens and artifacts, and photographs.

Using Another Ethnographer's Notes

Empathy and Identification: "Becoming the Other"

As I was not able to take copies of Wedgwood's notes into the field with me, before going to Manam I read through them to extract information about those topics and situations that were relevant to my research. Quickly, however, I became as interested in what I could learn about her, the ethnographer, as I was in the people and customs

2. Interior of Camilla Wedgwood's field house, Manam Island, New Guinea (1933). Courtesy National Library of Australia.

she was describing. At that point, prior to going to the field, the Manam themselves remained anonymous, faceless characters who soon merged into an undifferentiated group in my mind. Data about Manam culture remained a mass of decontextualized and therefore seemingly random and isolated social facts. I had been warned not to spend too much time studying Wedgwood's notes before going to Manam. This advice proved well founded.

My initial reading of her field journals and letters to friends, mentors, and family also captivated my attention less for their data about Manam society and culture than for what they could tell me about Wedgwood herself. This was more than simple curiosity. Like Wedgwood, I was a woman going into the field alone, and I easily identified with her. Since she was no longer alive to answer direct questions about what fieldwork on Manam had been like, I tried to read between the lines. I found myself searching for clues in this account from forty-five years earlier as to what a similar experience might hold in store for me.

Fieldwork, as the anthropological cliché states, is our profession's *rite de passage*. As we know, the initial stage of many rites of passage entails separation from one's former status and some form of instruction in the "mysteries" or secrets associated with the new status. As a graduate student preparing for my first major stint of fieldwork, in addition to reading Wedgwood's fieldnotes for information about Manam society, I came to realize that I also viewed her notes as a source of personal insight into the mysteries of the fieldwork endeavor on which I was about to embark. Reading her field materials and talking with relatives and colleagues who had known her provided me with a means of "becoming the other"—not, at least initially, of "becoming a Manam" but, through a process of empathy, becoming the *other ethnographer* to have worked on Manam.

Entree into the Field

There were many obvious ways in which access to Wedgwood's fieldnotes was helpful in beginning my own field research: they provided genealogical and demographic data, and they helped me to learn the language. But there were also unanticipated ways in which her ethnographic materials facilitated my entree into the field.

Because I intended to use her data as a baseline for the study of processes of culture change and the effects of culture contact on gender, economic, and political relations, I knew that I wanted to work in the same villages. Using the fieldnotes, I was able to seek out individuals who were still living with whom Wedgwood had been closely involved. Her notes related details—some intimate or humorous, others more mundane—about their lives and provided a way for me to build on her earlier relationships with them. It was fortunate, therefore, that the Manam had liked her and had no objection to having another anthropologist in their midst. By treating me categorically as if I were Wedgwood's granddaughter, they were able to fit me into their community and network of kinship relations with relative ease. Personal names in Manam are transferred from grandparent to grandchild; hence, I was given her Manam name—Idoge. This identity also provided me with membership in a particular clan and with an instant set of kinship relations—consanguineal and affinal.

In a sense, then, Wedgwood herself provided me with a logical structural position in the village and a means of kinship with the past. I also brought with me her photographs of some of the Manam's venerated ancestors, which elicited a deeply emotional response from their descendants. This event was what ultimately authenticated my presence and established a general level of rapport between many of the Manam and me. A ceremony was held in the village to honor those in the pictures who had died, and I made a pilgrimage around the island to show the photographs to people in other villages.

Establishment of rapport with strangers is one of the major challenges an anthropologist faces on first entrance into the field. This task was facilitated by the fictive connection the Manam created between Wedgwood and me. (Barth [1966] found the same sort of fiction useful in legitimizing his presence among the Marri Baluch when he conducted a brief fieldwork visit in order to help him edit Pehrson's fieldnotes. See also Stoller 1987.) More significantly, my presence on the island was quickly publicized and legitimized by the fact that I had brought photographs of deceased relatives and leaders who had been important to the Manam.

Using another person's fieldnotes can entail more, I learned, than simply culling facts and figures from them. Inscribed there also, in a sense, are specific social relations, the close involvement or rapport established with particular individuals. More diffusely, one's presence can be legitimized—that is, in some way rationalized—by the demonstration of a connection with the past. In my case, Wedgwood's fieldnotes and photographs provided me an identification both with the former anthropologist and with ancestors important to the present population.

"Liminal Phase": Betwixt and Between

After a year I left the field and returned to Australia, where I had a second opportunity to read through Wedgwood's fieldnotes. Having been submerged for the previous twelve months in Manam society, I now perceived Manam as a home in a way that neither Sydney or Canberra were. Because I knew that I would be returning to Manam after a month's absence, this reemergence into the world of Australia— where I had distant acquaintances, but no close friends or family—was a "liminal" period for me: I was betwixt and between the two more familiar and personal worlds of New York and Manam. To a large extent I was still "in" Manam during the time I was visiting in Australia, and from a broader perspective the entire period of research was liminal—in the sense that fieldwork in itself can be considered the liminal phase in the process of becoming a professional anthropologist.

Reading Wedgwood's notes was an entirely different experience the second time, for I was now reading with the interest and knowledge of an insider. The people and activities she described were now "local history" for me, a chronicle of past events some of which I had heard about in other contexts, others of which illuminated present events. They filled in gaps in my understanding of the reasons why certain things happened or were done in a particular way. Details about people, places, terms, and events had an importance and relevance for me that they could not have had before I had actually been in the field and spent time living with the Manam, studying their culture, and getting to know individuals among them.

Wedgwood herself, as author of the notes, faded into the background. I became less interested in her voice and her experience than in the Manam. Now that I recognized certain persons she was writing about, they were no longer merely a cast of faceless characters but individuals I had come to know personally or knew of indirectly through their descendants. Rather than identifying with Wedgwood in her role as ethnographer, I found myself identifying to a greater degree with the Manam. The liminal quality of this period also had an effect on my reading of the notes. The world that Wedgwood's words depicted had an immediacy and a reality that was more meaningful to me than the "real" world of Australia and the University of Sydney Library, where I was physically located in space.

Reintegration and Return

On my next return from the field I did not immediately read through Wedgwood's notes again. Instead, I was preoccupied for some time with organizing and analyzing my own field data and reaching my own conclusions about Manam society. Wedgwood's fieldnotes seemed less relevant to me during this stage of formulating an interpretation of Manam culture based on my own observations (Lutkehaus 1985).

However, I did refer frequently to the few articles she had published about Manam society immediately after she had left the field. Thus, unlike Wedgwood in her work with Deacon's notes, I had the benefit of some of her interpretations of her own data. In comparing my data with hers, it was apparent that in some respects she had misjudged the resiliency of certain aspects of Manam culture in the face of Western influence, and this raised interesting questions.

I entered into a dialogue—sometimes an argument—with her; I questioned some of her conclusions, pointed out what I felt were limitations and inconsistencies in her interpretations (Lutkehaus 1982). This seems to have been a necessary stage in defining myself as distinct from her, a part of the process of separating my identity from hers by asserting and establishing a difference between us. Just as a child or student needs to establish his or her own identity distinct from that of a parent or mentor, I needed to establish my own autonomy, now that I had successfully carried out my own fieldwork and was back in the relative security of my familiar environment. In the experience of fieldwork we were now equals. By asserting conclusions contrary to some of hers, I was establishing a new relationship of equality.

Finally, after my own interpretations and analysis of Manam society had deepened, I returned to her notes a third time. This time I was looking for data related to specific points in my conclusions about the organization of Manam society. In this reading the Manam again faded into the background, no longer important to me as the particular individuals I had come to know. Neither was I interested in focusing on the nature of Wedgwood's experience in the field. With regard to both the Manam and Wedgwood, I was less interested in empathetic relationships based on identification than in ascertaining certain social facts and the significance to the Manam of certain events, terms, and relationships. I now became more sensitive to the issue of the effect Wedgwood's own interests and interpretations may have had on the data she obtained and the way in which she recorded them.

Beyond Empathy to Understanding

I have chosen here to focus on the description and analysis of the changing nature of my relationship to Wedgwood's fieldnotes rather than on a discussion of the many specific ways in which the data in those notes were useful in my own research—although of course the two are interrelated. I have done so because I believe that the use of another's fieldnotes, in addition to involving the process of reading a specific kind of text, entails establishing a personal relationship with the notes. All fieldnotes represent an extension or projection of the individual who wrote them. This is the more significant when someone else actually uses those notes, especially if the person who produced them is no longer alive. Like other social relations established during the course of anthropological research, the relationship between the ethnographer as reader and the *other* ethnographer as author has to be negotiated. It is a relationship that changes with time as one's own experience as an ethnographer and one's understanding of the culture in question changes.

Some aspects of my use of Wedgwood's field materials were specific to my particular situation; for instance, not everyone who uses another anthropologist's fieldnotes is embarking on field research for the first time. But other aspects can be generalized. Joan Larcom, who used Deacon's fieldnotes as an adjunct to her own fieldnotes in the New Hebrides, also found that her response to his notes changed over time. Moreover, it is possible to interpret her account of "following Deacon" as the record of a process of negotiating a relationship between Deacon and herself, mediated by his notes. According to Larcom (1983: 176), she had to come to terms with "a ghost of [her] anthropological ancestors."

Although fieldnotes represent a form of text, the reader's interaction with them, as with more finely crafted texts, engages him or her in a phenomenology of reading, a process that has both intellectual and emotional dimensions. One must have the time and opportunity to "live" with another anthropologist's notes in order to establish a relationship with them. This is probably true of one's relationship with one's own fieldnotes as well.

Perhaps the most serious difficulty in the attempt to use another's fieldnotes relates to what they do *not* contain. Wedgwood's fieldnotes remain, for the most part, an example of Malinowski's "chaotic odds and ends of information." Before they could have full significance for me, I had to actually go to Manam myself and, finally, grapple with the process of analyzing and interpreting the data I collected there.

There is no doubt that having access to another ethnographer's fieldnotes can be advantageous. However, as I have tried to convey, there is a particular challenge associated with this opportunity. In addition to the task of learning to understand "the native's point of view" through the process of getting to know "the other," one must establish a relationship with the other ethnographer through the medium of the notes. This process entails moving beyond the establishment of empathy (or antipathy) in order to grasp the other ethnographer's point of view.[11] Ultimately, it becomes, as Rosemary Firth (1985: 22) has suggested, a matter of "the living and the dead [being] caught up together, in an operation of bringing order and significance to aspects of the present we feel we know, and of the past we try to apprehend."

APPENDIX: WEDGWOOD'S "PLAN OF BOOK"

In the same notebook in which she had written lecture notes about fieldwork in May 1932, while she was attending Malinowski's seminar at the London School of Economics, Wedgwood also wrote down the following detailed outline titled "Plan of Book."

Part I

Introduction: make this interesting; give own qualifications, scientific credentials, temperamental bias, length of stay, etc., etc.

Environment: general feeling of the people.
   a) Geographical environment: climate, fauna, flora; rainfall and seasons; maps.

Source: Undated notebook in Wedgwood Personal Archives, University Archives, University of Sydney.

[11] See Frank (1985) for a discussion of the contribution empathy can make to the goal of understanding in other aspects of anthropological research—in particular, the life history method and biographical interpretation.

b) Social environment: ie. account of neighboring tribes; contacts by war and trade, etc. just referred to. Contact with whites.
c) Demography: statistics, etc.

Part II

Social Morphology: give in rather formal, schematic way.
  (i) Territorial Groupings
      Tribe, sub-tribe; district; village or hamlet group; quarter of the village.
  (ii) Kinship Groups
      Moiety; phratry; clan; lineage; extended family; family.
  (iii) Status Groups
      Ranks, age groups, occupational groups, secret societies.

Part III

Descriptive Account of Daily Life
  (i) Place things into a definite scheme with the calendar—festive seasons, division of labour according to the seasons.
  (ii) Account of daily life—as shown at different seasons. Giving routine of work, hours of meals, etc.
  (iii) Play, singing, dancing and other recreations and sports.
  (iv) Ritual activities in daily and seasonal life—to be touched on.
  (v) Children and Adults—the seasonal and daily activities of children; work and play.
  (vi) Etiquette and social mores—ethical standards and the sanctions behind these.
  (vii) Legal elements of tribal life and their sanctions.
  (viii) Quarrels and strife within the village—types of offence which cause this.
(Note: [vii] and [viii] to be dealt with fully later)

Part IV

Kinship (Biographical Treatment)
Ideas concerning relations of the sexes: attitude of men and women towards each other; ideas concerning chastity; prenuptial conduct; postmarital sex freedom; etc.
The place of marriage in native life: status of the unmarried and married; value of fertility and of motherhood; value of fatherhood.
Courtship and Betrothal: arranging marriages; types of union; qualifications and prerequisites of marriage.
Marriage as a procreative contract: the marriage ritual and the legal aspect of marriage; period between birth and conception; conception—native theory, especially in relation to kinship; period of pregnancy, and attitudes towards it.
Birth: sociology of birth—where, who attends, etc.; ceremonial; period of mother and child isolation and their ritual release; naming (if done later—postpone); infanticide and abortion; twins, monsters, miscarriages, still-births, death of mother in childbirth; birth rate and infant mortality; fatherless children.
Lactation: duration of; nutritive aspects—how nursed, times of feeding, etc.; domestic aspect—how carried, cleaned, etc; social aspect—who tends it, etc.

The sociological awakening: the groups who surround the child as it awakens to its surroundings; constitution of the family and household; contact with other households; the linguistic side of this initial situation (first instalment of family terms); survey of the kinship situation; the endurance of the individual ties throughout life; the complexity of kinship and quasi-kinship bonds.

Marriage (from point of view of husband and wife): pre-requisites of marriage (cf. courtship); prescribed and proscribed unions;

Courtship: opportunities for individual selection; place of love and spontaneity; motives for marrying.

Character of relationship between husband and wife: domestic, economic, legal, religious, sexual (sexual exclusiveness and adultery), divorce.

New social contacts and obligations resulting from marriage: i.e. relations to kindred of the spouse; linguistic aspect of these; kinship terms for affinals.

Parenthood (cross-reference back): change of social status resulting from parenthood and how this marked; further changes of status through social growth of children (e.g. initiation; marriage; birth of 3rd generation).

The education period: way in which early tending passes into education; sociology of education (weaning, changes of dress, naming, etc.); education proper—technological and sociological; the child's social horizon: the home, the children's republic; other adults with whom it comes into contact; linguistic aspects of this: first extension of kinship terms; modes of address and reference by children amongst themselves and by children to adults and reciprocally.

The puberty periods (treat boys and girls separately): crisis of initiation—age, rites, etc.

Sociological side: performers; separation from the family and introduction to clan system; segregation of the sexes or marking of sex dichotomy (men and women's club-houses, etc.), rules of descent and principle of unilateral stress; introduction to adult life and activities—occupations, ritual life, mythology; linguistic aspect of this new social horizon (secondary extension of kinship terms).

Death: mortuary duties—sociology and procedure (deal with latter briefly here); cult of ancestors—by who carried out, and for how long.

Part V

Social Organization

(a) The House or Homestead: plan showing disposition of rooms, hearths, etc. How is it used and by whom; position in polygynous household (note social function of verandah, etc. where such is found). Sleeping, cooking, eating and working arrangements (distribution of household work—v. Economic life). Personnel of the household—arrangement for guests, etc. Authority in the household—in hands of one person or divided according to sphere of activity.

(b) The Village, Hamlet or Horde: plan of the village, showing arrangement of huts, adjacent gardents, wells, granaries, etc. Who occupies the houses—i.e. what relationships are the members of the households to each other; is the village or horde divided into "quarters" occupied by members of different kinship or other social groups? The place in the social life of the village square or clubhouse. The political organization of the village—headman, council, etc.

(c) The Hamlet Group: kinship, ritual, economic, social bonds between members of neighboring hamlets. Paths, etc. and their ownership and upkeep. Quarrels between the hamlets and how dealt with. Political organization, if any, of the hamlet group (as in [b]).

(d) The District: (as in [c]).

(e) The Tribe: (as in [c]).

[Statistics of population in (a)–(e)]

Part VI

The Economic Life (Ref. back to Part III)

(i) Land and Land Tenure: land used for different purposes; ownership of land—by the clan, village, etc. Use of boundary marks, etc., rights of using the land or its wild produce (note especially rights over trees).

Gardening rights: permanent and shifting; how acquired and how passed on; rights of clearing virgin bush.

Ritual aspects of land ownership and tenure: myths concerning rights over land.

Quarrels: concerning land (a) between fellow villagers; (b) between different villages—how they arise and how are they usually settled?

Map out the garden held by a village, showing what cultivated by whom and give history of different plots; also case histories of disputes over land and water rights.

(ii) Water: sea, reefs and foreshore, streams (as for [1]—note also regulation of water-rights in connection with irrigation).

(iii) Food-getting Activities:

(a) Gardening: different kinds of crops and different varieties of each; techniques and ritual of cultivation.

(b) Organization of labour: storing or distribution of crops. Rights over standing and harvested crops (e.g. of wayfarers, clansfellows, certain kindred to take what is required by them from the field). [Note: insert here detailed calendar of agricultural work.]

(b) Fishing: (as for [a])—where deep-sea fishing, note ownership and naming of canoes and tackle.

(c) Hunting: (as for [a])—note rights to kill if animal speared or dies in land of another village, in a garden, etc.; where organized hunting—use of dogs and position of owner of dogs used, etc. Note especially dividing of kill, which parts regarded as best.

(d) Domestic animals: what ones kept; attitude towards them; how owned; how cared for; if killed—when and on what occasions; if do damage to person or gardens, when and what extent is owner liable for this.

With reference to a, b, c, d, notice: social status of individuals excelling in a, b, or c, or particularly rich in d; setting up of trophies connected with them; myths concerning them.

(iv) Arts and Crafts: (very much as in [iii]—note existence of specialists and how special art handed on to next generation).

(v) The Exchange of Goods: nature of goods exchanged; occasion; between whom; existence of "valuables"; prestige and the ownership or exchange of goods. Ritual and mythology connected with exchange (also etiquette); social significance of exchange.

Part VII

The preservation of Law and Order
Warfare

Part VIII

Magic, Religion and Myth: general account of all aspects found in the society (Ref. to other parts); the morphology, dogma, ritual and sociology; ethics.

Part IX

Knowledge of the Arts: (This, especially the section on knowledge, will involve a lot of cross-referencing to other parts.)

Part X

Linguistics: texts and analysis of language; social contexts of dialects, etc.

Part XI

Problems of Contact

REFERENCES

Barth, Fredrik. 1966. Preface. In Robert H. Pehrson, *The Social Organization of the Marri Baluch,* comp. and ed. Fredrik Barth, vii–xii. Viking Fund Publications in Anthropology 43. New York: Wenner-Gren Foundation for Anthropological Research.

Clifford, James, and George E. Marcus, eds. 1986. *Writing Culture: The Poetics and Politics of Ethnography.* Berkeley: University of California Press.

Deacon, Bernard. 1934. *Malekula: A Vanishing People in the New Hebrides.* London: Routledge.

Firth, Rosemary. 1985. Bernard Deacon: An Intimate Memoir. (Review of Margaret Gardiner, *Footprints on Malekula: A Memoir of Bernard Deacon.*) *Anthropology Today* 1:21–22.

Frank, Gelya. 1985. "Becoming the Other": Empathy and Biographical Interpretation. *Biography* 8:189–210.

Gardiner, Margaret. 1984. *Footprints on Malekula: A Memoir of Bernard Deacon.* Edinburgh: Salamander Press.

Kaberry, Phyllis. 1957. Malinowski's Contribution to Field-work Methods and the Writing of Ethnography. In *Man and Culture,* ed. Raymond Firth, 71–92. New York: Humanities Press.

Keesing, Roger. 1981 [1976]. *Cultural Anthropology: A Contemporary Perspective.* 2d ed. New York: Holt, Rinehart & Winston.

Langham, Ian. 1981. *The Building of British Social Anthropology: W. H. R. Rivers and His Cambridge Disciples in the Development of Kinship Studies, 1898–1931.* Dordrecht: Reidel.

Larcom, Joan. 1983. Following Deacon: The Problem of Ethnographic Reanalysis. 1926–1981. In Stocking 1983b, 175–95.

Lutkehaus, Nancy. 1982. Ambivalence, Ambiguity, and the Reproduction of Gender Hierarchy in Manam Society. *Social Analysis* 12:36–51.

——. 1985. The Flutes of the Tanepoa: The Dynamics of Hierarchy and Equivalence in Manam Society. Ph.D. diss., Columbia University, New York.

——. 1986. She Was *Very* Cambridge: Camilla Wedgwood and the History of Women in British Social Anthropology. *American Ethnologist* 13 (4): 776–98.

Malinowski, Bronislaw. 1922 [1961]. *Argonauts of the Western Pacific.* New York: Dutton.

——. 1935 [1978]. *Coral Gardens and Their Magic.* New York: Dover.

Stocking, George. 1983a. The Ethnographer's Magic: Fieldwork in British Anthropology from Tylor to Malinowski. In Stocking 1983b, 70–120.

——, ed. 1983b. *Observers Observed: Essays on Ethnographic Fieldwork.* Madison: University of Wisconsin Press.

Stoller, Paul. 1987. Son of Rouch: Portrait of a Young Ethnographer by the Songhay. *Anthropology Quarterly* 60 (3): 114–22.

Wedgwood, Camilla. 1932–34. Wedgwood Personal Archives, University Archives, University of Sydney. Materials used by permission.

——. 1933. Girls' Puberty Rites on Manam Island, New Guinea. *Oceania* 4:132–55.

——. 1934a. Report on Research in Manam Island, Mandated Territory of New Guinea. *Oceania* 4:373–403.

——. 1934b. Sickness and Its Treatment in Manam Island, New Guinea: Part 1. *Oceania* 5:64–79.

——. 1935. Sickness and Its Treatment in Manam Island, New Guinea: Part 2. *Oceania* 5:280–307.

——. 1937. Women in Manam. *Oceania* 7:401–28; 8:170–92.

——. 1938. The Life of Children in Manam. *Oceania* 9:1–29.

——. 1959. Manam Kinship. *Oceania* 29:239–56.

ROGER SANJEK

Fieldnotes and Others

The primary relationship of fieldnotes is to their writer-reader, the ethnographer who produces them. Yet as objects they are seen, and sometimes read, by others. As Bond, Obbo, and Lutkehaus detail in this volume, these others are diverse—"the other" (as interpretationists are wont to call their informants) whom they are about; other "others" in the society studied but outside the immediate ethnographic range; and other anthropologists: teachers, colleagues, and those who may later read or even inherit and write from the original author's fieldnotes.

Informants, Publics, and Fieldnotes

Few anthropologists today, or even in the past, hide their researcher role as Mead did among the Omaha Indians. Most take notes openly—at least during ethnographic and formal interviews—though some ethnographers, like Whyte (1955, 1960), prefer not to write even scratch notes in front of informants but to rely later on their memory. Informants are aware of writing and its resultant documentary forms, if not of all the kinds of notes the anthropologist maintains. On some occasions, particularly rituals and ceremonies, the informants *expect* ethnographic note-taking (Powdermaker 1966: 87).

They also hear and see typewriters. The act of typing in the field, however—the reworking of scratch notes to typed or recopied field-notes—can dampen rapport when its desired privacy interferes with sociability. This was a particular problem for Jean Briggs, living in close quarters with an Eskimo family.

> I found it hard sometimes to be simultaneously a docile and helpful daughter and a dutiful anthropologist. Though Allaq appeared to accept my domestic clumsiness as inevitable, she may have felt less tolerant on the occasions when it was not lack of skill that prevented me from helping her but anxiety over the pocketful of trouser-smudged, disorganized field notes that cried out to be typed. [1970: 25]

Briggs eventually moved her typewriter, and later her residence, to a separate tent. The point of contention in the iglu had been between rapport and fieldnotes. The outcome, a sober lesson in what fieldwork is all about, makes one wonder why so few of the extended personal accounts discuss fieldnote writing with any candor at all, let alone the measure provided by Briggs.

In situations where informants can read, other anxieties may arise as well. John Adair, working at Zuni Pueblo in the late 1940s, was confronted by reaction to a newspaper article on sacred clowns based on Cushing's earlier account.

> I learned that one of the men of the house where I was living had entered my room during my absence and looked through the notes which I had been careful to hide under the mattress. . . . There he had run across the native name for these clowns in a life history I was taking. . . . This discovery didn't help me with my relations with my landlord or his veteran sons. [1960: 492]

Rumors spread about Adair, and for this and other reasons he moved to a new residence. He was aware, of course, of Zuni resistance to anthropologists and knew that "in 1941, the Tribal Council confiscated the field notes of an anthropologist and burned part of them. He was asked to leave Zuni within twenty-four hours" (Pandey 1972: 322n).

Experience or knowledge of social research methods is now common in many world areas and creates expectations about what an anthropologist should or should not be doing. In Adabraka, Ghana, in 1970–71, I remember vividly when a newspaper reporter living in the same building asked me when I was going to begin doing my questionnaire. Shah (1979: 31) deliberately chose to work in a Gujarat village where an economist had conducted a survey in 1930: "A few villagers who knew English would inspect our field notes and a few who did not asked us to translate them. The villagers gained confidence in us only after they could place us in the social categories with which they were familiar," those of both researcher and fellow Indian.

The Whittens chose to head off misunderstandings in Nova Scotia and avoid any loss of rapport. "We showed people our manner of writing and filing notes, our genealogies, maps and mechanical aids (typewriter)" (Whitten 1970: 382). Other ethnographers have deliberately read fieldnotes back to informants, as Osgood (1940: 53) did to Billy Williams, to verify and expand on them. Stanner, in perhaps the finest essay in all the fieldwork literature, relates that when in 1954 he went over his notes of twenty years earlier with his Australian Aborigine informant Durmugam, they stood up well and provoked valuable reflections from their original source (1960: 86).

Many informants, even those who are illiterate, well understand the permanency of written records and may enlist the anthropologist to put things of *their* choosing down on paper. The Bow Society priests directed Cushing to transcribe their prayers and songs in precise, archaic Zuni (Green 1979: 149). Mead writes:

> When I arrived among the Manus . . . they had already been quarreling for thousands of years about how many dogs' teeth [their currency] somebody had paid to somebody else. . . . So the first thing they said to me when I came along was, "Ah, now Piyap [Mead] can write it down. You write down every single transaction and we won't need to quarrel any more." [Howard 1984: 106]

Read (1965: 203) had a similar experience of being asked by New Guinea Highland informants to record transactions in his notebook.

The relativities of text and experience discussed with subtlety by George Bond have also had their equivalents for other ethnographers. Schapera, whose 1938 *Handbook of Tswana Law and Custom* was a product of *his* fieldnotes, found its distributed copies returned to him with annotations by Tswana chiefs for the second edition (Comaroff and Comaroff 1988: 563). Like the Yombe with Bond's ethnography, they had turned it into an open text in which to record *their* notes.

Christine Obbo's essay here relates interest in her fieldnotes by Kampala chiefs and officials curious about the neighborhoods and activities she was studying. She details her strategies to put them off, as well as her unsettling encounters with anthropologist and academic colleagues and their efforts to read her fieldnotes. Government officials, usually convinced that some greater secret than actually exists lies in fieldnotes, have attempted on occasion to read them elsewhere as well: in Ecuador, Ralph Beals's fieldnotes (Paul 1953: 229); and in India, those of Cora Du Bois, who left hers accessible to Indian intelligence officers to allay suspicions that she and her research team were American spies (1970: 224). According to Clifford's account (1988: 277–346) of the Cape Cod Mashpee Indian land claim trial, the threat of subpoena of an anthropologist-witness's fieldnotes was raised; and the fieldnotes of one anthropologist informant of Jean Jackson actually were subpoenaed.

Students and Colleagues

Few students arrive in the field ever having seen ethnographic fieldnotes. Mead, in her field methods course at Columbia, made a point of showing hers to her students (1972: 142–43); so do Ottenberg and Wolcott (1981: 256). Some anthropologists have also shared their notes with students working in the same field setting, such as Ottenberg with a student working among the Limba (this volume), Wolff (1960: 249n) with a student working in Loma, and Wagley (1977: 76) with Judith Shapiro working among the Tapirape. Foster opened his fieldnote files to three students working in Tzintzuntzan, requiring them to share their notes with him in return, and they may freely use and cite each other's data (Foster 1979: 178). The Comaroffs (1988: 559) have had access to Schapera's Tswana fieldnotes; as in the other instances, their mention bespeaks an amicable relationship.

All these cases, except Mead's, Ottenberg's, and Wolcott's teaching, illustrate a collegial practice of sharing field data rather than a didactic one of showing how to write fieldnotes. More usual (but one wonders) are situations in which a teacher reads a student's fieldnotes and reports as they are mailed home, or brought back from the field. Nancy Lutkehaus's essay in this volume discusses Malinowski's written responses to Wedgwood's field letters. Kimball and Partridge (1979) detail a similar dialogue founded on letters and reports more than on fieldnotes proper. Ruth Benedict's attention to students' fieldnotes was remarked upon by Mead (1974: 34, 59): "She made the most of her own field work, but I think she got greater enjoyment out of working over

her students' field notes, teaching them how to organize them and
trying to make a whole out of their often scattered observations." The
heartfelt acknowledgments in many dissertations and books no doubt
evidence similar attention from other anthropological teachers.

Reports of colleagues sharing fieldnotes are also few but usually
involve amicable relations, unlike the efforts at appropriation encountered by Obbo. Opler was given copies of fieldnotes by the other
students—John Gillin, Jules Henry, Regina Flannery Herzfeld, Sol
Tax—in a 1931 Laboratory of Anthropology field training party led
by Benedict among the Apache (Opler was committed to continued
work among the Apache, while the others were not) and also exchanged fieldnotes through the 1930s with another ethnographer of
the Apache, Grenville Goodwin (Opler 1973: 11–12, 13, 22). Scudder
and Colson, in their long-term Gwembe Tonga fieldwork in Zambia,
had an agreement:

> Each would supply a carbon of all field notes to the other and . . . each
> had the right to publish independently using the total body of informa-
> tion. This agreement still stands and has worked well. Over the years
> we have shared ideas as we read field notes, talked, and pooled experi-
> ence. [1979: 234]

Acknowledgments in ethnographies point to similar cooperation.
In *Navaho Witchcraft* Kluckhohn cites the fieldnotes of eleven anthropologists (1944: 244–52). Hildred Geertz (1961: 170) acknowledges
drawing on her colleague and husband Clifford Geertz's fieldnotes on
Javanese families. A for-the-record mention by Evans-Pritchard of
others' use of his Nuer fieldnotes a year before his first published
article appeared perhaps points to the power asymmetry in student-
teacher relationships: "The chapter on the Nuer (Chap. VI) in *Pagan
Tribes of the Nilotic Sudan,* by Prof. C. G. and Mrs. B. Z. Seligman,
1932, was compiled from my notebooks" (Evans-Pritchard 1940: 2
n.3; see also vii).[1] Are students ever free to deny fieldnotes to those
who sponsor their research? Fieldnote deposition was required of
researchers at the Rhodes-Livingstone Institute in then Northern Rhodesia and at the East African Institute of Social and Economic Research
in Uganda, although what was done with them by anyone other than
their authors is unclear (Richards 1977: 180).

---

[1] Evans-Pritchard's notes are duly acknowledged by the Seligmans in their book
(1932: xiii).

Teams

As discussed in "The Secret History of Fieldnotes" (Part III, this volume), the lone ethnographer designing, conducting, and writing up his or her own fieldwork adventure is mainly Malinowskian myth (though true in his case) and post-1960 individual grant practice. Until recent decades there have been more Argonauts than Jasons. Fieldwork in the classical period was less Odyssey than Iliad, organized in programs, projects, schemes, and teams, with larger purposes than those envisioned in single-investigator research designs.[2] After Samoa, Mead collaborated with Fortune in Manus, on the Omaha reservation, and in the Sepik region; and with Bateson and others in Bali and on her return to Manus. Fieldnotes were shared. Many of today's leading American anthropologists are products of organized research efforts. Harvard, home of teams, has housed the Yankee City, Ramah, Values in Five Cultures, Modjokuto, Six Cultures, Chiapas, and Kalahari Research projects. Team projects continue in anthropology, but they were much less central to the discipline in the 1970s and 1980s than earlier.

In team projects, the role of fieldnotes and their circulation varies with project organization. Mead's Bali research was unusual in its multimedia pattern of integration.

> The investigator may make a running record of the behavior of a group of individuals against a time scale. Where cooperative field-work is being done, a parallel photographic or Cine record, or a combination of the two may be added to this. The observations may be parceled out among a number of observers, one taking ceremonial behavior, another informal behavior not immediately oriented to the ceremony, another recording only verbatim conversations, or another following a single individual through the same period. (This is the method which is now being used in our Balinese researches by Mr. Bateson, Miss Jane Belo, Mrs. Katharane Mershon, and myself, with the addition of three trained

---

[2]In this context, I disagree with Marcus and Cushman (1982: 26) and Van Maanen (1988: 73–74) that the post-1960s personal accounts have "demystified" ethnographic fieldwork. This puts ethnography itself into a timeless "ethnographic present." The emphasis these writings place on *individual* experience and self-knowledge (Clifford 1986: 13–15; Van Maanen 1988: 106–9)—on fieldwork as "rite of passage" in a personal rather than professional sense—are "reflexive" of the decline of fieldwork project dominance since the 1960s, and the ascendancy of government funding of individual proposals. The historical "experimental moment" (Marcus and Fischer 1986) is historically determined.

literate native observers, I Made Kaler, Goesti Made Soemoeng, and
I Ketoet Pemangkoe, working in shifting cooperative combinations.)
[Mead 1940: 328]

The result of this fieldnoting/photographing/filming was unconven-
tional photograph-based behavioral analysis (see Mead 1970: 258–59,
Plates I–XVI; Whiting and Whiting 1970: 309–12). From Mead's
similar team fieldwork in Manus in 1953–54 (1956: 495–96), she returned to more traditional fieldnote-based prose ethnography.

Warner's 1930s Yankee City (Newburyport, Massachusetts) project
involved eighteen fieldworkers, who produced a wealth of records,
informal and ethnographic interviews, and "dictaphone" fieldnotes of
observations of events and organized behavior, filed according to categories and subcategories of the family, economic organization, associations, government, churches, and sports. One copy of his or her fieldnotes was retained by each fieldworker, and they all submitted another
copy, and weekly and annual written reports of their research. These
documents, with the files, were available to other field team members,
although direction of the project analysis, involving twenty-five persons, remained in Warner's hands (Warner and Lunt 1941: ix, 44–75).
The fieldworkers did not write their own ethnography; Warner was
author or senior coauthor of all five resulting volumes.

The control of fieldnotes in Oscar Lewis's Tepotzlan team project
was similar. He was sole author of the ethnographic volume resulting
from the work of his fifteen-person team; the only separately written
sections of *Life in a Mexican Village* (Lewis 1951) are a chapter on
Rorschach test results and appendixes on maize and potsherds, none of
these written by members of the field team. A much looser arrangement of a more tightly designed three-year research project in white
and Indian Minnesota communities allowed "substantial field-work
experience for eighteen graduate students in anthropology": the final
report of project supervisors Pertti Pelto and J. Anthony Paredes was
complemented by six master's theses, two doctoral dissertations, and
jointly and separately authored journal articles (Pelto 1970: 270–87).

This model of several coordinated fieldworkers in the same or
nearby locations, each writing his or her own ethnographic reports,
has marked most team projects from the 1940s through the present.
Fieldnote coordination, however, has varied. Kluckhohn's 1939–48
Ramah Navajo project (Lamphere 1979: 22–28) involved a score of
researchers, each pursuing individual projects published separately,

though a volume based on project fieldnotes about forty-eight children was coauthored by Dorothea Leighton and Kluckhohn, and Kluckhohn drew on other fieldworkers' notes in *Navaho Witchcraft* (1944). Project fieldnotes were filed at Harvard according to categories devised by Kluckhohn.

In 1948 Kluckhohn's Comparative Study of Values in Five Cultures Project (Lamphere 1979: 28–32)—comparing Navajo, Zuni, Mormons, Texans, and Spanish Americans—began with Rockefeller Foundation support. By its 1953 conclusion, thirty-seven fieldworkers had participated, again with separate projects and publications (a summary volume appeared only in 1966). From the beginning, a common-user organization of fieldnotes was adopted by the project.

> Field notes were typed on ditto masters, and the contents of each page of notes was analyzed in terms of the inventory of culture content devised by the Human Relations Area Files at New Haven. Each item in the inventory has its own code number, and so each page of notes acquired from one to half a dozen numbers, depending upon how its contents were analyzed. A copy of each page of notes was then filed under every content category involved. A participant in the project would then be able to refer quickly to the numbered heading in the file to see what others besides himself had recorded on a large number of predefined subjects. [Gulick 1970: 135n]

All Kluckhohn's Navajo files were moved to the Laboratory of Anthropology at Santa Fe in 1963. The pre-HRAF Ramah notes filed in Kluckhohn's own categories proved difficult for Lamphere (1979: 32) to use for later Ramah research: "It was as if the 'key' to the Ramah Files had died with Kluckhohn. Only hours of digging through 'cut up' field notes revealed facts that might easily have come to light in a conversation with him."

The HRAF categories, not tailored to a caste-divided community, were also used in a 1950s Cornell team study in an Indian village. Fieldworkers had their own projects and typed four copies of their notes for distribution to Lucknow, Cornell, the village field station, and back to the fieldworker. Though notes were available to all project members, including those who joined during later stages, the continual delays in typing up fieldnotes from scratch notes vitiated project intercommunication plans. No one read all the fieldnotes, and informal discussion in the field site proved the most important source of team integration (LeClair 1960; cf. Du Bois 1970: 222–23).

Such communication of headnotes, as well as fieldnotes, was maximized in the procedures developed by a group of five researchers in a mid-1970s ethnographic study of San Diego inner city hotels. Paul Bohannan, the project director, met with two or more fieldworkers at least every three weeks in "debriefing sessions," where detailed reports on fieldnotes were presented, discussed, and taped. Bohannan then took notes on the tapes, averaging twenty pages, and indexed them according to subjects and persons of interest to the project.

> These notes differ significantly from a fieldworker's notes. They contain not only data, but, clearly demarcated as such, formulations and preliminary analyses. Some of these latter points can be suggested to fieldworkers, more or less as assignments. Others go back to form the protodraft of analysis. [Bohannan 1981: 38]

As the project focus narrowed, life history interviews were conducted, and indexed by Bohannan according to the same project categories (1981: 40).

A complex use of fieldnotes marked the Six Cultures project in which two-person teams and local assistants conducted fieldwork simultaneously in Kenya, India, Mexico, New England, the Philippines, and Okinawa in 1954–55. In addition to general ethnographic coverage, they agreed to collect detailed data on child rearing, using a "Field Guide for a Study of Socialization," which all participated in drafting and which was later published. Copies of fieldnotes were sent to Beatrice Whiting at Harvard, who monitored the research (Whiting 1966: vii, ix). The six ethnographic studies, authored by the field researchers, appeared both in an edited volume in 1963 and separately in 1966 (see Fischer and Fischer 1966). Each ethnography was based on the researchers' own fieldnotes, but two analytic volumes were also published: *Mothers of Six Cultures* (Minturn, Lambert, et al. 1964), based on formal interviews; and *Children of Six Cultures* (Whiting and Whiting 1975).

The Whitings' volume analyzes fieldnotes on the behavior of 134 children between ages three and eleven, recorded in five-minute behavior sequences, with each child observed fourteen times or more over the course of several months (Whiting and Whiting 1975: 30–31, 39–42). Except in New England, local bilingual assistants translated what was said during the five-minute periods. Examples of the fieldnotes on which the analysis is based, and of the coding procedures, were published as well (1975: 187–220).

A unique team project was the study of Elmdon, a village of 321 people, fourteen miles from Cambridge University (Strathern 1981). It was begun in 1962 by Audrey Richards[3] and Edmund Leach as a student fieldwork training exercise; by 1975 nearly thirty anthropologists and other students had participated (Richards 1981). Most stayed for two weeks or less, residing at the home of Richards, who had moved to Elmdon in the late 1950s. They recorded family histories and genealogies; they made notes on casual conversations, village activities, pubs, and meetings. "Interviews were never more than loosely structured. Notes were often taken in the presence of the person talking, or jotted down immediately afterwards. The students usually indicated remarks recorded verbatim" (Strathern 1981: 271). A few students who spent longer fieldwork periods in Elmdon produced reports on local history, housing problems, and farming.

Richards retired in Elmdon in 1964. She also took notes, though intermittently and inconsistently and not with the short-term enthusiasm of a full-time fieldworker:

> The notes I took during a period of over twenty years' residence in Elmdon are not as systematic as those which resulted from two fifteen-month trips to Zambia in 1930–1 and 1933–4. I have, of course, a much richer supply of those stored memories and impressions on which anthropologists rely to give life to their descriptive work. [1981: xx]

In 1975 Richards published *Some Elmdon Families* as a work of local documentation. Still, with seventeen collective notebooks and other documents, she hoped to write

> something like an old-fashioned anthropological village study. . . . But a temporary run of bad health made me doubtful whether I would be able to complete the work. At this stage, Marilyn Strathern . . . offered to analyse our kinship data, which was complex owing to the degree of intermarriage in the village. However, it soon became clear that the book must be hers alone. She had developed very interesting ideas on

---

[3]In the Ghanaian sense, Audrey Richards was the Queen Mother of social anthropological fieldwork—from her discussion of censuses and quantitative approaches in 1935 and her paper on field methods (and "speech in action") in 1939 through her championing of anthropology in the Colonial Social Science Research Council, her assistance and direction to ethnographers of East Africa during 1950–56 as director of the East African Institute of Social Research, and the Elmdon study to the example of her Bemba and Ganda ethnography (Beattie 1965: 6, 37; Gladstone 1986; Richards 1935, 1939, 1977, 1981).

the phenomenon of the core families which were of greater complexity
and originality than my own would have been. *Kinship at the Core* is the
result. [1981: xxiii]

Strathern had worked in Elmdon in 1962 and returned briefly in
1977. She also drew on Richards's headnotes—on her "insights and
feelings about the village, quite as much as on her extensive data," and
on "an invaluable commentary on my first draft" (Strathern 1981:
xxxi, xxxiv).

Inheriting Fieldnotes

Few anthropologists have ever assumed the labor-of-love task of
producing an ethnography from fieldnotes written by others. When
they have done so, it has usually been to complete the work of those
who died young—Bernard Deacon, Buell Quain, Robert Pehrson,
Grenville Goodwin. Their ethnographic executors did not enjoy access to the original headnotes; they faced problems beyond those of
Marilyn Strathern, who had the collaboration of Audrey Richards as
well as her own brief fieldwork experience in Elmdon, or Robert
Smith, who benefited from the cooperation of Ella Lury Wiswell
(Smith and Wiswell 1982: ix–xii; Smith, this volume).

After fourteen months of fieldwork in the New Hebrides, Deacon
died in 1927 on the eve of his departure. As Lutkehaus explains,
Camilla Wedgwood had no easy task in editing his fieldnotes into
Malekula: A Vanishing People in the New Hebrides, published in 1934.
The notes were sketchy and disorganized, and some of them had also
vanished (Langham 1981: 235–36; Larcom 1983; Lutkehaus 1986). "To
reinterpret fieldnotes requires knowing something about what was
taken for granted when the notes were written—difficult enough for
the writer to deal with, let alone another reader" (Van Maanen 1988:
124). Wedgwood's Rivers-influenced Cambridge training, shared with
Deacon, provided the intellectual integument for the ethnography
(Larcom 1983; see also Langham 1981: 212–41); however, Larcom,
whose 1974 fieldwork was among one of the groups with whom
Deacon had worked, argues that a better approximation of Deacon's
evolving headnotes was contained in his letters from the field.

Quain died in Brazil in 1939 after four months of fieldwork among
the remote Trumai Indians the year before. His handwritten field-

notes, records, and journal (Murphy and Quain 1955: 1) were typed by his mother and turned over by Quain's friend Charles Wagley to Robert Murphy, who never knew Quain. Murphy faced the same dilemmas that Smith experienced upon receiving Wiswell's notes.

> It soon became clear that ordering and editing wre not enough [even though] the notes were rich in detail and insights. . . . he would have to read and re-read the notes, learn the names of the numerous informants and other individuals mentioned there and in the diaries, identify them as to age, sex, status, family membership, etc., familiarize himself with place names and Trumai terms just as a field investigator would have to do. [Wagley 1955: v–vi]

The headnotes Murphy brought to the writing were a combination of his own fieldwork experience among the Mundurucu Indians of Brazil, a theoretical orientation, and what he could glean from the fieldnotes of Quain's headnotes (Wagley 1955: vi): "It is impossible . . . to so neatly separate the Murphy from the Quain in this monograph, for Quain's interests and ideas have influenced my interpretation of the data" (Murphy and Quain 1955: 2). Murphy used the notes to formulate descriptive prose, quoting from them directly only once (1955: 95–96). The book was published under their joint authorship.[4]

When Robert Pehrson died in the field in 1955 (Barth 1966), Jean Pehrson, who had shared the fieldwork with her husband, typed 200 pages of his chronological fieldnotes on the Marri Baluch nomads of Pakistan. With letters, two papers by Jean Pehrson, and texts, they were turned over to Fredrik Barth, who had also received half a dozen field letters from his friend Pehrson. Yet despite their detail, the notes remained opaque, and Barth found writing from them frustrating—until in 1960 he spent five weeks in the locale where the well-remembered Pehrsons had worked. Their informants' knowledge of Pashto, which Barth had learned in his Pakistan fieldwork among the Pathans, made communication easy. With his own headnotes, Barth found Pehrson's fieldnotes "more tractable" and writing possible. For besides his own Marri Baluch fieldnotes, Barth concludes,

> clearly I had also accumulated data of other kinds, which were not recorded in the Pehrsons' notes but which are needed in anthropological

---

[4]Lévi-Strauss also drew upon Quain's fieldnotes for a contribution to the 1948 *Handbook of South American Indians* (Murphy and Quain 1955: 83).

analysis. . . . I believe [these critical supplementary data] are mainly connected with the concrete "stage" or setting in which social life takes place: the sizes of habitations, the uses of space, the physical as well as the conventional opportunities for communication. . . . The interpretation of actions, both in a strategic means-ends perspective and as messages of communication, depends on this knowledge, and case material remains highly ambiguous when it is lacking. [Barth 1966: x–xi]

With these physical coordinates, which Pehrson took for granted, now in mind, Barth wrote *The Social Organization of the Marri Baluch,* using Pehrson's materials (rather than his own fieldnotes) and quoting liberally from them in the text. The book was accordingly presented as "by Robert N. Pehrson, compiled and analyzed from his notes by Fredrik Barth" (Pehrson 1966).

The job of Keith Basso in editing Grenville Goodwin's fieldnotes for publication was much simpler than that faced by Wedgwood, Murphy, or Barth. Goodwin, who did fieldwork among the Apache of Arizona during the late 1920s and 1930s, had written *The Social Organization of the Western Apache* (1942) and several papers before he died in 1940 (Basso 1971: xi–xii, 3–25). Goodwin had outlined further monographs, and his widow, Janice Goodwin, organized the remaining fieldnotes and supervised their typing from longhand. The published volume (others are planned), *Western Apache Raiding and Warfare* (Basso 1971), consists of six verbatim narratives of elderly informants transcribed in 1931–32, plus other informant statements on several topics that Goodwin had used to organize his notes. These are highly readable texts, without Boasian linguistic literalism. Nonetheless, the considerable number of Apache terms used in the notes led Basso to conduct ten weeks of linguistic fieldwork (he had done earlier research in other Apache groups) to authenticate cultural translation. Historical rather than ethnological in aim, Goodwin's materials provide an Apache view of the unrest between the 1850s and the completion of United States pacification in 1890.

As more anthropologists return, like Lutkehaus, Lamphere, and Larcom, to scenes of earlier ethnography, and as we ask new questions about the discipline's history, access to fieldnotes will become more important. The archival homes of the papers of Cushing, Boas, Rivers, Malinowski, and Mead were not difficult for scholars to find, but the notes of other anthropologists are scattered (Kenworthy et al. 1985: 5–6; Raspin 1984). The process of archiving one's own fieldnotes and papers is an issue of uncertainty, ambivalence, and presumption for most ethnographers (see Ottenberg's and Wolf's essays in this volume). There are also practical issues—paper quality, preservation measures, the range of documents that make a useful collection—which few think about early enough (Kenworthy et al. 1985: 1–3, 10–11, and passim).

There remains the problem of how to preserve headnotes. More documentation of the stage coordinates that Barth identifies might help others make sense of fieldnotes. So, no doubt, do the letters from the field (as Larcom found for Deacon), those preliminary written releases of what Lederman terms the "sense of the whole" component of headnotes. Certainly, also, would more reminiscences of fieldwork tied to professional as much as personal aspects: that is, to writing in the field as well as to rapport and self-discovery. But the primary locus for the preservation of headnotes should be in their joint productions with fieldnotes: in published ethnography, the whole point of why fieldwork is done.

REFERENCES

Adair, John. 1960. A. Pueblo G.I. In Casagrande 1960, 489–503.
Adams, Richard N., and J. Preiss, eds. 1960. *Human Organization Research.* Homewood, Ill.: Dorsey.
Barth, Fredrik. 1966. Preface. In Pehrson 1966, vii–xii.
Basso, Keith, ed. 1971. *Western Apache Raiding and Warfare: From the Notes of Grenville Goodwin.* Tucson: University of Arizona Press.
Beattie, John. 1965. *Understanding an African Kingdom: Bunyoro.* New York: Holt, Rinehart & Winston.
Bohannan, Paul. 1981. Unseen Community: The Natural History of a Research Project. In Messerschmidt 1981, 29–45.
Briggs, Jean. 1970. Kapluna Daughter. In Golde 1970, 17–44.
Casagrande, Joseph B., ed. 1960. *In the Company of Man: Twenty Portraits of Anthropological Informants.* New York: Harper Torchbooks.
Clifford, James. 1986. Introduction: Partial Truths. In *Writing Culture: The Poetics and Politics of Ethnography,* ed. James Clifford and George E. Marcus, 1–26. Berkeley: University of California Press.
———. 1988. *The Predicament of Culture: Twentieth-Century Ethnography, Literature, and Art.* Cambridge, Mass.: Harvard University Press.
Comaroff, Jean, and John L. Comaroff. 1988. On the Founding Fathers, Fieldwork, and Functionalism: A Conversation with Isaac Schapera. *American Ethnologist* 15:554–65.
Du Bois, Cora. 1970. Studies in an Indian Town. In Golde 1970, 219–36.

Evans-Pritchard, E. E. 1940. *The Nuer.* Oxford: Oxford University Press.

Fischer, John L., and Ann Fischer. 1966. *The New Englanders of Orchard Town, U.S.A.* Six Cultures Series, vol. 5. New York: Wiley.

Foster, George M. 1979. Fieldwork in Tzintzuntzan: The First Thirty Years. In Foster et al. 1979, 165–84.

Foster, George M., Thayer Scudder, Elizabeth Colson, and Robert V. Kemper, eds. 1979. *Long-Term Field Research in Social Anthropology.* New York: Academic Press.

Freilich, Morris, ed. 1970. *Marginal Natives: Anthropologists at Work.* New York: Harper & Row.

Geertz, Hildred. 1961. *The Javanese Family: A Study in Kinship and Socialization.* Glencoe, Ill.: Free Press.

Gladstone, Jo. 1986. Significant Sister: Autonomy and Obligation in Audrey Richards' Early Fieldwork. *American Ethnologist* 13:338–62.

Golde, Peggy, ed. 1970. *Women in the Field: Anthropological Experiences.* Chicago: Aldine.

Goodwin, Grenville. 1942. *The Social Organization of the Western Apache.* Chicago: University of Chicago Press.

Green, Jesse, ed. 1979. *Zuni: Selected Writings of Frank Hamilton Cushing.* Lincoln: University of Nebraska Press.

Gulick, John. 1970. Village and City Field Work in Lebanon. In Freilich 1970, 123–52.

Howard, Jane. 1984. *Margaret Mead: A Life.* New York: Fawcett Crest.

Kenworthy, Mary Anne, Eleanor M. King, Mary Elizabeth Ruwell, and Trudy Van Houten. 1985. *Preserving Field Records: Archival Techniques for Archaeologists and Anthropologists.* Philadelphia: University Museum, University of Pennsylvania.

Kimball, Solon, and William Partridge. 1979. *The Craft of Community Study: Fieldwork Dialogues.* Gainesville: University Presses of Florida.

Kluckhohn, Clyde. 1944 [1967]. *Navaho Witchcraft.* Boston: Beacon Press.

Lamphere, Louise. 1979. The Long-Term Study among the Navaho. In Foster et al. 1979, 19–44.

Langham, Ian. 1981. *The Building of British Social Anthropology: W. H. R. Rivers and His Cambridge Disciples in the Development of Kinship Studies, 1898–1931.* Boston: Reidel.

Larcom, Joan. 1983. Following Deacon: The Problem of Ethnographic Reanalysis, 1926–1981. In *Observers Observed: Essays on Ethnographic Fieldwork,* ed. George W. Stocking, Jr., 175–95. Madison: University of Wisconsin Press.

LeClair, Edward, Jr. 1960. Problems of Large-Scale Anthropological Research. In Adams and Preiss, 28–40.

Lévi-Strauss, Claude. 1955 [1974]. Trans. John and Doreen Weightman. New York: Atheneum.

Lewis, Oscar. 1951. *Life in a Mexican Village: Tepoztlan Restudied.* Urbana: University of Illinois Press.

Lutkehaus, Nancy. 1986. "She Was *Very* Cambridge": Camilla Wedgwood and the History of Women in British Social Anthropology. *American Ethnologist* 13:776–98.

Marcus, George E., and Dick Cushman. 1982. Ethnographies as Texts. *Annual Review of Anthropology* 11:25–69.

Marcus, George E., and Michael M. J. Fischer. 1986. *Anthropology as Cultural Critique: An Experimental Moment in the Human Sciences.* Chicago: University of Chicago Press.

Mead, Margaret. 1940. *The Mountain Arapesh, II: Supernaturalism.* Anthropological Papers 37:317–451. New York: American Museum of Natural History.

———. 1956. *New Lives for Old: Cultural Transformations—Manus, 1928–1953.* New York: Morrow.

———. 1970. The Art and Technology of Fieldwork. In Naroll and Cohen 1970, 246–65.

———. 1972. *Blackberry Winter: My Earlier Years.* New York: Morrow.

———. 1974. *Ruth Benedict.* New York: Columbia University Press.

Messerschmidt, Donald A., ed. 1981. *Anthropologists at Home in North America: Methods and Issues in the Study of One's Own Society.* New York: Cambridge University Press.

Minturn, Leigh, William Lambert, et al. 1964. *Mothers of Six Cultures: Antecedents of Child Rearing.* New York: Wiley.

Murphy, Robert F., and Buell Quain. 1955. *The Trumai Indians of Central Brazil.* Seattle: University of Washington Press.

Naroll, Raoul, and Ronald Cohen, eds. 1970. *A Handbook of Method in Cultural Anthropology.* New York: Columbia University Press.

Opler, Morris, ed. 1973. *Grenville Goodwin among the Western Apache: Letters from the Field.* Tucson: University of Arizona Press.

Osgood, Cornelius. 1940. Informants. In *Ingalik Material Culture,* 50–55. New Haven, Conn.: Yale University Publications in Anthropology.

Pandey, Triloki Nath. 1972. Anthropologists at Zuni. *Proceedings of the American Philosophical Society* 116: 321–37.

Paul, Benjamin. 1953. Interview Techniques and Field Relationships. In *Anthropology Today,* ed. A. L. Kroeber, 430–51. Chicago: University of Chicago Press.

Pehrson, Robert H. 1966. *The Social Organization of the Marri Baluch.* Comp. and ed. Fredrik Barth. Viking Fund Publications in Anthropology 43. New York: Wenner-Gren Foundation for Anthropological Research.

Pelto, Pertti J. 1970. Research in Individualistic Societies. In Freilich 1970, 251–92.

Powdermaker, Hortense. 1966. *Stranger and Friend: The Way of an Anthropologist.* New York: Norton.

Raspin, Angela. 1984. A Guide to Ethnographic Archives. In *Ethnographic Research: A Guide to General Conduct,* ed. R. F. Ellen, 170–78. San Diego: Academic Press.

Read, Kenneth E. 1965. *The High Valley.* New York: Scribner.

Richards, Audrey I. 1935. The Village Census in the Study of Culture Contact. *Africa* 8:20–33.

———. 1939. The Development of Field Work Methods in Social Anthropology. In

The Study of Society, ed. F. C. Bartlett et al., 272–316. London: Routledge & Kegan Paul.

———. 1977. The Colonial Office and the Organization of Social Research. *Anthropological Forum* 4:168–89.

———. 1981. Foreword. In Strathern 1981, xi–xxvi.

Scudder, Thayer, and Elizabeth Colson. 1979. Long-Term Research in Gwembe Valley, Zambia. In Foster et al. 1979, 227–54.

Seligman, C. G., and Brenda Z. Seligman. 1932. *Pagan Tribes of the Nilotic Sudan.* London: Routledge.

Shah, A. M. 1979. Studying the Present and the Past: A Village in Gujarat. In *The Fieldworker and the Field: Problems and Challenges in Sociological Investigation,* ed. M. N. Srinivas, A. M. Shah, and E. A. Ramaswamy, 29–37. Delhi: Oxford University Press.

Smith, Robert J., and Ella Lury Wiswell. 1982. *The Women of Suye Mura.* Chicago: University of Chicago Press.

Stanner, W. E. H. 1960. Durmugam, a Nangiomeri. In Casagrande 1960, 63–100.

Strathern, Marilyn. 1981. *Kinship at the Core: An Anthropology of Elmdon, a Village in North-west Essex in the Nineteen-sixties.* Cambridge: Cambridge University Press.

Van Maanen, John. 1988. *Tales of the Field: On Writing Ethnography.* Chicago: University of Chicago Press.

Wagley, Charles. 1955. Foreword. In Murphy and Quain 1955, v–ix.

———. 1977. *Welcome of Tears: The Tapirape Indians of Central Brazil.* New York: Oxford University Press.

Warner, W. Lloyd, and Paul Lunt. 1941. *The Social Life of a Modern Community.* New Haven, Conn.: Yale University Press.

Whiting, Beatrice. 1966. Introduction. In Fischer and Fischer 1966, v–xxxi.

Whiting, Beatrice, and John Whiting. 1970. Methods for Observing and Recording Behavior. In Naroll and Cohen 1970, 282–315.

———. 1975. *Children of Six Cultures: A Psycho-Cultural Analysis.* Cambridge, Mass.: Harvard University Press.

Whitten, Norman E., Jr. 1970. Network Analysis and Processes of Adaptation among Ecuadorian and Nova Scotian Negroes. In Freilich 1970, 339–402.

Whyte, William Foote. 1955. Appendix: On the Evolution of "Street Corner Society." In *Street Corner Society,* enl. ed. 279–358. Chicago: University of Chicago Press.

———. 1960. Interviewing in Field Research. In Adams and Preiss 1960, 352–73.

Wolcott, Harry F. 1981. Home and Away: Personal Contrasts in Ethnographic Style. In Messerschmidt 1981, 255–65.

Wolff, Kurt. 1960. The Collection and Organization of Field Materials: A Research Report. In Adams and Preiss 1960, 240–54.

PART V

From Fieldnotes to Ethnography

I have long ago discovered that the decisive battle is not
fought in the field but in the study afterwards.

—E. E. EVANS-PRITCHARD

MARGERY WOLF

Chinanotes:
Engendering Anthropology

Perhaps more than any other, the last decade has brought anthropologists to the realization that their products, both uncooked (the fieldnote) and cooked (the ethnography), are but personal interpretations of others' equally nebulous realities. Our uncooked "facts," gathered so carefully in the field, are infected with the bacterial subjectivities of our own as well as our informants' particular biases. And our cooked descriptions, unlike other culinary concoctions, are even more likely to contain foreign particles if they jell into a pleasing whole. Reflexive anthropology, the latest treatment for our disease, seems to do little more than expose our wounds to light—a primitive cure that with more carnal injuries has had serious and even fatal consequences. Literary theorists, for all their exquisite tools, can dissect but offer us no hope of recovery.

Short of abandoning the patient, which I suspect few of us are prepared to do, how are we to proceed with the doing of anthropology? For starters, how are we to handle those apparently seriously compromised texts we call fieldnotes? Is there a way of continuing to collect field data that will preserve the contextual reality without

The comments and suggestions of Roger Sanjek and Robert J. Smith were very helpful in revising a talk into some semblance of an essay and are gratefully acknowledged.

requiring an explanatory essay for each observation? And how do we retrieve the various prejudicial influences that surrounded field data collected decades in the past, a past for this writer at least overlaid with too many other realities to provide hope (or desire) for resurrection? When I read back over my fieldnotes—some twenty-five years' accumulation of notebooks, five-by-eight cards, and other bits and pieces of paper—I also read back over my own life, but I suspect that only I can see the life that is in them.

Perceiving (as distinguished from seeing) what is in my fieldnotes—deconstructing or, more accurately, reconstructing the text—is an activity that was unanticipated when my original fieldnotes were made. This is in part because most of them were collected in a time when anthropology was less self-conscious about its process and in part because of the nature of my personal odyssey into anthropology. My first field experience was not as a graduate student in anthropology but as the wife of one. Arthur Wolf and I set out for Taiwan in 1958 with the overly ambitious intention of replicating and enlarging on the Six Culture Project designed by Beatrice Whiting, John Whiting, and William Lambert.[1] Our work required hundreds of hours of child observations, formal interviews with children and their parents, and the administering of questionnaires in local primary schools. All of these "instruments" were focused on a particular set of behavioral variables. I quickly became administrator and scribe, spending long hours typing and translating verbatim accounts of observations as they were brought in by the field staff.

In Chinese schools, students are required to commit vast amounts of material to memory, a skill on the part of our assistants that stood us in good stead in the field, for we soon discovered that they could observe up to four minutes of timed interaction among a group of children and repeat every word of it an hour later. They could make several of these observations and with the aid of only a few notes give us complete descriptions of verbal and physical interaction. We have literally thousands of typed pages of observations of this sort. The project also produced many hundreds of pages of open-ended inter-

[1]Data from the Six Culture Project might in itself be the basis of a study of the use of fieldnotes collected by others. There is now a long list of publications that derived from this project, but the first was the publication of six concise ethnographies with a similar format (Whiting 1963). It was followed by specialized studies by the senior investigators of parent and child behavior in all six cultures, as well as culture-specific studies by the field teams themselves.

view responses and some 700 questionnaires filled out by local school children.

But like all anthropologists of his generation, Arthur Wolf also hoped to produce a village ethnography from this trip, so we have some 600 closely typed pages of what we came to call G (for general) data. These notes include detailed descriptions of funeral ceremonies, intense interviews with unhappy young women, lengthy explanations by village philosophers, and rambling gossip sessions among groups or pairs of women and men. Neither Arthur nor I was present at all of the events and conversations recorded in these notes, for as our visit in this first village lengthened and we began to appreciate the qualities of our assistants, we frequently sent them out to gather particular kinds of information or simply to chat and observe and report back. Sometimes the conversations they memorized and repeated to us made no sense even to them, but often the pages I typed from their dictation recorded material that we as foreigners would have found difficult to elicit—not because it was particularly private but because it was pithier, more judgmental, less considered.

During this period, when I fancied myself a gestating novelist, I kept a journal, a very personal document; I would have been outraged had any of my co-workers attempted to read it. At the time I did not think of it as fieldnotes. My journal recorded my irritation with village life, some wild hypotheses of causation, an ongoing analysis of the Chinese personality structure, various lascivious thoughts, diatribes against injustices observed, and so forth. I expected the journal to keep the "real" fieldnotes free of my nonprofessional editorializing, to be fun to read when it was all over, and to tell me more about myself than about the society in which I was living.

By and large this turned out to be the case, with one exception. All the time we were in this first village—almost two years for me and longer for Arthur—we lived with the same farm family. My journal frequently recounted interactions with my housemates, as it would have wherever I had been living. But instead of shaking the youngest member of the Lim family, who never once woke up from a nap without imposing on us all at least a half-hour of peevish howling, I told my journal about his nasty character and declared he would come to no good end. (He is now, incidentally, a very successful engineer in Taipei, having graduated from university with honors. He is noted for his sunny disposition.) Rather than telling Tan A-hong what a cruel mother I thought her to be, I recorded in loving detail the gossip I heard around the village about her past and present and argued with myself about the nature/nurture causes of her (to me) reprehensible treatment of her poor daughters. I also pondered how my housemates could tell each other one thing, our local staff another, and the foreign anthropologist a third.

Returning to Cornell from this first field trip, I was fortunate enough to be given a small office and a pittance that allowed me to begin the long and extremely tedious task of coding the reams of child observations Arthur and I had collected. But I missed the Lim family and the daily drama of their quarrels and struggles. And I worried about them, for they were in a phase of the Chinese family cycle that was causing pain and distress to some family members and pride to others. I cannot for the life of me remember when I started or why, but at some point I began to sort through our G data, my journal, the mother interviews, and even the timed observations of their children to pull together all I knew about the Lims as individuals.

In this almost casual re-sorting of our fieldnotes, I found things that astonished me. Some items I had recorded myself and totally misunderstood; of others, recorded by Arthur or members of the field staff and in many cases typed by me, I had failed to see the import.[2] It seemed incredible that the Lims, fourteen of whom shared their house with us and with another fifteen who were in and out of it all day long, could have told us so much about themselves as individuals, as personalities. But it was only when I looked carefully at all the bits and pieces—the child observations that revealed solidarity among the children with one part of the family and hostility toward the other, the mother interview delineating the process by which a woman paid back her husband's battering, the misleadingly general discourse of the head of the household on the importance of face—that I began to see the history of their family and recognize the stress they endured in order to maintain a cultural ideal.

How is it that I could not have seen during those years in their household the inevitability of their family's division and the forces that were setting it in motion? I suppose at the time I was too involved with them as individuals who spent too long in the shared outhouse or used up all the hot water on bath night to see them as actors in the age-old

---

[2]See R. J. Smith's essay in this volume. There is a similarity in the methods we employed to free the voices in our fieldnotes, but the barriers against which we were struggling were different. Or were they?

and ever fresh drama of the Chinese family cycle. When I finally began to write *The House of Lim* (Wolf 1968), their story, I bitterly regretted the questions I had not asked but was equally gratified by all the seemingly purposeless anecdotes, conversations verging on lectures, and series of complaints that *had* been recorded.

Clearly, the presence of unfocused, wide-ranging, all-inclusive field-notes was essential to the success of this unplanned project, but so were the purposefully subjective "data" recorded in my journal and the so-called objective data recorded under the stopwatch in the child observations. From parts of each of them I pieced the puzzle together.

Yet another book (Wolf 1972) written out of this amorphous set of fieldnotes illustrates even more vividly the value of using a variety of methods to record details and conversations that may or may not seem to make sense at the time. (I must ask indulgence for further notes on my personal intellectual history.)[3] Political and intellectual transformations are fairly common to our profession but come to us as individuals in different ways. Some seem to wake up one morning with a whole new set of values and beliefs. Others change slowly, often without even noticing it themselves, their new world view emerging more like the metamorphosis of tadpole to frog than the apparently sudden transformation of chrysalis to butterfly. Me, I'm a frog. I swam around for a long time in the pond watching with interest as my sisters changed colors and lost their tails, not noticing until the mid-1970s that I too had lost my undulating tail and grown the more useful legs of the feminist.

In no small part, my recognition of this transformation came out of a long struggle with both the fieldnotes from my first field trip and the notes collected on a second trip, primarily by me and a woman assistant. To clarify this somewhat opaque statement and explain why I found myself in a relationship of struggle with my own fieldnotes, I must say a bit about the history of Chinese ethnology and the study of the Chinese family.

As an institution, the Chinese family has been subjected to study for many years—in fact, one could say centuries without much exaggeration—by historians, philosophers, theologians, sociologists, social

---

[3]Not surprisingly, in writing this essay I found it quite impossible to speak impersonally. Other contributors with whom I have spoken have had the same experience. Anthropologists with their fieldnotes seem to be much like novelists with their writing techniques: each thinks the relationship between product and process is personal and unique. But as Jean Jackson's survey shows, this is not the case.

reformers, novelists, and even some anthropologists. That it is a male-dominated structure and a male-oriented group is obvious; that it was primarily a male-studied subject was also obvious but deemed unimportant. The consensus seemed to be that Chinese women contributed to the family their uteruses, a few affines of varying degrees of influence, and considerable discord. Other than that, they were of minimal interest in any examination of the Chinese family's strengths, cycles, or romance. They added comic relief and provided support functions, but stage front was totally male.

I was vaguely aware of the invisibility of women at the time of my first fieldwork in Taiwan, but since my relationship to academia at that time was strictly marital, I was neither interested in nor constrained by the all-male paradigm. I hung out with the women, as did all women, and the understanding I acquired of the family was theirs. When I began to write, I dutifully read the important books about the Chinese family and then, turning to my fieldnotes, began the struggle in which I was ultimately defeated. In writing *The House of Lim* I assumed to some degree that the "unusual" influence of the women in the family resulted from the presence of some unusually strong personalities among the female Lims. But when I began to look at other families, my fieldnotes would not conform to the paradigm. Neither the words they recorded nor the voices they brought back fit the standard version of how things worked. At every turn of the family cycle, where the well-known anthropologists of China (see, e.g., Freedman 1961, 1970) debated the importance of the father-son relationship versus the solidary brothers against the father, my voices spoke of mothers-in-law in fierce competition with their sons' wives for the loyalty of the son-husband and, most important, of mothers and their children set in unflagging battle formation against what they saw as the men's family. I realized that I must either ignore my notes and see the Lim women as unique or ignore the received wisdom and let the women I knew give their version of the Chinese family and its cycle.

But that was only half the struggle. The other half was with my sisters, who were using their strong new feminist legs to stir up the mud in our pond and raise our consciousness. You will recall that during those years we were looking fiercely at women's situation, at our oppression, our subordination, our position as victims (see, e.g., Gornick and Moran 1971). Once again, the women's voices in my fieldnotes gave me problems. Of course they were oppressed; obviously they were victimized. But victims who passively accepted their fate they were not. Nor did they seem to see themselves as victims, although when it was to their advantage to evoke their powerlessness and their lack of influence, they certainly did so. Moreover, the women in my fieldnotes seemed considerably more analytic than the standard texts on the Chinese family assumed women to be. Events in the family cycle that were described by social scientists (usually but not always male) as the result of male interests and needs were seen by women—and by this woman as well—to have been manipulated by women with very definite personal goals in mind. If men were aware of women's goals, it was only vaguely, and they certainly did not see them as relevant to outcomes.

The blinders Chinese men wear result from the centrality of their gender and their institutions in society. Chinese women, structural outsiders who participate only peripherally in the major institutions, are much cooler, much less constrained by those institutions, and hence freer to work around them, within them, and eventually against them. My fieldnotes contain many examples of men solemnly discussing concepts such as filial piety and institutions such as ancestor worship. They are balanced by the voices of iconoclastic women, like that of one who advised another to spend her money on herself rather than save it for her funeral:

> So what are you worrying about? You have sons. If they can stand to let you sit in the hall and rot, then you shouldn't worry about it. You will be dead. Hurry up and spend your money and enjoy yourself. If you die and they do spend all your money to pay for a big funeral, people will just say, "Oh, what good sons they are. What a fine funeral they gave for her." They won't say you paid for it. If it were me, I'd spend every cent now, and if they could stand to just roll me up in a mat, that would be their worry. [Wolf 1968: 216–17]

Chinese men and perhaps some anthropologists dismiss these discordant voices as indicative only of women's ignorance; Chinese women would be quick to agree. They have found ignorance or the appearance of ignorance to be a valuable resource.

Fortunately, at about the same time the voices in my fieldnotes were forcing me to recognize the power of women, other feminist anthropologists were reaching similar conclusions. The recalcitrant fieldnotes from Taiwan no longer seemed aberrant. My revisionist perspective fit in well with the other essays in Rosaldo and Lamphere's now classic *Woman, Culture, and Society* (1974).

Nonetheless, even now, in attempting a broader consideration of fieldnotes and their forms and the effect they have on what we ultimately do with them, these Chinanotes from Taiwan leave me in a quandary. At least half of the notes used to write those two books were recorded by someone else (Arthur Wolf, and his field assistants) with another project in mind. Even the material I collected myself during the first field visit was in a sense recorded by another person, certainly not by a feminist looking for an alternative perspective on the Chinese family. How is it, then, that those prejudices or at least predilections did not obscure the strong themes I later found in the data? I do not suggest that somehow we managed in our data collection to reach the nirvana of objectivity—on the contrary. But perhaps because so many of our notes were records of conversations, they are open to a variety of analyses that a researcher with a single, sharper focus would have lost. Yet to advise a novice anthropologist to fill her empty notebooks with whatever she saw or heard and worry about its meaning after she got back to the university would be worse than no advice at all.

My early experience working as a research assistant to an experimental psychologist taught me to value (if not attain) the clarity of thought that comes from setting a hierarchy of hypotheses, defining variables, and establishing with caution the dimensions that measure them. Certainly the young anthropologist who goes to the field with a circumscribed problem and a clear picture of the kind of data that will address it will accomplish the task of dissertation research in half the time. Nonetheless, she must also consider whether it will be possible to return to those data to ask different questions, to search for solutions to conflicting explanations, or even to add to the general ethnographic literature. Such a limited research strategy should be employed only after a careful weighing of the advantages and disadvantages.

In 1980–81 I spent the academic year in the People's Republic of China and made use of this more focused approach—but not by my own choice. I would have preferred to do research in a single area, but for a variety of personal and political reasons I spent from four to six weeks each in six different sites spread across China. I came to this research carrying baggage different from what I had carried to Taiwan, having become openly feminist and pro-socialist. My goal was to look at the changes in women's lives, rural and urban, thirty years after the establishment of an officially feminist socialist society. I was armed with a set of basic questions and with warnings not to expect to find utopia. It was beyond a doubt the most difficult field research I have ever done. I was required to conduct formal interviews, always with a minimum of one government official present. In two of the six sites I was not allowed to interview in homes, and in others I was given little opportunity for small talk or casual observation. I was allowed a quota of fifty women and five men per field site. Obviously, there are ways of striking up informal conversations and making observations outside of working hours when one is living on a rural commune and I made full use of them, but being around for so short a time did not allow me to build the kinds of relationships with informants which give the deeper insights into individual lives. Nonetheless, the project was successful. It was not as complete as I would have liked, but I learned a great deal from the 300 women I talked with about their hopes, their disappointments, and the quality of their lives. As a side benefit, the two women who traveled with me throughout the research and heard the answers to my pointed questions in site after site gradually became radicalized and began to express, covertly of course, their indignation over the discrepancies between the slogans of gender equality and the realities they were encountering.

My informants in China were far more informative than either I or the officials who grudgingly allowed me to conduct my research had anticipated. A book (Wolf 1985) and a few essays resulted—but what of the fieldnotes? Will they have the same value in ten years that my early notes from Taiwan had after ten years? I doubt it very much. And if they do, it will be more as documents of a certain phase in the socialist transformation of Chinese society than as a source of new insights into women's lives. Even though I collected work histories and genealogical information for all the women and recorded their attitudes on a number of subjects other than gender, the focus was necessarily tight. I could not hope to get to know them well enough to evaluate independently their position in village or neighborhood society. Worse yet, I have no records of conversations initiated by them, for none was. Nor had I the advantage of hearing them talk about their interests rather than what I (sometimes mistakenly) took to be mine.

Rich as I believe these interviews are, they are frozen in time, individual statements only vaguely anchored in the social and historical context that created them. They are the responses of my informants to my questions, in no way a dialogue and in no sense a dialectic search for mutual understanding of a topic. One might reasonably say that in these fieldnotes I retained control of the subject matter, and my Chinese informants retained control of its content. I have information, but I must interpret it alone. By way of justification—or consolation, as the case may be—I can say that I had neither the luxury of repeated visits over a number of years nor the luxury of time that is required before one's informants *want* to tell you about themselves and their society. The situation in the People's Republic required all of us to compromise. My informants tried to satisfy me and their government; I tried to satisfy the goals of my research project. I was forced to write a different kind of fieldnote, and its form determined the kind of ethnography that resulted, an ethnography in which I must constantly remind my reader to question whether it is my informants or their government speaking.

The research in the PRC made me painfully aware of my own mortality and of the sensitive nature of fieldnotes. I see two issues about fieldwork as inextricably related: the protection of informants, and the sharing of fieldnotes. Over the years of doing fieldwork in Taiwan I have put a good deal of effort into attempts to protect the privacy of my informants. It never occurred to me when I wrote *The House of Lim* that in ten years I would find copies of the book staring at me in every tourist shop in Taipei. But because I used pseudonyms, changed the names of towns and villages, and even gave the compass a whirl when I wrote it, my efforts to protect informants have been successful at that basic level. Yet in the original fieldnotes for that village, even though we assigned everyone an identification number, the names of the individuals we knew best had a way of slipping in. The children we observed are now grown, and the so-called economic miracle of Taiwan has allowed some of the villagers to enter professions that make them socially and politically quite visible. One is even the director of an electronics facility in Silicon Valley in California. The responsibility I bear them will continue for many years to come and precludes my putting the fieldnotes in the public domain. Some of our systematic data would not be at all sensitive and with careful editing might be safely allowed in the hands of people I do not know, but that editing would be a big chore.

My data from the PRC are an even heavier burden. It is unfortunate but true that in China one can still suffer serious damage for the expression of an unpopular opinion, no matter how innocent that opinion may seem to the unwary outsider. For that matter, today's popular opinion may be tomorrow's heresy. In published material I have taken great care to be misleading as to who said what, particularly when the statement—however apolitical—was made by someone within the governmental apparatus who was speaking off the record. But, as with the Taiwan data, how am I to know that today's village woman will not in a decade be a provincial officer in the Women's Federation? I would be delighted if this were to come about, but, however unlikely such an event may be, I also feel constrained to conceal the fact that she once gave me her personal views on a touchy issue. The few names I have used in published material from the PRC are pseudonyms, and again the geography is moved about, but to expurgate these fieldnotes would be more difficult if not impossible. Much as I would like to make all our fieldnotes available to responsible colleagues for different kinds of analyses and alternative interpretations, my sense of my obligation to the people who gave me so much is that I would be breaking faith with them by doing so. Those who collect the fieldnotes are most fully aware of the damage to particular individuals that their irresponsible use could cause.

So what is to be the ultimate disposition of fieldnotes? After their collectors have turned to dust, are the notes to molder in attics and basements until some uninterested daughter or granddaughter recycles them? I hope not. We have all heard too many horror stories of the eager researcher who gets wind of a cache of invaluable records only to arrive a year or two after they have been consigned to the garbage heap. Perhaps all our notes should be turned over to the Smithsonian to be sealed in some attic room until they can do no harm to the living or the dead.

But is the sharing of fieldnotes—ignoring for a moment the pleasant feeling of generous altruism—really in the best interests of anthropology? Would we not be adding yet another level of complexity in our search for meaning? Would not the young anthropologist who looks at my old Taiwan notes have to make a quantum leap backward to understand the social, historical, political, and (equally important from my perspective) personal context in which those notes were written? And would she not also have to struggle to recreate the personality that had recorded them? Frankly, even I find that task more and more difficult as the years go by. Do we want to wish it on—indeed, trust it to—our descendants?

Should we perhaps treat our fieldnotes as ephemera, as texts created by anthropologist and informants in a particular space and time for a particular purpose: the creation of an ethnography or a research report which in itself becomes another kind of text with a set of long-established rules for its reading? Do we then write our memoirs and at the end of each day's writing stint sit in front of the fireplace and ceremoniously burn the notes we used that day? I don't think I could do that. And I am sure my historian colleagues would be horrified at the thought of such arson.

For arson it would be. However flawed, fieldnotes are not ephemera but documents that record one mind's attempt to come to understand the behavior of fellow beings. One day—fly specks, bacterial infection, and all—they must be part of the public record so that if the species should survive or be followed by some other postnuclear being cursed with curiosity, the fieldnotes can be reexamined for what they are: our feeble attempts at communication with one another. For however wanting anthropology may be, it has nonetheless served to create a sense of global humanity—cross-class, cross-culture, and cross-gender—that is sorely lacking in most other disciplines.

Considering the serious reassessment of anthropology currently under way, it may seem almost frivolous simply to muddle on, making superficial modifications in our old field methods. Perhaps the most we can do at this juncture is to attempt to be more aware of process, both in the field and while trying to make sense of what we bring back with us. Have we really any other choice? We must reflect on our work thus far, but we must not allow the inward gaze to blind us to the real achievements of our past. Recent trends in anthropology put us in danger of becoming more literary critics than creators of literature, more service workers than producers. Should we cease to produce fieldnotes and create ethnography, we will cease to do anthropology, for anthropology is dependent on fieldnotes and ethnographies for its existence. Theory is exciting and the source of growth, but untested theory will in time turn a discipline into an art form.

REFERENCES

Freedman, Maurice. 1961. The Family in China, Past and Present. *Pacific Affairs* 34:323–36.

———. 1970. Ritual Aspects of Chinese Kinship and Marriage. In *Family and Kinship in Chinese Society,* ed. Maurice Freedman, 163–87. Stanford, Calif.: Stanford University Press.

Gornick, Vivian, and Barbara K. Moran, eds. 1971. *Woman in Sexist Society: Studies in Powerlessness.* New York: Basic Books.

Rosaldo, Michelle Zimbalist, and Louise Lamphere, eds. 1974. *Woman, Culture, and Society.* Stanford, Calif.: Stanford University Press.

Whiting, Beatrice B., ed. 1963. *Six Cultures: Studies of Child Rearing*. New York: Wiley.

Wolf, Margery. 1968. *The House of Lim: A Study of a Chinese Farm Family*. Englewood Cliffs, N.J.: Prentice-Hall.

——. 1972. *Women and the Family in Rural Taiwan*. Stanford, Calif.: Stanford University Press.

——. 1985. *Revolution Postponed: Women in Contemporary China*. Stanford, Calif.: Stanford University Press.

ROBERT J. SMITH

Hearing Voices, Joining the Chorus: Appropriating Someone Else's Fieldnotes

Most anthropologists have enough trouble analyzing their own fieldnotes without taking on the extraordinarily complex task of dealing with someone else's. When they do so, it is usually because they plan to conduct research in a place where another anthropologist has already collected data. The would-be secondary user almost inevitably works alone, for in the most common case the writer of the notes has died, and there is no one to answer questions prompted by the discovery of ambiguities, lack of clarity, seeming contradictions, and simple illegibility likely to characterize such personal materials.

My motives for undertaking the enterprise I describe below had nothing to do with plans to conduct research in the place where the fieldwork was carried out. I did not even know of the existence of the materials until a few weeks before they passed into my hands. Furthermore, when I did at last begin the task of dealing with the remarkable journal that formed part of the collection, I enjoyed a distinct advantage: the woman who wrote it is very much alive and became an active participant in our joint effort to rescue it from oblivion.[1]

I am grateful to Ella Lury Wiswell and Margery Wolf for their comments on a draft of this essay.

[1] See the preface in Smith and Wiswell (1982: xxi–xxxviii). For an account of Wiswell's experiences at the fiftieth-anniversary celebration of the Embrees' study, organized and financed by the people of Suye in 1985, see Wiswell and Smith (1988).

I have chosen to give a fairly straightforward account of that rescue effort. At a time when many anthropologists are engaged in fevered reexamination of the foundations of our discipline, my approach may appear at best naive, at worst simply perverse. It is neither. I take the tack I do because it seems to me that the current concern with text, meaning, writing, and reflexivity is as much to be accounted for by its eruption in Western intellectual life in the 1970s and 1980s as by any particular relevance it may have to the ethnographic enterprise per se. The point is put with enviable elegance in an editorial comment on a set of papers dealing with one or another of the "crises" in anthropology:

> Anthropologists have become fond of writing about the culture of anthropology as a subject in itself and of including themselves in their fieldwork. The self-consciousness of a discipline seeking to understand the Other is hardly surprising, aside from the fact that it fits the tendencies of late-twentieth-century thought so neatly as to be a bit suspect. . . . Perhaps the problems of anthropology are less unique than its ambitions. [Grew 1986: 190]

We can only hope that Raymond Grew is right. However that may be, I set out here in some detail the circumstances that led to my involvement with the field materials and the process by means of which I tried to join the chorus of voices speaking through them. I apologize for the lengthy preamble but offer it because I think it otherwise difficult to see why I got involved in the first place.

In 1944, when I was seventeen, I joined a unit of the U.S. Army Specialized Training Reserve Corps at the University of Minnesota. It was one of several scattered about the country engaged in what were then called Japanese language and area studies. Among our courses was one on the ethnography of the peoples of the Pacific; it was taught by Wilson D. Wallis, with occasional guest lectures by his wife, Ruth Sawtell Wallis. In retrospect, it is not difficult to imagine what a struggle it must have been for these two anthropologists—one a specialist on the Micmac of the Canadian Maritimes, the other a physical anthropologist—to assemble a decent set of readings for the course. For Japan, however, there was one excellent book, John F. Embree's *Suye Mura: A Japanese Village* (1939). The field research on which it was based had been completed in 1936, just a few years earlier, and in addition to its scholarly merits the book had all the fascination of a nearly contemporary account of life in an enemy country. I found it interesting enough but had no reason to suppose I would ever refer to it again once the final examination in the Wallises' course was over.

So much for prescience. What had come to be widely touted as a hundred years' war ended abruptly several months later, and after spending most of 1946 in Japan, I was discharged from the army and returned to the University of Minnesota as an undergraduate majoring in anthropology. The very first quarter's schedule included a course on the ethnology of East Asia, taught by Richard K. Beardsley, himself a product of the U.S. Navy's wartime Japanese language program. Inevitably, the Embree book appeared on the list of required texts, and so I read it once more. In light of my own recent experience of Japan and its people, I found much in it that I had missed before. Eventually I learned that anthropologists do something called fieldwork on which they base ethnographies (I knew nothing of fieldnotes at the time), and it seemed to me that someone should do a similar study that would focus on what had happened in the countryside in postsurrender Japan.

After two years of graduate study at Cornell University, I found myself back in Japan to do just that under sponsorship of the Center for Japanese Studies of the University of Michigan, where Beardsley had gone from Minnesota. Soon after arriving, I moved into a village on the island of Shikoku, equipped with a portable typewriter (I had found out about fieldnotes long since), a dictionary, and a worn copy of *Suye Mura: A Japanese Village*. It was the summer of 1951, a few months after John Embree and his daughter Clare had been killed by a motorist who ran them down on a snowy street in Hamden, Connecticut. I had hoped to visit him at Yale before I left for Japan; now I had only his book and a few published papers on Suye to guide me in my research.[2] For several years after I took up my teaching post at Cornell in 1953, the book was a required text in my course on Japanese society and culture. It remains in print, a classic of the community study genre.

I knew nothing of Ella Embree, who had also been in Suye in 1935–36, save that in his preface John Embree had acknowledged that she spoke Japanese fluently, while his own command of the language was fragmentary. Then, in the summer of 1965, she came to Ithaca to visit one of his sisters, and we met for the first time. Ella Wiswell (she had

[2]The results of that research appear in severely abridged form in Cornell and Smith (1956: 1–112). Four community studies were conducted under the aegis of the University of Michigan's Center for Japanese Studies: two appear in Cornell and Smith 1956; the third is Norbeck 1954, and the fourth—capstone of the enterprise—is Beardsley, Hall, and Ward 1959. The Embree tradition was very much alive during this period.

by then remarried) proved to be a handsome woman, intense and vibrant, whose lightly accented English caught me by surprise. For some reason it had never occurred to me to wonder how the wife of an American anthropologist happened to be fluent in Japanese, but I should have guessed after having met so many expatriate Russians in Kobe just after the war. I think we must have ignored the other guests totally, so deeply involved were we in speaking of the Suye study, the tragic death of her husband and daughter, and my own research that had been inspired by his book.

It was late in the conversation that she raised an issue for which I was not prepared. When she left Connecticut for Honolulu to teach at the University of Hawaii in 1951, she said, she had tried without success to interest someone at Yale in taking over the Suye research materials. She could not bear to discard them, of course, but neither could she foresee any circumstances under which she would ever look at them again. They were stored in the attic of a friend's house in New Haven. Did I by any chance know of anyone who might be interested in looking at them to see whether they contained anything of value? I did.

When a number of cartons arrived in my office several weeks later, I unpacked them at once, astonished at their bulk. There were two albums of black and white photographs that I have since learned number 1,720 in all. Another set of albums contained carefully labeled advertising broadsides, notices of meetings of village organizations, school entertainment programs, paper charms and amulets from shrines and temples, and newspaper clippings—a galaxy of ephemera of the kind often discarded in the course of fieldwork. A batch of manila envelopes contained hamlet household census forms, copies of progress reports to the Social Science Research Committee of the University of Chicago (which had funded the study), some drafts of unpublished papers by John Embree and others, and correspondence relating to the research. In one folder there was an English-language typescript headed "The Diary of a Japanese Innkeeper's Daughter" with an introduction by John Embree and a note that the translation had been done by one Miwa Kai.[3] There was also the two-volume unedited manu-

[3]Shortly after we completed the manuscript of *The Women of Suye Mura*, Ella Wiswell reminded me of the existence of the diary. After looking it over again, I suggested that it be prepared for publication, and she put me in touch with Miwa Kai, who graciously agreed to the plan. With her indispensable assistance the diary appeared forty years after she had completed her translation of it during World War II (Smith and Smith 1984).

script of *Suye Mura: A Japanese Village* and a copy of the notes for the
lectures John Embree had given at the University of Chicago for the
Civil Affairs Training School for the Far East during the war. I put all
this wealth of material aside, however, when I found the core of the
collection: two typescript journals. John Embree's contained 1,276
pages; Ella's, 1,005.

Even that initial cursory inspection of the contents of the cartons
produced some surprises. The progress reports had been jointly in the
names of John and Ella Embree, for it turned out that under the terms
of the grant she had borne specific responsibility for collecting information on the lives of the women and children of the village. That
discovery cleared up the puzzle of why there were two research journals of impressive length but only one book. It was apparent that John
had written his dissertation from his notes, using his wife's hardly at
all, and revised it for publication. No book on the topic of the other
study (as I came to think of Ella's work) had ever seen the light of day.

My first task, I decided, was to read her journal. I was quite unpre-
pared to find that its information on Japanese women was absolutely
unique. One uses the word "unique" to describe anything Japanese
advisedly, for it is badly overworked and almost always inaccurate; in
this instance, however, it was entirely appropriate. Not only were the
Embrees the first foreign anthropologists to conduct research in Japan,
but they had also carried out the only study done to this date by a
husband-and-wife team residing in a rural community for a year. In the
mid-1930s no Japanese social scientist was collecting such material, and
nothing like the contents of her journal had appeared in any language in
the intervening years.

I wrote to her at once and so began a correspondence about how it
might be possible to make available at last the results of "the other
study." The Suye files had been put aside some thirty years before; that
the final result of my good intentions appeared only after another
seventeen years had passed can be explained if not excused. In 1969,
while on a visit to Austin, Texas, my wife and I narrowly escaped
meeting the fate of John and Clare Embree. Recovery from our extensive injuries was very slow, and when we finally returned to Ithaca, it
was to find Cornell's version of the campus revolution in full swing.
The years of turmoil that followed, rendered nearly insupportable by
my own greatly reduced level of energy, were academically unproduc-
tive. Then in 1973 came an unexpected opportunity to plan a restudy
of the place where I had lived on Shikoku, which led to fieldwork in

1975 and an extended period of writing and seeing a manuscript through to publication (Smith 1978).

Once more I returned to the Suye materials and arranged to be at the University of Hawaii for the fall semester of 1978. Retired long since, Ella Wiswell and her husband Frederick were living in Honolulu; it seemed a perfect chance to work together, and I took her journal with me. As I set about reading it once again, we talked over the many considerations that eventually led to our decision to publish *The Women of Suye Mura* (Smith and Wiswell 1982).

If I have been unduly discursive in this personal account, it is because I want to highlight several unusual features of my involvement with someone else's fieldnotes. First, they were given to me by their author, who from the outset entertained some doubt as to their value. Second, I never met John Embree, author of the basic ethnographic sources on the community in which the fieldwork had been carried out. Third, I have never visited the place or met any of its people. (In recent years I have come to suspect that I may well be the only American ethnologist of Japan over the age of fifty who has not gone there.) Insofar as I know the place and people at all, it is through the writings of John Embree and the numerous scholars who have made of restudies of Suye something of a cottage industry, and through the eyes, ears, and memory of Ella Wiswell.[4]

This essay is not about texts or presentation or re-presentation. It does not deal with writing or inscribing, pre-scription or de-scription. It *is* about voices, and in a purely nontechnical way it is about multi-vocality. It was Margery Wolf who said of *The Women of Suye Mura,* "You have given Ella Wiswell her voice." That is in fact what I hoped to do, but it now seems more appropriate to say I have helped her speak at least. Consider for a moment the object on which all that follows is based. The ethnographer—who continues to disavow the label—wrote down what she had seen and heard, and often what she thought about it, at the end of every day. The journal, which begins on December 20, 1935, and ends on November 3, 1936, is written in English, although she might equally well have used Russian or French. As we shall see, and as those who have read our book will know, hers is a powerful voice. Indeed, so powerful is it that as secondary user of her fieldnotes, I initially found it a serious problem.

---

[4]The major restudies include Kawakami 1983; Raper et al. 1950; Ushijima 1958, 1971; and Yoshino 1955.

In my earliest readings of her journal I became fascinated with its author, whom I had then met only once and so barely knew. Only gradually did it dawn on me that the voice I had come to hear so clearly in the pages of the journal was not that of the woman I had met but rather that of a young woman in her mid-twenties, a foreigner conducting research in a land she thought of as home by virtue of having spent much of her youth there and where her family still lived. She was educated at Berkeley and the Sorbonne and had been a graduate-student wife at the University of Chicago. The experience in Suye recorded in her journal was filtered through a highly cosmopolitan screen indeed.[5] I took no comfort in comparing her background with my own when at about the same age I had taken my purely American perspective with me into a similar research situation. To add to my discomfort there was the far more obvious problem of the difference of gender. The author of the journal spoke in a woman's voice, and much of what she wrote about concerned other women. For some time I wrestled with what I saw as linked problems. The first was how to extract from this inconceivably rich and impossibly copious record the parts that ought to be published. The second was how to get past the ethnographer, for whom my admiration and respect increased with each reading, to the ethnography.

I made several false starts, each abandoned a short way into the enterprise, and then one day it came to me that I had overlooked the most painfully obvious central problem. The journal was not *mine* in any sense other than that it had ended up on my desk. Lacking any system of cross-referencing, it was in some respects very like a diary. Its author had lived in one place for over a year, so that every day's entry was based on her accumulating experience. As a reader—one kind of spectator or auditor—I simply could not keep things straight. A woman who figured in a domestic quarrel reported in a December entry, for example, would appear again and again in other circumstances and as a participant with many other people in a variety of activities. With each appearance her character and personality became more palpable, more rounded, better understood, and her voice more audible. The difficulty was that increasing familiarity led the journal's author to use shorthand references to individuals and places. This meant that the woman identified early on as Mrs. Sawada Taki of

---

[5] I find it difficult to see how one reviewer of the book came to the conclusion that she was "a fairly ordinary housewife-cum-scholar who spoke excellent Japanese" (Moeran 1984).

Oade or Otsuka's daughter Taki is referred to simply as Taki in later entries and occasionally as Mrs. Sawada with no mention of her hamlet of residence. Furthermore, there were scores of women to keep track of; sometimes they were identified by full name, occasionally by surname only, and frequently by given name alone. In some passages there were no names at all; in most of these there was some clue to the identity of the person being written about, but the clue often pointed in more than one direction. The more deeply I got into the journal, the more completely at sea I felt.

How could I make the journal mine? To pose the question was to answer it—there seemed to be no way. What I needed was some means of diminishing the powerful presence of the ethnographer so that the people of whom she wrote would emerge more clearly. Here I must acknowledge membership in that generation of academics who write some of our manuscripts in longhand and type others. In either case I compose as I go along, and each revision, whether hand- or typewritten, is also a recomposition. The solution I arrived at reflects these preferences and habits; because it seems to have served its purpose well, I report it here. I photocopied the entire journal, marked every passage in the copy not devoted to the weather, recipes, and the like, and sat down at my typewriter. For weeks I spent most of every day retyping the marked passages verbatim, beginning with the first entry. Before I was well into this stultifying task, I began to know the people in a new way. Some of the payoff was purely technical. For example, for the first time it became clear to me that Mrs. Higuchi of the store (February 13, 1936), Ayako at the village shrine festival (November 27, 1935), old man Sakata's daughter (May 29, 1936), and almost certainly the unnamed object of some unrestrained gossip on an outing (July 1, 1936) were all the same woman. What is more, by the time I got to the gossip about her, it came as no surprise. When I was finally done, I had learned enough to spot continuities and inconsistencies, resolve most of the occasional ambiguities, and see how passages that had appeared to be unrelated (or unrelatable) to anything or anyone did in fact connect with what had gone before or came after.

My aim had been to appropriate the journal, which has many passages that begin with something like "It must have been she they were talking about at the market in town last week," or "If that is what she meant, then Sakata has got it all wrong or was trying to mislead me." As they became part of *my* fieldnotes, all such journal entries were transformed into references to conversations and observations I had typed up myself. In the innumerable lengthy indirect quotes and many direct ones I began to hear familiar voices and recognize characteristic manners of expression. My growing sense of confidence was rooted in my own fieldwork in another village in Japan just fifteen years after the Embrees left Suye. Although a catastrophic war and vast social changes had intervened, it seemed to me that I had spent a year with farmers and shopkeepers who in many respects were very like their counterparts in prewar Suye. Ella Wiswell's shy young women, philandering husbands, neighborhood scolds, hardworking household heads, and indulged children were familiar figures. I confess that the people of Suye discussed some matters in ways that did afford me an occasional jolt; otherwise, the landscape was easily recognizable. This discovery was reassuring, for it suggested that despite all our differences in background, we had nonetheless encountered very similar kinds of people. It seemed highly unlikely that we had merely created them.

So I am led to make the audacious claim that the voices of the women of Suye could be heard more clearly once I had interposed myself between them and their ethnographer, who now was far less salient in my perception of the place and its people. Nevertheless, I was left still with nothing more than a year of narrative. In my abridgment the story lines were easier to follow, but I did not know what to do with it. Certainly I had no desire to try my hand at writing something like "*My Year with Japanese Village Women* by Ella Lury Wiswell as told to Robert J. Smith." Once or twice I flirted with the idea of "*Ella Lury Wiswell: An Anthropologist at Work* by Robert J. Smith," but quickly concluded that for better or worse, we were not Ruth Benedict and Margaret Mead.[6]

In some despair I went through my newly typed fieldnotes again, studied the carefully captioned photographs that allowed me to put names with faces, and the for the *n*th time reread John Embree's book. The effect was startling. A work I had always found appealing for the sense it gave of life as lived by Japanese farmers now seemed curiously lifeless, almost bland. All the important topics were covered, but there

---

[6]The allusion is to Mead 1959, of course. About this time a suggestion came from an entirely different quarter that the complete journals of the Embrees be translated into Japanese to mark the fiftieth anniversary of their arrival in Suye in 1935. Valuable as the data are, this seemed an idea virtually guaranteed to trivialize their accomplishment; it was not pursued.

were fewer *people* than I had remembered. Indeed, the text was hardly populated at all; the people of Suye were blurred, their individual voices indistinct in this highly normative picture of the place.

John Embree cannot be faulted, however, for accomplishing precisely what he had set out to do. The "First Report on Field Work: Suye Mura, Kumamoto, Japan" by John and Ella Embree, dated February 15, 1936, opens with this paragraph:

> We have now been in Suye three and a half months. We have learned that a community of sixteen hundred is much more than two people can ever hope to know personally. We are making progress by concentrating on about a fourth of the village as individual households and studying the activities as a whole only as they are expressed in those more formal units of the school and village office.

Further on, John writes:

> Ella has been picking up most of *the living social order* [emphasis supplied] by means of conversations with housewives. The numerous drinking parties make it easy to become acquainted.

The goal of the remaining nine months of fieldwork, he adds, is "to have enough material for a fairly good picture of a Japanese village," including data on the kinship system and life-cycle rites, the hamlet-level cooperative system, the economy, social classes and cliques, and religion.

I was struck by the aptness of the phrase "the living social order." It is echoed in Plath's review (1984: 340) of *The Women of Suye Mura*: "If John Embree's book is a sort of official group photograph of the people of Suye, Ella Wiswell's journal is an album of snapshots of those people milling around before and after they struck a pose for the lens of science." To recast this characteristically astute observation in my own metaphor, John Embree takes us to the public performance of the village chorus made up mostly of men who hold the sheet music firmly before their eyes; Ella Wiswell gives us material of which only a fraction is incorporated into the concert, for there was much singing, whistling, and humming offstage, especially by women who never got to perform in public at all. Not everyone can read music or carry a tune, after all, and whether sharp or flat, the off-key singer is seldom welcomed into the chorus. The Ella Embree who wrote the journal would probably have added some caustic comment to the effect that the women were there only to serve tea and refreshments to the male public performers anyway.

And so we have returned to the ethnographer. I cannot imagine that my efforts would have come to anything had I not been able to consult with her time and again. Perhaps the most egregious request I made of her was that she reread her journal, for it must have been a wrenching experience. While she was so occupied, I set about deciding how to reorganize the narrative I had appropriated in such a way that the pages of John Embree's book would be peopled, however disorderly the crowd and ragged its voices. The standard chapter headings of his study would not do, for they are not what Ella Wiswell had been about in Suye. I ended up by repackaging, telling myself that by and large the categories I developed from my fieldnotes had congealed out of the array of topics most extensively reported in her journal.

There remained the problem of multivocality. Concerned to keep the identity of the speaker clear and to retain her words verbatim, insofar as that was possible, I adopted a necessarily cumbersome technique, an account of which appears in Smith and Wiswell (1982: xii):

> The passages in double quotation marks are taken directly from the journal, edited to reduce redundancy and to clarify where necessary. Materials between single quotation marks within these passages are quotations from conversations and comments made by the villagers. Parenthetical passages are in the original. Bracketed ones are mine, as is the balance of the text. Thus:
>
> That was precisely what had happened. "Of the Maehara change of wives the women thought favorably. This one is said to be a good worker and not 'an *okusan* type' [by implication a lady] like the one who has left. She gave a *kao mishiri* [a 'face-showing' party given by one who moves into a new community] when she arrived. 'At Maehara's,' they laughed, 'they had to throw such a party because the wives change so often.' (I learned later that his real wife—the first one—is not officially registered as such.)"

The first draft of the manuscript I sent to Ella Wiswell, therefore, was the journal dismembered, cut and pasted, its pieces patched together with transitional passages and observations provided by the ultimate outsider—a man who had never even been near the small world of which she had written. The cutting and pasting had introduced a new kind of order; the transitions and observations introduced a new voice. Along with the draft I sent a list of questions about many matters that still puzzled me. Had I got this particular dispute right? Had I confused two women because they bore the same given name? Was a certain marriage really between cousins? Was this woman's husband her second or third? She could not answer them all, for as any ethnographer knows or will learn, despite the early conviction that you will never forget anyone or anything encountered during your first extended fieldwork, memory fails with alarming speed. Small wonder, then, that forty-five years after the event Ella Wiswell could not even recall some of the individuals whose activities take up many pages of her journal. But memory is selective, of course, and for the most part I found hers phenomenal, refreshed as it was by rereading her journal.

Waiting for her reaction to the manuscript was an anxious time, for I was concerned to know whether I had got the tone right. Had I been true to the character of particular individuals she had known so well? Had I given this or that event the proper emphasis? Did I overinterpret here? Most important, I wondered whether she would feel that the manuscript revealed too much about ethnographer and villager alike. Those who have read the book will know that it reveals a great deal. What had been muted voices now speak quite loudly in some of its passages, and occasionally what had been a whisper has been raised to the level of full-throated declamation. For the most part, however, I felt confident that the voices were telling us what the speakers wanted Ella Wiswell to hear and see, which is some version of what everybody—or nearly everybody—in Suye already knew. But that was then, and this was forty-five years later. The young village women of that time had become today's grandmothers or joined the ancestral spirits of their house. Had we revealed too much in light of the sensibilities of Suye people in the 1980s? In the end we decided that in only one instance had we gone too far and at the last minute deleted eight pages from the copyedited manuscript.[7] Those pages dealt with what anyone who has done extended fieldwork will recognize as perhaps the most painful period: the several days just prior to leaving

---

[7]See Smith and Wiswell (1982: xi, 273–281) for our justification of the decision to publish the book in its present form. In the final version of the manuscript I adopted the familiar tactic of changing all personal names, confusing directions, shuffling people and places, and otherwise misleading the reader. When Ella Wiswell complained that *she* could no longer keep the people straight, I felt I had succeeded in this exercise in dissimulation.

the place. The difficulty of disengaging yet leaving the tempers and dignity of all parties intact is a matter far less frequently dealt with in courses on "field methods" than how to "gain entry" and "build and maintain rapport." It can be a highly stressful time for all concerned; how stressful and in what ways it was so for the Embrees and the people of Suye, we have chosen not to say.

We went to press. Unlike other books that exploit the fieldnotes of another,[8] the prologue to this one is entirely in the fieldworker's voice (Smith and Wiswell 1982: xxi–xxxviii). I do not remember how we came to decide against making it an epilogue, but I think our instincts were right. Once again the voice of the ethnographer dominates, as Ella Wiswell of the 1980s tells us how it came about that she went to Suye and, in retrospect, what that long-ago year was like. In the chapters that follow, using the awkward notation system described above, I tried to make hers only one voice among the many speaking from the past. On occasion the outsider speaks, touching on what seems to be the larger meaning of an event, drawing comparisons, and offering presentiments of things to come. The introduction of the intruder's voice, clearly distinguished from all the others, can be justified only to the extent that it is doubly alien.

Neither of us has ever imagined for a moment that this account is the only conceivable version of what rural Japanese were like some fifty years ago. Hers is a very personal voice, as is the one I adopt in my appropriation of her journal. Furthermore, Ella Wiswell's reading of it in the 1980s is not the same one that Ella Embree would have given it in the 1930s, nor is my own more distanced one of the 1980s like the reading I would have given the journal in the 1950s—for despite fashionable claims to the contrary, most anthropologists I know think of what they write as highly informed opinion rather than Holy Writ. Yet however defective a record it may be and however colored by the fieldworker's personality and interests, her journal nonetheless has this ultimate value: it is the only contemporary account of the lives of rural women in Japan at that moment in history. Thanks to her fieldwork, we are not forced to try to imagine what their lives were like then, nor need we ask people today to try to remember how they lived. She set

---

[8] I know of only one exception, which involved the editing and annotating of a manuscript of formidable length written by E. Michael Mendelson and put aside ten years earlier and fifteen years after the fieldwork was carried out. Mendelson gave John P. Ferguson, the editor, access to his fieldnotes and personal diary as well. Details are given in two prefaces, one each by editor and author (Mendelson 1975: 15–20).

down in her journal what she saw and heard, thinking the material would be published only insofar as John Embree drew on it in writing his dissertation. The form in which it has finally appeared was calculated to provide a setting in which the voices of women, men, and children could be heard publicly for the first time. The account is no less instructive for being accompanied by two other voices from another time and two very different worlds.

If we are to continue to do ethnography at all, I cannot see that we have any other option than to listen carefully to what people say, watch what they do, and keep our voices down. I find offensive the recent tendency to refer to fieldwork as a *rite of passage*. Not only is the label variously dismissive or derisive, depending on the point being made; it also signals a shift of focus that bodes ill for the discipline. Its use reveals a concern for the fieldworker's experience so exclusive as to render the people among whom the ethnographer lives irrelevant save as instruments to facilitate career transitions. The implication is demeaning to people who deserve more respect; the transformation of our informants into hapless victims of alleged careerist machinations is the high price we pay when we stop writing anthropology and start writing about it and ourselves. The subjects of ethnographies, it should never be forgotten, are always more interesting than their authors.

In the end, the blend of voices in our compositions will be uneven. How could it be otherwise? We can at the very least take care to identify each singer clearly, for in our fieldnotes is the only record of the only performance they will ever give.

REFERENCES

Beardsley, Richard K., John W. Hall, and Robert E. Ward. 1959. *Village Japan*. Chicago: University of Chicago Press.

Cornell, John B., and Robert J. Smith. 1956. *Two Japanese Villages*. Occasional Paper 5. Ann Arbor: University of Michigan Center for Japanese Studies.

Embree, John F. 1939. *Suye Mura: A Japanese Village*. Chicago: University of Chicago Press.

Grew, Raymond. 1986. Editorial Foreword. *Comparative Studies in Society and History* 28:189–90.

Kawakami, Barbara. 1983. The Position of Women in Rural Japan: Tradition and Transition in Suye Mura. M.A. thesis, University of Hawaii, Honolulu.

Mead, Margaret. 1959. *An Anthropologist at Work: Writings of Ruth Benedict*. Boston: Houghton Mifflin.

Mendelson, E. Michael. 1975. *Sangha and State in Burma: A Study of Monastic Sectarianism and Leadership.* Ed. John P. Ferguson. Ithaca: Cornell University Press.

Moeran, Brian. 1984. Review of *The Women of Suye Mura* by R. J. Smith and E. L. Wiswell. *School of Oriental and African Studies Bulletin* 47:2.

Norbeck, Edward. 1954. *Takashima: A Japanese Fishing Community.* Salt Lake City: University of Utah Press.

Plath, David W. 1984. Review of *The Women of Suye Mura* by R. J. Smith and E. L. Wiswell. *Journal of Asian Studies* 43:339–42.

Raper, Arthur F., et al. 1950. *The Japanese Village in Transition.* Report 136. Tokyo: General Headquarters, Supreme Commander for the Allied Powers, Natural Resources Section.

Smith, Robert J. 1978. *Kurusu: The Price of Progress in a Japanese Village, 1951–1975.* Stanford, Calif.: Stanford University Press.

Smith, Robert J., and Kazuko Smith, eds. 1984. *The Diary of a Japanese Innkeeper's Daughter.* Trans. Miwa Kai. Cornell University East Asia Paper 36. Ithaca: East Asia Program, Cornell University.

Smith, Robert J., and Ella Lury Wiswell. 1982. *The Women of Suye Mura.* Chicago: University of Chicago Press.

Ushijima, Morimitsu. 1958. Suye Mura in Transition. M.A. thesis, University of Atlanta.

———. 1971. *Henbō suru Suye mura* (Suye Mura in Transition: A Fundamental Study of Sociocultural Change). Kyoto: Minerva-shobō.

Wiswell, Ella L., and Robert J. Smith. 1988. Suye Mura Fifty Years Later and Postscript. *American Ethnologist* 15:369–84.

Yoshino, I. Roger. 1955. Selected Social Changes in a Japanese Village. Ph.D. diss., University of Southern California, Los Angeles.

DAVID W. PLATH

Fieldnotes, Filed Notes, and the Conferring of Note

"But these are your notes," screamed Miss Clovis, snatching a half-burned sheet from the edge of the fire.

" 'They did not know when their ancestors left the place of the big rock nor why, nor could they say how long they had been in their present habitat . . .'," she read, then threw it back with an impatient gesture. "Kinship tables!" she shrieked, "You cannot let *these* go!" She snatched at another sheet, covered with little circles and triangles, but Alaric restrained her and poked it further into the fire with his stick.

"Esther, it's no good," he said. "I shall never write it up now. If Catherine hadn't encouraged me, I don't think it would ever have occurred to me that I could be free of this burden for ever."

—BARBARA PYM, *Less than Angels*

One of my books about Japan came out recently in Japanese translation. The publisher issued the book with an advertising wrapper, and on that wrapper printed the tease line "Field Notes of an Anthropologist!!" The Anglo phrase "field notes" slipped into the local vocabulary

Several colleagues provided valuable comments on what was a much cruder version of this essay. My thanks to Edward M. Bruner, Janet Dougherty, Elizabeth Hurley, Charles Keller, and Robert J. Smith. And my extra special thanks to Jacquetta Hill and Roger Sanjek.

some time ago, nativized as *fuirudo nōto*. Educated Japanese are familiar with the term. But most of the populace will only recognize its two component words separately—both have been in everyday Japanese speech for decades—and then will wonder what connection to make between *nōto* as in notebook and *fuirudo* as in baseball. The publisher, however, is evidently betting that a substantial number of Japanese not only know what fieldnotes are but have an appetite for reading them.

Such are the paradoxes of ethnography when it intersects with the show biz of trade publishing. I did actually carry on field interviewing for a year as part of the line of inquiry that eventuated in that book (Plath 1980; for remarks on how I did the study, see chap. 2). But I slogged on for seven more years at home before the book was finished. And there are not seven pages in it that I now could trace back, even circuitously, to *fuirudo nōto* if fieldnotes are the jottings I put into a journal then and there.

Suppose I stretch the definition, counting as fieldnotes all the other artifacts, verbal or visual or whatever, I brought back from that year in Japan—even then only about half the book is derived from field materials. The rest was composed from filed notes.

So here we have an ethnographer who went out and coaxed some natives to tell him *their* unrehearsed life stories. He translated and edited those stories, embedding them in information that puts them into cultural and historical context for the benefit of a foreign reader. But now, people in the host culture are being promised that the ethnographer's book offers *his* unrehearsed reactions to their way of life.

A number of issues are twined together in this situation. I want to extract and examine two of them.

First, for all the honor we accord to fieldwork and fieldnotes as emblems of professional uniqueness, we spend most of our anthropological energy doing filework. Fieldnotes may contain the makings of an ethnographic story, but that story somehow has to be teased out of them and given form.

Second, we believe—well, most of the time—that we do our work out of motives of personal curiosity as channeled by professional norms and habits. But for most of our public audiences, that work blurs into the larger enterprise of the mass media: the work of providing "documentaries" that depict the human condition as we moderns suppose it to be "in reality." All of mankind is becoming caught up in this mythos of documentary reality. Natives or anthropologists, all of us are budding para-mediacs. We bandage our images and nurse our conduct, whether in the field or in the files, to suit the canons of the new realism.

Neither of these issues is high on the agenda when we discuss ethnography as a scholarly craft. Neither of them, I venture, has become obfuscated by an oversufficiency of debate.

Filework

The totemic value of the fieldworker and his fieldnotes as images good to think derives from the idolatry of early modern science. The nineteenth century had a magnificent obsession with the image of the scientist as fact-knapper. Under the new dispensation of empiricalism he would collect and disburse those packets of real data that would once and for all cure mankind of the errors of perception that had become embalmed in custom.

In the nineteenth-century phrasing of Thomas Henry Huxley, the Scientist is "secretary to the universe, taking down its dictation." The occupation probably was higher on the scale of manliness then, when scribes and secretaries were mostly male. Gender-linked or not, the job implied a shift in the locus of work. In the new scientific study of nature or of human history it would not suffice to do one's work only *in camera,* so to speak—in one's study or laboratory. The Scientist himself must become a camera, automotive and ideally autofocusing as well.

This accent on the empirical is no special property of the anthropologist. It reverberates through the offices of grant agencies and campus research committees. They too have been spooked by the ghost of Huxley's secretary for so many decades that they would much rather provide a thousand dollars for "collecting primary data" than a hundred for "secondary analysis" or as much as ten dollars for "mere write-up." Filework is not even on their list of fundable activities, though now and then they may make money available for "preservation of archives."

To be fair to the grants committees, they are caught in a structural contradiction. Filework flows on in long waves of activity, but committees must hop to the pulsebeat of an annual budget. A committee of course wants its grantees to prove they have been productive over some short interval, usually labeled "FY [fiscal year] such and such."

For fieldwork you can count up pages of notes, hours of tapes, feet of film. For filework, on the other hand, over the short run—particularly during the composition of a monograph or a visual documentary— your best indicator of activity may be not output but outthrow. In documentary movie or TV production, for example, you will normally shoot at least ten or fifteen feet of film for each foot of final program. Sometimes the ratio can go as high as 30:1. The task of sifting through so much material can become daunting. For weeks, even months, you may have nothing to show as proof of effort expended. Sometimes you feel like the Curies, boiling down tons of pitchblende, bucketful by bucketful, just to obtain a splash of luminosity.

Filework is the outward manifestation of an inward pledge that most of us make to continue striving to understand a particular people or region or issue, or all of the above. Our files include fieldnotes, of course. But they tend to include many more notes that are not of field provenience, and even vaster amounts of material that is not verbal at all: films, slides, maps, music recordings, artifacts—all the cumulating detritus of our years of trying to document some scene in the human comedy. Filework, like psychoanalysis, has no self-generating point of conclusion—another reason why it makes deans and grants committees so jittery.

Less easy to explain is our shyness about even mentioning filework when we publicly discuss our professional activities. We cheerfully dilate on fieldwork methodologies or analytical paradigms but never on filework. The only commentary on the subject that I have ever seen is one by C. Wright Mills in his essay "On Intellectual Craftsmanship" (1959: 195–226). Describing his own file, he asks how it is used in "intellectual production." He answers that "the maintenance of such a file *is* intellectual production." And he goes on to say that his files are "a continuously growing store of facts and ideas, from the most vague to the most finished. . . . all projects with me begin and end with them, and books are simply organized releases from the continuous work that goes into them" (1959: 199, 200–201).

My own ratio of effort on that recent Japan book—about seven parts filework to one part fieldwork—is probably close to the general guild average. But if you read those guidebooks on how ethnography is done, you might well conclude that the ratio is just about the reverse. If such is needed, a guidebook author could cite ancestral precedent: Franz Boas chiding Margaret Mead for spending too much time in the field and not enough on write-up (Howard 1984: 192). But although guidebook authors may talk about "analysis," they do not put it in a time frame. They leave the impression that the phenomenon called write-up generates itself by autocombustion the day after the ethnographer is home again and unpacked.

Ethnography, it would seem, is really all a matter of field technique. The guidebooks praise our endurance as field marshals. They denounce the timid, who venture *ex camera* too briefly, if at all: the hit-and-run news reporters and travel writers, or the slash-and-burn survey sociologists. Guidebook authors are of the same persuasion as authors of sex manuals. They provide emphatic detail on how to position yourself vis-à-vis the Other but offer almost no help at all when you are thinking about the whole business afterward.

Is filework unmentionable for reasons of ethics or decorum? Is it such an unsanitary enterprise that the public should be discouraged from even looking on—a corollary to Bismarck's dictum that the public ought not be present during the making of either its laws or its sausages? To be sure, there is ample scope for flummery in the file room, for faking data and fudging results. But the strongest odors I ever nose from the scene are not those of corruption but those of the tears and sweat of effort sustained.

Most of the time, what I see going on in the file room is the intellectual counterpart of Weight Watchers: people trying to slim their corpus of fact and make it presentable. Which suggests to me that the problem with filework is not morality but visuality. In an era saturated by visual mass media, fieldwork is full of action and scene changes, is easy to dramatize on camera. Filework offers all the dramatic tension of watching paint dry. Fieldwork, as Captain Cousteau demonstrates every week, is the scientific spectator sport that holds the viewer's eye.

From Discovery to Documentary

A symposium or book on fieldnotes as the makings of anthropology probably should have a follow-up session or volume on filed notes as the bakings of anthropology. Once we are home again we have to conduct those shake-and-bake operations that fuse field and filed materials into documentaries that we hope will make sense to others. "To document" surely need not mean only to assemble words on paper. It can also mean offering lectures and seminars and courses on the subject, or producing exhibits of photos and artifacts, as well as preparing documentaries of the more usual kind using film or videotape or audiotape.

While doing fieldwork, we can focus our attention on "taking down" reality as we perceive it. While composing and editing our documentaries, we have to focus on putting reality back up again into some form that will communicate. New criteria come into play as we select among our materials. We begin viewing the content of some piece of information in a new context, the context of presentation. Factuality, narrowly defined, may become subordinate to purposes of use: does this bit of evidence move the story along? Will it play in Peoria? Perhaps it suggests a different story entirely. Listen to Mills again:

> If you write solely with reference to what Hans Reichenbach has called the "context of discovery" you will be understood by very few people; moreover, you will tend to be quite subjective in statement. To make whatever you think more objective, you must work in the context of presentation. At first, you "present" your thought to yourself, which is often called "thinking clearly." Then when you feel that you have it straight, you present it to others—and often find that you have not made it clear. Now you are in the "context of presentation." Sometimes you will notice that as you try to present your thinking, you will modify it—not only in its form of statement but often in its content as well. You will get new ideas as you work in the context of presentation. In short, it will become a new context of discovery, different from the original one, on a higher level I think, because more socially objective. [1959: 222]

Such was the situation as I went about writing that book of supposed *fuirudo nōto*. Along the way the story took off in a different direction, unanticipated. The book I originally had in mind would have had a much higher proportion of field materials.

I had gone to Japan to compile a series of life histories of middle-aged men and women. I hoped to document how their lives had taken form through a twofold set of long engagements—to show how they had molded themselves on the Japanese heritage of ideas about maturity, and concurrently been molded by involvements with their significant others.

My plan was to collect a set of case records, each consisting of lengthy interviews with every member of a household that included a middle-aged couple. I soon realized that I'd do well just to obtain paired life histories from some sets of spouses. By the time I had several such sets on tape, along with a number of solo cases (one spouse but not yet the partner), my field year was already over.

Going home meant plunging back again into full-time teaching and administrative duties. But when I could find the time, I reread the interview transcripts, listened again and again to the tapes, and began to rough-sketch verbal portraits of each life. Before long I knew I had a problem. Most of the narrative pairs were coming out unbalanced. He was articulate but she was not, or vice versa. She talked of many things but never of her life with him, or vice versa. And so on.

For a while I thought of activating a cultural explanation. Quite a number of scholars, Japanese as well as foreign, claim that Japanese husbands and wives live in "separate worlds." The idea may fit the marital milieu of Japan's managerial elite, but I doubt that it applies to much of the rest of the populace. I strongly suspected that the imbalance in my narratives resulted from the way the interviews had been conducted.

I did have two cases in which her story and his moved well in duet, but here I had a different problem of imbalance. The wives in these two cases were salaried employees of large corporations. I had no equally rich narrative pairs in which the woman was a "professional housewife"—the normative situation in Japan—or in which husband and wife collaborated in running a family business. Since I wanted to document these other female pathways in adulthood also, my only option seemed to be to use some of the women's life histories in solo.

To do that would force me to downplay or drop the whole theme of significant others. I wasn't pleased with the prospect but comforted myself with the idea that the book would at least contain the most vivid among my narratives.

After all, like any ethnographer I was powerfully reluctant to leave out so much as a page of the material I had collected. Already I had paid too high a price for that material. Paid in the hundreds of hours of riding commuter trains, so that I could meet my interviewees in their homes or offices or other familiar settings. Paid with guilty worries that I was neglecting my family in favor of the study. Gone into debt socially to colleagues and friends who provided introductions to potential interviewees—debts I would have to repay at some future date. And continued to pay, back home, with the evenings and weekends of work needed to fabricate readable narratives out of the disjointed information in the interviews.

Sometime during this phase of the enterprise a new idea began to seep into awareness. It came not from fieldnotes but from other notes—in this instance, reading notes—in my "project file." I've forgotten much of what went on during that period except its clouds of frustration. But I am fairly sure I rejected the idea the first few times it arose, so eager was I to make use of all the field news that was fit to print. For weeks I had plodded along almost obsessively reshuffling the narratives, trying to come up with a winning combination. But I did something else as well, something I often do when disillusioned with an outline I have been following. I dumped the contents of all the folders in the project file into one big heap and began sorting them afresh. In the heap were abstracts and excerpts from a number of modern Japanese novels—and those were where the idea was coming from.

Why not—I said to myself—set aside the spouse pairings and instead pair each life history with the life story of a character from a novel? After all, a novelist who wants to depict believable persons cannot stray far from the cultural concepts and sensibilities that people use in order to comprehend their own real-time lives. The virtue of this new format was that it brought cognitive and symbolic aspects of adulthood to the foreground. The great drawback, however, was that I could effectively match only a few of the life histories I had with stories that the novelists happened to have written. The book has fewer field narratives than I had originally planned to include. Fieldnotes lost out again.

If many of us have a special attachment to our fieldnotes, it may not be only because we paid so much to get them. The notes are not just some set of rubbings we crayoned against reality "out there." They are promissories we made to ourselves, pledges to be redeemed later, during documentary production, with all the ethnographic imagination we can muster. In his essay in this book Robert J. Smith tells how he painstakingly retyped Ella Wiswell's fieldnotes until they became "his" notes; only then could he shape them into a story. I sometimes find myself retyping sections of my *own* notes, even though I was their scribe of first instance. In the context of presentation they become different. Borrowing what Samuel Beckett said of memory, we might say of fieldnotes that they are as much an instrument of discovery as of reference.

Our Documentary Consciousness

Whether in the field or in the files, our most important instrument of understanding continues to be our human sensibility, searching for "the cruel radiance of what is" (James Agee's phrase, Agee and Evans 1941: 11) *and* struggling for ways to communicate it. Our anthropological heritage guides that search by declaring certain phenomena to be fittest for survival in the symbolic environment of scholarly data. But in making fieldnotes and composing documentaries we are not just capturing and transmitting information. We are involved in social acts that confer note upon particular peoples and particular aspects of their lives (as well as, by reflex, upon our own lives). But our anthropological activities are only auxiliary to that imperial apparatus that modern mankind employs to document reality and confer note upon itself, the media of mass communication.

One need not acknowledge McLuhan's wild dicta that the medium "is" the message, or that the media world already has swallowed all previous versions of mythos. But one must as an anthropologist acknowledge that the documentary consciousness has to some degree percolated into all cultures, thereby shaping people's efforts at self-understanding, individual or collective. This consciousness is most evident in the public operations of the mass media, but it pervades our private lives as well. We are intoxicated to the point of substance abuse with documentary forms for perceiving and representing the reality of our human habitat.

"Just like a movie," we say of an event we witnessed—such as an auto crash. More assertively, we script our lives so that they can be replayed for us in media-documentary modes. Across many parts of the world today, for example, weddings are consecrated not by the gods, clergy, relatives, or officials of the state but by the authoritative (and often authoritarian) presence of the official photographer. And if photo albums and videotapes will not capture enough of the event for you, some wedding shops also will publish a pseudo–newspaper extra that chronicles the ceremony in print and is ready for distribution to the guests as they leave. As natives or as anthropologists we produce and direct our lives in myriad ways, simple and elaborate, so as to situate them within the web of moral and aesthetic possibilities opened by this new world of communicable dreams.

Consider an example from the life of Marilyn Monroe, whose whole life became such a mass media creation. Marilyn Monroe the private person never graduated from high school, and she apparently felt her life to be incomplete because of it. Not long before she died, it is reported, she hired a photographer to make a set of pictures of her posing as she would have posed for the school yearbook had she ever been a high school senior.

Or consider Margaret Mead, so often as eager to document her own life as to chronicle the lives of the Manus or Balinese. Jane Howard (1984: 208) records that when Mead was about to give birth to her daughter Catherine, "the delivery was delayed for ten minutes until the arrival of the photographer." A movie cameraman was already in position. Others in attendance included "the obstetrician, several nurses (all of whom, at Mead's request, had seen the Bateson-Mead film 'First Days in the Life of a New Guinea Baby'), a child development psychologist, . . . and the pediatrician Dr. Benjamin Spock."

When the public media turn their attention upon a community or person or event, they thereby impute social significance to it, and potential power. Anybody sensitized to these operations of the media—and that must include almost all of humankind today—can be expected to transfer such sensibilities to the more novel situation that arises when attention is conferred instead by the presence of an ethnographer.

Ethnographers may pride themselves—rightly, I think—that they are more than just media agents. But they should not be surprised when people react as if that is what they are—flashing a smile the moment a camera is unsheathed, for instance, or, if they are young Japanese, smiling and also waving in the fieldworker's face the two-finger V-sign. Historically associated with Winston Churchill in Euro-America during World War II, in Japan lately the V-sign is widely used as a greeting by television "talent" (in Japanese, *tarento*). Or people may react to the researcher's equipment itself, or lack of it, or his or her inability to obtain broadcast-quality results with it. When I arrived in a Japanese community on one recent sortie, the locals wondered out loud if they were going to be subjected to old-fashioned research by this technologically backward American. I had not brought along a video camera.

A colleague who *was* making videotapes—not in Japan but in rural Latin America—encountered the following reaction. Striving to be authentic, he was recording the craft techniques of a group of wood-carvers in their own village workshop. But the village has no electricity, so he was obliged to rely on battery packs and available light in the dim shop room. Quite unimpressed by what they saw coming up on his monitor, the craftsmen stopped working and persuaded him to follow them to a nearby town. There they arranged to borrow somebody else's workshop, and then could watch themselves performing their skills on TV in a setting that afforded electric power and good lighting.

Fieldwork itself has become a media event. To see deutero-documentaries, films of an ethnographer filming the natives, is no novelty any more. Perhaps one can still escape the local media in remote parts of the Third World but not in media-saturated high-tech countries such as Japan. Liza Dalby comments that during the year she was a geisha–ethnographer performing in Kyoto, she "was interviewed almost as often as [she] conducted interviews" (1983: xv). By October 1986 her year in Kyoto had been transmuted into a two-hour CBS docudrama called *American Geisha*. So far as I know, this is the first dramatic film with an ethnographer as protagonist, though Hollywood has given feature roles to archaeologists since well before the invention of Indiana Jones.

I find that even when I am doing research in remote locales in Japan and am making an effort to avoid the media, I am nevertheless contacted by a reporter or producer on an average of once a week. On the scene the media crew will inevitably insist that I "play anthropologist," posing for their lens as if they had just caught me in the act of asking questions of the natives or of making *fuirudo nōto*.

All this media involvement in the field can take on further levels of complexity if we become involved back home in producing documentaries—which in turn may be seen by native audiences as well as home ones. Though we may have a good passive comprehension of the modern documentary language, we may not have active command of its rules of syntax and style. We may have to learn by committing a solecism.

I once served as consultant to a television team that produced a series of educational programs on Japanese history and culture. It was a million-dollar enterprise that resulted in fourteen hours of programming plus auxiliary study guides, audiotapes, and readings. Our policy was to keep new filming to a minimum. We composed programs by assembling excerpts from films and videotapes that we were allowed to copy from the files of the Japanese networks and film libraries. We wanted our programs to be authentically Japanese, at least in their visual sensibilities.

The project took more than three years to complete. This meant that by the time the programs were finally ready to be broadcast, much of the visual material was several years old. When we shipped a set to Tokyo to get reactions from a panel of Japanese advisors, one of their first responses was, "Are you trying to make American audiences believe that Japan is still technologically a step behind? All the automobiles in your programs are five years old or more—where are the latest models?" In the mythos of modern documentary reality, what matters most is how things seem. Nothing is so dated as yesterday's edition of the news, or last year's car models.

There are issues here waiting to be debated by our committees on professional ethics. We are in some general agreement about norms for protecting the privacy of informants, for example, or for collaborating with government agencies. But what are our obligations toward the media? And do those obligations differ toward native or local media in contrast to Western or world media?

At home I usually welcome the attention that the media may confer on my work. Being cast in a stereotyped "expert" role or hearing an explanation of mine decapitated and broadcast as a mere "sound bite" may rankle, but I am awed by the power of the media to reach out to such vast audiences. At home, however, I feel relatively free to refuse involvement if my work is going to be disrupted too much or if the topic is one about which I have nothing to say. In the field, all of this becomes much more complicated.

Japanese media agents, for example, know their own culture well enough and are shrewd enough that they often arrive bearing an introduction from an acquaintance to whom I owe a favor. Then again, disruptive as the incursion may be, I can rationalize it as enlightened self-interest: it will further my own work or at least be appreciated by "my people." The locals may not be impressed by my scholarly credentials, but they can relate to the idea that if the media are spotlighting the ethnographer, then he must be up to something important. Or people may simply be gratified because, thanks to my presence, the media are finally giving their community the attention they always knew it deserved anyway.

This sort of pride is not at all peculiar to high-tech countries. Often I accompany my wife on her field trips to a Lahu village in northern Thailand. These Lahu are illiterate and helpless with print media, but they are sophisticated about audio. Pleased by the sound quality of our cassette recorders, they urged us to submit our tapes of their singing and instrumental music to the Lahu Hour on Chiang Mai radio. They were jealous that the honor of being broadcast had so far always gone to musicians from other villages.

The picture that emerges, then, is of a Burkean human barnyard filled with critters, including the anthropologist, some of them pathetic and some comic, all of them braying for note. Our usual discourse about the makings of anthropology tends to turn this into a problem primarily of the ethnographer's consciousness, to cast the issues in terms of personal honesty and professional integrity, which work together to produce an authentic cultural portrait. I am suggesting that in today's world we need to extend the discourse to include everybody's involvement in the mythos of documented reality, in the media that institutionally celebrate it, and in the cultural politics of authenticity.

Ethnography and Notability

Positivism is once again the epithet of choice in some ethnographic guildhalls in the 1980s. In my own reading of Franz Boas or Ruth Benedict or Edward Sapir I have never found them mute about the positivist self-delusions of scientific objectivity. So there are days when I wonder if the jackleg preachers of "reflexivity" and "sensory ethnography" should be invited to do a little more homework in the history of their discipline.

On other days I am ready to discount the buzzwordy "querying of realist models" as a cohort phenomenon. The me-too generation has come of age professionally. I am not yet convinced, as some are, that this new generation is any more crassly careerist than its predecessors. But like every generation new-fledged, it does seem uncertain about what it stands *for* and yet quite sure of what it is *agin*.

On still other days a different explanation comes to mind. Is this anthropological self-preening of the 1980s a sign, instead, of a historical drift? Not a new cohort grooming itself for roles in the profession but a whole profession grooming itself for survival as an adjunct of the documentary media? Is each of us already hiding in his or her knapsack not the Napoleonic baton of the future field commander but the contact lenses of the future media talent?

What about some of the new cults of analysis such as *textualisme*? As I understand its proponents, they want to reduce culture to recorded utterances ("textualization") and anthropology to "literary therapy" (Marcus 1986: 264–66). Is this some form of mono-mediac Ludditism, a reaction against the pressures of our polymorphously perverse era of multichannel capacity for communication?

And then what about Margaret Mead? Is it just coincidence that the most impassionate ethnographic disputes of the decade are swirling around the figure of her who was first mother of Media Anthropology?

Our present attention to fieldnotes arises in a climate of concern, outside anthropology as well as in, over which forms of the documentary are the more true-to-life, the more authentic, real. Perhaps the dreamy world of the media is as needful to us in our era as were the Dreamtimes of an earlier era's mythology then. But as professionals we are thrust into minor confusions such as that stirred by my Japanese publisher, who advertises my studied sentences as if they were raw—authentic—fieldnotes, words that enable the reader to reach beyond the artifice of media events and touch somebody real.

Our major paradox is that whatever authenticness there is in those notes got there only through filework, with its attendant conjuring up and warding off of personal, professional, and public demons. Fieldnotes emerge, and find their purpose, only through a soap opera of scenes in which we and others compete and collude in conferring note upon our little lives.

REFERENCES

Agee, James, and Walker Evans. 1941 [1980]. *Let Us Now Praise Famous Men.* Boston: Houghton Mifflin.
Dalby, Liza Crihfield. 1983. *Geisha.* Berkeley: University of California Press.
Howard, Jane. 1984. *Margaret Mead: A Life.* New York: Fawcett Crest.
Marcus, George E. 1986. Afterword: Ethnographic Writing and Anthropological Careers. In *Writing Culture: The Poetics and Politics of Ethnography,* ed. James Clifford and George E. Marcus, 262–66. Berkeley: University of California Press.
Mills, C. Wright. 1959. *The Sociological Imagination.* London: Oxford University Press.
Plath, David W. 1980. *Long Engagements: Maturity in Modern Japan.* Stanford, Calif.: Stanford University Press.
Pym, Barbara. 1982. *Less Than Angels.* New York: Harper & Row.

ROGER SANJEK

On Ethnographic Validity

What is "writing up?"

"*Having* notes—all neatly typed or bound, all stored safe and sound—is one thing," Rena Lederman writes. "But *using* notes is quite another." In this essay I examine the procedures by which fieldnotes are used in constructing ethnography. Despite the now voluminous size of the fieldwork literature, "the production of fieldnotes [and] the processes by which these are transformed into 'analysis' . . . are still poorly covered" (Ellen 1984b: 3). As an ethnographic practitioner, I am concerned more with writers and writing, with ethnographic craft, than with the art of Authors (Geertz 1988: 17–20). More is involved than ethnographic impressionism (though that counts too), more than running off the numbers and tests of data gathered according to the experimental model (if that may also have its place). My aim is to demonstrate that "Yes, Virginia and Virgil, there *is* an ethnographic method."

Our problem is to make this method visible, and "this requires essentially what we might call an ethnography of ethnography: a description of exactly how ethnography is done" (Berreman 1968: 368–69). The essays in this volume take us much of the way. Clifford and Lederman identify general and specific forms of writing in fieldwork. The Johnsons discuss the conscious and unconscious decisions that ethnographers make about what to observe, hear, and write down. Ottenberg stresses the priority of headnotes over fieldnotes in writing once one is back home (see also Mayer 1978). Wolf recounts how her evolving feminist headnotes interacted with fieldnotes in the writing of her three China books. Smith and Plath bring us into the hurly-burly and nitty-gritty of organizing and reorganizing fieldnotes and of writing from them.

Writing ethnography is not always the first act of writing for which fieldnotes are read and used. Reports from the field, a form of "gray" or sub-ethnography, may draw upon fieldnotes. But many reports, like letters from the field, are no doubt primarily releases of headnotes. The most important first form of writing is a skeletal one, an outline written from, for, and sometimes inscribed directly on fieldnotes. This is indexing, and it involves major decisions that will structure later prose ethnography (Davis 1984: 305–8; Ellen 1984c: 285–88).

Indexing

The need to index wide-ranging fieldnotes before beginning ethno-graphic writing can be explained no better than it was by James Mooney, a contemporary of Cushing, in defending the Bureau of American Ethnology's practices before a Smithsonian investigation in 1903:

> I am talking to an Indian . . . about his shield, and he tells me that this shield was dreamed by a certain man. Then I get a dream origin for my myth note-book; I get a name with a translation for my . . . glossary, and I get a statement on name giving for some other investigation, and before I am done with it, he may mention a plant, and some use for that plant, and there may be some origin for that, and after an hour's talk with him, I have probably struck a dozen threads for investigation; and that would all be on two or three pages. And the rest of those same lines or threads would be on other pages in other notebooks. Now, when it comes to writing those out for final publication, it must be all over-hauled, and all the material from the different places put together. [Qtd. in Hinsley 1981: 222]

There are early indexers and late indexers, detailed indexers and general indexers. Records, like Mooney's "myth note-book," are in-dexed fieldnotes, kept separately from the chronological mass, already grouped according to a scheme. Cases and topical interview records, like those Lederman maintained, reflect a theory of significance as well as a significant theory, usually that from which the fieldwork problem derives (see Lederman 1986: ix–x, 14–18, 117–18). Records pre-index and consequently prefigure what is observed and heard.

A few ethnographers, like Honigmann (1970a: 40) in his 1963 urban Eskimo fieldwork, know from the start that certain topics are of interest and record their data under these headings directly. Most others, aside from any records, only later index their chronologically entered fieldnotes. Some during the 1940s to 1960s, including Kluckhohn, Foster, and others (Dentan 1970: 96; Force 1960: 179; Foster 1979: 169–70; Gulick 1970: 135n; Honigmann 1970a: 40; Lamphere 1979: 31), adopted Murdock's *Outline of Cultural Materials* or Human Relations Area Files (HRAF) categories, and thus a theory of culture and society. I suspect this has been less common in the 1970s and 1980s. Malinowski apparently abandoned topical fieldnotes taken in Mailu for chronological notes in the Trobriands. It is a pity that we have no diary of the writing period in Australia between his Trobriand field trips; how he indexed and organized his fieldnotes as he wrote "Baloma" and drafts on the *kula* would be revealing of his emerging "functional" theory of fieldwork materials (cf. Clifford 1988: 111).

The handful of ethnographers who have written about their personal indexing procedures tell us much about how ethnography is constructed. On her teacher Malinowski's advice, Powdermaker wrote her notes by hand in small ($4\frac{1}{2}''$ by $7\frac{1}{2}''$) notebooks.

> When a book was filled, I indexed it according to a detailed outline made before I left London. On every page I marked with a red pencil the appropriate number and letter for each topic and sub-topic, such as childhood (birth, nursing, weaning, play), economics, mortuary rites, and so on. On the last pages of each notebook was an index with topic headings and the pages which had the relevant data. . . . The typing— two copies—was done . . . under the topics and subheadings, which had cross references to each other. . . . There was thus a preliminary organization of data while in the field, and I could see some of the gaps reading the typed notes. [1966: 95]

Powdermaker was a member of Radcliffe-Brown's Rockefeller-funded Australian National Research Council cohort; she mailed the second copy of her typed fieldnotes to him. Considering Powdermaker's two mentors, her account may expose what was common indexing practice among social anthropologists in the years around her 1929–30 Lesu fieldwork.

Whyte decided soon into his 1937–40 Boston fieldwork that he wanted to subdivide his chronological fieldnotes. He organized them in folders on the basis of the groups he was studying, rather than such topics as the church, politics, or the family. But

> as time went on, even the notes in one folder grew beyond the point where my memory would allow me to locate any given item rapidly. Then I devised a rudimentary indexing system: a page in three columns containing, for each interview or observation report, the date, the person or people interviewed or observed, and a brief summary of the interview or observation record. Such an index would cover from three to eight pages. When it came time to review the notes or to write from them, a five-to-ten-minute perusal of the index was enough to give me a reasonably full picture of what I had and of where any given item could be located [1955: 308–9]

This two-stage indexing work structured the ethnography that would emerge (Whyte 1943; 1955: 307–8, 322–23).

In his 1944 study of a Spanish-speaking southwestern United States community, Wolff (1960) deliberately avoided the categories of *Notes and Queries on Anthropology* or the HRAF. After typing eighty pages of chronological fieldnotes, he began to develop a topical classification, producing some sixty-six headings. He then cut up the carbon copy of his notes and filed each piece in one of sixty-six envelopes; cross-references between envelope categories were written on the envelope fronts. After completing four and a half months of fieldwork, he had 500 pages of notes in both chronological and topical form. The sixty-six topics were grouped in seven categories: background materials, culture change, social relations, social institutions, evaluations and/or interpretations, clues to patterns, theory and methodology. These formed chapter headings or titles for separate papers, but the full ethnography was never written (Wolff 1964).

Whether preformulated by others or self-formulated, indexes may undergo revision as fieldwork proceeds. Beattie, on arrival in Uganda in the early 1950s, first visited the East African Institute for Social Research and received "a Malinowskian 'culture outline'" (Director Audrey Richards no doubt had a hand in this):

> Typical broad headings were Environment, History, Material Culture, Political Structure, Legal Rules and Norms, Values; and each of these was subdivided into a number of subheadings. . . . Much material collected under one of these subheads might equally well be included

under other heads. . . . The fieldworker is encouraged to keep constantly in mind the possible implications for one another of the various institutions he studies. [1965: 6]

Malinowskian indeed. Beattie prepared file folders according to heads and subheads. As expected, this was a good way to start, but "by the end of my first year in the field my filing system had been very largely reorganized; some heads had proved redundant and had been discarded, others had been subdivided, and a number of new ones had been made" (1965: 7, 41). In his essay in this volume, Ottenberg mentions similar revisions of the index he devised in Afikpo: "It is now the heart of my written notes. . . . It has paid off in the writing stage." Indeed it has, in four books and a score of articles.

The Johnsons discuss computer indexing for those who use a word-processing program to type their fieldnotes. Even without special indexing software, I have found the computer-aided flexibility of my MuliMate Elmhurst-Corona fieldnotes a godsend. Event accounts, and paragraphs within them, can be copied, moved, rearranged, and printed easily, while their original chronological order still anchors my sequential memories. Yet the tasks of index categorization and entry, on paper or by computer, and inevitable revision and expansion are "intensive, tedious work" (Boissevain 1970: 79, 81–82), however essential for fieldnote-based ethnography.

Writing Ethnography

Writing is sometimes a socialized process. After preparing detailed outlines, Malinowski dictated his writing, shared it with his students, read it in his seminar, and enjoyed the assistance of his wife, Elsie, in its editing (Comaroff and Comaroff 1988: 557; Firth 1957a: 10; 1981: 106–7; Fortes 1957: 157; Wayne 1985). Friedrich (1986: 221, 222, 224) similarly talked about his developing ethnographic drafts with colleagues and read them aloud to students. Between their Manus and Arapesh fieldwork, Mead and Fortune each wrote three books in New York during 1929–31: "In the evening each would read what the other had done during the day or we would read aloud to each other" (Mead 1972: 184). Elwin (1964: 188) wrote most of his 1955 Saora ethnography, *The Religion of an Indian Tribe,* in the field, where he could interact with informants and verify his analysis. Wolcott's ethnography of

Rhodesian beer gardens also was written in the field, he recounts (1975), with several drafts read critically by medical specialists, welfare workers, and academics all concerned with beer consumption. "I am in favor of joining the writing task with fieldwork rather than making it subsequent to it. . . . I begin writing to bring order to what I have done and efficiency to the fieldwork that will continue" (Wolcott 1981: 259–60).

More characteristically, ethnographic writing is done after field-work, alone, with just fieldnotes and headnotes. It is the loneliness of the long-distance writer that we shall focus upon. Input from col-leagues, such as Lederman enjoyed at conferences of the Association for Social Anthropology in Oceania, most often comes after a major ethnographic writing act is accomplished.

As Plath explains (this volume), writing takes the ethnographer from "the context of discovery," in which fieldnotes are written, to "the context of presentation" (see also Plath 1980: 28–37). Becker (1986a: 17) picks up this point, too, in the context of an excellent discussion of the psychology of writing.

Malinowski's continual analysis of his fieldnotes in the field proba-bly exceeded that of most who have followed him. He clearly moved to "the context of presentation" while still in the Trobriands.

> Now to method in fieldwork: . . . the first layer of approach . . . consists in the actual observing of isolated facts, and in the full recording of each concrete activity, ceremony or rule of conduct. The second line of approach is the correlating of these institutions. The third line of ap-proach is a synthesis of the various aspects. [1935, vol. 1: 456]

In his fieldnotes, he tells us, this sequence is demonstrated in his developing analysis of Trobriand land tenure. And he makes it clear that this process was guided by theory: "Long before I went to the field I was deeply convinced that the relation between religious and magical belief, on the one hand, and economic activity, on the other would open important lines of approach" (1935, vol. 1: 318–40, 456, 457). Yet functionalism, and the series of institutional monographs, foiled presentation itself. The analysis Malinowski refers to, which Leach considers "the most intelligible account of the total social struc-ture of Trobriand society which Malinowski gives us," is in *Coral Gardens* (Malinowski 1935, vol. 1: 327–81) and "occupies the *last* 50 pages of the *last* book he published on the subject" (Leach 1957: 134).

In one of his last papers, Honigmann attempted to defend "the personal approach" of wide-ranging ethnographic fieldnotes before the scientific, quantitative onslaught of the 1970s. Though presented in highly general, if embattled, terms, Honigmann's argument does summarize the essentials of the ethnographic method. Unlike Malinowski, however, he acknowledges no guiding role for theory.

> Anthropologists have given the matter little attention, partly no doubt because the process as it has traditionally been carried out is individually variable and highly inexplicit. My attempt to make explicit how features come to be selected for patterns, in view of the sparsity of information about how others do it, relies on recollection of my own procedures. . . . Pattern recognition begins with the anthropologist's inspection of a series of . . . field notes, or other fieldwork documents, . . . and abstracting from them one or more general features recognized in the event. . . . The features recognized in a set of events need not be present in every event of the set. . . . The technique of constructing such patterns . . . calls for considerable intuition, speculative ability, and speculative freedom as well as abundant, detailed data. . . . since anthropology contains no recognized body of rules for standardizing the construction of patterns, this basic level of analysis offers considerable scope for the personal approach. . . . Patterns reflect not what is in the external world, but the features the observer conceptualized and incorporated in the field notes. . . . If an ethnographer does not adhere closely to field notes . . . there is danger that the creative faculties will motivate the invention of data unrelated to events observed. . . . An anthropologist is responsible for being prepared if called upon to support patterns by providing evidence from field notes. . . . anthropologists following the personal approach . . . possess . . . a heightened, or deliberately cultivated, sense of responsibility to their original observations (i.e., carefully recorded, detailed field notes and other memoranda). [Honigmann 1976: 247–48, 257]

It is unfortunately true that information about "how others do it" is sparse. The contributors to this volume provide major exceptions. Yet a few comments from more theoretically self-conscious ethnographers help flesh out Honigmann's sketch. Agar, who relies more on transcripts of ethnographic interviews than on speech-in-action, is procedurally explicit.

> The first thing to do is to read the transcripts in their entirety several times. Immerse yourself in the details, trying to get a sense of the interview as a whole. . . . You, the analyst, now seek to categorize the different segments of talk . . . marking off stretches of talk that cohere because they focus on the same topic. This is not an automatic pro-

cedure by any means. . . . Cut up a copy of the transcripts according to the new topic-oriented code. Each group of talk can then be read to check for consistency within each informant and variation across informants. You can also see what was talked about and, more important, what was *not* talked about. [1980: 103–4; see also Agar 1986b]

Agar's ethnography of independent truckers (1986a) demonstrates the power of this form of interview-driven ethnography.

Like Smith with Wiswell's notes, Barth at first worked without headnotes and thus came to appreciate the processes of writing ethnography more consciously than many others. He chose the theoretical problem of "the organization and maintenance of camps" as the organizing framework for Pehrson's Marri Baluch fieldnotes.

I have written up the material block by block, going through the complete notes each time and marking all information relevant, for example, to kinship, working up a classification under subtopics and a crude index, and completing the kinship chapter before going through the whole process again for the next topic. [Barth 1966: xi]

Whyte is a master ethnographer who moves to presentation efficiently, having published *Street Corner Society* by 1943. Just as he did for fieldwork (1955), he provides one of the clearest and most succinct statements about writing in describing his writing method, closely related to his indexing, for an ethnographic study of restaurants.

In writing a report we can work directly from the index to the outline of the paper. A few minutes spent in rereading the whole index gives a systematic idea of the material to be drawn on. Then, for each topic covered in the report, we can write into the outline the numbers of the interviews and the page numbers of relevant material. For example, in writing a section on relations between hostesses and waitresses, we write in the outline some general heading referring to the supervision of waitresses. Then we note in the outline all interviews where we find in the index "waitresses-hostess"—plus the page numbers of those particular interview sections. This may refer us to a dozen or more interviews. Perusal of the index will refresh our memory on these interviews, and we will recall that some of them merely duplicate each other. We pull out of the file perhaps a half dozen interviews, turn to the sections where "waitresses-hostess" is marked on the margin, reread these sections, and finally use materials from three or four. [Whyte 1984: 118]

Reliability versus Validity

Anthropologists are their own worst critics of the ethnographic method.

> Many social scientists—anthropologists and others—see ethnography as methodologically unsophisticated, intuitive, journalistic, and unfocused, and they therefore call for increased rigor. [Berreman 1968: 368]

> The traditional anthropological attitude to methodology has led to a non-accumulative or very slowly accumulating tradition which is more akin to that in the humanities than that of the sciences. [Cohen and Naroll 1970: 3]

The Peltos (1973: 269) point to "much criticism of impressionistic, non-quantifiable field methods." Agar (1980: 112) writes, "In my opinion, field notes are the most overrated thing since the Edsel."[1] Lewis (1953: 7n), more charitably, concludes nonetheless, "That anthropologists sometimes guess brilliantly is to their everlasting credit."

This indictment is powerful. Unfortunately, we have few places toward which to point the uncharitable external skeptic, or the trusting anthropology student. And as ethnography is increasingly appropriated and frequently denatured by newcomers beyond anthropology and our sociological fieldworker cousins (Agar 1980: 123, 197; Van Maanen 1988: 24, 40–41), we cannot afford to be so silent, and secretive, about fieldnotes. Others need to know that the emperor is not naked.

The answer to the charges is not to give in to the "quantitative extreme." The "mix of methods" many advocated in the 1970s confined the ethnographic method to an "exploratory" stage; the hypothesis-testing, experimental model—"the standard model of research" (Whyte 1984: 266)—overpowered any mix. The result was in fact capitulation (see Brim and Spain 1974; cf. Agar 1986b: 16).

---

[1] Agar (1980, 1986b) comes from a linguistic anthropology background and focuses, as we have seen, on transcribed texts of interview speech. But he clearly brings powerful headnotes from his fieldwork (Agar 1986a), including sensitivity to speech-in-action. And unlike Malinowski, who went on no *kula* canoe expeditions, Agar drove by night with the truckers. In this research he also took fieldnotes (1986b: 66–67).

The 1960s and 1970s "humanist" response—"letting the problems emerge from the data"; "insight at the expense of verification" (see Berreman 1968: 368)—drifted in the 1980s to what Clifford in his essay here identifies as "ethnography less concerned to separate itself from 'subjective' travel-writing . . . registering the circumstantial situations of an interpreting subject, noting events and statements as part of a passing sojourn of research."

Both scientists and interpretationists lost sight of the ethnographic method (even if many ethnographers of the 1970s and 1980s, consciously or unconsciously, did not: see the Appendix to "The Secret Life of Fieldnotes," in Part III). In a battle between strict thinking and loose thinking, ethnography loses. There is another way.

Interpretationists hold no brief for reliability; what one sees is what you get. Scientists of the hypothesis-testing, experimental mold, however, are preoccupied with reliability (Brim and Spain 1974: 19–24), "the repeatability, including interpersonal replicability, of scientific observations" (Pelto and Pelto 1978: 33; see Agar 1980: 64). Reliability is extremely important in laboratory work: in physics and chemistry, and in medical and product safety research. We want to be certain that other investigators performing the experiment or test get the same results; we expect and hope that other investigators in fact do so before reliability is accorded and a new product or treatment is marketed.

In ethnography, "reliability" verges on affectation. We cannot expect and do not hope that another investigator will repeat the fieldwork and confirm the results before they are published. Reliability is flashed to show the integrity or ingenuity of research design; it is not meant as an invitation to go to "my village" and do it over again. As Honigmann (1976: 246) correctly puts it: "Speaking realistically, there is practically a zero probability of ever testing the reliability of a comprehensive ethnographic report, so one ought to stop talking about replication as a technique of verification" (see Johnson and Johnson, this volume).

Reliability was *not* the issue when the findings of Robert Redfield and Margaret Mead were disputed by later investigators Oscar Lewis and Derek Freeman. The challengers came to different conclusions because they used different methods (more revealing ones, they claimed), not because they failed to get Redfield's and Mead's results by using the same methods (Clifford 1986b: 101–3; Lewis 1951: xi–xxvii; Weiner 1983). It was *validity* that they challenged, "the degree to which scientific observations actually measure or record what they purport to measure" (Pelto and Pelto 1978: 33). Validity lies at the core of evaluating ethnography.

Anthropology speaks in the language of validity: institution, pattern, configuration, outline, structure, web, organization, relations, network, system, map, domain, grid, schema; holes in the data, gaps, lacunae, breakdowns. The results ethnographers present in such language aim for validity: does it say what I claim it does? (see Agar 1980: 64).

Ethnography is a potentially validity-rich method, fully as scientific as the reliability-rich experimental, hypothesis-testing method. As Powdermaker (1966: 306) put it, "A scientific attitude ignores no level of understanding." The method requires loose-strict-loose-strict thinking.[2]

The historic development of the ethnographic method, although underexposed, is *not* "non-accumulative." Nor is the method "intuitive, journalistic, unfocused, impressionistic" or merely "brilliant guesswork." The validity of ethnography should be evaluated in its own right, as more than just an "exploratory" phase preceding "real science." How, then, is ethnography to be validated? Ethnographic validity may be assessed according to three canons: theoretical candor, the ethnographer's path, and fieldnote evidence.

The First Canon: Theoretical Candor

Ethnographic fieldwork involves a series of choices. These choices and the theoretical reasons for them need to be presented explicitly to establish ethnographic validity. Significant theories, those in books and journals, determine the place, problems, and record objectives

---

[2]We should also turn the tables and ask how the hypothesis-testing, experimental, and survey research that stresses reliability establishes validity. The abstract confirmation procedure does not generate the variables and values; it only measures the likelihood of their correlation (see Johnson and Johnson). How scientists do science, an important area of research (Agar 1986b: 70; Caws 1969; Crick 1982: 28–29; Woolgar 1988), does not always involve the "rigor" that reliability insinuates. Where do behavioral scientists and survey researchers get their variables and values? From newspapers, "the literature," ethnographies (Van Maanen 1988: 30)? Their procedures for establishing validity are often inexplicit. And much survey research, the honest will admit, involves fabrication at the grassroots (see Srinivas 1987: 182–84; Whyte 1984: 143–45, 207–8). Whyte (1984: 266–67) also raises questions about the validity of currently favored quantitative research that works over old data-sets: its theoretical conclusions relate to places and people its authors have never seen.

brought to the field. Theory at this level relates the fieldwork to the "larger social, political, symbolic, or economic issues" (Van Maanan 1988: 127) which give an ethnography purpose and meaning and make it "a critical tale of the field."

Critical, political, and theoretical awareness precedes ethnography and structures the research proposals that fieldworkers nowadays most often prepare themselves. Yet the "grain of the field" cannot be discounted, and "in many cases a detailed research design turns out to have little relationship to the research that finally emerges from a field trip" (Pelto 1970: 252). In the early stage of fieldwork the ethnographer "opportunistically" records wide-ranging fieldnotes about whatever goes on, but the objective is not to continue doing this forever (Honigmann 1970b: 269; Powdermaker 1966: 61; Saberwal 1975). This charting of the ethnographic terrain is filtered through theory so that more selective and systematic participant observation will follow. The net of people, places, and activities studied opportunistically may continue to widen in fieldnotes, but theory-guided research activities will narrow at the same time. Sampling begins; other opportunities are forgone (Agar 1980: 124, 134; Honigmann 1970b: 268–70; Whiting and Whiting 1970: 283–84, 286–88).

In addition to significant theories, the fieldworker develops terrain-specific theories of significance about people, events, and places. These determine much of the looking and listening that are recorded in fieldnotes and, in turn, confirm, extend, or revise the significant theories. In a paper more revealing of the ethnographic method than most book-length "personal" accounts, Saberwal (1975) provides a rich and instructive professional account of how this process worked in his study of caste and mobility in a Punjab town. Candid exposition of when and why locally developed theories of significance are adopted enhances ethnographic validity.

Validity-rich ethnography must make explicit as many of both sorts of theoretical decisions as possible by reporting when and why judgments of significance are made. Readers need to know both the "theory of events" (Agar 1980: 115) with which the ethnographer structures the fieldwork and the larger significant theories this relates to (cf. Marcus and Cushman 1982: 58).

In the small Mountain Arapesh village of Alitoa, Mead attempted to study the whole culture; she lists the specific types of "significant events" her fieldnote "Record" was designed to capture, and the validity of her work may be judged accordingly. Firth (1966: 360–61) and

Colson (1967) collected 100 percent samples of selected activities or informant data, and they are specific about the theoretical rationale for what their fieldnotes and records contain. The Johnsons, for theoretically explicit purposes, advocate random household visits to gather particular information, as well as for opportunistic listening and observation (Johnson 1978: 87–91, 106–10; Johnson and Johnson, this volume). Werner (1984: 85–86) used this method to obtain what wide-ranging fieldnotes normally record but also to give "a sense of order to my fieldwork." My own use of systematic interviews about daily interaction (Sanjek 1978) was related to politically charged theories of class and ethnicity. In a busy urban setting of daily dispersal, it provided a measure of the comprehensiveness that Mead achieved with direct observation and questions in Alitoa, and the Johnsons and Werner could accomplish with random visits to Indian village households in the Amazon basin.

Validity may also be established by the decision to follow linked events and activities systematically in order to verify or falsify theoretically significant patterns. It is "essential to see group members in different situations, not just during a brief interview. . . . An ethnographer learns something new, and then tries to understand how it connects with other aspects of the situation" (Agar 1980: 70, 75). Thus, Malinowski (1935, vol. 1: 327–39) charts the fieldnote course by which he worked out his analysis of Trobriand land tenure. Middleton's *Study of the Lugbara* is an excellent short account of how this validity-building process works: "What the fieldworker does in essence is to build up hypothetical structures or patterns as he goes along. Every new fact that he gathers can either be fitted into that structure, or if not, he is forced to change the structure" (1970: 47).[3]

As Mead argued, an anthropologist "follows rules different from those employed in other social sciences but doesn't operate totally without discipline" (qtd. in Honigmann 1970b: 272; cf. Evans-

[3]"The Lugbara made sacrificial offerings of cattle, goats, sheep, chickens and grain; they offered them to ghosts, ancestors . . . and to several categories of spirit; they made these sacrifices in response to various kinds of sickness, associated with various kinds of sins and offenses. There were thus four sets of variables (oblation; spiritual agent; sickness; and offense) for which I assumed there would be a neat pattern of relationships. I spent many months seeking this pattern, but it eluded me. . . . Finally I saw that the key factor in the pattern was the historical development of the sacrificing group, so that I had to turn to the study of the cycle of development of lineages and sections in order to understand the pattern in the organization of sacrificial rites" (Middleton 1970: 60).

Pritchard 1950: 139–54).[4] There has been too little formal discussion of ethnographic "discipline" as it applies to wide-ranging fieldnotes. Validity depends upon a more explicit discussion of how theory guides fieldwork than most ethnographies include. As Agar explains, "Good ethnographers, of course, always try to falsify their conclusions, but they often do so in informal ways that are not reported in their published works" (1980: 134). Making such procedures and their related theories explicit is essential. Most often they remain unrevealed, buried within the fieldnotes. Yet here lies ethnographic validity.

"Where theory?" In the field and out of the field. "When theory?" Significant theories while planning fieldwork, and theories of significance as it takes shape and direction. "Why theory?" To give ethnography meaning and purpose and to avoid opportunistic study of "everything." "Which theory?" Consult your political and critical values.

The Second Canon: The Ethnographer's Path

Ethnographic research is an intensely personal experience for the fieldworker. She or he meets people, is introduced to still others, locates a range of informants, develops a variety of relationships, and enters data about and from this set of persons into fieldnotes. In his comment on Nash and Wintrob (1972), Dwight Heath remarked upon this ethnographer's path through field research and its significance for ethnographic validity.

> My point is simply that (a) any effective anthropologist develops his own social network in the process of fieldwork; (b) the nature of this network is, at the same time, both a determinant and an outcome of the research enterprise; (c) therefore, it would provide a valuable additional perspective if this network were specified in more detail than has been done to date. The "additional perspective" . . . would be valuable to the readers who eventually attempt to understand and evaluate the field-

[4]Rejecting "science" and "positivism" as models for anthropology, Evans-Pritchard saw history as the nearest neighbor in method: "It does not follow from regarding social anthropology as a special kind of historiography rather than as a special kind of natural science that its researches and theory are any the less systematic" (1950: 152). The historians Bloch and Carr present methodological discussions consistent with the view of ethnographic validity developed here: theory guides observation; selection of facts studied must be explicit and complete to achieve validity; observation and analysis are in constant interplay (Bloch 1953: 65, 69, 71; Carr 1961: 10, 22, 32, 35). See also Honigmann on "history" and "science" (1976: 244).

worker's findings. . . . Looking at networks in greater detail might do much to answer such fundamental questions as, for example: What are the significant channels of communication through which data were secured concerning topics A, B, C? [1972: 536]

"Key informants" not only provide quantities of information but introduce the fieldworker to other informants. From fieldnotes, every ethnographer could reconstruct a diagram of informant contacts opened directly, their introductions and leads to others, and the universe of informants, with an assessment of its relationship to the population of the social unit studied in terms of gender, age, institutional participation, and other characteristics.

Heath (1972: 536) suspects that "many (if not most) studies nowadays are based on a sample that is insignificant . . . and with a major portion of the data collected from relatively few 'key informants' on each of the various aspects of the research." It is not necessary to be as cynical as Heath to see that readers would be in a much better position to assess ethnographic validity if they had a road map of the ethnographer's path. To the extent that Heath is correct, the secrecy surrounding fieldnotes and the emotions they arouse may in part be understood.

The most thorough description I know of an ethnographer's path is in Gluckman's classic analysis (1940) of a bridge opening in Zululand. We meet his range of white and African informants and contacts, from Zulu royals through policemen, Zulu Christians and "pagans," missionaries, government officers, traders, and recruiting agents to the laborers who built the bridge. The validity of Gluckman's analysis can be weighed by our understanding of those he talked to and observed.

Hildred Geertz's appendix to *The Javanese Family* (1961: 161–71) is another detailed portrait of an ethnographer's path. She explains carefully how her sample of forty-five families grew from its beginning with the family of her landlord, and she identifies the dilemma for furthering her work caused by this household's class position. She charts her path to fourteen other families with whom "she worked intensively, seeing them between fifteen and forty times," and provides the class and religious background of her total sample. Ethnographic validity is considerably enhanced by this straightforward presentation.

Powdermaker (1966: 129–98) describes her path into the black and white societies of Indianola, Mississippi, in her 1932–33 fieldwork and points out the significance of key contacts for establishing credibility and for gaining introductions to particular segments of each racial group. The "Uganda Trio" of fieldwork accounts (Beattie 1965; Middleton 1970; Robertson 1978) are also effective portrayals of the ethnographer's path in fieldwork. This in fact provides the major narrative structure for Robertson's *Community of Strangers: A Journal of Discovery in Uganda* (1978), as much as ethnographic as a personal account. In contrast, Rabinow's *Reflections on Fieldwork in Morocco* (1977) is less an account of his fieldwork path than a personal journal, ranging beyond the fieldwork itself.[5]

The importance of the ethnographer's path goes far beyond its size and range. As Holy's cogent argument (1984) implies, an assessment of the interpretive power of ethnography also requires that we understand the ethnographer's path.[6] As a measuring stick of ethnographic validity, accounts of an ethnographer's fieldwork path should be incorporated in ethnographic writings.

The Third Canon: Fieldnote Evidence

A synopsis of the ethnographer's theoretically guided fieldwork decisions and a description of the path connecting ethnographer and informants are two of the legs on which ethnographic validity stands. These correspond to the list of collections chosen for consultation and their locations and access codes that historians provide as part of the resulting work they produce (Bloch 1953: 71). One who questions the validity of the historian's conclusions knows what places he or she

[5]One can do other things in the field than ethnography. These other things may make interesting, even compelling reading, as in Lévi-Strauss's *Tristes Tropiques,* or Rabinow's *Reflections,* or Barley's *Adventures in a Mud Hut* (1983). They may be better reads than ethnography, though to me, most other personal accounts are not. But if it doesn't walk like a duck, quack like a duck, and look like a duck, it isn't a duck. Travel impressions are one genre; ethnography is another (see Pratt 1986).

[6]"In interpretative social science, the validity of the researcher's account is not tested against the corpus of scientific knowledge. It is tested against the everyday experience of the community of people. . . . When the anthropologist discusses with the actors 'what is going on' in the search for the meaning of the encounters in which they are jointly engaged and the situations they are jointly confronted with, s/he is engaging with them in negotiated meaning. Through this process, a competence at meaning construction equal to theirs is gradually acquired. . . . To do this, s/he must participate in the lives of subjects in the sense of actively interacting with them, for only through interaction can we gain any insight into the meaning construction in the culture studied" (Holy 1984: 30, 33. Also see Clifford 1983: 128–29; and Rosaldo 1980).

decided to visit and which documents were used. The skeptic may then examine the historian's sources. And here the anthropology/history parallel ends (in most cases). Headnote evidence is manifested in the ethnography, but rarely are fieldnotes open to anyone's inspection. An accounting of the relationship between fieldnotes and the ethnography based upon them is the third canon of ethnographic validity.

In a very few cases, fieldnotes *are* actually there. As we have seen (in "The Secret Life of Fieldnotes," Part III of this volume), Mead provided the fieldnote evidence itself in *The Mountain Arapesh,* as did Kluckhohn in *Navaho Witchcraft,* and Tax's fieldnotes for *Penny Capitalism: A Guatemalan Indian Community* were made available on microfilm. Boas's Kwakiutl volumes were his and Hunt's fieldnotes, with little analysis. Roberts's *Zuni Daily Life* (1956) is a dense, nearly unreadable presentation of minute behavioral fieldnote accounts of one day's activities in three households and two days at a sheep camp, again with minimal analysis (cf. Whiting and Whiting 1970: 284, 288, 292, 297–307).

There is also a handful of first-rank ethnographies that are organized around masses of fieldnote materials. Condominas's *We Have Eaten the Forest: The Story of Montagnard Village in the Central Highlands of Vietnam* is a chronological account of a year's agricultural cycle in the village of Sar Luk; the author tells us that the account consists of "unedited material from notebooks I kept during my stay" (1957: xviii). The prose is smooth—a stage or two beyond retyped scratch notes—and includes some material interpolated later than the events presented (1957: 29). There is minimal introductory text (1957: 3–18, 119–20), and extensive subject indexes are provided for the specialist reader. The account is selective, with holidays and rituals highlighted, and the chronological chapters are organized thematically, almost as short stories. Conventional ethnological analysis is published elsewhere. Condominas's purpose is clear: "to render reality as it was lived while being observed" (1957: xix).

Van Velsen's *Politics of Kinship: A Study in Social Manipulation among the Lakeside Tonga of Nyasaland* is a theoretically oriented study organized around twenty cases of marriages, disputes, political doings, and deaths, each ranging from one to seventeen pages. "From the fieldworker's notebooks" (1964: xxv), the cases are amalgams of observation, informant statement, and interpretation, and they include reconstruction of past events. The presentation both addresses larger issues in kinship and political theory and seeks to reproduce the theory of significance that van Velsen developed in the field: "to describe the Tonga social system by the same process whereby I gained my own insight" (1964: xxvii). Accordingly, the principals reappear from case to case, cross-referenced in footnotes, in what van Velsen terms "situational analysis" or the "extended-case method" (1964: xxv–xxvi, 8; 1967).

The remarkable story of how *The Women of Suye Mura* (Smith and Wiswell 1982) was written is told in Smith's essay here. Ella Lury Wiswell's fieldnotes, edited into topical chapters by Smith, constitute the bulk of the book, with punctuation indicating carefully what is original fieldnote and what was written by Smith. Smaller-point, indented text is the device used by Agar to present the extensive quotations from his life history interview material in *Independents Declared: The Dilemma of Independent Trucking*. Substantively, the book is oriented to ethnographic description and political and symbolic issues. In an appendix, Agar explains:

> In the five hundred double-spaced pages of transcript that underlie this book, there are a total of 403 segments. . . . 58 percent of them were accounted for by the analysis, . . . either directly quoted or referred to in the text. . . . Looking at the amount of the transcript rather than number of segments [one finds that] the material included in the analysis rises to 66 percent. [1986a: 178–79]

Few ethnographers have ever been as precise in describing the relationship of fieldnotes to ethnographic text.

Long Engagements: Maturity in Modern Japan (1980) is the book whose birth Plath describes in his essay. At the opposite extreme from the ethnographies we have just mentioned, less than seven pages derived directly from fieldnotes. An extraordinarily artful and crafted ethnography, *Long Engagements* meets all three canons of validity; the first two chapters detail the theoretical background, the strategies and path of fieldwork, and the fieldnote evidence from which the book was written.

Most ethnography contains only as much fieldnote material as Plath's, or less. "Public display might occur more often than it does, but it is difficult and requires much space" (Agar 1980: 134). Fieldnotes and informant voices are regularly "filtered out" (to appear sometimes in personal accounts), as the distanced ethnographer narrates the account (Clifford 1983: 131–32; Marcus and Cushman 1982: 31–32).

Direct fieldnote evidence has not been a criterion of ethnographic renown; in fact, reviewers complained that van Velsen's *Politics of Kinship* was "burdensome" (see Gluckman 1967: xvi). Normally, "the public, colleagues as well as others, finds the results credible or otherwise useful to the extent that the argument, reasoning, and presentation are plausible, persuasive, clear, and without obvious contradictions or illogic" (Honigmann 1976: 244). My own admiration of the fieldnote-rich ethnographies is obvious, but the canon of fieldnote evidence requires only that the relationship between fieldnotes and ethnography be explicit. Ethnographic validity is served by, but does not require, extensive fieldnote documentation.

Narrative and rhetorical decisions—now coming more into ethnographers' consciousness as a result of the textualist assist (Clifford 1983; Conkling 1975; Geertz 1988; Marcus and Cushman 1982; Van Maanen 1988)—dominate "writing up." Yet when validity knocks and fieldnotes reappear, often for narrative or rhetorical reasons, they bring the baggage of outward-facing incomprehensibility that Lederman, Bond, and Smith point to. They are not always so easy to use.

> An author, if he has something to say, will want to convince his readers. The truth, however, rarely looks veracious. Arranged truth, which is no longer truth but a striving for effect, has a much greater semblance of veracity. . . . On occasions, in one's own work one feels the necessity to brace oneself against such concessions to one's reader. After all, our aim is not to turn out a flawless piece of work calculated to achieve a maximum of effect, but rather to report as truthfully as possible. [Den Hollander 1967: 25; cf. Marcus and Cushman 1982: 57]

Defending van Velsen's ethnography, Gluckman (1967: xvi) admitted that "heavy demands are indeed made on the reader by this kind of analysis."[7]

Davis (1984: 303–4) presents the choice between a generalized account and presentation of a single case from fieldnotes as a matter of rhetorical preference, not validity. Much of the small-print use of fieldnotes as "apt illustration" (Gluckman 1961: 7–8) in ethnographies indeed reflects rhetorical concerns, as Clifford's discussion (this volume) of Geertz's use of fieldnotes in *The Religion of Java* indicates. Spicer's quotation from his fieldnotes to portray two major informants in the introduction to *Potam: A Yaqui Village in Sonora* (1954: 5–7) could

---

[7]In my article on network analysis, "in order to illustrate the results of the interviews" (Sanjek 1978: 260)—to provide validity—I included a sample four-day network in the submitted version. In revisions it was cut to one day by the editor. My heart was broken, but the decision was understandable.

as well have been written in polished prose. It meets the rhetorical demonstrations of "I-witnessing" and "Being There" (Geertz 1988; Marcus and Cushman 1982: 29, 33, 39; Pratt 1986) more than it does the fieldnote evidence canon of ethnographic validity. (No other quotations occur in the rest of the monograph.) Srinivas's extensive fieldnote quotations in two papers on disputes in Rampura (1987: 139–74) are just the opposite. They are the foundation of his validity-rich ethnographic analysis; like van Velsen's cases, they are demanding and work rhetorically against slick description.

Gluckman's preference for the connected cases of situational analysis over discrete fieldnote "apt illustration" speaks to a concern for validity over rhetoric (1961, 1967; cf. Marcus and Cushman 1982: 35). In his theoretical exposition of the approach, van Velsen (1967) hovers between seeing it as a refinement of Radcliffe-Brownian social structuralism—"it was there in the fieldnotes, if not the ethnographies"—and recognizing the extended-case method as a new, generative approach to fieldwork-based social description. Bond identifies the horns of this dilemma from a viewpoint that is different from but compatible with rhetoric versus validity. Extended cases are *still* apt, if lengthy, illustrations of the ethnographer's analysis; placing authority in fieldnotes only masks the responsibility of the anthropologist for the theoretical soundness and political bias of the ethnography.

The potential of wide-ranging fieldnotes under theoretical control to generate ethnographic description (see Johnson and Johnson, this volume) has been most effectively presented by the sociologists Howard Becker and Blanche Geer (1960), drawing upon their field study of a medical school. They describe how they continuously analyzed their eventual 5,000 single-spaced fieldnote pages by applying indexing, coding by topic, quantification of "qualitative" observations and listening, and sorting of fieldwork evidence from most powerful (observations and speech-in-action among ongoing groups) to least powerful (formal interview responses). I must agree with Agar (1980: 9) that sometimes "ethnographically oriented authors from other disciplines do a better job [of] articulating ethnography than we do." The third canon of ethnographic validity is here given a standard that anthropologists cannot afford to neglect.

Fieldnote Voice(s)

This essay owes homage to James Clifford's "On Ethnographic Authority" (1983) for more than its title alone. Clifford's paper is an incisive look backward and forward at ethnography.[8] It identifies four modes of authority. Two of them, the experiential and interpretive, together compose the ethnographic method; they will approach and refine each other more intimately in the return to ethnography of the 1990s and later (see Marcus and Cushman 1982: 38–39, 61–62; Marcus and Fischer 1986: 186 n.6). The other two, the dialogic and polyphonic, are more problematic when viewed from fieldnotes "up."

I see the dialogic mode as a narrowing of ethnographic practice and results. It erases speech-in-action as a source of understanding the informant's point of view and moves ethnography off the informant's turf (see Marcus and Cushman 1982: 42–43) to "discourse" on the ethnographer's turf—whether borrowed, rented, or otherwise appropriated. It places ethnographic work within a Western/middle-class (WM) "language event"—dialogue/discourse/interlocution—usually with a tape recorder, which is not the way most informants talk to each other. As in the Western therapy encounter, which it mirrors, the "other" is encouraged to "tell me what you *really* think; tell me all about yourself," and a good informant is one who performs accordingly: "Nisa was quite unusual in her ability to recall and explain her life" (Clifford 1986b: 105). It does not suppose, as Briggs (1986) advises, "learning to ask" in the local speech-event forms, some of which may approach "dialogue" and "interlocution" but most of which have different conventions, constitutions, and microcultures (Clifford 1986b: 103–6).

While the interpretive mode (Clifford 1983: 128–29; Holy 1984) shares Briggs's logic, the dialogic mode retains all the WM baggage of its field weapon, "the interview" (Clifford 1983: 133–34). As an exclusive or dominant method of ethnographic inquiry, the dialogic mode locks the informant into an ethnographic present defined by WM "discourse" and alienates her or him from the historical, interpenetrating settings that informant and ethnographer may come to share (Clifford 1986b: 107–9). The "critical flavor" and "political angle"

---

[8]My only quibble with Clifford's starting premises is his identification of ethnography with "translation," ethnography as "a means for producing knowledge from an intense, intersubjective engagement" (1983: 119, 142 n.1). This is only part of the picture. I follow Evans-Pritchard (1950: 148): "But even in a single ethnographic study the anthropologist seeks to do more than understand the thought and values of a primitive [*sic*] people and translate them to his own culture. He also seeks to discover the structural order of the society, the patterns, which, once established, enable him to see it as a whole. . . . Then the society is not only culturally intelligible . . . but also becomes sociologically intelligible." We need a "systematic sociology" (Ortner 1984) as well as cultural interpretation.

(Ortner 1984: 147, 149) are lost. Speech is removed from "action" and from its accustomed environments.

Rosaldo's conversion to participating in Ilongot narrative speech events (1980), rather than missionizing them with "dialogue" and "interlocution" (Clifford 1983: 135–36; Marcus and Fischer 1986: 98–101), suggests the deep methodological gulf between dialogic and interpretive modes of ethnography. "Dialogic" ethnography must be handled with care. Undoubtedly useful for carefully defined research objectives, it is best deployed by those who are trained in both ethnographic and psychoanalytic methods, and who integrate observation and speech in action with the results of their deliberate interviewing (Marcus and Fischer 1986: 48–54).

The polyphonic mode seeks to share ethnographic authority with the voices of informants (see Clifford 1986b). This idea has not sat well with anthropological commentators on Clifford's advocacy of poly-phonic ethnography (see Marcus and Fischer 1986: 68–69; Van Maanen 1988: 137).

> Obviously the anthropologist would also admit to being in control of the final text. However much multiple authorship is acknowledged, using people's experiences to make statements about matters of anthro-pological interest in the end subordinates them to the uses of the disci-pline. But that does not mean it is a worthless exercise. [Strathern 1987: 289]

Shokeid (1988: 42) notes, "Ethnographic texts are mainly orchestrated through the anthropologist's towering voice"; Clifford's "suggestion that anthropologists will increasingly have to share their texts and authorship with their indigenous collaborators" is "utopian." And Geertz (1988: 140) writes:

> The burden of authorship cannot be evaded, however heavy it may have grown; there is no possibility of displacing it onto "method," "language," or (especially popular at the moment) "the people them-selves" redescribed ("appropriated" is probably the better term) as co-authors. . . . The responsibility for ethnography, or the credit, can be placed at no other door than that of the romancers who have dreamt it up.

They are all correct, but so is Clifford. He begins with reference to "the polyphonic novel" of a Dickens or Dostoevski but then admits that the polyphonic novel written by a single author is not the best example of what he has in mind (1983: 136–39). As in fieldnote-rich ethnography, he writes, "quotations are always staged by the quoter," the point Bond makes in his critique of the extended-case method and the one made by Strathern, Shokeid, and Geertz.

Clifford turns, at the conclusion of his essay (1983: 140–41), to what he truly advocates: enlisting the informant as writer, and publishing the informant's texts along with those of the ethnographer. This moves away from the criticism of Geertz and from most, but not all, of that of Strathern and Shokeid. What remains is their uneasiness about the "sharing" that occurs in texts for which the anthropologist remains the editor and perhaps still transcriber, as in the two examples Clifford cites. Control is still asymmetrical.

The fieldnote perspective may help move us beyond this impasse, and even beyond Clifford's ultimate solution (1983: 146 n.65), where the example is given of finally publishing "George Sword, an Oglala warrior and judge," whom ethnographer James Walker encouraged decades ago to write his own account of his culture (see also Clifford 1986a: 15–17).

In the end, the line between ethnographer and "other" cannot be held. It never was held easily. The tension Boas felt when working with Hunt in 1894 eased in later decades as Hunt was acknowledged as author of his own work. How different the history of anthropology would be if it were written not only about the awakening of anthropological interest in other cultures by Western/middle-class/white/males (WMWM) but also about the awakening of cultural awareness and ethnographic self-reflection by people of color, with the stimulus and assistance of (but also appropriation by) WMWM anthropology.

There needs to be written a "Secret History of Assistants," beginning with a biography of Hunt. Others would include Muntu, Sulli, Ahuia Ova, Billy Williams—and, as writers, Carmelo, with whom Wagley (1983: 8–15) worked in Guatemala in 1937 and who wrote his own fieldnotes of interviews he conducted; Phiri, with whom Powdermaker (1966: 260–62, 270–71, 283) worked in Zambia in 1953–54, who wrote fieldnotes and a 45-page autobiography, and who later went to England to study "community relations"; and I Made Kaler (Howard 1984: 186–88; Mead 1972: 229–36), with whom Mead and Bateson worked in Bali in 1936–38 and who wrote to Mead in 1938:

> Anyhow with this letter I do you a request. But when you think it will be bad for your Bali book, I won't do it. Do you think I can write a short article about the cockfight. . . . But I tell you if you think this action will

be a bit bad for your book, I won't do it. I don't want to make profit of
any of the stuff we have collected. It belongs all to you. [qtd. in Mead
1977: 238]

Where is the Balinese analysis of the Balinese cockfight? "The stuff
we have collected belongs all to *you*." We, anthropologists and informants, have lost something irreplaceable here. A profound sadness
grips me when I read this letter.

The answer must not be just to append, edit, transcribe, or co-create
the writings of informants. We must break each of the four legs of
WMWM anthropology and radically widen the discipline's membership as we look to the 1990s and beyond. The days when "those who
were informants in the field rarely saw the finished anthropological
texts" (Crick 1982: 17) are almost gone, and their end should be
hastened. We need to "think of an ethnography which is not predicated
on a dichotomy between the self and other. . . . the former subjects or
objects of study are not only becoming an audience, and a critical one
at that, but they are becoming anthropologists themselves" (Caplan
1988: 17). From a "fieldnotes up" view of anthropology, we can see
that "they" have been becoming anthropologists for almost one hundred years, and if we change "anthropologist" to "ethnographer,"
"they" have been writing fieldnotes and more extended ethnographic
texts for one hundred years as well. "They" are "we" already, if "we"
are not yet fully "they."

The poignant story of Paul C. P. Siu and his book *The Chinese
Laundryman: A Study in Social Isolation* (1987) is one of an ethnographer
whose work was "not predicated on a dichotomy between self and
other" but who did not live to see the finished text. The major ethnographic research for this fieldnote-rich book, which belongs among
the great ethnographies of the classic period, was conducted in Chicago in the late 1930s. Siu did not find a place within academia till the
1950s. He completed seventeen of the study's eighteen chapters in
1945 when he took a social work position; the dissertation was accepted in 1952. At that time the University of Chicago Press declined
to publish it, believing that a study of Chinese laundry workers was
unmarketable.

The work was rediscovered by historian John Kuo Wei Tchen in
1980; Tchen edited the manuscript in consultation with Siu, who died
just before its publication in 1987. Tchen (1987: xxxiv) remarks, "His
career strongly suggests that he received less recognition for his talents

than comparably educated and accomplished white colleagues." Siu remained loyal to an ethnographic establishment that perhaps deserved less. A substantial base-broadening of WMWM professional ethnography is required if the method is to continue into the next century. We have no choice. The "others" do.

We may compare *The Chinese Laundryman* with *Silenced: Talks with Working Class West Indian Women about Their Lives and Struggles as Domestic Workers in Canada* (1983) by Makeda Silvera, a Jamaican and activist-organizer in Toronto. Both books document low-status service occupations to which their incumbents find no alternative. Silvera's book consists of oral accounts of the life and work experiences of ten women. It is not based upon the ethnographic method and is not an academic product. It *is* a powerful, rich, moving book. In the 1980s those outside the WMWM (or WMWF) establishment no longer need subordinate themselves to the university (cf. Clifford 1986a: 10). Today a range of alternative forms of documentation and publication is more open than in Siu's time. Community-based oral history like Silvera's is flourishing. Other "para-ethnographic genres" such as "the non-fiction novel, the 'new journalism', travel literature, and the documentary film" may also give "voice" (Clifford 1983: 143). And as ethnography seeps outside anthropology and sociology, it is often less demanding, easier to claim.

The ethnographic method is a gift we must pass on, not a hot potato to toss away. My own ties through Marvin Harris and Lambros Comitas to Wagley, Mead, and Boas and through van Velsen to Gluckman and Malinowski are relations I value and feel responsible to transmit to new bearers. Clifford is correct in calling for a new polyphonic ethnography, but the polyphony must be not only in texts but in a rainbow company of ethnographers themselves.

Keep Hope Alive

We steer a middle course. Ethnographers have learned that they need not be "mimic physicists or closet humanists. . . . Instead they [can] proceed with their vocation, trying to discover order in collective life" (Geertz 1983: 21). And our loose-strict-loose-strict operations draw from both shores.

We collect cargo from the humanist shore. We value the "telling" case as much as the typical one (Mitchell 1984: 239); we "understand

people not as units but as integral parts of systems of relationships"
(Wallman and Dhooge 1984: 239); we depend on "personal involvement, chance, and all the characteristics which are rejected within the
positivist tradition" (Tonkin 1984: 220).

We receive goods on the scientific bank as well. We know that a
fieldwork decision about "systematicity"—to make the plunge and
test out an emerging theory of significance—"is one of the more
creative moments of ethnographic research" (Agar 1980: 134). We
must realize, and no longer tolerate, "how many anthropological texts
are accepted as knowledge when their authors say virtually nothing
about the methods they employed to get their data" (Crick 1982: 18).

We may call on both banks, but we dwell on neither. In the fray of
schools, movements, anti-antirelativism, and anti-antiscience, many
of ethnography's most acute observers still sense that we hold our own
course. From Britain, Strathern writes: "Social anthropology still
continues to know itself as the study of social behavior or society in
terms of systems and collective representations. If these constitute a
paradigm, then it is largely intact" (1987: 281). And from the United
States, Johnson observes: "The fact is, interpretation does not cancel
the need for quantification, or vice versa" (1987: 30).

In our continuing attention to the ethnographic monograph on our
intellectual journey, anthropology is pre-paradigmatic, not (yet) a
science (Kuhn 1962: 20–21); an admired ethnographic work enhances
rather than impairs an anthropologist's career. Gluckman (1961: 16)
wished more than a quarter-century ago that this tradition would
continue, and there is no reason today why he cannot rest in peace.

If not fully a science, the ethnographic method certainly is a practice. It was discovered by Cushing, Boas, and Rivers, but each turned
away from it. It was rediscovered, consolidated, and "took"—when
the conditions were right—with Malinowski and Mead. It was challenged from the bank of science by Murdock (who respected it) in the
1930s and by many more in the 1950s to 1970s. It was challenged from
the bank of humanism by Evans-Pritchard (who practiced it) in the
1950s and by many more interpretationists in the 1970s and 1980s.
These challenges have enriched the ethnographic method and will
strengthen its continuation in the 1990s and beyond.

In a fascinating recent paper, Howard Becker sketches a sociology
of the current relativist mood in intellectual life, and ethnography as a
practice finds its place as one way of "telling about society."

Any representation of social reality—a documentary film, a demo-graphic study, a realistic novel—is necessarily partial, less that what one would experience and have available for interpretation in the actual setting. . . . The same reality can be described in an enormous number of ways, since the descriptions can be answers to any of a multitude of questions. . . . We only ask the same question when the circumstances of social interaction and organization have produced consensus on that point. This happens when . . . people . . . see certain problems as common, as requiring certain kinds of representations of social reality on a routine basis, and [these conditions] thus lead to the development of professions and crafts that make those representations. [1986b: 125, 134. See also Hughes 1960; Clifford 1986a]

Like Agar, "sometimes I think ethnography is to social science as jazz is to music" (1980: 92). My aesthetic sensibility is rooted in American music, especially jazz and African American song (Sanjek 1988). In the 1980s both these art forms have enjoyed an "in the tradition," "retro nuevo" florescence; older styles and recorded performances are valued and preserved and attract audiences as much as newer ones. (The same is true of country music.) Roy Eldridge, Jack DeJohnette, Gil Evans, Joe Venuti, Jackie MacLean, Charlie Haden, Charles Mingus, Wardell Gray, Eric Dolphy, Elvin Jones, Craig Harris, and Amina Myers are all appreciated. One can enjoy Dinah Washington, the Clovers, Tina Turner, Johnny Otis, Stevie Wonder, Aretha Franklin, James Brown, Maxine Brown, Sheila Jordan, Andrae Crouch, Sam Cooke, Sweet Honey in the Rock, and Patti LaBelle. I think ethnography will enjoy similar advances and consolidations in the 1990s.

Jazz innovator Miles Davis is known to have told band members: "You need to know your horn, know the chords, know all the tunes. Then you forget about all that, and just play." Knowing the anthropo-logical tradition, knowing the range of fieldwork methods, and know-ing what constitutes ethnographic validity are essential, but they do not produce ethnography. Like jazz, ethnography requires the person who improvises the performance, who not only knows how to do it but does it.

It is not surprising to me that the word "art" is used by several ethnographers in their deepest meditations about their calling (see Clifford 1986a: 4, 6). Wagley explains:

I would not go so far as to say that fieldwork is an "art"; but like an art there are basic rules of the form within which the artist-anthropologist

is working. The research anthropologist in the field must know, respect, and play with these rules. Beyond that, fieldwork is a creative
endeavor. [1983: 16]

Sounds like Miles to me!

Evans-Pritchard (1951: 82–85) believed that "social anthropology is
best regarded as art and not as a natural science."

> The work of the anthropologist is not photographic. He has to decide
> what is significant in what he observes and by his subsequent relation of
> his experiences to bring what is significant into relief. For this he must
> have, in addition to a wide knowledge of anthropology, a feeling for
> form and pattern, and a touch of genius.

The crux, he thought, was the question "whether the same results
would have been obtained had another person made a particular investigation."

> While I think different social anthropologists who studied the same
> people would record much the same facts in their notebooks, I believe
> that they would write different kinds of books. . . . One can only
> interpret what one sees in terms of one's own experience and of what
> one is.

A master jazz musician knows the horn, the chords, and the tunes.
Yet it takes only a few tenor saxophone phrases to tell whether you are
listening to "Body and Soul," or the blues, from Coleman Hawkins,
Ben Webster, Lester Young, Arnette Cobb, Paul Gonsalves, Gene
Ammons, Eddie Lockjaw Davis, Sonny Rollins, John Coltrane, Yusef
Lateef, Booker Ervin, Eddie Harris, George Coleman, or David Mur-
ray.

Ethnography is not dead, nor is it dying (Geertz 1988: 139; Van
Maanen 1988: 71 n.13). As it progresses, attention to ethnographic
validity—What did you do and why? Who did you talk to and learn
from? What did you bring back to document it?—will deepen the
growing appreciation outside our ranks of ethnography's value as a
way of "telling about society." But to register fully the ethnographic
method's potential, we need radical expansion of ethnography's ranks
and the promotion of assistants to "ethnographer," as well as the
recognition that ethnographers also may be "assistants" to their informants.

As we follow the middle course, we need to remember, with Smith, that the subjects of ethnography are more interesting than the authors and, with Ottenberg, that the inward turn of the 1970s and 1980s was also a turn away from disappointments and tragedies on the turfs of many of the classical period's informants.

Luckily, we have navigation charts to guide our course. *Coral Gardens and Their Magic, The Mountain Arapesh, Street Corner Society, Navaho Witchcraft, We Have Eaten the Forest, The Politics of Kinship, The Women of Suye Mura,* and *The Chinese Laundryman* are not airport-rack "easy reads." They are not novels, not plays, not journalism. They are to be evaluated by different canons. They are ethnography, and made from fieldnotes.

REFERENCES

Adams, Richard N., and J. Preiss, eds., 1960. *Human Organization Research.* Homewood, Ill.: Dorsey.
Agar, Michael H. 1980. *The Professional Stranger: An Informal Introduction to Ethnography.* New York: Academic Press.
———. 1986a. *Independents Declared: The Dilemmas of Independent Trucking.* Washington, D.C.: Smithsonian Institution Press.
———. 1986b. *Speaking of Ethnography.* Beverly Hills, Calif.: Sage.
Barley, Nigel. 1983. *Adventures in a Mud Hut: An Innocent Anthropologist Abroad.* New York: Vanguard Press.
Barth, Fredrik. 1966. Preface. In Robert H. Pehrson, *The Social Organization of the Marri Baluch,* ed. and comp. Fredrik Barth, vii–xii. Viking Fund Publications in Anthropology 43. New York: Wenner-Gren Foundation for Anthropological Research.
Beattie, John. 1965. *Understanding an African Kingdom: Bunyoro.* New York: Holt, Rinehart & Winston.
Becker, Howard. 1986a. *Writing for Social Scientists.* Chicago: University of Chicago Press.
———. 1986b. Telling about Society. In *Doing Things Together: Selected Papers,* 121–35. Evanston, Ill.: Northwestern University Press.
Becker, Howard, and Blanche Geer. 1960. Participant Observation: The Analysis of Qualitative Field Data. In Adams and Preiss 1960, 267–89.
Berreman, Gerald D. 1968. Ethnography: Method and Product. In *Introduction to Cultural Anthropology: Essays in the Scope and Methods of the Science of Man,* ed. James A. Clifton, 336–73. Boston: Houghton Mifflin.
Bloch, Marc. 1953. *The Historian's Craft.* New York: Vintage Books.
Boissevain, Jeremy. 1970. Fieldwork in Malta. In Spindler 1970, 58–84.
Briggs, Charles. 1986. *Learning to Ask: A Sociolinguistic Appraisal of the Role of the Interview in Social Science Research.* New York: Cambridge University Press.

Brim, John A., and David H. Spain. 1974. *Research Design in Anthropology: Paradigms and Pragmatics in the Testing of Hypotheses.* New York: Holt, Rinehart & Winston.

Caplan, Pat. 1988. Engendering Knowledge: The Politics of Ethnography. *Anthropology Today* 4 (5): 8–12; 4 (6): 14–17.

Carr, Edward Hallett. 1961. *What Is History?* New York: Vintage Books.

Caws, Peter. 1969. The Structure of Discovery. *Science* 166: 1375—80.

Clifford, James. 1983. On Ethnographic Authority. *Representations* 1 (2): 118–46.

———. 1986a. Introduction: Partial Truths. In Clifford and Marcus 1986, 1–26.

———. 1986b. On Ethnographic Allegory. In Clifford and Marcus 1986, 98–121.

———. 1988. *The Predicament of Culture: Twentieth-Century Ethnography, Literature, and Art.* Cambridge, Mass.: Harvard University Press.

Clifford, James, and George E. Marcus, eds. 1986. *Writing Culture: The Poetics and Politics of Ethnography.* Berkeley: University of California Press.

Cohen, Ronald, and Raoul Naroll. 1970. Method in Cultural Anthropology. In Naroll and Cohen 1970, 3–24.

Colson, Elizabeth. 1967. The Intensive Study of Small Sample Communities. In Epstein 1967, 3–15.

Comaroff, Jean, and John L. Comaroff. 1988. On the Founding Fathers, Fieldwork, and Functionalism: A Conversation with Isaac Schapera. *American Ethnologist* 15:554–65.

Condominas, Georges. 1957 [1977]. *We Have Eaten the Forest: The Story of a Montagnard Village in the Central Highlands of Vietnam.* Trans. Adrienne Foulke. New York: Hill & Wang.

Conkling, Robert. 1975. Expression and Generalization in History and Anthropology. *American Ethnologist* 2:239–50.

Crick, Malcolm. 1982. Anthropological Field Research, Meaning Creation, and Knowledge Construction. In *Semantic Anthropology,* ed. David Parkin, 15–37. London: Academic Press.

Davis, John. 1984. Data into Text. In Ellen 1984a, 295–318.

Den Hollander, A. N. J. 1967. Social Description: The Problem of Reliability and Validity. In *Anthropologists in the Field,* ed. D. G. Jongmans and P. C. W. Gutkind, 1–34. New York: Humanities Press.

Dentan, Robert K. 1970. Living and Working with the Semai. In Spindler 1970, 85–112.

Ellen, R. F., ed. 1984a. *Ethnographic Research: A Guide to General Conduct.* San Diego: Academic Press.

———. 1984b. Introduction. In Ellen 1984a, 1–12.

———. 1984c. Notes and Records. In Ellen 1984a, 278–93.

Elwin, Verrier. 1964. *The Tribal World of Verrier Elwin: An Autobiography.* New York: Oxford University Press.

Epstein, A. L., ed. 1967. *The Craft of Social Anthropology.* London: Social Science Paperbacks.

Evans-Pritchard, E. E. 1950 [1962]. Social Anthropology: Past and Present. In *Social Anthropology and Other Essays,* 139–54. New York: Free Press.

———. 1951. *Social Anthropology.* New York: Free Press.

Firth, Raymond. 1957a. Introduction: Malinowski as Man and as Scientist. In Firth 1957b, 1–14.

——, ed. 1957b. *Man and Culture: An Evaluation of the Work of Bronislaw Malinowski.* New York: Harper Torchbooks.

——. 1966. *Malay Fishermen: Their Peasant Economy.* Hamden, Conn.: Archon Books.

——. 1981. Bronislaw Malinowski. In *Totems and Teachers: Perspectives on the History of Anthropology,* ed. Sydel Silverman, 101–39. New York: Columbia University Press.

Force, Roland. 1960. *Leadership and Cultural Change in Palau.* Chicago: Chicago Natural History Museum.

Fortes, Meyer. 1957. Malinowski and the Study of Kinship. In Firth 1957b, 157–88.

Foster, George M. 1979. Fieldwork in Tzintzuntzan: The First Thirty Years. In Foster et al. 1979, 165–84.

Foster, George M., Thayer Scudder, Elizabeth Colson, and Robert V. Kemper, eds. 1979. *Long-Term Field Research in Social Anthropology.* New York: Academic Press.

Freilich, Morris, ed. 1970. *Marginal Natives: Anthropologists at Work.* New York: Harper & Row.

Friedrich, Paul. 1986. *The Princes of Naranja: An Essay in Anthrohistorical Method.* Austin: University of Texas Press.

Geertz, Clifford. 1983. *Local Knowledge: Further Essays in Interpretive Anthropology.* New York: Basic Books.

——. 1988. *Works and Lives: The Anthropologist as Author.* Stanford, Calif.: Stanford University Press.

Geertz, Hildred. 1961. *The Javanese Family: A Study in Kinship and Socialization.* Glencoe, Ill.: Free Press.

Gluckman, Max. 1940. Analysis of a Social Situation in Modern Zululand. *Bantu Studies* 14:1–30.

——. 1961. Ethnographic Data in British Social Anthropology. *Sociological Review* 9:5–17.

——. 1967. Introduction. In Epstein 1967, xi–xx.

Gulick, John. 1970. Village and City Field Work in Lebanon. In Freilich 1970, 123–52.

Heath, Dwight. 1972. Comment. *Current Anthropology* 13:536.

Hinsley, Curtis M., Jr. 1981. *Savages and Scientists: The Smithsonian Institution and the Development of American Anthropology, 1846–1910.* Washington, D.C.: Smithsonian Institution Press.

Holy, Ladislav. 1984. Theory, Methodology, and the Research Process. In Ellen 1984a, 13–34.

Honigmann, John J. 1970a. Field Work in Two Northern Canadian Communities. In Freilich 1970, 39–72.

——. 1970b. Sampling in Ethnographic Fieldwork. In Naroll and Cohen 1970, 266–81.

———. 1976. The Personal Approach in Cultural Anthropological Research. *Current Anthropology* 17:243–61.

Howard, Jane. 1984. *Margaret Mead: A Life*. New York: Fawcett Crest.

Hughes, Everett. 1960 [1971]. The Place of Field Work in Social Science. In *The Sociological Eye: Selected Papers*, 496–506. Chicago: Aldine.

Johnson, Allen. 1978. *Quantification in Cultural Anthropology*. Stanford, Calif.: Stanford University Press.

———. 1987. The Death of Ethnography: Has Anthropology Betrayed Its Mission? *The Sciences* 27 (2): 24–31.

Kuhn, Thomas S. 1962. *The Structure of Scientific Revolutions*. Chicago: University of Chicago Press.

Lamphere, Louise. 1979. The Long-Term Study among the Navaho. In Foster et al. 1979, 19–44.

Leach, E. R. 1957. The Epistemological Background to Malinowski's Empiricism. In Firth 1957b, 119–37.

Lederman, Rena. 1986. *What Gifts Engender: Social Relations and Politics in Mendi, Highland Papua New Guinea*. New York: Cambridge University Press.

Lewis, Oscar. 1951. *Life in a Mexican Village: Tepoztlan Restudied*. Urbana: University of Illinois Press.

———. 1953. Controls and Experiments in Fieldwork. In *Anthropology Today*, ed. A. L. Kroeber, 452–75. Chicago: University of Chicago Press.

Malinowski, Bronislaw. 1935 [1978]. *Coral Gardens and Their Magic*. New York: Dover.

Marcus, George E., and Dick Cushman. 1982. Ethnographies as Texts. *Annual Review of Anthropology* 11: 25–69.

Marcus, George E., and Michael M. J. Fischer. 1986. *Anthropology as Cultural Critique: An Experimental Moment in the Human Sciences*. Chicago: University of Chicago Press.

Mayer, A. C. 1978. *The Remembered Village*: From Memory Alone? *Contributions to Indian Sociology* 12:39–47.

Mead, Margaret. 1972. *Blackberry Winter: My Earlier Years*. New York: Morrow.

———. 1977. *Letters from the Field, 1925–1975*. New York: Harper & Row.

Middleton, John. 1970. *The Study of the Lugbara: Expectation and Paradox in Anthropological Research*. New York: Holt, Rinehart & Winston.

Mitchell, J. Clyde. 1984. Case Studies. In Ellen 1984a, 237–41.

Naroll, Raoul, and Ronald Cohen, eds. 1970. *A Handbook of Method in Cultural Anthropology*. New York: Columbia University Press.

Nash, Dennison, and Ronald Wintrob. 1972. The Emergence of Self-Consciousness in Ethnography. *Current Anthropology* 13:527–42.

Ortner, Sherry. 1984. Theory in Anthropology since the Sixties. *Comparative Studies in Society and History* 26:126–66.

Pelto, Pertti J. 1970. Research in Individualistic Societies. In Freilich 1970, 251–92.

Pelto, Pertti J., and Gretel H. Pelto. 1973. Ethnography: The Fieldwork Enterprise. In *Handbook of Social and Cultural Anthropology*, ed. John J. Honigmann, 241–88. Chicago: Rand McNally.

———. 1978. *Anthropological Research: The Structure of Inquiry.* 2d ed. New York: Cambridge University Press.

Plath, David. 1980. *Long Engagements: Maturity in Modern Japan.* Stanford, Calif.: Stanford University Press.

Powdermaker, Hortense. 1966. *Stranger and Friend: The Way of an Anthropologist.* New York: Norton.

Pratt, Mary. 1986. Fieldwork in Common Places. In Clifford and Marcus 1986, 27–50.

Rabinow, Paul. 1977. *Reflections on Fieldwork in Morocco.* Berkeley: University of California Press.

Roberts, John M. 1956 [1965]. *Zuni Daily Life.* New Haven, Conn.: Human Relations Area Files Press.

Robertson, A. F. 1978. *Community of Strangers: A Journal of Discovery in Uganda.* London: Scolar Press.

Rosaldo, Renato. 1980. *Ilongot Headhunting, 1883–1974: A Study in Society and History.* Stanford, Calif.: Stanford University Press.

Saberwal, Satish. 1975. The First Hundred Days—Leaves from a Field Diary. In *Encounter and Experience: Personal Accounts of Fieldwork,* ed. Andre Beteille and T. N. Madan, 42–63. Honolulu: University of Hawaii Press.

Sanjek, Roger. 1978. A Network Method and Its Uses in Urban Anthropology. *Human Organization* 37:257–68.

———. 1988. Preface. In Russell Sanjek, *American Popular Music and Its Business: The First Four Hundred Years,* 1:v–vii. New York: Oxford University Press.

Shokeid, Moshe. 1988. Anthropologists and Their Informants: Marginality Reconsidered. *Archives Européennes de Sociologie* 29:31–47.

Silvera, Makeda. 1983. *Silenced: Talks with Working Class West Indian Women about Their Lives and Struggles as Domestic Workers in Canada.* Toronto: Williams-Wallace.

Siu, Paul C. P. 1987. *The Chinese Laundryman: A Study of Social Isolation.* New York: New York University Press.

Smith, Robert J., and Ella Lury Wiswell. 1982. *The Women of Suye Mura.* Chicago: University of Chicago Press.

Spicer, Edward H. 1954. *Potam: A Yaqui Village in Sonora.* American Anthropological Association Memoir 77. Menasha, Wis.: American Anthropological Association.

Spindler, George D., ed. 1970. *Being an Anthropologist: Fieldwork in Eleven Cultures.* New York: Holt, Rinehart & Winston.

Srinivas, M. N. 1987. *The Dominant Caste and Other Essays.* Bombay: Oxford University Press.

Strathern, Marilyn. 1987. An Awkward Relationship: The Case of Feminism and Anthropology. *Signs* 12:276–92.

Tchen, John Kuo Wei. 1987. Introduction. In Siu 1987, xxiii–xxxix.

Tonkin, Elizabeth. 1984. Participant Observation. In Ellen 1984a, 216–23.

Van Maanen, John. 1988. *Tales of the Field: On Writing Ethnography.* Chicago: University of Chicago Press.

Van Velsen, Jaap. 1964. *The Politics of Kinship: A Study in Social Manipulation among the Lakeside Tonga of Nyasaland.* Manchester: Manchester University Press.
———. 1967. The Extended-Case Method and Situational Analysis. In Epstein 1967, 129–49.
Wagley, Charles. 1983. Learning Fieldwork: Guatemala. In *Fieldwork: The Human Experience,* ed. Robert Lawless, Vinson H. Sutlive, Jr., and Mario D. Zamora, 1–17. New York: Gordon & Breach.
Wallman, Sandra, and Yvonne Dhooge. 1984. Survey Premises and Procedures. In Ellen 1984a, 257–67.
Wayne (Malinowska), Helena. 1985. Bronislaw Malinowski: The Influence of Various Women on His Life and Works. *American Ethnologist* 12:529–40.
Weiner, Annette. 1983. Ethnographic Determinism: Samoa and the Margaret Mead Controversy. *American Anthropologist* 85:909–19.
Werner, Dennis. 1984. *Amazon Journey: An Anthropologist's Year among Brazil's Mekranoti Indians.* New York: Simon & Schuster.
Whiting, Beatrice, and John Whiting. 1970. Methods for Observing and Recording Behavior. In Naroll and Cohen 1970, 282–315.
Whyte, William Foote. 1943. *Street Corner Society.* Chicago: University of Chicago Press.
———. 1955. Appendix: On the Evolution of "Street Corner Society." In *Street Corner Society,* enl. ed. 279–358. Chicago: University of Chicago Press.
———. 1984. *Learning from the Field: A Guide from Experience.* Beverly Hills, Calif.: Sage.
Wolcott, Harry F. 1975. Feedback Influences on Fieldwork; or, A Funny Thing Happened on the Way to the Beer Garden. In *Urban Man in Southern Africa,* ed. Clive Kileff and Wade Pendleton, 99–125. Gwelo, Rhodesia [Zimbabwe]: Mambo Press.
———. 1981. Home and Away: Personal Contrasts in Ethnographic Style. In *Anthropologists at Home in North America: Methods and Issues in the Study of One's Own Society,* ed. Donald A. Messerschmidt, 255–65. New York: Cambridge University Press.
Wolff, Kurt. 1960. The Collection and Organization of Field Materials: A Research Report. In Adams and Preiss 1960, 240–54.
———. 1964. Surrender and Community Study: The Study of Loma. In *Reflections on Community Studies,* ed. Arthur J. Vidich, Joseph Bensman, and Maurice R. Stein, 233–63. New York: Wiley.
Woolgar, Steve. 1988. *Science: The Very Idea.* New York: Tavistock.

Index

Compiled by Maria Matteo

Library of Congress Cataloging-in-Publication Data
Fieldnotes : the makings of anthropology / edited by Roger Sanjek.
    p. cm.
   Includes rev. versions of some papers presented at the AES Invited
Sessions at the American Anthropological Society meetings in
Washington, D.C., 1985.
   Includes bibliographical references.
   ISBN 0-8014-2436-4 (alk. paper). — ISBN 0-8014-9726-4 (pbk. :
alk. paper)
    1. Ethnology—Field work—Congresses.   2. Ethnology—Research—
Congresses.   I. Sanjek, Roger, 1944– .   II. AES Invited Sessions
(1985 : Washington, D.C.)   III. Title: Field notes.
GN346.F52   1990
306'.072—dc20   89-46169